T0238132

Lecture Notes in Computer Science 5895

Commenced Publication in 1973
Founding and Former Series Editors:
Gerhard Goos, Juris Hartmanis, and Jan van Leeuwen

Raghunath Nambiar   Meikel Poess (Eds.)

Performance Evaluation and Benchmarking

First TPC Technology Conference, TPCTC 2009
Lyon, France, August 24-28, 2009
Revised Selected Papers

 Springer

Volume Editors

Raghunath Nambiar
Hewlett-Packard Company
11445 Compaq Center Dr W
Houston, TX 77070, USA
E-mail: raghu.nambiar@hp.com

Meikel Poess
Oracle Corporation
500 Oracle Parkway
Redwood Shores, CA 94065, USA
E-mail: meikel.poess@oracle.com

Library of Congress Control Number: 2009938720

CR Subject Classification (1998): C.4, D.2.8, D.2, D.4.8, H.3.4, K.6.2

LNCS Sublibrary: SL 2 – Programming and Software Engineering

ISSN	0302-9743
ISBN-10	3-642-10423-1 Springer Berlin Heidelberg New York
ISBN-13	978-3-642-10423-7 Springer Berlin Heidelberg New York

springer.com

© Springer-Verlag Berlin Heidelberg 2009
Printed in Germany

Typesetting: Camera-ready by author, data conversion by Scientific Publishing Services, Chennai, India
Printed on acid-free paper   SPIN: 12792528   06/3180   5 4 3 2 1 0

Preface

First established in August 1988, the Transaction Processing Performance Council (TPC) has shaped the landscape of modern transaction processing and database benchmarks over two decades. Now, the world is in the midst of an extraordinary information explosion led by rapid growth in the use of the Internet and connected devices. Both user-generated data and enterprise data levels continue to grow exponentially. With substantial technological breakthroughs, Moore's law will continue for at least a decade, and the data storage capacities and data transfer speeds will continue to increase exponentially. These have challenged industry experts and researchers to develop innovative techniques to evaluate and benchmark both hardware and software technologies.

As a result, the TPC held its First Conference on Performance Evaluation and Benchmarking (TPCTC 2009) on August 24 in Lyon, France in conjunction with the 35th International Conference on Very Large Data Bases (VLDB 2009). TPCTC 2009 provided industry experts and researchers with a forum to present and debate novel ideas and methodologies in performance evaluation, measurement and characterization for 2010 and beyond.

This book contains the proceedings of this conference, including 16 papers and keynote papers from Michael Stonebraker and Karl Huppler.

A number of people have contributed to the success of this conference. I would like to thank the members of TPC and the organizers of the VLDB 2009 conference for their support and sponsorship. I would also like to thank members of the Program Committee, Publicity Committee, the authors and the conference participants for their contributions in making this conference a big success.

November 2009   Raghunath Nambiar

TPCTC 2009 Organization

General Chair

Raghunath Nambiar (Hewlett-Packard)

Program Committee Chair

Meikel Poess (Oracle)

Publicity Committee Chair

Nicholas Wakou (Dell)

Program Committee

Alain Crolotte (Teradata)
Berni Schiefer (IBM)
Krithi Ramamritham (IIT Bombay)
Masaru Kitsuregawa (University of Tokyo)
Mike Molloy (Dell)
Murali Krishna (Hewlett-Packard)
Omer Trajman (Vertica)
Paul Larson (Microsoft)
Yicheng Tu (University of South Florida)

Publicity Committee

Jerrold Buggert (Unisys)
Matthew Lanken (Oracle)
Peter Thawley (Sybase)
Forrest Carman (Owen Media)
Michael Majdalany (L&M Management Group)

Keynote Speakers

Michael Stonebraker (MIT)
Karl Huppler (IBM)

About the TPC

Introduction to the TPC

The Transaction Processing Performance Council (TPC) is a non-profit organization that defines transaction processing and database benchmarks and distributes vendor-neutral performance data to the industry. Over the past two decades, the TPC has had a significant impact on industry and on expectations around benchmarks. Vendors and end users rely on TPC benchmarks to provide real-world data that are backed by a stringent and independent review process.

TPC Memberships

Full Members

Full Members of the TPC participate in all aspects of the TPC's work, including development of benchmark standards and setting strategic direction. The Full Member application form can be found at: http://www.tpc.org/information/about/app-member.asp

Associate Members

Certain organizations may join the TPC as Associate Members. Associate Members may attend TPC meetings, but are not eligible to vote or hold office. Associate membership is available to non-profit organizations, educational institutions, market researchers, publishers, consultants, governments and businesses that do not create, market or sell computer products or services. The Associate Member application form can be found at: http://www.tpc.org/information/about/app-assoc.asp.

Academic and Government Institutions

Academic and government institutions are invited to participate in the TPC's bimonthly meetings, and a special invitation can be found at: http://www.tpc.org/information/specialinvitation.asp.

Contact the TPC

TPC
Presidio of San Francisco
Building 572B (surface)
P.O. Box 29920 (mail) San Francisco, CA 94129-0920
Voice: 415-561-6272
Fax: 415-561-6120
Email: info@tpc.org

How to Order TPC Materials

All of our materials are now posted free of charge on our website. If you have any questions, please feel free to contact our office directly or by email at info@tpc.org

Benchmark Status Report

The TPC Benchmark Status Report is a digest of the activities of the TPC and its technical subcommittees. Sign-up information can be found at: http://www.tpc.org/information/about/email.asp.

TPC 2009 Organization

Full Members

AMD, Bull, Dell, Fujitsu, Fusion IO, HP, Hitachi, IBM, Ingres, Intel, Kickfire, Microsoft, NEC, Netezza, Oracle, ParAccel, Sun, Sybase, Syncsort, Teradata, Unisys, Vertica, VMware and XSPRADA

Associate Members

Ideas International, ITOM International Co and TTA

Steering Committee

Karl Huppler (IBM), Chair
Charles Levine (Microsoft)
Jerrold Buggert (Unisys)
Mike Molloy (Dell)
Raghunath Nambiar (Hewlett-Packard)

Public Relations Committee

Nicholas Wakou (Dell), Chair
Jerrold Buggert (Unisys)
Matthew Lanken (Oracle)
Peter Thawley (Sybase)
Raghunath Nambiar (Hewlett-Packard)

Technical Advisory Board

Mike Brey (Oracle), Chair
Jamie Reding (Microsoft)
Matthew Emmerton (IBM)
Mike Molloy (Dell)
Omer Trajman (Vertica)
Rick Freeman (Unisys)
Wayne Smith (Intel)

Table of Contents

Transaction Processing Performance Council (TPC): Twenty Years Later – A Look Back, a Look Ahead

Raghunath Othayoth Nambiar[1], Matthew Lanken[2], Nicholas Wakou[3], Forrest Carman[4], and Michael Majdalany[5]

[1] Hewlett-Packard Company, 11445 Compaq Center Dr. W, Houston, TX-77070, USA
Raghu.Nambiar@hp.com
[2] Oracle Corporation, 500 Oracle Parkway, Redwood Shores, CA-94065, USA
Matthew.Lanken@oracle.com
[3] Dell Inc., One Dell Way, Round Rock, TX-78682, USA
Nicholas_Wakou@dell.com
[4] Owen Media, 3130 E. Madison St., Suite 206, Seattle, WA-98112, USA
forrestc@owenmedia.com
[5] LoBue & Majdalany Magt Group, 572B Ruger St. San Francisco, CA- 94129, USA
majdalany@lm-mgmt.com

Abstract. The Transaction Processing Performance Council (TPC) [1] is a non-profit corporation founded to define transaction processing and database benchmarks and to disseminate objective, verifiable TPC performance data to the industry. Established in August 1988, the TPC has been integral in shaping the landscape of modern transaction processing and database benchmarks over the past twenty years. Today the TPC is developing an energy efficiency metric and a new ETL benchmark, as well as investigating new areas for benchmark development in 2010 and beyond.

Keywords: Industry Standard Benchmark.

1 Industry Standard Benchmarks

Historically, robust and meaningful benchmarks have been crucial to the advancement of the computing industry. Without them, assessing relative performance between disparate vendor architectures is virtually impossible. Demands for audited and verifiable benchmarks have existed since buyers were first confronted with a choice between purchasing one piece of hardware over another, and have been driven by their desire to compare price and performance on an apples-to-apples basis.

Over the years, benchmarks have proven useful to both systems/software vendors and purchasers. Vendors use benchmarks to demonstrate performance competitiveness for their existing products and to improve/monitor performance of products-under-development; in addition, many buyers reference benchmark results when considering new equipment. Finally, benchmarks help vendors improve their products through competition.

The two most prominent industry standard benchmark organizations to emerge from the 1980's are the Transaction Processing Performance Council (TPC) and

R. Nambiar and M. Poess (Eds.): TPCTC 2009, LNCS 5895, pp. 1–10, 2009.
© Springer-Verlag Berlin Heidelberg 2009

Systems Performance Evaluation Corporation (SPEC) [2]. The TPC's primary focus is total system performance under a database workload, including: hardware, operating system, and I/O system. All results have a price-performance metric audited by an independent TPC certified auditor. Like the TPC, SPEC "develops suites of benchmarks intended to measure computer performance. These suites are packaged with source code and tools and are extensively tested for portability before release."[7] Unlike the TPC, SPEC results are peer audited.

2 Transaction Processing Performance Council

The TPC is a non-profit corporation founded to define vendor-neutral transaction processing benchmarks and to disseminate objective, verifiable performance data to the industry. Omri Serlin and Tom Sawyer founded the TPC in 1988 as a response to the growing problem of "benchmarketing," the inappropriate use of questionable benchmark results in marketing promotions and competitive comparisons. At the time, two frequently referenced benchmarks were the TP1 benchmark, originally developed by IBM, and the debit-credit benchmark, which appeared in a 1985 Tandem Computers Inc. technical article that was published by a team led by Jim Gray. With no standard body oversight, vendors took such liberties with these benchmarks that muddied the waters even further [3].

The TPC's first benchmark was TPC-A, which was a formalization of the TP1 and Debit/Credit benchmarks. However, while a formal and accepted benchmark for system performance now existed, there continued to be many complaints of benchmarketing. In response, the TPC initiated a review process wherein each benchmark test had to be extensively documented and then carefully vetted by an independent auditor before it could be published as a formal TPC benchmark result. Today, all published results of TPC benchmarks have been audited and verified by TPC certified auditors.

2.1 User and Vendor Benefits

Over the past two decades, the TPC has had a significant impact on the industry and expectations around benchmarks. TPC benchmarks have permanently raised the bar; vendors and end users rely on TPC benchmarks to provide real-world data that is backed by a stringent and independent review process. The main user and vendor benefits of TPC benchmarks are listed below.

- **A trusted and respected auditing process.** TPC-certified independent auditors verify all results as a requirement for publishing a benchmark result. Additionally, after a benchmark result is published the TPC allows for a peer review process –for 60 days every company in the TPC has the right to challenge any published result based on technical correctness.
- **An objective means of comparing price and price/performance.** The TPC has been the most successful benchmarking group in developing a standard means of comparing the price and price/performance of different systems. All TPC testing requires vendors to detail their hardware and software components, along with the associated costs and three years of maintenance

fees, in order to provide the industry's most accurate price and price/performance metrics.

- **Standard benchmarks for corporate and governmental acquisitions.** Typically, as corporations and governments develop their request for proposals(RFPs) to purchase new systems, they scramble to find an objective means of evaluating the performance of different vendor architectures, technologies and products. Prior to the TPC, these users would spend enormous time and resources trying to define a custom benchmark and convincing the vendor community that it was technically sound and fair to all parties. Using a TPC benchmark already accepted by the user and vendor communities eliminates much of this wasted time and resources.

- **Complete system evaluation vs. subsystem or processor evaluation.** The TPC benchmarking model has been the most successful in modeling and benchmarking a complete end-to-end business computing environment. This has helped TPC benchmarks gain recognition as credible, realistic workloads. Most past and many current benchmarks only measure the hardware performance (processor and memory subsystem). TPC benchmarks have led the way in developing a benchmark model that most fully incorporates robust software testing.

- **Objective engineering tools which spur real hardware and software improvements.** TPC benchmarks, especially TPC-C and TPC-H, are well-understood, stable workloads that engineers use on a continuous basis to eliminate hardware and software bottlenecks that lead to real-world performance improvements for users.

2.2   What Makes the TPC Unique?

Since its formation, the TPC has had a marked impact on the server performance industry. It boasts a membership that is who-is-who in the computer industry. These companies can be considered to be business rivals and yet they willingly work together to showcase and compare their products using the TPC organization. Given the marketing stakes, why do companies trust the TPC to fairly validate their claims? What makes the TPC unique?

First of all the TPC provides cross-platform performance and technology comparisons. The organization provides, manages, and maintains the benchmark specification. The results' sponsors independently decide on the best test configuration to showcase their system as long as it complies with the benchmark specification. This has enabled fair and verifiable cross-platform and technology comparisons.

The TPC is the only benchmark organization that requires price/performance scores across all of its benchmarks. This is a realization of the fact that performance has its costs and those costs have to be declared. The price/performance metric has encouraged test sponsors to be more realistic in their test configurations because cost affects purchasing decisions. The availability date of all components of the test configurations has to be declared. These components have to be orderable at the time the result is published. This has limited test configurations to commercially available and viable products.

Furthermore, all results have to be verified and certified by an independent Auditor prior to publication. Next, a 60-day peer review period begins where the result can be challenged.

All tests require full documentation of the components, applications under test and benchmark procedures to enable test replication by any interested party. This full disclosure makes it possible to question and challenge a result and ensures that all published results are credible and verifiable.

The TPC is the foremost database performance verifying organization. Most of its benchmarks are database-centric and database agnostic and a wide variety of databases have been showcased and compared.

Furthermore, all TPC benchmarks demand that a system support ACID (atomicity, consistency, isolation, and durability) requirements for the database system to demonstrate they can meet the reliability and security features required for real systems. Each benchmark defines a series of tests that are administered by the auditor before each benchmark result is published.

In 2006 TPC introduced a common pricing specification across all its benchmarks that is designed to allow a fair and honest comparison for customers to review. It was created in order to guide the customer, the vendors implementing a benchmark, and the auditors on what is acceptable pricing for the purposes of publication.

The TPC pricing specification does not attempt to dictate or exclude business practices in the marketplace. There may be some restrictions on pricing for publication (such as excluding sales and closeouts) that are different from some business transactions that actually take place in the marketplace, but those restrictions are intended to make publication both tractable and comparable during the lifetime of the publication for the majority of customers and vendors.

Several factors make TPC's pricing specification unique and creditable. Pricing must be based upon some pricing model that the sponsoring company actually employs with customers. Furthermore, the published price must be a price that any customer would pay for the priced configuration, and the methodology used must generate a similar price for a similar configuration for any customer.

Pricing must also be verifiable. In a competitive environment, aggressive discounting may occur in certain situations, so the pricing model employed for TPC Benchmark publications might not represent the best or lowest price some customer would pay. It must, however, represent the pricing that could be obtained by any customer in a request for bid to a single vendor.

Situations that occur when requests for bids go out to multiple vendors, and then those bids are used in multiple negotiations to get a better price, are not represented.

2.3 TPC Organization

At the helm of the TPC organization is the General Council, which is composed of all member companies. To expedite the work of the TPC, the General Council has created two types of subcommittees: standing and technical subcommittees. Standing subcommittees are permanent committees that supervise and manage administrative, public relations, and documentation issues for the TPC. The technical subcommittees are formed to develop a benchmark proposal, maintain the benchmark, and evolve the benchmark after development work is complete.

- **General Council:** All major decisions are made by the General Council. Each member company of the TPC has one vote, and a two-thirds vote is required to pass any motion.
- **Steering Committee:** Consists of five representatives, elected annually, from member companies. The Steering Committee is responsible for overseeing TPC administration, supporting activities, and providing overall direction and recommendations to the General Council. The General Council, however, has the final decision in all substantive TPC matters.
- **Technical Advisory Board:** This subcommittee is tasked with maintaining document and change control over the complex benchmark proposals and methodologies. In addition, the TAB studies issues involving interpretation/ compliance of TPC specifications and makes recommendations to the Council.
- **Public Relations Committee:** This subcommittee is tasked with promoting the TPC and establishing the TPC benchmarks as industry standards.
- **Technical Subcommittees**
  - **Benchmark Development Subcommittees:** A development subcommittee is the working forum within the TPC for development of a Specification.
  - **Benchmark Maintenance Subcommittees:** A maintenance subcommittee is the working forum within the TPC for developing and recommending changes to an approved TPC Benchmark Standard.

The TPC organization adheres strictly to the TPC Bylaws [4] and the TPC Policies [5].

2.4 TPC Membership and Benefits

The TPC has two classes of members, full members and associate members. While only select organizations are eligible for associate membership, all members enjoy the rights and benefits detailed in the TPC bylaws and policies. The following types of organizations are eligible for associate membership: non-profit organizations, educational institutions, market researchers, publishers, consultants, governments, and organizations and businesses that do not create, market or sell computer products or services [6].

Benefits of membership include:

- **Influence in the TPC benchmarking development process.** Given the TPC's tremendous influence on the competitive arena, members have an opportunity to help the TPC decide which benchmarks to consider for future development, and how the current set of benchmarks should evolve. TPC member participation also provides advance, detailed knowledge of upcoming changes to the TPC benchmarking process. These changes can have a profound impact on how the market perceives products and product performance. Members gain insight into how products will be measured in advance of actual benchmark publication.

- **Timely access to ongoing proceedings.** The TPC's membership roster is virtually a "Who's Who" list of commercial computing, featuring many prominent computer system vendors, software database vendors, market research firms and systems integrators. TPC membership provides access to the TPC's internal Web site, which contains all day-to-day rulings, along with ongoing discussions and member proposals.
- **Product Improvement.** Some organizations participate in the TPC's benchmarking process for the same reasons car companies participate in Formula 1 racing. In the world of racing, many of the new components and technologies applied to producing the fastest Formula 1 cars are incorporated into consumer car design. Similarly, the TPC testing process enables members to produce more robust, higher performing retail products. TPC benchmarks are designed to put systems under maximum stress. Since TPC benchmarks model the basic types of operations that a typical transaction processing system might use, they have a wide-range of applicability to customers' environments.

Since the inception of the TPC, the organization's membership roster has grown substantially. In 1988, the TPC had eight members, while in 1994 the organization had 45 members. After many acquisitions and mergers, the TPC now has 25 full members and three associate members.

3 TPC Benchmark Standards: Past and Present

Over the past two decades, the TPC has had a significant impact on the industry and expectations around benchmarks. Prior to the late 1980's, the industry lacked objective, verifiable benchmarks that were relevant to real world computing. TPC benchmarks quickly raised the bar for what the industry came to expect in terms of benchmarks themselves.

Vendors and end users now rely on TPC benchmarks to provide real-world data that is backed by a stringent and independent review process. TPC benchmarks have encouraged the comparison of price and price/performance on an apples-to-apples basis.

3.1 TPC Benchmark Standards Overview

The TPC's primary focus has been on online transaction processing (OLTP) benchmarks. Over the years, the original TPC benchmarks evolved into new benchmarks or were ultimately retired. The chart below, created by TPC associate member IDEAS International, illustrates the progression of TPC's benchmarks over the past 20 years.

TPC Evolving Benchmarks
- TPC-A evolved into TPC-B, and was ultimately replaced by TPC-C.
- TPC-E is a new OLTP benchmark, which currently coexists with TPC-C.

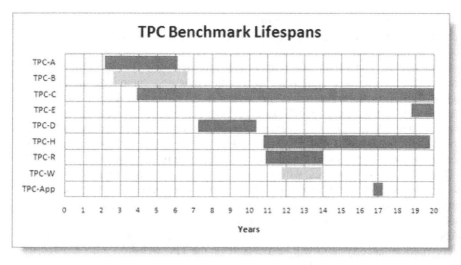

Fig. 1. TPC Benchmark Lifespans [7]

- TPC-D was the first Decision Support benchmark, which as evolved into TPC-H and TPC-R.
- The TPC also developed a web server benchmark, TPC-W, which was later replaced by TPC-App.

TPC Retired Benchmarks

- TPC-R and TPC-W were retired due to lack of industry acceptance.
- TPC-S, TPC-Enterprise and TPC-CS benchmark development efforts were aborted due to lack of support.

TPC "Undecided" Benchmarks

- TPC-DS is the next generation Decision Support benchmark designed to overcome some of the limitations of TPC-H but TPC is unable to reach consensus on TPC-DS.

TPC Current Benchmarks

- TPC-C and TPC-E for OLTP workloads.
- TPC-H for decision support workloads.
- TPC-App for Application Server and Web services.

The TPC-C and TPC-H benchmarks continue to be a popular yardstick for comparing OLTP performance and Decision Support performance respectively. The longevity of these benchmarks means that hundreds of results are publicly available over a wide variety of systems. TPC-E is also gaining momentum.

3.2　TPC Current Developments

Since 1988, the TPC has developed nine benchmarks, each addressing requirements of industry demands. Currently, the TPC's metrics-under-development include the TPC Energy Specification and the TPC-ETL benchmark [8].

3.2.1 The TPC Energy Specification

Performance and price/performance metrics are key criteria in data center purchasing decisions, but the demands of today's corporate IT environment also include energy consumption as one of the most important considerations. Energy efficiency has become one of the most significant factors in evaluating computing hardware. To address this shift of IT purchasers' priorities, the TPC is developing a new Energy Specification to enhance its widely used benchmark standards. The addition of energy consumption metrics to the TPC's current arsenal of price/performance and performance benchmarks will help buyers identify the energy efficiency of computing systems to meet their computational and budgetary requirements.

The TPC Energy metrics will provide an additional dimension to computing systems' performance and price. As with the TPC's price/performance metrics, which rank computing systems according to their cost-per-performance, the TPC Energy metrics will rank systems according to their energy-consumption-per-performance rates, and will take the form of watts/performance. The ranking of the Top Ten energy/performance systems will be available on the TPC website.

Buyers now demand an objective method of comparing all three factors to select equipment that best meets their changing requirements, and the TPC's Energy Specification is being carefully designed to address this need. Like the TPC Pricing Specification, the TPC Energy Specification is a supplement to existing TPC benchmark standards, rather than a standalone measurement framework. This means that it is intended to be compatible with TPC benchmark standards currently in use, including TPC-App, TPC-C, TPC-E and TPC-H. The result will be metrics that enable comparison of systems on all three axes: price, performance and energy consumption.

3.2.2 The TPC-ETL Benchmark

The TPC-ETL (extract, transform and load) benchmark committee was formed in November 2008. The TPC's intent is to develop an ETL environment workload, which manipulates a defined volume of data, preparing the data for use in a traditional data warehouse (DW). In particular, data extracted from an online transaction processing (OTLP) system is transformed along with data from ancillary data sources (including database and non-database sources), and loaded into a data warehouse. The source and destination schemas, data transformations and implementation rules have been designed to be broadly representative of modern ETL systems. The TPC is encouraging companies interested in participating in the development of this benchmark to join the TPC.

4 Benchmark Development Process

The TPC encourages industry experts and the research community to submit draft standard specifications in a format similar to other TPC benchmark standards. The proposal can be a new benchmark in a new domain (e.g. TPC-ETL), a new benchmark in an existing domain (e.g. TPC-E in OLTP domain where TPC-C is a standard) or a refinement of an existing benchmark (e.g. TPC-Energy initiative, adding and energy metric to all TPC benchmarks).

After the TPC Steering Committee reviewed all submitted benchmark proposals for contents, applicability and viability it presents recommendations to the TPC General Council, identifying advantages/disadvantages for each submission and a proposed course of action. The TPC General Council may then vote to formally accept the proposal for future work.

If approved, the TPC General Council establishes and empowers a subcommittee to develop a formal benchmark specification. To speed up the benchmark development cycle, the subcommittee is empowered to brief non-members on their benchmark in order to obtain timely feedback.

At each General Meeting, the subcommittee provides a status update on its work, including a working draft of the specification. The TPC General Council may provide direction and feedback to the subcommittee to further their work.

The TPC General Council may also authorize the release of a draft specification to the public. Principal goals include encouraging companies to implement the draft specification, gathering more experimental data, and speeding up specification approval.

Once the specification is of sufficient quality, the subcommittee will submit it to the General Council for formal review and approval. During this phase, the specification will be made available to all members and the public. All comments and proposed changes will be posted to the TPC's private Web site and considered by the subcommittee for resolution.

The subcommittee will propose resolution of comments as an updated specification, which is then reviewed by the General Council. The General Council approves the updated specification by voting to send the specification out for mail ballot. To become a benchmark standard, the specification must be approved by a mail ballot in accordance with policies.

After the specification has been approved by mail ballot, the General Council will establish a corresponding maintenance subcommittee, which will automatically supersede the development subcommittee. Results on different versions of a TPC benchmark standard are considered comparable unless the General Council stipulates restrictions for publicly comparing older version results with newer version results.

Such complex development and approval processes are necessary to the benchmark development process. Creating carefully designed, robust metrics takes a considerable amount of time and resources, and the TPC's extensive review process is designed to minimize potential future revisions.

5 A Look Ahead

The world is in the midst of an extraordinary information explosion, and the need for industry standard benchmarks remains crucial to the computing industry. To meet industry demands, the TPC is exploring potential areas for benchmark development in 2010 and beyond.

The following areas are considered high-priority for future benchmark exploration:

- Appliance
- Business Intelligence
- Cloud computing
- Complex event processing
- Database performance optimizations
- Green computing
- Data compression
- Disaster tolerance and recovery
- Energy and space efficiency
- Hardware innovations
- High speed data generation
- Hybrid workloads or operational data warehousing
- Unstructured data management
- Software management and maintenance
- Virtualization
- Very large memory systems

In the 1980's, the TPC established the basic framework for price and price/performance metrics based on industry need, and ultimately many of the TPC's original benchmarks have evolved and are still in widespread use today. Now, with its first ever Technology Conference on Performance Evaluation and Benchmarking, the TPC is again laying a basic framework for the development of future benchmarks. This conference is meant to solicit new ideas and to provide a discussion forum for the research community and industry experts. The TPC's Technology Conference on Performance Evaluation and Benchmarking is a concrete step towards identifying and fostering the development of the benchmarks of the future. Tomorrow's metrics will likely have as profound an impact on systems/software vendors and purchasers, as the TPC's price and price/performance benchmarks have today.

Acknowledgements

The authors would like to thank the past and present members of the TPC, especially Jerry Buggert, Andreas Hotea, Charles Levine, Mike Molloy and Kim Shanley for their contributions to documents referenced in this paper. Additionally, the authors would like to thank Meikel Poess for his comments and feedback.

References

1. Transaction Performance Council website (TPC), http://www.tpc.org
2. Standard Performance Evaluation Corporation website (SPEC), http://www.spec.org
3. Shanley, K.: History and overview of the TPC,
   http://www.tpc.org/information/about/history.asp
4. TPC Bylaws,
   http://www.tpc.org/information/about/documentation/bylaws.asp
5. TPC Policies,
   http://www.tpc.org/information/about/documentation/
   TPC_Policies_v5.17.htm
6. TPC Invitation to Join, http://www.tpc.org/information/about/join.asp
7. IDEAS International,
   http://www.ideasint.blogs.com/ideasinsights/2008/10/
   twenty-years-of.html
8. TPC Benchmark Status Report,
   http://www.tpc.org/reports/status/default.asp

A New Direction for TPC?

Michael Stonebraker

Computer Science and Artificial Intelligence Laboratory (CSAIL)
Massachusetts Institute of Technology
Cambridge, Ma
Stonebraker@csail.mit.edu

Abstract. This paper gives the author's opinion concerning the contributions the Transaction Processing Council (TPC) has made in the past, how it is viewed in the present by me and my colleagues, and offers some suggestions on where it should go in the future. In short, TPC has become vendor-dominated, and it is time for TPC to reinvent itself to serve its customer community.

Keywords: Transaction Processing, Data Warehousing, Benchmarking, Standards.

1 Introduction

TPC has now been in existence for more than 20 years. It started its existence serving a great need of the user community on a problem of great relevance to them, as we will see in Section 2. Moreover, TPC-A encouraged the vendors to improved performance dramatically on OLTP. As such, it was a client-focused benchmark oriented toward encouraging vendors to improve their products.

Over time, TPC appears to have been taken over by the commercial vendors. At the present time, most of TPC's benchmarks have been politically engineered through vendor negotiation, and therefore lack relevance to any real world problem. Moreover, TPC has become slow moving and ponderous. Instead of encouraging the vendor community to do better, they are oriented toward preserving the positions of the current vendors. As such I conclude that TPC has "lost its way", as will be explored in more detail in Section 3.

In contrast, there are many areas crying out for either different DBMS features or better DBMS performance. In this paper I will highlight traditional areas (data warehousing and OLTP) as well as a couple of new ones, including science applications and RDF. This discussion appears in Section 4.

As such, the recommendation of this paper is that TPC reorient its mission back to its roots; namely finding areas where there is significant pain in the user community and then constructing benchmarks that encourage the vendor community to address these needs. In other words, TPC should become customer-focused and not vendor-focused.

R. Nambiar and M. Poess (Eds.): TPCTC 2009, LNCS 5895, pp. 11–17, 2009.
© Springer-Verlag Berlin Heidelberg 2009

2   A Look at TPC History

I want to note clearly that this is my interpretation of events from a long time ago, and others may have a different recollection. In 1985 Jim Gray did two terrific things. First, he wrote down a debit-credit benchmark, and then got all his friends to be coauthors on this paper [1]. This benchmark was a reasonable approximation to cashing a check at a bank, and resonated clearly with users and researchers alike. It was simple, consisting of 5 commands that could be coded up quickly in most any system. Lastly, at the time Jim could not find a DBMS that could execute more than 25 debit-credit transactions per second, obviously a paltry number. At the time it was obvious that the user community wanted something much better.

The second terrific thing Jim did was to start the High Performance Transaction Processing Workshop (HPTS) at Asilomar as a forum to discuss ideas for making DBMSs faster on OLTP. The goal of HPTS was to figure out how to achieve 1000 transactions per second, at the time a factor of 40 better than could currently be done. I remember thinking at the time that this was an unbelievably aggressive number.

The first few HPTSs generated lots of ideas on how to go faster on "bread and butter" OLTP. DBMS vendors started touting benchmark numbers on debit-credit, which were obviously never "apples-to-apples". As a direct result of Jim's efforts, the Transaction Processing Council (TPC) was created three years later. TPC set about firming up the specifications for debit-credit, which would ultimately become TPC-A.

Within a few years, performance on TPC-A leaped from 25 per second to 1000 per second, mostly by using techniques such as group commit and multiple lock tables, that were stimulated by HPTS.

I consider the early work of TPC on debit-credit to be noteworthy for the following reasons:

1)   There was a pressing user need
2)   TPC benchmarks were simple and relevant to the user need
3)   The result was a 40-fold improvement in OLTP performance over a few years

In effect, TPC found a user pain, publicized the pain and encouraged the vendor community to fix it. Although Jim Gray had a lot to do with this early process, nevertheless, I believe that the path he put TPC onto is the right one, and is the most effective way to encourage vendor improvement.

3   The Current Situation

I will now take a quick look at TPC-H, TPC-DS and TPC-C on the three scales mentioned above; namely user need, user-relevance, and simplicity.

3.1   TPC-H

There is clear and obvious pain in the user community in the data warehousing area. In my opinion, this comes in six areas:

a) Users are forced into dividing the day into a load window followed by a query window. This "batch processing" operation is forced on them by the structure of the current products from the major vendors. Specifically, all current systems allow simultaneous read and update, and have a lock management system to sort out transaction management. Read operations set read locks while write operations set write locks. A transaction must block if it cannot acquire the lock for an object it wants to read or write. Business intelligence queries tend to entail substantial numbers of reads. Data loads are similarly substantial numbers of writes. If both are run concurrently, the chances of a lock conflict are high. In this case, one or more transactions will block, holding substantial numbers of locks. If this occurs the data base will likely "freeze", i.e. nobody will be able to get any work done. A primitive solution is to force a static division of the day into a read phase and a write phase.

b) In addition, business analysts want to run collections of "what if" scenarios on the same data set. For example, in a retail scenario, an analyst might want to compare sales of certain items today against comparable sales yesterday. Receiving the answer, he might be inclined to ask the same question about other items. The goal is to have the two answers be comparable – i.e. computed from the same data. However, if the data can change between successive queries, then the results cannot be compared "apples-to-apples".

A batch load window solves this problem, by ensuring there are no updates between successive reads. However, there are much more elegant options, including named versions and time travel. Such advanced features are not in the products from most vendors, so batch operation is forced on users.

c) As a result of a) and b), many users are in pain because they are having trouble loading their data within the batch load window allotted. Even if a user can currently load his data, the future is often problematic. Data volumes are increasing at most data warehouses, while the load window is fixed, which indicates trouble is coming. I have talked to numerous users who can predict within few days when they will hit the "load window wall".

d) Business analysts are relentless in their desire for more complex queries on more data. The correlations that analysts want to run are moving from ordinary statistics queries to more complex clustering and data mining tasks. Moreover, users are relentless in their desire to correlate more data elements. This is one of the reasons data warehouse sizes are going up so rapidly.

As a result, most warehouse hardware configurations cannot keep up. Warehouse administrators are in pain because they must say "no" to user requests for service.

e) Scalability. Several data base offering from major vendors have serious scalability problems, that limit the ability of users to add processing horsepower to current configurations. These tend to be vendors that are running on shared memory multiprocessor or shared disk configurations. For users of these products, there is a "query processing wall".

In contrast, "shared nothing (or MPP) vendors tend to scale much better than vendors on older architectures.

f)   The "out of box" experience is awful for most current products. It is too hard to install the system, too hard to design a schema, too hard to load data, and too hard to learn and manipulate the tuning knobs to optimize performance. My experience with the major vendor's products is that it takes weeks to months to perform the above steps. It should take less than one day. Also, the current tuning aids do not appear to be very helpful in the systems I have used.

TPC-H has no data loading, and therefore there is no test for load performance or consistent read in a "trickle load" environment. There is no focus on "out-of box" experience. There is no requirement to test scalability. Moreover, test configurations for TPC-H tend to have absurd numbers of disks for the data stored. For example, a recent published test used a disk system with 32 times the disk space required for the benchmark; i.e. TPC-H is being run on a hardware environment that no user in his right mind would set up.

Moreover, the schema for TPC-H is well known as an example of terrible schema design [2]. Lastly, TPC-H has been "jiggered" (presumably by the vendors) to disallow materialized views, one of the very common ways to improve query performance in data warehouses.

As such TPC-H is a bad schema with no data load and materialized views disallowed. As such, it is hardly relevant to any real world problem.

Although it consists of only 22 queries, TPC-H is not simple. Explaining some of these queries to undergraduates in a DBMS course is not a trivial task. In my opinion, it could be a lot simpler.

Although these problems with TPC-H have been known for years, TPC has been very slow to do anything about them. More ominously, their recent response (to start exploring TPC-DS) is a step in the wrong direction. It still does not have a requirement for incremental load and has been ballooned to 99 queries (the last time I looked), hardly responsive to user relevance or simplicity. Also, TPC-DS has been in the works for years, hardly an example of a speedy response to a problem.

As such, I consider TPC to have lost its way in the warehousing space. The way forward, in my opinion, would be put the user community in control of the process, not the vendor community.

3.2 TPC-C

I want to make 2 very brief comments about TPC-C. First, the record holder for performance on TPC-C is running more than 6M new orders per minute; i.e. about 100,000 new orders per second. I know of no retailer on the planet running at this volume of orders. Hence, performance on the benchmark has exceeded the needs of retail users in its current form. As such, it addresses no real world pain issue.

Second, the schema does not conform to any real world problem I know of. Again, the schema has been "jiggered" by the vendors, presumably for political compromise.

Notice clearly that I am not saying there is no OLTP pain; quite the contrary. Most "web 2.0" companies are in major pain in the OLTP area. One company has major needs in the multi-tenancy area, which are not addressed by any TPC activity. Several other companies are "sharding" (partitioning) their data in user-level code to get their OLTP performance requirements met. The reason for user-level sharding is either because the multi-node performance of their chosen DBMS is unacceptable or because their chosen DBMS has no multi-node support. However, no TPC activity (that I am aware of) is addressing either of these issues.

In addition, every OLTP application I am aware of wants 7 x 24 x 365 x 10 years. I.e they want their application to never fail. Twenty years ago this was too expensive to contemplate; now applications are happy to pay for the data redundancy and network bandwidth to achieve non-stop operation. However, this universal requirement is not reflected in TPC benchmarks.

In addition, high volume retailers on the web are building high performance OLTP systems that look nothing like TPC-C. They are willing to sacrifice transactional consistency in favor of eventual consistency [3] so as to achieve high availability. Again, this is an ominous sign that TPC-C is no longer relevant.

3.3 Summary

In this section I want to make a collection of comments, that should cause TPC to reassess its mission.

Current TPC rules make it very expensive to run the benchmark. Hence, this discourages small vendors from participating, and most do not. Hence, TPC is becoming a club open only to large vendors.

The major data warehouse vendor (Teradata) does not use TPC-H. In fact, the majority of the data warehouse DBMS vendors do not run TPC-H, obviously because their customers have decided it is not relevant to their decision making process. This is a sign that TPC has lost its relevance in the data warehouse sector.

A similar comment can be applied to the OLTP sector.

Lastly, more than one analyst has decided that TPC is no longer relevant to user needs [4, 5].

One option would be for TPC to "declare success" in accomplishing its mission, and cease operation. However, there are a substantial collection of good things TPC could choose to focus on. The next section offers some ideas on future directions for TPC to address the issues above.

4 What Should TPC Do?

I have two suggestions for TPC in this section, one concerning traditional markets, and one concerning new applications.

4.1 Traditional Markets

In both the data warehouse and OLTP markets, there is considerable pain that is not being addressed by TPC. There are also plenty of smart people who can articulate this pain. In the warehouse space, to be relevant, the following are required:

a) one button install
b) much better "out-of-box" experience
c) schemas that make sense
d) trickle load

e)   "what if" scenarios on consistent data
f)   failover on crashes, including a "pull the plug" stress test
g)   petabyte workloads
h)   scalability to 100 nodes now, more in the future

In the OLTP area, unmet needs exist in the area of:

a)   multi-tenancy
b)   failover
c)   disaster recovery
d)   parallelism to 10's of nodes
e)   relaxed consistency rules

Most of the vendor products are not very good at these features, and TPC could play a major role in articulating these needs and encouraging the vendors to do much better. I. e. TPC could play the same role they played 20 years ago with TPC-A. To move in this direction, a new political process would have to be constructed. This process would have to represent user requirements rather than vendor wishes.

4.2 New Areas

As I wander through the world, I am constantly struck by the number of users with incredibly hard data management problems. These exist both in areas that the current vendors pay attention to and in new areas. Recently, I spoke with a financial services firm who wanted to compute the **real time** value of credit derivatives (called "toxic" assets here in the US) for 30,000 such instruments. The computation and data management scale of this problem is mind-boggling. Multiple financial services firms desperately want to solve this problem, so they can manage the financial strategy of their firm to acceptable risk levels.

TPC should be actively trolling for the "new problems" in traditional areas, such as this one.

Secondly, consider science data bases. It is hard for me to find a science person who is happy with relational data bases. Most refuse to use them, relying on "bare metal" solutions instead. This is true in big science projects, such as the Large Hadron Collider (LHC) as well as in smaller ones. Under Jim Gray's guidance, the astronomy community has put the Sloan digital sky survey into a DBMS, and the results have been noteworthy. However, even in astronomy, there are many unmet needs [6].

If the planet is going to be saved, it will be the science community which leads the way. Our DBMS community has pretty much ignored their requirements. TPC should do its part in defining and publicizing this unmet need.

A similar comment can be made about RDF data in the bio-pharm community.

4.3 A Call to Action

In my opinion, it is time for TPC to reinvent itself. Instead of continuing with the current political process of slow moving benchmarks that are complex and not relevant to user needs, TPC should return to its roots of looking for user pain and then publicizing this pain to the vendor community, so that future systems will be better than current ones. Obviously, this requires a change in the current TPC process.

In addition, TPC must move at the speed of the industry today. From beginning to end a standard should consume not more than 6 months, a radical improvement from today's process. Presumably this will require benchmarks to have champions of the stature that Jim Gray brought to TPC-A.

In addition, TPC should reach out to the research community, which has extensive experience in designing benchmarks for a variety of purposes, to get their involvement. This workshop is a good step in the right direction. For example, there is at least one science DBMS benchmark that TPC might be able to leverage [7]. Similarly, there are at least a couple of RDF benchmarks [8] and a Hadoop-oriented benchmark [9]. Put differently, the research community is working on cutting edge applications, and TPC should take careful note of these efforts.

Moreover, the research community often has talent (e.g. graduate students) which TPC could leverage under certain circumstances. This could move benchmark activities forward at a quicker rate.

My hope is that this workshop will spend at least part of its time on how to address this call to action.

References

1. Anon, et al.: A Measure of Transaction Processing Power, Datamation (March 1985)
2. O'Neil, P.: https://www.cs/umb.edu/~poneil/StarSchemaB.pdf
3. Vogels, W.: Eventually Consistent. ACM Queue (April 15, 2009)
4. http://www.forester.com/Research/Document/Exerpt/0.7211.53871.00.html
5. http://www.dbms2.com/2009/06/22/the-tpc-h-benchmark-is-a-blight-upon-the-industry/
6. Szalay, A.: Private communication
7. Stonebraker, M., et al.: A Standard Science Benchmark. SciDB.org website, http://scidb.microartsdev.com
8. Abadi, D., Marcus, A., Madden, S., Hollenbach, K.: Scalable Semantic Web Data Management. In: Proc. 2007 VLDB Conference (August 2007)
9. http://www.database.cs.brown.edu/sigmod09/

The Art of Building a Good Benchmark

Karl Huppler

IBM Corporation
IBM MS XQK
3605 Highway 52 North
Rochester, MN 55901
huppler@us.ibm.com

Abstract. What makes a good benchmark? This is a question that has been asked often, answered often, altered often. In the past 25 years, the information processing industry has seen the creation of dozens of "industry standard" performance benchmarks – some highly successful, some less so. This paper will explore the overall requirements of a good benchmark, using existing industry standards as examples along the way.

1 Introduction – Building a Good Benchmark

Why so many benchmarks? The cynic would say "They haven't got it right, yet." The pessimist would say "They'll never get it right, but they keep on trying." The realist knows "The computing industry is so vast and changes so rapidly that new benchmarks are constantly required, just to keep up."

R. Nambiar and M. Poess (Eds.): TPCTC 2009, LNCS 5895, pp. 18–30, 2009.
© Springer-Verlag Berlin Heidelberg 2009

Unfortunately, just because a benchmark is "new" doesn't mean that it measures the "right stuff." The design and implementation of a good performance benchmark is a complex process – often compromising between contrasting goals.

There are five key aspects that all good benchmarks have, to some degree. It is not necessary to be perfect in each of these. In fact, it is impossible to be so. Most good benchmarks have clear strengths in one or two areas, and accommodate the others. The five characteristics are:

- Relevant – A reader of the result believes the benchmark reflects something important
- Repeatable – There is confidence that the benchmark can be run a second time with the same result
- Fair – All systems and/or software being compared can participate equally
- Verifiable – There is confidence that the documented result is real
- Economical – The test sponsors can afford to run the benchmark

Often, in order to satisfy the last four of these items, a benchmark developer must choose to give up on some of the first. This is not all bad, as long as one understands the choices being made. In fact, as we explore each of these items in greater detail, along with discussions of compromise between them, we will also look at the dangers of (believe it or not) doing too good a job in creating a benchmark.

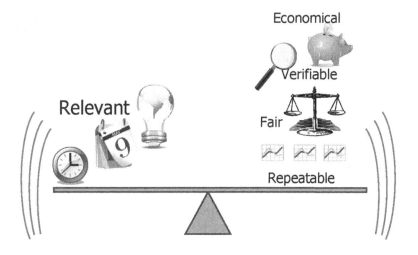

2 Relevant

There are a number of characteristics that can make a benchmark relevant, or irrelevant. Some of them are:

- Meaningful and understandable metric
- Stresses software features in a way that is similar to customer applications
- Exercises hardware systems in a way that is similar to customer applications
- Longevity – leading edge but not bleeding edge
- Broad applicability
- Does not misrepresent itself
- Has a target audience that wants the information

First, the **metric of the benchmark must be understood by the reader** – or at least be perceived to be understood. For example, the metric of SPEC's (Standard Performance Evaluation Corporation) SPECjbb_2005 benchmark is "SPECjbb bops". It isn't difficult for the casual reader to determine that the "ops" is "operations per second", and they might guess that it is "business operations per second", there is no doubt that it is "business operations per second as measured with the SPECjbb benchmark" and one might even infer that the "jbb" stands for "java business benchmark", even though you won't find this phrase in SPEC's documentation for the benchmark. The view that this is a throughput measure of merit for server-side transactional java where bigger is better is quickly understood – and this is a strength of the benchmark.

It parallels another great benchmark, TPC Benchmark C (TPC-C), whose primary performance metric is simply "tpmC" – transactions per minute in Benchmark C – simple, yet elegant: This is a transactional benchmark, measuring throughput, where a larger value is better. That the "C" stands for the third benchmark produced by the Transaction Processing Performance Council (TPC) may be a little obscure, but this can be forgiven for the most successful transactional database benchmark in the industry. A student of the benchmark will find that "tpmC" is really a measure of "New Order Transactions per minute", where the New Order transaction is only one of 5 business transactions in TPC-C, but this is fine, since the ratios of the transaction mix are tightly controlled in the benchmark.

Two more benchmark metric examples: The TPC-H benchmark performance metric is "QphH@xxxGB" where "xxx" is a value that represents the database size that was measured. One can infer that this is also a throughput measure, one of queries per hour in Benchmark H (No, the "H" doesn't represent the 8th benchmark produced by the TPC – it stands for "ad Hoc"). If you study the benchmark, you find that the metric isn't the actual number of queries that are executed per hour, because the metric is actually the geometric mean of the throughput measure

$$\sqrt{\frac{3600*SF}{\sqrt[24]{\prod_{i=1}^{i=22} QI(i,0) * \prod_{j=1}^{j=2} RI(j,0)}}} * [(S*22*3600)/Ts *SF]$$

times the database size and the database size divided by the geometric mean of the individual query times - - Confused? Sure, but for the casual reader, QphH@dbsize means it is a measure of throughput capacity in Benchmark H for queries run against a particular size of database - - - and for all intentional muddying of the formula, here, it truly does relate to that very thing!

My final example is the SPECcpu2006 suite (SPECfp2006, SPECfp_rate2006, SPECint2006 and SPECint_rate2006). Here, the metric is - - - a number. There are no units, because this metric is essentially a ratio of the ability of the system under test to perform in a suite of intensive processor-oriented operations and functions in comparison to a reference point. To make matters more obscure, there are potentially 8 numbers, for "base" and "peak" measures of each of the two ways to run each of the two independent suites in the benchmark suite. One might ask "How can something that seems to measure something so esoteric be a good benchmark?" The answer is that the SPECcpu suite is so overwhelmingly strong in other aspects that it is far and above the most popular performance benchmark in the world.

The next "relevance" point is the **use of software features in a realistic way**. This can be one of the most challenging aspects of a benchmark, and one that leads to a fairly short life-span for benchmark relevance – because software is constantly evolving. As each software supplier delivers features and functions on an independent schedule, it can also run directly against the "fair" requirement for benchmarks.

The appropriate use of software features is *perhaps the most important requirement* of benchmark development, even though it is also one of the least obvious to the casual observer. It is easy enough to tag a benchmark with terms like "Database", "OLTP", "Decision Support", "Numeric Intensive", "Compute Intensive" and the like. Such terms may make a benchmark appear to be exercising relevant software paths. However, if the benchmark does not use software features in the way that a "typical" customer application will, it can prevent computer providers from delivering optimal solutions to their customers. If a benchmark becomes popular, computer providers <u>will</u> invest skills and money to improve the benchmark results. If the benchmark uses a very limited software path or if the benchmark uses a path that is seldom used by consumers, this investment is made *at the expense* of development that might improve real consumer applications.

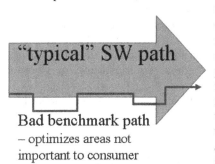

Bad benchmark path
– optimizes areas not important to consumer

On the other hand, when a benchmark exercises features realistically, it can be an absolute boon for consumers, because it gives development organizations the incentive to optimize paths that the consumer wants to take. The hallmark example of this is TPC-C. When it was delivered in 1992, it represented database transaction processing in a way that many,

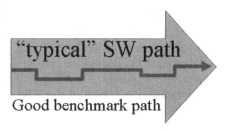

Good benchmark path

many consumers accomplished that function. At that time, I examined a database that IBM maintained that had performance data from thousands of AS/400 customers (running the operating system that was the predecessor to the IBM i operating system that is one of the options on IBM Power Systems, today.) The assessment showed that the overall path length of a TPC-C New Order was at approximately the 70th percentile of IBM AS/400 customer applications and exercised database and workstation features in a way that was very similar to our customer's OLTP applications. TPC-C has enabled the industry to provide customers with optimizations that are important to their applications, such as improved logging, improved serialization locking, optimal transaction processing paths, optimal transaction control, task/resource affinity, optimal interaction between customer workstations, middle-tier servers and database servers and overall improved path length for many key transaction processing functions. On several occasions, I have observed customer applications that had expanded with customer growth that would have experienced bottlenecks that would slow them down, except that our development team had already removed those bottlenecks to help optimized TPC-C. The relevant paths of the benchmark allowed us to optimize features ahead of when our customers needed them, helping them to expand without stressing the computer systems that they relied on to run their businesses.

There are other examples of similar improvements that benchmarks have provided for consumers: TPC-H provided opportunities to greatly improve parallel processing for large queries. The SPECcpu suite helps to improve compilers, arithmetic operations, string operations, and others. Versions of SPECjbb help with just-in-time (JIT) compilation for Java code. The list goes on.

Next on the "relevance list" is the **use of hardware in a manner that is similar to consumer environments.** As with software, it is important that a benchmark exercise hardware components and subsystems in a meaningful way, but it is even more important that a benchmark does not exercise hardware in ways that are not realistic. For example, a benchmark that does nothing but exercise a floating point accelerator might cause undue investment in that area, at the expense of investments in more general hardware improvements. On the other hand, a benchmark that exercises a mixture of floating point arithmetic, integer arithmetic, cache, memory, string manipulation and vector manipulation might provide a very satisfactory measure of the processor and related components in a system.

The benchmark of reference is, again, the SPECcpu suite of benchmarks. The members of the Open Systems Group CPU (SPECcpu) committee within SPEC spend a great deal of time and effort making sure that the individual test cases used within the suite stress a variety of relevant hardware and software functions within the processor nest. This is not to say that the benchmark tests that make up the SPECcpu suite are the end-all measure of hardware functions. In fact, these benchmarks do not exercise all hardware  functions – by design. This leads, briefly, into a discussion of **appropriate representation.** A strength of the SPECcpu suite is that it says what it does and it does what it says. There is no implication that superior performance in SPECint_rate2006, for example, will translate to superior performance in an environment that requires massive numbers of user-tasks simultaneously competing for processor, memory, cache and I/O resources on the system – but there is a strong indication that it will work well for the portions of the processing that require substantial time to be spent manipulating integers in a variety of ways.

For focus on a broader spectrum of hardware components in an environment with massive numbers of competing tasks that exercise processor, memory, cache, NUMA

characteristics, network I/O and storage I/O, the benchmark of choice has, for years, been TPC-C. One could argue that the sands of time have eroded the software relevance of TPC-C. Applications of today are far more complex than those developed in 1992, when TPC-C was first introduced. However, TPC-C continues to be a premier engineering tool for ensuring that an overall hardware design (and the associated firmware and OS kernels that run on it) is capable of supporting robust multi-user, multi-tasking environments. In this regard, the TPC's two transaction processing benchmarks compliment each other, with TPC-C enabling and encouraging strong affinity and non-uniform allocation of system resources and TPC-E requiring a more uniform allocation of resources across the entire system with less focus on affinity. Both environments are important to consumers, and a combination of the two benchmarks can lead to strong innovation in processor technology and associated hardware components.

Another aspect of **appropriate representation** is taking the steps necessary to ensure that the benchmark is not misused to represent something that was not intended. This can be a challenge, since one of the strengths of a benchmark is to deliver a metric and exercise software and hardware in ways that are meaningful. The natural inclination of a user of the benchmark is to generalize this to assume that the benchmark represents *everything* associated with the environment that it emulates.

I recently had an experience with SPECjbb2005 that highlighted this. The benchmark is "server-side java" and "transactional", with a metric that includes "operations per second". The inclination is to assume that it can be used to represent *all* transactional java environments that run on a server with multiple users – even though the benchmark intentionally does not include network I/O, storage I/O, database or a user interface. In the situation I encountered, someone was attempting to use SPECjbb2005 to examine power management routines when the system is not running at full speed. The way to reduce system utilization with SPECjbb2005 is to run fewer jobs than there are logical processors – which focused some jobs on processors running at nearly 100% utilization while other processors sat idle.

Clearly, this is not the way that a real transactional environment would work at moderate system utilization, and the result of the experiment were not what would be expected in a real environment. I should note that SPEC's SPECpower committee addressed this very point when creating SPECpower_ssj2008. This committee used the SPECjbb2005 application as a base for the SPECpower_ssj2008 benchmark, but altered it to more appropriately distribute work across the entire system at lower utilization points.

The next item on my "relevance" list is **longevity.** A benchmark whose usefulness lasts only one year is not a benchmark – it is a workload for a white paper. To a large degree, longevity is accomplished by creating a successful benchmark with other qualities described in this paper. In addition to satisfying these requirements "today", however, there needs to be a perception that the benchmark will satisfy them "tomorrow". In order to build a base of comparative performance information, a benchmark needs to be relevant for several years. This means that the software concepts that are exercised must be modern enough that they will still seem current 5 years hence, but not so modern that they will go through rapid change as they mature – The benchmark must be leading edge, but not bleeding edge. It also means that benchmark development must be accomplished in a reasonable time. Innovations in computing technology will likely stay current for five years and may stay current for ten, but if it takes seven years to develop a benchmark, chances are the opportunity for the benchmark to remain relevant over time is very limited.

There is another way to look at **longevity** – that being the longevity of the benchmark suite. Both the SPEC and TPC organizations have recognized that as technology changes, benchmarks may need to change with it. SPEC, in particular, has done an excellent job of initiating discussions for the next version of a benchmark almost as soon as a new version is released. Thus, while the results from the SPECcpu95 suite are not comparable with those of SPECcpu2000 or SPECcpu2006, the concept of what the benchmark is trying to achieve has been retained, maintaining longevity while upgrading the currency of the benchmark suite. The TPC has done this to some degree, too, with changes to the pricing and storage rules for TPC-C and the growth of TPC-D into TPC-R and TPC-H, although one could argue that the next change is overdue.

There are two items left in the "relevant" list: **broad applicability** and **having a strong target audience.** Both seem simple and straightforward, but both create challenges.

Certainly a benchmark application that focuses on the electronic examination of dental x-rays would not be considered to have a broad interest base, and yet if it does not include some of the functions that are important for this, the target audience may not include dentists who are looking to upgrade their information technology. On the other hand, a benchmark that makes use of a variety of imaging techniques could build a target audience that includes dentists, physicians, x-ray specialists, meteorologists, seismologists, geologists, natural resource engineers, crime investigators, and security specialists. The key is to retain sufficient specific use of hardware and software functions and features to stay "real", while broadening the application to be appropriate for a wide number of uses.

A couple more points on the identification of a **strong target audience:** The target audience must be interested in receiving the information. Suppose the key selection criteria for a computer solution for the groups listed above center around software functionality, hardware stability and customer service, with the assumption that the application design and hardware capacity are capable of handling the required workload. If the target audience doesn't need the information to help with their purchase decisions, the benchmark is of little use.

Finally, I must note that the "target audience" does not need to be "customers". Taking advantage of the many strengths that are listed throughout this paper, the SPECcpu suite has developed a huge audience – in the very people who run the benchmark – engineers, programmers, scientists, academics. Because the benchmark does not require sophisticated software support, it is also an outstanding tool for early processor development. While the benchmarks within the suite are most certainly used to help sell systems, this is almost an afterthought, once the real audience for the benchmark results completes its study.

3 The Other Side of the Coin

Thus far, I have spent a good deal of time on the need for performance benchmarks to be relevant. Indeed, without relevance, the benchmark will be worthless, at best, and at the worst will cause damage by forcing bad investments. However, just being relevant is insufficient to label a benchmark as "a good benchmark."

An often used phrase is "The best benchmark is the customer's application". This may be true as long as one accepts a target audience of one, but it may not be true, even then. The other four main criteria also enter in. If the benchmark results cannot be **repeated** again and again, the value of the measurement information is in question. Often a customer environment has data that change in a nonuniform way, making it difficult to run the benchmark over and over without doing a full system save/restore operation. If the benchmark cannot be run on different systems with different software packages driving it, it cannot be used to **fairly** evaluate different solutions. If there is no way to **verify** that the results are accurate and the benchmark was run correctly, the confidence in the result is questionable. If the benchmark cannot be run **economically,** without making a massive investment, there is little incentive to run it.

It is well worth discussing these four criteria further, including some examples of how successful benchmarks have implemented them.

3.1 Repeatable

It sounds so simple – You run the same code on the same system, so you should get the same answer, right? In most cases, this is not so. Database applications grow (or shrink) data and consequently grow and change indices, which means "identical" queries have different paths and process different numbers of rows. Java applications can JIT repeatedly, causing the identical "code" to perform more effectively over time, but they also build up garbage in the java heap that must be cleaned out. Even physical entities are not immune: rotating disk can   become less efficient when filled, because seek times will be longer and writes to newly formatted solid state storage are typically faster than over-writes of space that has been previously used to store information.

Benchmark designers must trade some aspects of "reality" to ensure repeatability and consistency – both from run to run and from minute to minute. One of these trade-offs is the creation of a steady-state period within the benchmark. Real applications are hardly steady in the way that they generate work on the system, but a benchmark where results will be compared requires either that the application and associated performance does not change over a period of time (such as with TPC-C, SPECjbb_2005 and SPECweb2005) or that the exact same (or nearly exact same) "dynamic" work flow runs for each iteration of the benchmark (such as with the SPECcpu suite and TPC-H) In TPC-H, updates are made to tables, but in key ranges that do not affect the queries that are the main focus of the benchmark, and in a way that lock contention from the inserts does not affect the read-only queries. In TPC-C, although the History, Order and Order_Line tables continue to grow throughout the benchmark run, empirical data demonstrates that they do not grow so much as to affect the processing of the benchmark application. And, while the TPC-C New_Order table is increased at the same rate that rows are removed by the Delivery transaction, care is taken to reset the database at least after every 12 hours of benchmark execution, because that is the point when the Delivery transaction will begin to process new orders that were created during the benchmark run, rather than the nicely compressed and ordered information that comes in the prebuilt database.

3.2 Fair/Portable

This is another requirement that seems blatantly obvious, but is truly a challenge to accomplish. Portability is less of an issue today that it was two decades ago when the primary benchmark consortias were formed. The use of standard C, C++ and Java languages and the use of standard SQL data access methods allows benchmark applications  to be run on a wide variety of platforms. However, being "portable" does not mean that the benchmark is automatically "fair".

Consider the wide variety of database products that exist in today's market – from traditional row-oriented structures, to newer columnar organization, to in-memory environments, to database accelerator appliances – each with specific strengths and potential weaknesses. How, then, can any single application fairly represent the ability of each of these products to perform in a more general environment? The answer is, of course, "It can't." However, benchmark implementers can make compromises that help the situation.

At the extreme, these compromises can take a benchmark to a "lowest common denominator" situation, where they include only tried and true functions that almost all products have had a chance to optimize already. This can be self-defeating, making the benchmark old before it is even introduced. The key is to select functions that are viewed as important in the environment that the benchmark attempts to emulate and to assume that, for products that are weak in some areas, the benchmark can be used to help optimize those products for the general benefit of their customers. The phrase on application currency, "leading edge but not bleeding edge," also applies to the creation of fair benchmarks.

Another aspect of fairness comes, not with the specific benchmark design, but with the designers. If a benchmark is developed and prototyped only on one operating environment, it will naturally tend to be optimized for that environment, at the expense of others. This has been true for some benchmarks from SPEC's Java/ClientServer committee in the past, which focused initially on UNIX-related environments and the TPC's TPC-App benchmark, where development was focused on Windows environments. These benchmarks naturally flowed toward the environments of choice for the benchmark developers, and were not necessarily "fair" to the other environments – even though part of this is because of the choice of the specific vendors involved to simply not participate.

Some compromises can be avoided by not relying on a single benchmark, but instead using multiple benchmarks that may appear to operate in the same space. As previously mentioned, TPC-C is structured to stress features that can take advantage of partitioning and strong affinity between processes and the data they manipulate, whereas TPC-E is structured to reflect applications that are not as easily divided. TPC-E uses standard SQL with portions of the application logic being dictated by the benchmark, much like a business management software package might run, whereas TPC-C allows a broader range of data access methods and complete control over the transaction application code, much like a custom "roll your own" application would use. TPC-H focuses on ad-hoc queries, while its prior sister benchmark, TPC-R, focused on the kind of report generation that can be achieved with pre-defined materialized views that are formed with prior knowledge of the kind of queries that will execute. (TPC-R was retired by the TPC, not because it was poorly implemented, but because it did not generate a sufficient target audience to warrant active continuation of the benchmark.) This is also one of the reasons there is a SPECint2006 and a SPECfp2006 instead of a SPECcpu benchmark.

3.3 Verifiable

A benchmark result is not very useful if there is not a high degree of confidence that it represents the actual performance of the system under test. Simple benchmarks can be self-verifying, providing high confidence as soon as the result is delivered. More complex "system level" benchmarks have greater requirements for verification because there are more things that can change. One possible answer is to take the route that the TPC has taken, requiring benchmark results to be reviewed by a TPC-certified auditor who is very familiar with the benchmark and can identify  when an implementation does not follow the benchmark requirements.

SPEC's approach is to simplify benchmarks when possible, to provide automatic verification routines when possible, and to assign final verification to the committee that created the benchmark and is charged with considering revisions in the future.

Both approaches are designed to deliver confidence to the receiver of benchmark results and both have merit. The TPC could learn from SPEC in the creation of self verification routines and the simplification of benchmarks when complexity is not required. As SPEC works toward more complex environments, such as Service Oriented Architecture and Virtualization, they may find that volunteer reviews of results are insufficient without the benefit of the dedicated scrutiny of an independent professional.

3.4 Economical

This is the final item in my list of primary criteria. It is too often overlooked during initial benchmark development, because the initial phases of development are focused on emulating reality to provide the necessary relevance for the benchmark. Indeed, to be relevant, one might expect a benchmark to be realistic; and to be realistic often means to be complex; and to be complex invariably means to be expensive. This is clearly another opportunity for compromise, if one wants to create a successful benchmark.

The term, "economical", does not mean "cheap", but rather "worth the investment". Consider IBM's leading TPC-C result (6,085,166 tpmC, $2.81USD/tpmC, available December 10, 2008) which employed the use of 11,000 disk drives and 128 middle-tier client systems. Clearly, the return on the investment was worth it. The benchmark was implemented and the result published, after all. On the other hand, it isn't something one wants to do every week! In fact, as systems become more and more powerful, the cost of supporting equipment in the TPC-C benchmark has been one of the contributing factors in a decline in benchmark publishes.

Other benchmarks, like TPC-E, TPC-H, SPECjAppServer2004, SPECweb2005 and some SPEC and TPC benchmarks that are currently under development require robust system configurations that will require investments to run them. However, as with TPC-C, the existence of storage, memory and networking components is key to the business model for these benchmarks, so the trade-off must be the degree to which the business model is satisfied.

In contrast, SPECjbb2005 and SPECfp2006/SPECint2006 enjoy large numbers of benchmark publishes – in part because it is not necessary to establish a massive data center to support them. College students can run these benchmarks on their laptops. They might not want to play too many video games while they wait for SPECfp2006 to complete, but the point is that the benchmarks are very affordable. Both benchmarks make conscious trade-off decisions – They select only a slice of the computing industry's "total reality", in return for the appeal of being inexpensive to run, easy to run and easy to verify. As long as they are not used out of the context of their intent, they also meet the requirements for relevance, fairness and repeatability.

4 You Don't Want All Items Satisfied

Can a benchmark be too perfect? I think so. When TPC-C was introduced in 1992, it satisfied a hunger for a meaningful, robust benchmark that was representative of the kind of database transaction processing that existed in the industry. It had (and still has) a business model that was easily understood. It used software and hardware in a representative way. It was (and is) verifiable. It was (and is) repeatable. At the time, it was relatively economical (The first benchmark results topped out at 33.81 tpmC and 54.14 tpmC, requiring somewhat fewer resources than the results of today.) The target audience was - - - Everyone! Many companies do different things with their computing technology, but ALL businesses must do some kind of database transaction processing to run their business. TPC-C grew to be the premier benchmark of the industry. Marketing teams and customers asked for results in TPC-C first and considered other benchmarks as an afterthought.

TPC-C became such a force in performance benchmarks that it was extraordinarily difficult to change or introduce new, "competing" benchmarks. It became an almost generic measure of computer power, regardless of whether a target application was similar to the TPC-C business model or not. The TPC had several development efforts that would have built on the strengths of TPC-C, while upgrading the characteristics of the benchmark to keep pace with the times. Of these, the newest TPC benchmark, TPC-E, was the only successful one, and although the rate of publishes of TPC-E has now exceeded those of TPC-C, one could argue that they continue to be slowed by the continued strength of the TPC-C benchmark.

How many TPC-C's does it take to run that geothermal analysis application?

In contrast, while SPEC benchmarks were far from obscure, these benchmarks have not been viewed under the brightest of spotlights that was, for a time, reserved for TPC-C, and the engineers who created them have enjoyed the freedom to maintain currency by reviewing and revising them.

5 In Summary

What can we learn from all of this? The first point is that benchmark developers must keep these five primary criteria in mind from the beginning of the development process. Benchmarks must have some component of relevance, repeatability, fairness, verifiability and economy. Perhaps more important is the reality that all of these should not (and likely cannot) be totally satisfied. It is more important to understand the compromises made to enable one strength over another than it is to satisfy every possible criterion.

It is equally important to ensure that the consumers of benchmark information understand the strengths and limitations of each benchmark. It may be better to spend 2 years developing a benchmark that stresses a single subsystem than it is to spend 6 years developing a total system benchmark, but not if the subsystem benchmark is used to represent the "total system."

The industry continues to move rapidly, which implies that new benchmarks are needed and old ones should be considered for retirement. There will likely be some mainstays – Linpack, for one, TPC-C for another, but there is also a need for new tools to evaluate and optimize the features and functions that are growing in importance in today's environment.

Finally, we need to learn from each other. The TPC has an outstanding reputation for building robust, full system benchmarks. As SPEC moves in that direction (particularly with their efforts in virtualization), they could learn a few things from the TPC. SPEC has an outstanding reputation for "rapid" (still measured in years) development and enhancement of benchmarks, and for making conscious compromises I recommend to make benchmarks more manageable in scope and therefore more readily accepted by those who are interested in using them to measure computer systems. The TPC could well learn from this example.

Trademarks: *TPC* and *TPC Benchmark* are copyrights of the Transaction Processing Performance Council. The *SPEC logo, SPEC, SPECjbb, SPECsfs, SPECmail, SPECint, SPECfp, SPECweb, SPECjAppServer, SPECjms and SPECjvm* are registered trademarks of the Standard Performance Evaluation Corporation. *BAPco and SYSmark* are registered trademarks of the Business Applications Performance Corporation. *SPC Benchmark* is a trademark of the Storage Performance Council.

Database Are Not Toasters: A Framework for Comparing Data Warehouse Appliances

Omer Trajman[1], Alain Crolotte[2], David Steinhoff[3],
Raghunath Othayoth Nambiar[4], and Meikel Poess[5]

[1] Vertica Systems, 8 Federal St., Billerica, MA-01821, USA
Omer@Vertica.com
[2] Teradata, 17095 Via del Campo, San Deigo, CA-92127, USA
Alain.Crolotte@teradata.com
[3] ParAccel, 9920 Pacific Heights Blvd. Suite 450, San Diego, CA-92121, USA
david.steinhoff@paraccel.com
[4] Hewlett-Packard Company, 11445 Compaq Center Dr. W, Houston, TX-77070, USA
Raghu.Nambiar@hp.com
[5] Oracle Corporation, 500 Oracle Parkway, Redwood Shores, CA-94065, USA
Meikel.Poess@oracle.com

Abstract. The success of Business Intelligence (BI) applications depends on two factors, the ability to analyze data ever more quickly and the ability to handle ever increasing volumes of data. Data Warehouse (DW) and Data Mart (DM) installations that support BI applications have historically been built using traditional architectures either designed from the ground up or based on customized reference system designs. The advent of Data Warehouse Appliances (DA) brings packaged software and hardware solutions that address performance and scalability requirements for certain market segments. The differences between DAs and custom installations make direct comparisons between them impractical and suggest the need for a targeted DA benchmark. In this paper we review data warehouse appliances by surveying thirteen products offered today. We assess the common characteristics among them and propose a classification for DA offerings. We hope our results will help define a useful benchmark for DAs.

Keywords: Appliances, Benchmark Development, Databases, Data Warehousing, Database Systems Standard.

1 Introduction

Business Intelligence continues to be a top priority of Chief Information Officers today because organizations gain a competitive edge by successfully leveraging integrated enterprise business intelligence. This capability helps them better understand customers, streamline their supply chain, and improve financial performance. Enterprise BI systems require larger data warehouses to support them, meaning more data, tables, users and query complexity. In today's market vendors

R. Nambiar and M. Poess (Eds.): TPCTC 2009, LNCS 5895, pp. 31–51, 2009.
© Springer-Verlag Berlin Heidelberg 2009

offer three types of data warehouse configurations: traditional custom configurations, reference architectures configurations and data warehouse appliances.

Traditional data warehouse systems are custom-built to meet individual customer requirements. Such configurations are highly flexible and provide high performance to meet demanding data warehouses while providing for potentially unlimited scalability for future growth. Custom-built configurations have a high pre-sale, implementation and support price tags.

Reference architecture configurations are best practice building blocks that are pre-tested and documented. Such components are typically designed to support varying scenarios at multiple levels of data and query scaling. Some immediate benefits for deploying data warehouse solutions based on reference configurations include:

- Simplified product selection and sizing process
- A predefined set of core components to simplify purchasing
- Simplified, rapid deployment with predictable performance
- Off-the-shelf components to enable repurposing and lower risk

Alternatively, data warehouse appliances are designed around scalable design principles, delivered with preconfigured hardware and software pre-installed, and are ready to run at a specified performance level out of the box.

In this paper we attempt to analyze the product offerings, not as a marketing exercise, but to attempt and discern the properties that data warehouse appliance vendors themselves offer and believe are lacking in the traditional offerings. The remainder of section one covers a brief history of how database appliances have been portrayed by analysts and vendors. Section two is an analysis of the common properties of database appliances based on a market survey conducted by the authors of appliances available today. The survey is included in full as Appendix. Section three attempts to classify and construct a test for what customers may consider an appliance. Section four describes future work including the need for an industry standard benchmark by which the market can assess key properties that are unique to appliances.

The primary motivation of this study is to determine what features data appliances have in common in order to facilitate the process of defining a data appliance. Wikipedia proposes the following definition for a data warehouse appliance: "a data appliance consists of an integrated set of servers, storage, operating system(s), DBMS and software specifically pre-installed and pre-optimized for data warehousing." [1] They go on crediting Teradata and Britton-Lee as the first appliances on the market – both companies were founded on 1979. Britton-Lee was acquired by Teradata which itself was acquired later on by AT&T/NCR and then spun off. The company who can be credited with "popularizing" the concept of data appliance is Netezza in the early 2000s. There has been a flurry of start-ups in the current decade most benefiting from open source PostgreSQL or Ingres. They implement traditional relational architectures or vertical technologies. All traditional database vendors have recently joined the bandwagon with special-purpose bundles either software running on some specific vendor hardware or proprietary hardware/software combinations.

Numerous analysts as well as vendors have attempted to find a single definition for a database appliance (or an IT appliance in general). Foster Hinshaw, arguably the father of the modern data warehouse appliance, used the benefits of an appliance to attempt a definition [2]. Gartner in 2006 found that vendors began misusing the word appliance starting in the late 1990s and created a set of questions to evaluate an appliance [3]. Microsoft published a review of many database appliances in the market in the context of comparing them to SQL Server 2008 using openness and cost-effectiveness as their criteria [4]. The whitepaper is a market positioning paper that argues that systems from older vendors such as Teradata, IBM and Oracle are costly to operate. The paper further maintains that newer systems are too specialized and immature, and vendors have provided little or no public support network. The whitepaper fails to acknowledge or analyze market demands driving appliance vendors to introduce new products that address limitations in traditional data warehousing solutions.

These definitions are relatively recent, but already appear to be outdated as the pace of new product offerings continues to develop. The increasing number of vendors offering dedicated appliances or appliance variations of their solutions makes it clear there is a wide market demand for an alternative to classic "do it yourself" data warehouse solutions. Despite some common characteristics across the vendors described in this paper, the rapid progress of appliance market presence continues without clear industry wide technology convergence.

2 Survey Analysis

Surveying the vendor offerings available in the market today we distilled a catalog of common properties attribute by the various vendors to their appliance offerings. We describe these properties and introduce a matrix (see Table 1) that summarizes which solutions offer each property. This analysis is not a validation of the properties that each vendor promotes, rather an extrapolation of how vendors perceive appliance offerings differently from custom configurations and reference configurations. This classification is also not intended as an exhaustive enumeration of the properties that the market demands of data warehouse appliances. This list does highlight some of the key properties which are later analyzed in the context of existing benchmarks.

2.1 Efficiency and Energy Efficiency

Data warehouse appliances are preconfigured not only for performance and cost, but also for energy efficiency and physical size. Many appliances are designed to offer "out of the box" efficiency relieving the user of balancing different hardware and software configurations. Whereas an assembled system may have additional CPU that the software cannot take advantage of or more disks that are necessary for the workload, appliances are balanced to maximize resources. For example, a system that requires ten disks for warehouse type workloads on 1TB of data would ship with ten appropriately configured disks of the correct capacity and speed. A custom-built system could easily be over or under provisioned leading to degradation in performance or unnecessary space and power consumption.

2.2 Large Volumes/Capacity of Data

Data warehouse appliances are primarily geared towards large volumes of data. While some appliances focus at smaller volumes (less than 1TB) or medium volumes (1-10TB), many are designed for environments with 100s of terabytes. Constructing data warehouses at the larger scales is a complex project that can consume system design resources over an extended period of time. To date only the most sophisticated organizations have been able to construct 100TB warehouses, always with substantial assistance from hardware and software vendors. As smaller organizations look to store and analyze more data, an appliance model - pre configured and tested at scale can be very attractive. A pre-built system with a shipping capacity of 100TB simplifies much of the provisioning, design and installation required in a self-built system.

2.3 Expandable in Modular Units

Data warehouse appliances are designed with integrated modular components. An expandable appliance is well suited to environments where data volume, numbers of users, workload or performance requirements grow over time. Some appliances are complete (closed) configurations that have fixed capacity with limited or no expansion capability. Other appliances are designed for limited or continual modular expansion at the storage system, server or rack level. A modular system allows expansion starting at a smaller size such as 1TB system all the way up to some maximum capacity such as 100TB or even 1PB+. Similar to the advantages of a fixed appliance configuration, an expandable appliance alleviates the ongoing system design burden from the user that needs to scale the system.

2.4 Single SKU

While it may appear trivial, the value of a single SKU when assembling a complex data warehousing system can greatly simplify the purchasing and maintenance process for a large system. Ordering separate hardware and software can often lead to weeks of analysis, comparing the different components that are available at any given point in time. Often times the disks, additional CPUs and memory upgrades are priced separately. Some RDBMS software requires packages on top of the base software when deploying specifically for data warehousing. Similarly when upgrading a system, different components may be available resulting in dozens of changes to a purchase order.

2.5 Single Vendor/Support

Traditional data warehouse systems are composed of various combinations of hardware and software components. For instance, a general purpose RDBMS may run on any suitable hardware/OS platform chosen by the user. In a single-vendor system the hardware and the software are sold by the same vendor. The single vendor is responsible for the entire system delivery and support. A single-vendor system resolves many of the contentious issues that can arise when troubleshooting a large complex system. For example, data warehouse workloads often involve large disk scans. Poor performance may result from a software issue that has incorrectly laid out data on disk, a disk firmware issue that is incorrectly buffering data. A single vendor takes responsibility for resolution regardless of the source of the issue.

2.6 Specialized Hardware

While some data warehouse appliances are constructed using industry standard hardware that is also used for other applications, some appliances are constructed with specialized hardware. This may be a chip that is designed specifically for warehousing queries or a disk that is programmed to primarily read and write data sequentially. Since the specialized hardware is design and built specifically for the appliance it is typically not sold as a separate component. For certainly types of workloads, specialized hardware may provide a particular advantage or may complement the software provided in the appliance.

2.7 Specialized Software

General purpose DBMS software is designed to run on a variety of different types of hardware. This flexibility in software that can run on a variety of hardware platforms can lead to missed opportunities to optimize for a specific tested configuration. Some data warehouse appliances offer specialized software, designed only for their appliance offerings. The specialized software is tuned and embedded into a custom hardware design to maximize performance and scalability of the appliance solution. The specialized software is not available other then as part of the data warehouse appliance.

2.8 Special Purpose or Purpose Built

Often Data warehouse appliances are specifically designed to handle certain types of workloads. For example data warehouses usually have large volumes of data, are primarily ready only, compared to transaction processing systems, and handle workloads ranging from reporting to ad-hoc analytic queries. To accommodate these use cases, some appliances are designed from scratch or tuned in such a manner that the software and hardware configuration is optimized for warehousing workloads. This may require sacrificing performance for non-warehousing workloads, such as transaction processing.

2.9 Pre-installed

Different major versions and minor revisions of database software, operating system, drivers and interoperability can cause confusion and interoperability challenges. Specific bug fixes addressed by software may be unnecessary following hardware revisions (and vice versa). Commonly with data warehouse appliances, all software and hardware components are pre-installed and tested for compatibility with specific version of each component. While not necessarily an official certification, the packaging of each version combined with the support (and presumably quality assurance tests) result in a higher guarantee of function and performance for the appliance user.

2.10 Pre-configured or Fast Deployment

Custom Data Warehouses and warehouses built from reference architectures require significant planning, design and implementation effort. The larger the system the more complex these requirements become and the longer they will take to design and implement. Most data warehouse appliances are delivered as configurable software or complete software/hardware systems that require only basic connection and setup installation. Unlike traditional custom-built data warehouse configurations, data warehouse appliance hardware is pre-installed (servers, storage, disk arrays) to specification from the factory and shipped directly to the customer. Pre-configured application software may be bundled with the system, as well. The complete appliance speeds everything from provisioning to installation and deployment.

2.11 Massively Parallel

Massively parallel processing refers to a system in which independent units execute operations on separate data in parallel. In the context of a database system MPP generally equates to a "shared-nothing" architecture where units have their own memory and their own data on disk. For redundancy purposes however, certain processing units and I/O subsystems can be arranged in clusters sharing data. A combination of modularity and scalability, MPP is a common architecture for data warehousing and data warehouse appliances.

2.12 Packaged Database and Application

Data warehouse solutions require not only hardware, operating system and database software, but also application software to load and query the database. A few data warehouse appliances have entered the market with combined database and application software. These are sometimes loosely coupled with joint marketing, packed together and per-configured. Others have specific optimizations and are sold as a single turnkey system.

2.13 Packaged Database and Hardware

Most Data warehouse appliances are pre-packaged with database software, operating system and hardware. From design through sales, marketing and support these appliances function as a single solution rather than a combination of products.

2.14 Bundled Solution vs. Appliance Only

Data warehouse appliances may be configured and delivered the pre-installed OS and database product components. Bundled solutions extend beyond the basic appliance to include general purpose or pre-configured vertical product software. These may include general or specialty applications, connection/interface components for variable data environments or external storage components. Appliance only solutions are comprised of components that are not sold separately. Often appliance only solutions include specialized hardware and software.

2.15 Self Managing or Self Tuning

While the data warehouse appliance that arrives from the factory is tuned for a specific size and workload. Both the composition of the appliance and the target workload may change over time. A self-managing system is able to re-balance based on changing workloads and data. Similar to a device that can self-align, the self managing or self tuning appliance stand in contrast to a user assembled data warehouse that often requires manual maintenance and tuning both out of the box and as an ongoing task.

2.16 Bundled Pricing

Bundled pricing refers to a commercial practice whereby a single line item is provided to the client for the entire system including hardware, software and maintenance. The appliance bundle can be accompanied by a detailed list of items that constitute the bundle (a requirement for TPC pricing for example) though not necessarily for single-vendor bundles. A typical bundle could be for instance: System X with software version Y and 3-year maintenance for Z dollars.

Table 1. Analysis of different appliances

A. Greenplum/Sun	H. Microsoft/DATAllegro
B. HP/Neoview	I. Netezza
C. HP/Oracle	J. Oracle
D. HP/Vertica	K. ParAccel
E. IBM	L. Sybase
F. Ingres	M. Teradata
G. Kickfire	N. Vertica

System Characteristics	A	B	C	D	E	F	G	H	I	J	K	L	M	N
Efficiency and Energy Efficiency	X	X		X		X	X				X	X		X
Large Volumes/Capacity of Data	X	X	X	X	X		X	X	X	X	X		X	X
Expandable in modular units	X	X	X	X	X			X	X		X		X	X
Single SKU	X	X	X				X	X	X		X		X	X
Single Vendor/Single Support	X	X		X	X	X	X	X	X		X	X	X	X
Specialized hardware			X				X	X	X				X	
Specialized software			X			X		X	X		X			
Special purpose or purpose built	X	X	X	X		X	X	X	X	X	X	X	X	X
Pre-installed	X	X	X	X	X	X	X	X	X	X	X	X	X	X
Pre-configured / Fast deployment	X	X	X	X	X	X	X	X	X	X	X	X	X	X
Massively Parallel	X	X	X	X				X	X	X	X		X	X
Packaged database plus application						X					X	X		
Packaged database plus hardware	X	X	X	X	X		X	X	X	X	X	X	X	
Bundled Solution vs. Appliance		X	X			X					X	X		
Self managing or self tuning			X						X	X	X			X
Bundled pricing	X	X		X							X	X		

3   A Data Warehouse Appliance Test

In the first two sections of this paper we reviewed the existing market demand for data warehouse appliances, appliance offerings from over a dozen vendors and the properties that each of these vendors ascribed to their appliance offerings. In this section we extrapolate from these properties a test that consumers can use to identify whether an offering meets a commonly accepted criterion for an appliance. We do not claim an absolute definition of a data warehouse appliance rather we have relied on the collective research of these vendors to make our assessment.

A brief glance at table 1 shows some clear consensus among vendors as to the qualities of a data warehouse appliance. DAs are targeted at large volumes starting at 100GB or greater and expandable in modular units. Appliance vendors provide a single source of support or at least a single point of contact for purchase and return. Most appliances are specially designed or customized for data warehousing and all are pre installed and pre configured for warehousing type workloads. Finally, nearly all appliances are offered as packaged database and hardware.

While these seven most popular criteria are not an absolute definition of an appliance, it seems that most consumers expect the scalability and simplicity of an appliance to include most if not all of these features. Where vendors differ is in the nine other properties – either due to design decisions or to offer competitive differentiation. For example, a common but not universal property of data warehouse appliances is massively parallel processing. Ten out of fourteen solutions employ this architecture in their appliance offerings. Similarly, seven vendors have some specialized software or hardware that is designed specifically for their appliance solution while only three vendors offer additional bundled application software that is not included in their non-appliance offering. Though bundled pricing is not espoused as an appliance feature, an informal inquiry revealed that discounts among appliances are common.

The trend among these key properties is that at first glance most are not easily compared quantitatively. Yet the quantitative measures tested in existing benchmarks including performance and price/performance are absent from the list of key appliance properties. While many data warehouse vendors often claim price and price/performance measures of their custom-built configurations, only those that exclusively sell appliances do so of their DA offerings. This dichotomy leads us to speculate that there is a need for some evaluation of the defining properties for data warehouse appliances.

Existing benchmarks such as the TPC-H decision support benchmark and its predecessors emphasize query performance and overall price performance. These benchmarks require that submitters record load times but do not factor them into the results. Nor do the benchmarks measure setup time or scalability of a single solution. In fact, comparison across scales is expressly forbidden [15]. While we cannot claim that existing benchmarks provide a disincentive to run appliances, it is telling that only three appliances have been run since the concept first became popularized ten years ago. In particular vendors who sell both appliance and non-appliance solutions have generally opted to run their non-appliance solutions.

4 Need for a Data Warehouse Appliance Benchmark Specification

The distinguishing factors in data warehouse appliances fall under two broad categories: scalability and simplicity. The consensus among vendors appears to be that the market demands a solution that can grow in modular units from 100s of gigabytes to 100s of terabytes or greater by simply plugging in new components purchased from a single vendor. The proliferation of data warehouse appliances from both new and established vendors indicates that this demand is not met by traditional custom configurations or even reference configurations.

We believe there is a strong market demand for a suite of tests that benchmark data warehouse appliances. The warehousing decision support benchmarks that exist today, while satisfactory for comparing custom and reference configurations do not test for the properties that embody data warehouse appliances. Rather than focus exclusively on traditional workloads and timing aspects, this assessment should also focus on appliance specific factors and account for the properties outlined in this paper.

A simple proposal could begin with extending or supplementing an existing benchmark to create quantitative measures that capture the essence of scalability and simplicity. For example, the TPC-H benchmark could be augmented to encourage comparisons across scale as a measure of modularity and change in price/performance across different volumes of data. Scalability testing might be performed without reloading instead appending new data as a customer would. Simplicity could be measured by including the load timings, including a random query generation phase or even comparing the amount of configuration information provided to the system for setup.

We encourage bodies such as the TPC to take on this future work to define a data warehouse appliance benchmark specification that assess scalability and simplicity of a packaged solution. The benchmark should also definitively articulate the un-measurable qualities of an appliance solution to facilitate evaluation by consumers.

Acknowledgements

The authors would like to thank Karl Huppler, Michael Corwin, Kannan Govindarajan for participating in the survey.

References

1. Wikipedia contributors, Data warehouse appliance. Wikipedia, The Free Encyclopedia, http://en.wikipedia.org/wiki/Data_warehouse_appliance (accessed June 20, 2009)
2. Hinshaw, F.D.: Tera-Scale Data Appliances for Business Intelligence. The Data Administration Newsletter (April 1, 2003), http://www.tdan.com/view-articles/5075
3. MacDonald, et al.: Findings: Not All Appliances' Are Appliances. Gartner Research (September 12, 2006)
4. SQL Server Technical Article: Data Warehouse in the Enterprise, A Competitive Review of Enterprise Data Warehouse Appliances and Technology Solutions, Microsoft web site (January 2009), http://tinyurl.com/18b4x6
5. Greenplum website: The Data Warehouse Appliance, http://www.greenplum.com/partners/data_warehouse_appliance/ Sun, Greenplum Unveil Data Warehouse Appliance, http://www.hpcwire.com/offthewire/17886374.html?viewAll=y
6. HP Neoview Enterprise Data Warehouse, http://www.hp.com/go/neoview
7. HP Oracle Database Machine, http://www.hp.com/go/exadata, http://www.hp.com/go/exadata
8. A Next-Generation Teramart™ Solution from Vertica, HP & Red Hat, http://www.vertica.com/appliance
9. Shanley, K.: History and Overview of the TPC, http://www.tpc.org/information/about/history.asp
10. IBM Business Intelligence, http://ibm.com/bi
11. InfoSphere Balanced Data Warehouse, http://www-01.ibm.com/software/data/infosphere/balanced-warehouse/
12. Microsoft DATAllegro: DATAllegro Data Warehouse Appliance, http://www.datallegro.com/data_warehouse_appliances/data_warehouse_overview.asp
13. Netezza Marketing Collateral: Data Warehouse Appliance, http://www.netezza.com/data-warehouse-appliance-products/dw-appliance.aspx
14. The ParAccel Analytic Database, http://www.paraccel.com/data_warehouse_resources/library.php
15. TPC Policies v5.17, http://tinyurl.com/l88ykx

Appendix Data Warehouse Appliance Survey

This section surveys an array of solutions that may be viewed as appliances in today's market place. In order to perform an unbiased survey we contacted twelve vendors and their partners to contribute a one-page description of their appliance solution, which have been included in unedited form, except for formatting changes to comply with publisher guidelines.

Table A.1. Contacted Vendors/Partners and Products offered

Vendor/Partner	Product Offering
Greenplum/Sun	The Greenplum Data Warehouse Powered by Sun
Hewlett Packard	HP Neoview Enterprise Data Warehouse
Hewlett Packard/Oracle	HP Oracle Database Machine
Hewlett Packard/Vertica	The Vertica Analytic Database Appliance
IBM	IBM InfoSphere Balanced Warehouse
Ingres	Ingres Icebraker Appliance
Kickfire	Kickfire Analytic Appliance for the Data Warehouse Mass Market
Microsoft	DATAllegro Appliance
Netezza	Data Warehouse Appliance
Oracle	Oracle Optimized Warehouse
ParAccel	ParAccel Analytic Database
Sybase	Sybase Analytic Appliance
Teradata	Teradata Data Warehouse Appliance
Vertica	The Vertica Virtualized Analytic Database

We received product descriptions from Hewlett Packard, IBM, Kickfire, Oracle, ParAccel, Sybase, Teradata and Vertica. For those vendors who did not contribute a description we have researched their website and press releases and compiled a short description. These descriptions may not fully reflect the features and capabilities of these products. The intention is to come up with a list of appliance properties commonly claimed by vendors.

A.1 The Greenplum Data Warehouse Powered by Sun

Sun-Greenplum Data Warehouse Appliance [5] is open source software and general purpose systems powered by the Solaris 10 Operating System (OS) and PostgreSQL. The solution combines Sun Fire X4500 data server powered by dual-core AMD Opteron processors with Greenplum's massively parallel distribution of PostgreSQL, Bizgres MPP, in a single turnkey appliance. With its Query-In-Storage design, the solution is capable of scanning 1 terabyte of data in 60 seconds and can scale to hundreds of terabytes of usable database capacity. Sun claims the data warehouse system is one of the most energy efficient solutions in the industry, at only 90W per terabyte. The solution offers the following key attributes:

- Performance - Massively parallel processing, made possible by the performance scalability of the AMD Opteron processor with Direct Connect Architecture, leverages a high-performance interconnect and moves processing to where the data resides.
- Openness - Powered by open source software including the Solaris Operating System, PostgreSQL, and Solaris ZFS. Supports industry standards and interfaces (SQL, ODBC, JDBC).

- Value - An acquisition and ongoing administration cost of less than $20,000 per usable terabyte. Small footprint (up to 50 TB per rack) and low power requirements (4.5 kW per rack) reduce operating costs.
- Ease-of-use - Integrated and turnkey appliance reduces system complexity, for easy implementation and maintenance.

A.2 HP Neoview Enterprise Data Warehouse

HP Neoview enterprise-class data warehousing platform [6] is designed to meet the needs of a 24x7 operational BI environment, where massive amounts of information are analyzed in seconds. This pre-configured, pre-integrated and pre-tested platform is built to help simplify the deployment process. It includes startup and deployment services that enable users to begin loading data as soon as the system is powered up.

Table A.2. Neoview features and benefits

Neoview feature	Key customer benefit
Parallel execution across hundreds of servers	Handles complex queries, mixed workloads, and high concurrency
Massive scaling to hundreds of terabytes	Allows complete analysis of large volumes of data, maximizing business insight from all information assets
Innovative optimization engine	Delivers unparalleled performance
Built-in system-wide fault tolerance	Provides mission-critical 24x7 capabilities and mitigates risk
Remote management and monitoring from HP	Simplifies administration and reduces maintenance costs
Single vendor solution	Provides accountability and simplicity so that you achieve your goals and mitigate risk
Priority driven workload execution and user defined service levels and rules	Gives consistent performance to meet service levels of varied mixed workloads
Industry-standard components	Protects investment and facilitates data center integration. Allows component reuse.
Completely integrated and preconfigured hardware, software, and services	Assures faster time to operation. Provides simplicity that lowers cost of operations.
Fully compatible with leading data integration, ETL, query, analysis, and reporting tools	Allows easy integration into an existing environment and preserves investment in tools, training, and process

There are fourteen HP Neoview platform models. The Cxxx model family uses 146 GB user data disks and the Exxx model family uses 300 GB user data disks.

A.3 HP Oracle Database Machine

The HP Oracle Database Machine [7] is a complete system, including software, servers, networking and storage designed to run multi-terabyte data warehouses. At the heart of this system, is the HP Oracle Exadata Storage Server, which has smart storage software that offloads data-intensive query processing from database servers closer to the data. This results in much less data getting sent over fast InfiniBand interconnects, dramatically improving both query performance and concurrency. It's simple and fast to implement, very cost-effective, and can linearly scale storage capacity, processing power and network bandwidth as your data warehouse grows.

HP Oracle Database Machine is pre-configured for performance, pre- tuned, and certified for Oracle Business Intelligence Enterprise Edition tools and Oracle Real Application Clusters. Complete configurations can be ordered from Oracle, with hardware support by HP. The HP Oracle Database Machine is a high-performance system configured for data warehousing that includes a grid of eight database servers featuring: 64 Intel processor cores, and Oracle Enterprise Linux; and a grid of 14 HP Oracle Exadata Storage Servers that include up to 168 terabytes of raw storage and 14 GB/sec data bandwidth to the database servers, when accessing compressed data, the effective throughput for a single rack can be 50 GB per second or more. Up to eight Database Machines can be networked together without requiring additional InfiniBand switches, and larger configurations can be built with the addition of external switches.

A.4 HP Vertica Analytic Database Appliance

The HP Vertica Analytic Database appliance [8] is a pre-configured HP c-class BladeSystem delivered as a single unit with integrated compute and storage blades. The HP BladeSystem c3000 or c7000 enclosure is designed as a balanced system with either 4 or 8 database nodes, each comprised of a compute blade paired with a storage blade. The Vertica software and RedHat Linux operating system are pre-installed and configured, delivering an instant out of the box database experience. In addition to the benefits of a single fully configured system, the HP Vertica appliance also delivers a dense and efficient real time data warehousing solution. A single c3000 can accommodate up to 20TB of user data with a c7000 scaling to 40TB or approximately 2TB per 1U of rack space[1].

The HP c-class BladeSystems are expandable by simply plugging in new pairs of blades or new enclosures and registering them with the running system. For example, a c7000 enclosure can be purchased with half capacity (c3000 equivalent) and then expanded by adding compute and storage blade pairs. A full c3000 or c7000 based Vertica Appliance can be connected over Ethernet or InfiniBand to any number of additional appliances for additional capacity. Since each enclosure is self contained, each compute blade and storage blade forms a single unit and each Vertica nodes functions in a shared-nothing configuration, appliances can be sized as small or as large as the customer requires, up to four c7000 enclosures or 32 Vertica nodes per full rack capable of warehousing a full 160TB of user data.

As with all configurations of the Vertica Analytic Database, the HP Vertica appliance is designed to be always on. Since each of the nodes functions as a peer in the database operation so users can connect to any node and see a single system image, regardless of the number of nodes. The nodes all support high availability so

---

[1] 20TB c3000 or 40TB c7000 is fully configured with pairs of BL460c and an SB40c with 6x 300GB SFF SAS.

that one or more blade failures do not bring down ten rest of the cluster. When adding and removing nodes or while the database is self-tuning, users can continuous load and query data against the appliance.

A.5 IBM InfoSphere Balanced Warehouse

The IBM® InfoSphere Balanced Warehouse™ is the complete data warehousing solution comprised of pre-tested, scalable and fully-integrated system components of InfoSphere Warehouse, Server and Storage. It takes the best attributes of appliance-like solutions, while still maintaining the flexibility of typical relational database servers. Like an appliance it offers the ease of deployment and configuration. The building-block approach in Balanced Warehouse™ allows for easy growth to handle additional workload and data in a data warehouse. This is unlike many "appliance" data warehouse solutions. And, while the configuration comes with a set of tools designed to make the implementation and maintenance of a data warehouse easy to accomplish, the customer also has the complete power of DB2 available to use as they need. Included in the IBM® InfoSphere Balanced Warehouse™ are:

- InfoSphere Warehouse software: Including tooling and infrastructure to help data warehouse architects and administrators efficiently design, deploy and maintain an enterprise data warehouse.
- A preconfigured, fully installed server
- A fully installed storage subsystem
  - Currently, the IBM® InfoSphere™ Balanced Warehouse™ has three basic building blocks:
- IBM® InfoSphere™ Balanced Warehouse™ C4000, comprised of:
  - InfoSphere Warehouse Intermediate Edition software
  - IBM System x3850 M2
  - IBM System Storage DS3200
  - Optional EXP3000 Storage
- The IBM® InfoSphere Balanced Warehouse™ D5100 includes:
  - InfoSphere Warehouse software
  - IBM System x 3650
  - IBM System Storage DS3400
  - Optional EXP3000 Storage
- The IBM® InfoSphere Balanced Warehouse™ E7100 includes:
  - InfoSphere Warehouse software
  - IBM System p 570 (on POWER6)
  - IBM System Storage DS4800
  - Optional EXP810 Storage

The D5100 and E7100 are available in the form of five flexible modules, designed to deliver affordable scaling that meets a customer's needs:

- Foundation (includes all the function needed to manage the data warehouse)
- Data (for flexible scaling of data and data access capabilities)
- User (for extending the user access capabilities)

- Failover (for high availability solutions)
- Application (portals to a variety of data warehousing applications)

For more information on the IBM® InfoSphere Balanced Warehouse™ see [10][11].

A.6 Ingres Icebraker ECM Appliance

Ingres web site states that today's general-purpose databases and operating systems include a huge array of features, most of which are not used by all applications. Features that are not marketed as optional are included in products by default. Customers have to pay, install and maintain them. This may contribute not only to an unnecessarily high license fee, but also to an increased cost for deployment, configuration maintenance and security.

The Icebreaker Software Appliances try to simplify installation, reduce security risks and, simplify deployment to improvements in efficiency and cost savings. Simplicity is achieved by reducing the layers in the appliance to the bare essentials. Additionally, Ingres takes responsibility for the integration of the various components within the appliance. The provided setup utility installs and configures the complete set of technologies as one unit. Ingres provides maintenance for the entire Icebraker Appliance.

Reducing the components used in a database reduces the risk of exposure to security vulnerabilities. Additionally, securing the environment is greatly simplified because of less number of components that may interact. Lastly, the Ingres Icebraker Appliance only opens ports that it requires, only creates the minimum number of accounts and only starts the services and demons that are required.

Being designed from the ground up, Ingres' Software Appliances take advantage of the latest advances in hardware and software solutions, which are preinstalled and configured on a particular hardware configuration.

Ingres' appliances take advantage of Virtualization Technologies resulting in high efficient systems while also reducing cost. Especially since they are supplied as a unit, they greatly reduce the cost of installing, configuring, deploying and maintaining these solutions.

A.7 Kickfire Analytic Appliance for the Data Warehouse Mass Market

Kickfire™, Inc., delivers the first analytic appliance that affordably delivers the high-performance capabilities of large commercial database systems to the mass market. The data warehousing mass market constitutes those deployments in the gigabytes to low terabytes which, according to IDC, represent over three quarters of the total market.

This market presents significant challenges to traditional vendors. Customers need performance but are very price-sensitive. They have limited data warehousing expertise and few IT resources with which to deploy solutions. Finally early-stage data warehousing deployments, typical in the mass market, often include mixed workload characteristics.

Kickfire has addressed these challenges the first analytic solution based on a parallel-processing SQL chip. Kickfire chose to package the solution as an appliance because this has proven to be an attractive deployment model for customers in the mass market. The key characteristics of the Kickfire appliance are summarized below.

Kickfire's appliance combines the industry's first SQL chip, which packs the power of 10's of CPUs, and an advanced column-store engine with full ACID compliance, it achieves low price/performance based on rigorous benchmark tests and ensures complete data integrity. The small form factor and low power consumption of the device are designed for today's cost- and green-conscious customers. Some properties of Kickfire's appliance are:

- An integrated and optimized solution down to the operating system level with features like Active System Monitor which notifies users of any potential system anomaly.
- Runs standard MySQL Enterprise™.
- Built to scale to the needs of the mass market in terms of data volumes, user concurrency and workload type, handping data sizes from the gigabytes to the terabytes.
- Offers high-user concurrency on a single node, supporting 100 concurrent users and 1,000 active users.
- Fast bulk loading as well as fast incremental loading to handle traditional as well as operational workloads.

As highlighted above, Kickfire's solution delivers all the benefits of an appliance, namely price/performance, ease of use, and manageability. Additionally, the Kickfire Appliance enables the mass market to scale in terms of data capacity, user concurrency, and workload type.

A.8 Microsoft DATAllegro Appliance

Prior to acquisition by Microsoft in July of 2008, DATAllegro sold a data-warehouse appliance named DATAllegro v3 [12].The DATAllegro appliance was created to enable rapid deployment of hundreds of terabytes of data at relatively low cost. The architecture was designed to offer both flexibility and scalability using a modular and open, standards-based technology. DATAllegro v3 utilized EMC storage, Dell servers and Cisco InfiniBand switches. Each server contained Intel multi-core CPUs and was powered by the Ingres open source database. Combined, these technologies allowed DATAllegro to offer a low cost, high performance appliance as well as a reliable and scalable solution.

Traditionally, SAN based data warehouse storage solutions offers slow query performance and reduced disk space available for user data. This is because traditional warehouses were optimized to put data only on the fastest parts of the disk and to deploy as many small capacity spindles as possible to maximize IOPs. DATAllegro employed at RAIDW technology to maximize overall I/O performance as well as provide built in fault tolerance across all system components, not just the storage.

The disk patters underlying most data warehouse solutions resemble random I/O, requiring a high number of IOPs, achieved with a very large number of spindles. This is due to the number of indexes, and the complex disk infrastructure required to support different hard ware platforms and operating systems. By developing Direct Data Streaming technology, DATAllegro was able to optimize query execution to use sequential disk I/O and minimize the need for tuning.

DATAllegro also reduced network traffic using their USN parallel database design. USN configured the database to maximize co-located joins across all nodes in the system. This minimizes network traffic and improves performance for most query types. Additionally, the use of multi-level partitioning reduces the amount of data read for each query. DATAllegro also supported indexes as required for queries that accessed a small number of rows each.

A.9 Netezza

Netezza Performance Server is a data warehouse appliance combining database, server, and storage, based on Linux and PostgreSQL. It uses a patented massively parallel architecture. The following is a copy the first page of Netezza's description of a data warehouse appliance [13]: "To eliminate the need for constant tuning and the technology bottlenecks caused by slow disk transfer I/O rates, slow network transfer rates and inefficient caching, Netezza developed a system designed specifically for analytical processing on extremely large amounts of data. We call our system an "appliance" because, like a network or storage device, it was designed to do one thing extremely well. It is very straightforward – when you plug it in and load your data, it analyzes it very fast. And because the Netezza appliance is an integrated database-server-storage system, you are no longer faced with building your own system out of disparate components, or maintaining these different piece parts.

Netezza's patented massively parallel architecture takes a different approach than traditional database architectures to processing queries. Where standard computing architectures are targeted at operations on individual data elements, the Netezza architecture is all about "streaming" processing. Rather than shuttling data between disk and memory for processing once a query comes in, which creates the bottleneck, data streams off the disk and through query logic loaded into an FPGA (field programmable gate array). The FPGA and processor (a PowerPC chip), together with 400 GB of disk storage, reside on each of the massively parallel nodes that Netezza calls snippet processing units (SPUs). Each of our Netezza racks contains 112 of these SPUs. Queries are optimized across the SPUs for maximum performance and power efficiency A Linux host server aggregates SPU results and manages query workload and the results are returned to the user. It is this different approach to the growing analytic processing challenge that provides our customers with a high-performance database engine that brings simplicity to what has become a very complicated process.

The Netezza 10000 product line starts with the 10050 with 56 SPUs (half a cabinet) rated at 6.25 TB of user data (12TB with compression). A basic 10100 (one cabinet) is rated at 12.5TB of user data with 112 SPUs. The other models are multipliers of the 10100 – a 10x00 with x=2, 4, 6 or 8 is composed of x 10100 cabinets and the number of SPUs and the amount of user data are x times that of the 10100. In summary Netezza emphasizes modularity, ease of use and lack of tuning chores

A.10   Oracle Optimized Warehouse Initiative

The Oracle Optimized Warehouse Initiative is a joint development between Oracle and its partners to provide customers with a choice of easy-to-implement, high performance and scalable data warehousing solutions. It provides optimized data warehouses that combine the world's most popular database for data warehouses, Oracle Database, with server, storage and networking components from HP, IBM, SUN, Dell, EMC and SGI. The Oracle Optimized Warehouse Initiative provides customers flexibility of choice to meet their different scale of requirements:

- Reference Configurations are a best practice guide to choosing the right server, storage and networking components to build an Oracle data warehouse. These best practice guides help customers take the risk out of implementing a data warehouse as Oracle and its partners have encapsulated years of configuration expertise.
- Oracle Optimized Warehouses provide customers with a pre-built, optimized data warehouse, complete with Oracle software, servers, storage and networking components ready to load data and run queries and reports. Available from Oracle's partners, Optimized Warehouses have been fully tested and validated.

There are a wide range of Reference Configurations available from HP, IBM, SUN, Dell, EMC and SGI to suit the different needs of all customers. These range in scale from 500GB to over 100TB data warehouses available on single and clustered servers to support tens to thousands of users with a wide choice of operating systems including Linux and Unix depending on specific partner reference configurations and Oracle Optimized Warehouses available.

Configurations and Oracle Optimized Warehouses are designed with modular scalability in mind to incrementally add more storage and processing power as demand grows.

Any Business Intelligence tool that is supported with Oracle Database can be used with the Optimized Data Warehouse. These include, OLAP, Data Mining, Oracle Business Intelligence Enterprise and Standard Editions, Hyperion, Business Objects, Cognos and many more.

Oracle Warehouse Builder, a feature of Oracle Database, is a core component of Oracle Optimized Warehouse Initiative enabling transformation of raw data from disparate sources into high-quality information for business reporting and analytics.

Oracle Enterprise Manager Database Control, a feature of Oracle Database, is used in the Oracle Optimized Warehouse Initiative solutions to automatically monitor the data warehouse environment and to help proactively resolve issues before they turn into emergencies.

The HP Oracle Exadata Storage Server, a combination of the HP DL180 G5 storage server and smart software from Oracle optimized for use with Oracle Databases, is part of the Oracle Optimized Warehouse Initiative. Its massively parallel architecture delivers outstanding query performance for data warehousing applications.

A.11 ParAccel Analytic Database

The ParAccel Analytic Database (PADB) is a purpose-built analytic DBMS that is available as both traditional enterprise software or as a software appliance that can be implemented on a variety of configurations of any brand of industry standard hardware. The Ultra-Fast Data Warehouse powered by Sun and ParAccel, was the world's first analytic appliance to publish TPC-H benchmarks (October 2007).

As a software appliance, PADB offers both the flexibility of server choice that people enjoy with traditional DBMSs and the convenience of a purpose-built appliance with its simplicity and lower cost of ownership (e.g., load-and-go installation, single point of contact for troubleshooting, etc.).

PADB installs with minimal setup overhead in environments with data volumes ranging from 100s of gigabytes to multi-terabytes, on configurations with variable numbers of servers based on standard multi-core x86 compatible CPUs. Despite the variable degree of configuration options, PADB uses a failover strategy that minimizes downtime and guarantees data integrity through intelligent mirroring, and the appliance's integrated SAN storage option. The SAN configuration also offers guaranteed disaster recovery capability in the unlikely event of multiple simultaneous systems failures.

PADB differs from most traditional DBMSs in that it assumes an analytic processing environment. PADB is built on a linearly scalable MPP shared-nothing architecture that uses columnar storage to optimize query performance, and data compression to minimize storage and access overhead. PADB includes support for advanced analytics defined by the SQL 2003 standard, complex multi-level aggregations, correlated sub-queries, and a patent-pending join strategy that allows the system to handle hundreds of tables in a single query. Another difference between PADB and many traditional DBMSs is that they were often designed for operational work and thus require many redundant structures or specialized design techniques (star schema, materialized view, indexes, summaries) to offer reasonable analytic query ability. PADB does not require these performance enhancement and tuning mechanisms to deliver record-setting performance for applications based on a wide range of schema, data and query requirements.

ParAccel is also available as vertical application appliance (e.g., Autometrics Pulse). Finally, PADB differs from all other databases (appliance and non-appliance) in how it integrates into SAN environments. Patent-pending blended scan features leverage both server- and SAN-based storage for higher overall performance than either storage type alone. The scalable analytical appliance (SAA), bundled with SAN, is available as a single SKU.

A.12 Sybase

In the analytics space, Sybase offers both an appliance and a software-only solution. Sybase opted for this route to cater to what they believe are two almost independent markets. Increasingly, some customers are exploring "black-box" solutions to analytic and data mart types of use cases. Sybase believes there are several value propositions, which are driving some of their customers to choose an appliance solution over separate components. Briefly, these are:

- Faster time to "Value"
  - No system integration work required, especially with respect to storage;
- Full solution stack:
  - the server and storage appliance already appropriately sized & configured (multiple options available based on data volumes and concurrent user estimates;
  - the DBMS software appropriately sized & configured;
  - Data modeling and development software to automate modeling and acquisition of source schemas as well as the creation of target schemas within the appliance;
  - ETL software to automate the extraction, transfer and load of production data into the appliance;
  - Top business intelligence tool to gain immediate business insight from the data;
  - a unified systems management console for the entire appliance.
- Single vendor support model:
  - No additional database tuning required
  - One vendor services the entire solution

Sybase also believe this market is particularly well suited to column-based RDBMS products because the vast majority of customers are really trying to get solutions to the business faster than IT can deliver. In these environments, Sybase find that the degree of ad-hoc, what-if scenario queries is significantly higher than in data warehouse / data mart use cases with traditional IT-based (non-COTS) applications. Column-stores inherent "index-everything" model is generally better suited to these types of environments.

A.13 Teradata

Teradata entered the appliance market in 1984 with the original Teradata DBC/1012, a Database Computer with integrated storage, servers, and RDBMS all supplied by a single vendor and purpose built for Decision Support processing. Today, although best known for the customized Active Data Warehouse 5550 platform, Teradata offers three appliance models.

- Data Mart Appliance 551P, suitable for entry-level data warehousing, data mart, or test and development systems up to 2.6 TB user data.
- Extreme Data Warehouse 1550, designed for very high-volume (100+ TB), non-enterprise data/analysis requirements for a small number of power users.
- Data Warehouse Appliance 2550, designed for entry-level data warehouses or analytical data marts.

Although all run the same Teradata RDBMS and SuSE Linux OS, each appliance has different disk subsystems and packaged software to suit their different purposes. All Teradata appliances are pre-configured and staged for quick installation. System options are minimized and simplified for easy configuration and ordering.

A.14   Vertica Analytic Database

The Vertica Analytic Database is a high performance SQL database, written from scratch to provide the best performance possible for data warehousing, business intelligence and analytic applications. Vertica's database management system is a massively parallel, compressed columnar system with a sophisticated design that provides built in high availability, continuous load and query capabilities and self-tuning technologies in an always-on system.

Vertica offers two version of the Vertica Analytic Database configured as a database appliance. Vertica's Analytic Database Appliance is a pre-configured system that includes industry standard hardware from vendors such as HP, Dell or Sun with an operating system and the Vertica Analytic Database pre-installed. Customers can purchase the Vertica Analytic Database Appliance and experiences a plug and play high performance database. Additional capacity can be added on the fly but plugging in new appliance nodes and registering them with the system.

The Vertica Virtualized Analytic Database is a VMware virtual machine image that includes a pre-installed copy of the Vertica Analytic Database. With a pre-installed operating system, a fully configured Vertica Analytic Database and the Vertica Webmin Administration tools, customers can deploy a full database solution near instantly. Using VMware vSphere, users can easily add capacity by starting new virtual machines.

Vertica's Web-based administration tools allow point and click addition of new nodes to the cluster – either physical or virtual. Adding and removing nodes is a fully on-line operation and data can be loaded, offloaded and segmented across the cluster all while users are continuously loading and querying data. As a shared nothing database, each Vertica nodes is connected to independent storage. This is directly attached to the nodes of a Vertica Analytic Database Appliance and provisioned at deployment time for the Vertica Virtualized Analytic Database.

All versions of the Vertica Analytic database include the automatic Database Designer, which creates an optimized physical designs using the data and query workloads as users begin to load and query data. The designer can run in the background as users continue to manage data and will optimize for new data or new workload patterns.

The Vertica Analytic Database appliances also include built in management and monitoring tools. With SNMP for critical events and remote monitoring capabilities, the Vertica Analytic Database appliance runs in a completely headless configuration. Vertica requires little to no administration and can be backed up using standard enterprise backup solutions.

The State of Energy and Performance Benchmarking for Enterprise Servers

Andrew Fanara[1], Evan Haines[2], and Arthur Howard[2]

[1] US EPA
MC: 6202J, Ariel Rios Building 1200 Pennsylvania Avenue, NW Washington, DC 20460
fanara.andrew@epa.gov
[2] ICF International
9300 Lee Highway, Fairfax, VA 22031
{ehaines, ahoward}@icfi.com

Abstract. To address the server industry's marketing focus on performance, benchmarking organizations have played a pivotal role in developing techniques to determine the maximum achievable performance level of a system. Generally missing has been an assessment of energy use to achieve that performance. The connection between performance and energy consumption is becoming necessary information for designers and operators as they grapple with power constraints in the data center. While industry and policy makers continue to strategize about a universal metric to holistically measure IT equipment efficiency, existing server benchmarks for various workloads could provide an interim proxy to assess the relative energy efficiency of general servers. This paper discusses ideal characteristics a future energy-performance benchmark might contain, suggests ways in which current benchmarks might be adapted to provide a transitional step to this end, and notes the need for multiple workloads to provide a holistic proxy for a universal metric.

1 Introduction

All day, every day, servers process and deliver increasing quantities of video, voice, and data through a vast global network to several billion devices, where that data is consumed and often stored for posterity. In this context, if computing is the heartbeat of a global network, servers are the muscle. It can be argued that the quality of life for the billions of people who rely upon ubiquitous computing would suffer without access to continually evolving computing technology. A variety of industries have invested tremendous resources to enhance the reach, richness, and speed of digital information, but the rapid growth of energy consumption by these enhanced services warrants increased scrutiny. As broad segments of the world economy increase their focus on energy efficiency, this scrutiny will help to ensure that continued increases in computing performance can be achieved without a run away increase in energy consumption.

The current market shows a discernable trend towards the improvement of operational productivity of computing systems, and data center operators around the

R. Nambiar and M. Poess (Eds.): TPCTC 2009, LNCS 5895, pp. 52–66, 2009.

world are taking an increased interest in energy performance when procuring IT equipment. While this has not yet become a universal management imperative, there is little doubt that organizations that embrace an energy efficiency strategy will minimize future risks to their business with the most sustainable data center operations. Building on the substantial progress made in this industry to date, additional tools are needed to uniformly assess and improve the efficiencies of IT equipment. One such tool would be a universal metric for server efficiency which is applicable to a majority of the server market. Such a generalized metric would provide end users with a window into the energy performance of systems under consideration and provide the data center industry with a stepping stone toward the smarter procurement of efficient servers.

1.1 Energy Constraints in the Current Data Center

The energy efficiency of information technology (IT) equipment and data center facilities has dramatically increased in importance over the past decade in response to the rapid growth in the number and size of data centers and the power and cooling constraints of the associated infrastructure. Consider the following:

- *Rising Data Center Costs.* McKinsey Consulting estimates that the cost of running data centers is increasing by as much as 20 percent a year, while overall IT spending is increasing by only 6 percent.[1]
- *Power Grid Capacity.* In a report to Congress, the EPA estimated that ten new power plants would be required to meet the additional energy demand from data centers by 2011.[2] Evidence of this trend is already mounting; a utility provider in Virginia estimates that by 2012, 10 percent of all the energy it supplies to northern Virginia will be consumed by data centers.[3]
- *Load and Demand.* EPA estimates 6X growth in server capacity and 69X growth in storage capacity in this decade.[4]

Available energy at the server-, rack-, row-, or building-level is often a bottleneck that hinders an organization's ability to meet the computing capacity demands of an increasingly digital economy. Ample supply of electricity is an important prerequisite for selecting the location of a new data center facility. Existing facilities can be haunted by the risk of grid congestion and peak power concerns. Moreover, if variable real time electricity pricing becomes commonplace data center operational expenses could rise well above current levels, especially during peak periods. While server compute performance may continue to be defined using contemporary rating systems, a clear metric for the work performed per unit of energy consumption has yet to be universally established. The development and adoption of such standard metrics would greatly improve the ability of data center operators to increase efficiency by maximizing the work completed by servers for a given energy consumption. Furthermore, greater access to detailed power information would facilitate better

---

[1] Forrest 2008.
[2] US EPA 2007.
[3] Garber 2009.
[4] US EPA 2007.

capacity planning for increased efficiencies in data centers. Breaking down the barriers obscuring this information is essential in order to provide clear indications of the energy-performance balance rather than the *perceptions* often reported on the market today.

1.2 Benchmarks, Metrics and Reducing the Total Cost of Ownership

The computing industry has long used software benchmarks as a basis for comparing the performance of competing server products. Such software benchmarks are developed to measure the output of servers as they perform standardized, representative workloads. The results of these benchmark tests allow products to be directly compared in a way not easily achieved in an actual operating environment. Software benchmarks output a metric indicating the server's ability to complete the workload's tasks, typically represented by the system's speed (e.g. operations per second). The resulting data provides the industry with a meaningful tool to compare competing systems or quantify improvements on a single system.

The rising cost of energy and corresponding increases in energy consumption together drive the need for server benchmarks with a broad focus on both speed-oriented performance and associated energy consumption. Existing benchmark methodologies vary in their ability to meet this need. Maximized computational performance will remain an important goal for server development, but a benchmark that solely focuses on compute performance does not easily fit into the total cost of ownership (TCO) calculation. In this case, analysis of both performance and energy require additional end user research or testing.

As an alternative to strict performance-based metrics, a second benchmark approach present on the market compares computational performance to a measure of TCO only including hardware and maintenance costs. This approach, which provides insight into how a server meets the day to day operational needs of the data center, makes it possible to compare cost-effective performance of various products. Still, this risks the under-representation of the broader operational cost of running a server; energy remains a missing component, and a significant omission: the 2007 *EPA Report to Congress on Server and Data Center Energy Efficiency* noted at that time that server energy costs would exceed the hardware purchase cost of a server by 2008.[5]

The addition of standardized energy measurement during benchmark testing expands the scope of a benchmark to include a more holistic view of the server in operation. A number of benchmarking organizations have undertaken efforts to include energy measurement methodologies within their processes; a few examples will be discussed in Section 4. The existence of these efforts points not only to the market's desire for this information, but also to the intrinsic strength of benchmarking organizations as trusted information resources. As performance benchmarks have evolved over time to serve a competitive and diverse market seeking standardized test methodologies, the development processes surrounding them have incorporated characteristics that support expansion into meaningful energy comparison:

---

[5] US EPA 2007.

- *Consortium-based development processes* provide input into workload development by a range of industry stakeholders with knowledge of available technologies, industry trends and developments in the market.
- *Pre-determined and transparent testing methodologies* ensure comparable results using agreed upon procedures for standardized energy measurements.
- *Structured versioning and revision schedules* allow for periodic updates to ensure continued applicability of energy metrics as technologies mature and change.
- *Established presence in the market* with well-understood workloads that provide context to associated energy measurements.

With these building blocks in place, there is clear context to provide the needed tools to address server efficiency and to contribute to the reduction of energy consumption, thereby reducing the long term TCO.

2 Current State of Server Performance Metrics and Benchmarks

2.1 Traditional Benchmarking: Determining Maximum Capability

Server benchmarks set a proxy by which computing performance can be consistently measured, quantified and understood. Benchmarks also facilitate ranking systems based on stable underlying testing conditions and settings. These two roles are closely tied. Though a particular workload may either be synthesized to exercise hardware under artificial conditions (synthetic workload) or designed to run a series of processes based on an end-use application mix (application-based workload), the repeatability and standardization of the process allows for direct comparisons of relative performance.

The proxy and ranking functions have traditionally been associated with maximized performance conditions. Vendors have responded by developing and aggressively marketing servers which can attain the highest benchmark scores. This focus leads to an emphasis on the highest *achievable* result instead of the *actual* performance that may be observed in a real end-use application in the data center. Though these benchmarks effectively illustrate maximum performance potential, they underemphasize the performance (and efficiency) of products as they would actually be used in the market. The maximum case does little for an end user seeking information on expected performance of the system once installed at their facility.

2.2 The Future Role of Benchmarks: Incorporating Both Efficiency and Performance

Integration of efficiency measurements into performance benchmark results can effectively extend the applicability of existing benchmarks to more realistic end-use scenarios. In the hypothetical example presented in Table 1, three systems have completed a benchmark where data is presented in terms of performance (completed operations), efficiency (operations per watt consumed), and average idle power measurements. Server 1 is the clear winner in terms of pure computational performance. However, a closer look at the data presented in this manner shows that Server 2 produced the more efficient completion of the workload per watt of power

Table 1. Example of holistic benchmark results

	Completed Operations @ 100% Utilization	Completed Operations per Watt	Average Server Idle Power	Best-Suited Use
Server 1	400,000	1000	165	Maximum Performance
Server 2	250,000	1200	110	Efficient Operation
Server 3	200,000	950	70	Underutilized Applications

consumed. Server 3 was inferior to 1 and 2 in both completed operations and operations per watt but had a significantly lower idle power measurement.

While hypothetical, this example illustrates how unique selection criteria by different audiences may yield diverse interpretations of the same set of data. An end user with business needs driven solely by computing performance might select Server 1, though they will have been made aware of the energy consumption penalties associated with this choice. A second user with similar computational needs but a tight power or density budget might choose Server 2, since it provides the best balance of energy use to workload performance. Finally, a third user with light application loads who expects long periods of idle time might find that Server 3 provides acceptable performance while also minimizing power consumption in the most common mode for expected applications. All three of these audiences are able to act on the cost-performance analysis most appropriate to their specific business needs.

With the growing emphasis on both energy and performance in the data center, the measurement of energy for existing benchmarks will be necessary to meet end-user expectations. Rather than highlighting only the fastest systems, there will also be demand to identify the most efficient systems, including models or configurations previously overlooked in benchmark results or by industry marketers. From a benchmark development organization's perspective, a greater demand for benchmarking data may result from a new audience looking for efficiency data rather than just maximum performance data. It is illustrative to consider a future scenario in which such benchmark development might result in a universal or generalized, metric for server efficiency. In the next section, ideal characteristics of such a unified approach are considered.

3   Development of a Generalized Energy and Performance Benchmark

In this section we consider a few important considerations for the development of a generalized metric for server energy efficiency and computing performance. These considerations include discussions of power versus energy measurement, synthetic versus application-based workloads, and other factors.

3.1 Power versus Energy Measurements

It is important to contextualize the differences between instantaneous power measurements, time-scaled energy measurements, and averaged values of each measurement as important elements of a power and performance benchmark. Marketing claims regarding energy efficiency for IT equipment are more prevalent in recent years; and while such efforts may meet the information needs of end users, marketing materials often use the terms energy and power interchangeably. It is important that the implications of each term are understood as they apply to benchmarks and metrics.

It is potentially less complicated to use instantaneous power measurements when performing a benchmark test, yet care must be taken to properly frame the periodic nature of a typical computing workload. Averaged power reporting over time can be effective as a proxy for the expected power consumption of a workload exhibiting stabilized or cyclic behavior. Selecting an appropriate sampling rate for power measurements is critical to the quality of the measurement; if readings are not taken frequently enough, one risks overlooking important system events that have a significant effect on average power consumption.

In contrast, measuring energy accumulated over time requires either (1) that instantaneous readings be abstracted to apply to an expected usage case, or (2) that the selected workload is truly representative of actual server operation. One risk with the accumulated energy approach is that end users may make incorrect assumptions about the relationship between watt-hour output and utility pricing. To mitigate this risk, data on the time taken to complete the workload and the instantaneous power consumption during the test should be provided along with the accumulated energy data to ensure that the test results are taken in proper context.

In general, it is critical to the success of the benchmark metric that workload weightings and measurement inputs are made available to the end user. Transparency preserves the context of the data and enables end users to assess the relevance of the results to their specific application environment. As an example, the Version 5.0 ENERGY STAR Computer Specification includes an efficiency metric based on kWh ratings.[6] In addition to publishing the calculated kWh "score," the ENERGY STAR program makes transparent the equation used to calculate the score and requires vendors to report the measured power inputs entered into this calculation. While the standard efficiency equation is weighted based on statistically relevant data, this transparent reporting structure provides a means for end users to estimate their own energy costs based on the specifics of their application.

3.2 Synthetic versus Application-Based Workloads

Two common workload structures for benchmarks are *synthetic workloads* that drive the server to complete as many artificially-derived tasks as possible in a given amount of time, and *application-based workloads* that measure the server's ability to complete predetermined operations based on real applications. A generalized server efficiency benchmark could make use of either type of workload, but any results would have to be carefully annotated to ensure that they are interpreted properly by

---

[6] ENERGY STAR 2009.

Table 2. Comparison of different benchmark characteristics

	Synthetic Workload	Application-Based Workload
Power Measurement	• Opportunity to meet the steady-state condition necessary to support averaged power measurement. • The number of operations most likely varies between tests. It is reasonable to report averaged power, but also to frame the power levels with information on utilization during the test.	• May not meet the steady state condition since transitions between applications or the realistic variations in power necessary to complete tasks will vary from test to test. • The number of operations may vary similarly to the situation for a synthetic workload. Averaged power is again useful to report. Associating the average power measurements to the applications in the workload can provide insight into architecture's ability to handle elements within the workload.
Energy Measurement	• A set time period can provide structure to energy measurement, but results are best weighted with the number of operations completed during the time period. • Since operations vary from test to test, this workload structure is not easily positioned to report a generalized "expected energy consumption."	• As systems improve in performance, a task may initiate and conclude too rapidly to derive a meaningful energy measurement. • Since the server is completing the same set of tasks and may vary in utilization during the workload, energy data provides more of the expected variety important for development of a generalized energy consumption model.

end users. The impact of each structure on the marketing of power and energy results is considered in Table 2.

3.3   The Use of a Generalized Server Efficiency Benchmark

Widely used server performance benchmarks typically mimic or replicate intended workloads in the data center. An effective *generalized* benchmark – one applicable for a wide variety of system applications – should give end users an indication of how a particular server ranks compared to others in general operation through an assessment relevant to different workload types. Because workloads within data centers vary widely, there will never be a perfect correlation between the work performed in a benchmark workload and that which is performed in an end-use application. There is no true substitution for testing a server with an actual application workload, but for buyers without the resources to conduct such in-depth testing, an effective generalized benchmark should provide insight into server performance under a variety of operating conditions.

Examples of typical workloads run by servers and represented by available benchmarks are *high performance computing (HPC)*, *web services or other accessed services*, *email services*, *database management*, and *shared file services*. These five categories represent a broad cross-section of server uses and illustrate the types of workloads that could be assessed by a generalized benchmark. Examples of benchmarks used to approximate these workloads are available in Section 4. Although these workloads are expected to cover the majority of the server market, other common and niche application workloads may exist.

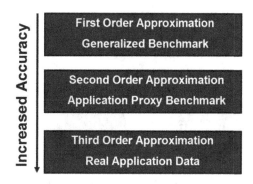

Fig. 1. Hierarchy of Different Benchmarking Approaches

An available benchmark that produces general indication of broad-based server efficiency and performance is currently missing from the market. Such a benchmark – capable of representing more than one workload type – might be thought of as a *first-order* approximation of the energy efficiency of a server; benchmarks based on one of the five referenced workload types might be thought of as a *second-order* approximation, providing greater accuracy for a specific workload type. A *third-order* approximation of energy efficiency could be achieved by testing a server in its intended application, affording more precision at the cost of additional testing resources. Server purchasers might rely on a mix of first, second, and third-order approximations depending on available resources.

For example, large organizations might use a first-order approximation to narrow down a list of hardware platforms for more detailed benchmarking or application testing, while a smaller buyer looking for a general workhorse server to run a number of different applications might use a first-order approximation as their sole purchasing criteria.

3.4 Technical Characteristics of a Generalized Benchmark

Most servers can be thought of as consisting of a few key components and capabilities that will affect the performance and energy consumption of that server, which have been summarized in Table 3.

Table 3. Capability factors in server performance benchmarks

Capability	Component(s)	Description
Compute	Processors and system memory	Performing operations, i.e. switching 1s and 0s
Storage	Hard drives, solid state drives, etc.	Long term storage of data, i.e. keeping 1s and 0s
Input and Output (I/O)	Network cards, RAID/SAS controllers, etc.	Transferring data in and out of devices, i.e. moving 1s and 0s

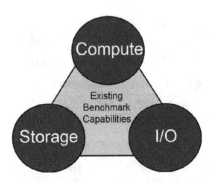

Fig. 2. Capability factors in server performance benchmarks

Different workloads require a different mix of these basic capabilities. For example, an HPC application will be almost all compute, while file services, in contrast, will be very storage and I/O intensive. A conceptual illustration of this concept is included in Figure 2.

A truly generalized benchmark would test relative energy and performance efficiency for each of the three factors, using a combination of the relative efficiencies of each capability to arrive at a generalized system efficiency. A server with high compute efficiency (e.g., with high efficiency processors and/or memory) and a low efficiency I/O device would receive a moderate efficiency rating on the generalized scale, while a server with high efficiency in all three factors would rate much higher. If the specific efficiencies of each capability could be separately assessed, this benchmark could also be used to identify servers ideal for more specific workload scenarios. A generalized benchmark capable of evaluating a server in this way could be developed with either a synthetic benchmark designed to stress each factor in turn, or with a carefully-selected set of application code designed to concurrently assess the performance of each factor.

3.5   Other Important Elements of a Generalized Power and Performance Benchmark

A benchmark is only useful if there is a low barrier to entry for its use and it is adopted by a large segment of the industry it is intended to serve – there must be a critical mass of test results available to allow purchasers to make meaningful comparisons to support their purchasing decisions. To lower this barrier to entry, there are many other criteria a successful benchmark must meet to maximize its effectiveness in the market:

- Able to operate on a wide variety of system architectures and operating systems.
- Low cost to run and report data in a standard way.
- Scalable with system size.
- Easily configured for consistent, repeatable results.
- Consistent with current standards for operation of equipment in data centers.
- Able to assess the relative efficiency of multi-node and blade systems.

4 Using Existing Benchmarks to Assess Generalized Server Efficiency

Many benchmarks exist in the current market to measure the performance of systems under various workloads. This section will focus on benchmarks intended for general servers and how such benchmarks might be combined to create a generalized metric for server efficiency.

4.1 Selection of Current Benchmarking Organizations

Transaction Processing Council (TPC)
TPC is a non-profit corporation and industry consortium which focuses on benchmarks for data base systems and transaction processing. Transactions measured and tested by TPC involve common business processes. A typical transaction, as defined by the TPC, would include the updating of information in a database system for purposes such as inventory control, airline reservations, or banking transfers. Systems relevant to TPC benchmarks are often large database systems composed of many subcomponents (e.g., servers, external storage, and networking) which create the larger systems. Certain TPC benchmarks already include metrics for $/operation, and the organization is currently engaged in ongoing efforts to include energy measurements for the benchmarks, so that their metrics include a true measure of TCO (including energy costs) for all benchmarks. Draft energy measurements are expected in 2009.[7] Further information on TPC and their benchmarks can be found at www.TPC.org.

Standard Performance Evaluation Corporation (SPEC)
SPEC is a non-profit corporation and industry consortium which focuses on the creation of server benchmarks for a variety of standard data center applications. The SPEC benchmarks are typically aimed at individual server systems and specific subsystems. A SPEC subcommittee has recently developed a standard protocol for measuring and reporting power consumption as part of the measurement and reporting process for its benchmarks. SPEC released the first such benchmark (SPECpower_ssj2008) in 2008 and the second (SPECweb_2009) in 2009, and will continue to revise its other benchmarks to include power consumption measurements.[8] Further information on SPEC and their benchmarks can be found at www.SPEC.org.

Green 500
The Green 500 is a ranking of the most energy efficient super computers in the world. The Green 500 uses the LINPACK benchmark along with associated power measurement techniques to measure floating point operations per watt.[9] Further information on Green 500 and their benchmarks can be found at http://www.green500.org/

---

[7] Transaction Processing Performance Council.
[8] Standard Performance Evaluation Corporation.
[9] The Green500.

4.2 Available Benchmarks by Data Center Workload Category

Table 4. Typical data center workloads and available benchmarks. Additional details of the available benchmarks are included in Appendix A of this report.

Data Center Workload Category	Available Benchmarks
High performance computing (HPC)	LINPACK, Green 500*, SPEC_CPU2006
Web services or other accessed services	SPECpower_ssj2008*, SPECweb2009*, TPC-App
Email services	SPECmail2009
Database management	NNA Server Power Efficiency*, NNA Server Transaction Throughput Benchmark, TPC-C, TPC-E, TPC-H
Shared file services	SPECsfs2008

(*) denotes benchmarks that currently integrate power measurement into results/procedures.

4.3 Measuring Power Using Existing Benchmarks

If existing benchmarks are to be used as a proxy to measure the energy efficiency of servers, it will be necessary to develop standardized procedures for adding power and/or energy measurements to some existing benchmarks. The EPA set the stage for this work in the 2006 release of an initial *Server Energy Measurement Protocol*[10] and in the 2009 release of the *ENERGY STAR Test Procedure for Determining the Power Use of Computer Servers at Idle and Full Load*, as Appendix A to the ENERGY STAR specification for Computer Servers[11]. As described in the SPEC procedures and *Server Energy Measurement Protocol*, benchmark tests should, where possible, be performed at a number of different load points, including at a minimum full load (100%) and idle (0%), in order to allow for the development of a power and performance load curve. An example load curve from a SPECpower_ssj2008 result has been included in Figure 3 to illustrate this approach. In order to use existing benchmarks to assess generalized server efficiency, more investigation may be necessary to ensure that existing practices can be applied to some current benchmarks which do not yet include energy or power measurements.

4.4 Creating a Generalized Server Efficiency Metric from Existing Benchmarks

The development of an ideal generalized efficiency benchmark for servers as described in Section 3 could be a lengthy and challenging process. However, the recent emphasis on efficiency and energy management in the data center illustrates that there is momentum in both the manufacturer and end-user communities to support such an effort.

---

[10] Koomey, *et al* 2006.
[11] ENERGY STAR 2009.

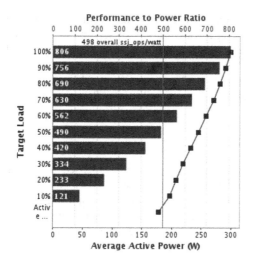

Fig. 3. Example SPECpower_ssj2008 result showing a measured load curve[12]

In the short term, this suggests an opportunity to bring together the efficiency metrics referenced above to develop a hybrid metric to assess server energy efficiency. Since servers can be expected to operate under a variety of applications and workloads, this hybrid metric would integrate elements from a variety of workloads. These workloads, as well as appropriate benchmarks which act as proxies to server performance, could be chosen from Table 4 in Section 4.2. A possible scenario would be to select a single, representative benchmark from each category for inclusion in the hybrid metric; this scenario would minimize the testing burden on manufacturers and ensure uniformity in results between systems. Once a list of appropriate workloads and benchmarks was selected, data could be collected to assess different options for a generalized efficiency metric. The following approaches could be considered:

- Measure the relative efficiency of each benchmark separately, to allow end users to determine which metric is most suited to their particular application;
- Weight each benchmark to calculate a single hybrid efficiency metric based on the combined test results; or
- Identify a preferred benchmark that served as the best proxy for all additional benchmarks (i.e. select the single benchmark that best preserves the relative ranking of server efficiency for all benchmarks).

Data gathered during the development and implementation of a metric based on existing benchmarks could then form the basis for development of a more advanced generalized efficiency metric that meets the intent and ideal requirements identified in Section 3.

---

[12] Standard Performance Evaluation Corporation. *SPEC and the benchmark name SPECpower_ssj2008 are registered trademarks of the Standard Performance Evaluation Corporation. For the latest SPECpower_ssj2008 benchmark results, visit http://www.spec.org/power_ssj2008/results/*

Regardless of the approach used to leverage existing benchmarks, a new emphasis should be placed on testing a wider variety of servers, as configured for shipment to the end customer, with their associated benchmark scores disclosed. Greater disclosure of consistent, accurate performance data – including energy consumption – across a diverse set of server product lines will enable smarter procurement practices and stimulate competition while continually propelling market transformation.

5 Conclusion

Performance benchmarks have traditionally focused on measuring maximum computing performance without regard to energy efficiency. However, the importance of environmental issues related to computing is prominently discussed in the business community today. While the use of TCO as a purchasing tool has increased, more transparency is needed to identify operating costs that are specifically attributable to energy consumption, and to highlight the role of inefficient computing practices in exacerbating these costs.

The community responsible for server performance benchmarks is well-positioned to contribute to the development of new metrics which include energy efficiency in addition to computing performance. The consortium-based development structures and open process for sharing performance data that are the hallmarks of performance metrics would also serve the development of energy efficiency metrics. Numerous benchmark organizations have already recognized this opportunity by developing independent methods to collect energy or power information as a standard practice.

This paper reviewed the current state of server energy and performance benchmarking, highlighting important issues for consideration in further benchmark development. The server industry as a whole, however, continues to focus primarily on setting new benchmark records for maximized workloads. By incorporating energy measurement into benchmark results, the industry can help mainstream product configurations become more competitive in the marketplace based on optimized operational and efficiency performance.

While it can be argued that data derived from a discrete set of workloads is not representative of actual server performance in all cases, the very nature of benchmarks as a standardized evaluative set of methodologies does provide a means for end users to make meaningful comparisons of different server products. It will be important for benchmark development organizations to continue efforts to standardize energy measurement methodologies in a manner that is consistent with how products are actually operated in the field, so that benchmark results are repeatable and relevant to real world conditions.

A generalized benchmark, applicable for a wide variety of data center applications, will remain a valuable objective for the server industry. Current and forthcoming efforts to enhance existing performance benchmarks will provide the foundation on which to build a generalized assessment tool, and will provide an ongoing catalyst for continued energy efficiency improvements in servers. The benchmark community should continue to seek out opportunities to integrate energy measurement into standard benchmark procedures, and should standardize the collection of power and/or energy data in benchmarking procedures. By making energy measurements a common and accepted part of performance measurement, the benchmarking community will be able to reach a wider audience, broaden the scope of systems that can be measured with existing benchmarks, and serve their customers needs for insight into expected energy performance.

References

1. ENERGY STAR Program. ENERGY STAR Program Requirements for Computer Servers (2009)
2. Forrest, W., Kaplan, J., Kindler, N.: Data Centers: How to cut carbon emissions and costs. McKinsey on Business Technology 14, 6 (2008)
3. Garber, K.: The Internet's Hidden Energy Hogs: Data Servers. US News and World Report (2009)
4. The Green500 List, http://www.green500.org
5. Hass, J., Monroe, M., Pflueger, J., Pouchet, J., Snelling, P., Rawson, A., Rawson, F.: Proxy Proposals for Measuring Data Center Productivity. The Green Grid: Beaverton, OR (2009)
6. Koomey, J., Belady, C., Wong, C., Snevely, R., Nordman, B., Hunter, E., Lange, K., Tipley, R., Darnell, G., Accapadi, M., Rumsey, P., Kelley, B., Tschudi, W., Moss, D., Greco, R., Brill, K.: Server Energy Measurement Protocol. Analytics Press, Oakland (2006)
7. Koomey, J., Brill, K., Turner, W.P., Stanley, J.R.: A Simple Model for Determining True Total Cost of Ownership for Data Centers. The Uptime Institute, Santa Fe (2007)
8. Neal Nelson & Associates, http://www.nna.com
9. Standard Performance Evaluation Corporation, http://www.spec.org
10. Stanley, J.R., Brill, K., Koomey, J.: Four Metrics Define Data Center "Greenness" Enabling Users to Quantify "Energy Efficiency for Profit" Initiatives. The Uptime Institute, Santa Fe (2007)
11. Transaction Processing Performance Council, http://www.tpc.org/information/about/abouttpc.asp
12. United States Environmental Protection Agency: Report to Congress on Server and Data Center Energy Efficiency, Public Law 109-431 (2007)

Appendix A: Available Performance Benchmarks

Benchmark Name (*Organization*)	Intended Workload	Workload Category	Performance Metric	Power/ Energy Meas.?*
LINPACK (*N/A – Public*)	Floating point operations	High Performance Computing (HPC)	MFLOPs	No
LINPACK (*Green 500*)	Floating point operations per Watt	HPC	MFLOPs / Watt (peak performance divided by average power)	Yes
NNA Power-Efficiency Benchmark (*Neal Nelson and Associates*)	WWW transaction requests	Database Management	Watts for a given transaction rate	Yes
NNA Server Transaction Throughput Benchmark (*Neal Nelson and Associates*)	WWW transaction requests	Database Management	Transactions / minute	No
SPEC_CPU2006 (*SPEC*)	Integer speed (*SPECint2006*), integer rate (*SPECint_rate2006*) and floating point speed (*SPECfp2006*), floating point throughput (*SPECfp_rate2006*)	HPC	N/A – unitless mix of various performance measurements from multiple workloads	No
SPECmail2009 (*SPEC*)	Corporate mail server workloads based on number of users	Email Services	Sessions / hour	No
SPECsfs2008 (*SPEC*)	File server throughput and response time	Shared File Services	Throughput (ops/sec), response time (msec)	No
SPECpower_ssj2008 (*SPEC*)	Java based applications	Web/Accessed Services	Operations / watt (ssj_ops/watt)	Yes
SPECweb2009 (*SPEC*)	Http transactions including: Banking, ecommerce and support	Web/Accessed Services	Simultaneous user sessions (SUS) / watt	Yes
TPC-App (*TPC*)	Application server and web services	Web/Accessed Services	Web Service Interactions / second (SIPS), price / interaction ($/SIPS)	Pending
TPC-C (*TPC*)	New-order transactions	Database Management	Transactions / minute (tpmC), price / transaction ($/tpmC)	Pending
TPC-E (*TPC*)	On-Line Transaction Processing (OLTP): workload of a brokerage firm	Database Management	Transactions / second (tpsE), price / transaction ($/tpsE)	Pending
TPC-H (*TPC*)	Decision support benchmark of business oriented queries	Database Management	Query-per-Hour (QphH@Size), price / query ($/QphH@Size)	Pending

* Denotes status of power/energy measurement as an integral methodology within the benchmark.

From Performance to Dependability Benchmarking:
A Mandatory Path

Marco Vieira and Henrique Madeira

CISUC, Department of Informatics Engineering
University of Coimbra, Portugal
{mvieira, henrique}@dei.uc.pt

Abstract. The work on performance benchmarking has started long ago. Ranging from simple benchmarks that target a very specific system or component to very complex benchmarks for complex infrastructures, performance benchmarks have contributed to improve successive generations of systems. However, the fact that nowadays most systems need to guarantee high availability and reliability shows that it is necessary to shift the focus from measuring pure performance to the measurement of both performance and dependability. Research on dependability benchmarking has started in the beginning of this decade, having already led to the proposal of several benchmarks. However, no dependability benchmark has yet achieved the status of a real benchmark endorsed by a standardization body or corporation. In this paper we argue that standardization bodies must shift focus and start including dependability metrics in their benchmarks. We present an overview of the state-of-the-art on dependability benchmarking and define a set of research needs and challenges that have to be addressed for the establishment of real dependability benchmarks.

Keywords: Benchmarking, dependability, performance, metrics.

1 Introduction

The ascendance of networked information in our economy and daily lives has increased the awareness of the importance of dependability features. In fact, due to the impressive growth of the Internet, some minutes of downtime in a server somewhere may be exposed as loss of service to thousands of users around the world.

Computer benchmarks are standard tools that allow comparing different systems or components according to specific characteristics (performance, robustness, dependability, etc). Computer systems industry holds a reputed infrastructure for performance evaluation and the set of benchmarks managed by TPC (Transaction Processing Performance Council [1]) and by SPEC (Standard Performance Evaluation Corporation [2]) are recognized as the most successful benchmarking initiatives. However, dependability evaluation and comparison have been absent from the TPC and SPEC benchmarking efforts.

Performance benchmarks have contributed to improve peak performance of successive generations of systems, but in many cases the systems and configurations

R. Nambiar and M. Poess (Eds.): TPCTC 2009, LNCS 5895, pp. 67–83, 2009.

used to achieve the best performance are very far from the systems that are actually used in the field. The major problem is that the results tend to portrait rather artificial scenarios, as dependability-related mechanisms are not adequately configured (or are configured for the minimum impact on performance) and the characterization of the effectiveness of dependability features is totally disregarded.

The fact that many businesses require very high dependability for their systems shows that it is necessary to shift the focus from measuring pure performance to the measurement of both performance and dependability. This way, the tight dependence between performance and dependability in modern systems urge the definition of benchmarks to compare different products in a more realistic scenario. Above all, it is important to include in the benchmarks new measures that show the benefit of adding better mechanisms in the system or configuring the available mechanisms to achieve the best performance and dependability.

Research on dependability benchmarking started in the beginning of this decade, having already led to the proposal of several benchmarks (see Section 4). However, in spite of the pertinence of having dependability benchmarks for computer systems, the reality is that no dependability benchmark has yet achieved the status of a real benchmark endorsed by a standardization body or corporation, in a clear contrast with performance benchmarking, where TPC and SPEC have very successful initiatives.

In this paper we argue that standardization bodies must include dependability characterization in their benchmarking initiatives. A dependability benchmark is a specification of a standard procedure to measure both the dependability and performance of computer systems or components. Comparing to typical performance benchmarks, which consist mainly of a workload and a set of performance measures, a dependability benchmark adds two key elements: 1) **measures related to dependability**; and 2) a **faultload** that emulates real faults experienced by systems in the field.

In the same way performance benchmarks have contributed to improve peak performance of successive generations of systems, we believe that dependability benchmarking represents a possible way to improve dependability of future systems. In fact, a dependability benchmark shall be largely useful in several scenarios:

1. Help **end-users** and **system administrators** to choose the system that best fit their requirements by comparing the dependability features of alternative systems.
2. Assist **system vendors** in promoting their products. In addition, a dependability benchmark may be a very important tool to help the system vendors to detect possible dependability problems on their computer systems/components.
3. Help **system integrators** to choose the best components for a given solution.
4. Provide **researchers** a tool to evaluate new prototypes.

The outline of this paper is as follows. Section 2 presents basic concepts on computer benchmarking. Section 3 introduces the well-established performance-benchmarking field. Section 4 discusses the dependability-benchmarking concept and presents an overview of the state-of-the-art on dependability benchmarking. Section 5 presents an example of a dependability benchmark for transactional systems and Section 6 proposes a set of research needs and challenges that have to be addressed for the establishment of real dependability benchmarks. Finally, Section 7 concludes the paper.

2 The Computer Benchmarking Concept

Computer benchmarking is primarily an experimental approach. As an experiment, its acceptability is largely based on two salient facets of the experimental method: 1) the *ability to reproduce* the observations and the measurements, either on a deterministic or on a statistical basis, and 2) the *capability of generalizing the results* through some form of inductive reasoning. The first aspect (ability to reproduce) gives confidence in the results and the second (ability to generalize) makes the benchmark results meaningful and useful beyond the specific setup used in the benchmarking process.

In practice, benchmarking results are normally reproducible in a statistical basis. On the other hand, the necessary generalization of the results is inherently related to the representativeness of the benchmark experiments. The notion of representativeness is manifold and touches almost all the aspects of benchmarking, as it really means that the conditions used to obtain the measures are representative of what can be found in the real world.

The key aspect that distinguishes benchmarking from existing evaluation and validation techniques is that a benchmark fundamentally represents an agreement (explicit or tacit) that is accepted by the computer industry and by the user community. This technical agreement is in fact the key that turns a benchmark into a standard. In other words, a benchmark is something that the user community and the computer industry accept as representative enough of a given application domain to be deemed useful and to be generally used as a (standard) way of measuring specific features of a computer system and, consequently, a way to compare different systems.

The concept of benchmarking can then be summarized in three words: *representativeness, usefulness,* and *agreement*. A benchmark must be as representative as possible of a given domain but, as an abstraction of that domain, it will always be an imperfect representation of reality. However, the objective is to find a useful representation that captures the essential elements of the application domain and provides practical ways to characterize the computer features that help the vendors/integrators to improve their products and help the users in their purchase decisions.

To achieve acceptance by the computer industry or by the user community a benchmark should fulfill a set of key properties: representativeness, portability, repeatability, scalability, non-intrusiveness, and simplicity of use. These properties must be taken into account from the beginning of the definition of the benchmark components and must be validated after the benchmark has been completely defined.

The work on performance benchmarking has started long ago. Ranging from simple benchmarks that target a very specific hardware system or component to very complex benchmarks focusing complex systems (e.g., database management systems, operating systems), performance benchmarks have contributed to improve successive generations of systems. Research on dependability benchmarking boosted in the beginning of this decade, having already led to the proposal of several dependability benchmarks. Several works have been carried out by different groups and following different approaches (e.g., experimental, modeling, fault injection).

3 Performance Benchmarking: A Well Established Field

Performance benchmarks are standard procedures and tools aiming at evaluating and comparing different systems or components according to specific performance measures. The work on performance benchmarking as started many decades ago and the two most prominent organizations currently working on the performance benchmarking business are TPC (Transaction Processing Performance Council) [1] and SPEC (Standard Performance Evaluation Corporation) [2].

Whetstone programs, the first general-purpose benchmarks that did set industry standards for computer system performance, started almost four decades ago with the HJC11 benchmark [3], which was written in Algol 60 in 1972 at the National Physical Laboratory in the United Kingdom. Whetstone is a very well known synthetic benchmark for evaluating the performance of computers in terms of instructions executed per second.

Several performance benchmarking initiatives were launched in the 70's and 80's. The Wisconsin benchmark [4] was launched in 1983 and marked the beginning of a new generation of performance benchmarks targeting complex database systems. In fact, the work on performance benchmarking of database systems (and transactional systems in general) boosted, and two years after the Wisconsin benchmark, the TP1 and Gray's DebitCredit [5] benchmarks were launched. These benchmarks settled the foundations for the Transactions Processing Performance Council (TPC) benchmarking initiative, which started in 1988, when the TPC organization has been formed [1].

The **Transaction Processing Performance Council (TPC)** is a non-profit organization whose goal is to define and disseminate benchmarks for databases and transactional systems in general. TPC also verifies the results announced by benchmark performers in order to make those results official. TPC is composed by the major vendors of systems and software from the transaction processing and database markets (detailed information on TPC can be obtained at [1]), and has currently four active benchmarks: TPC-C and TPC-E for OLTP (On-Line Transaction Processing) systems, TPC-App for application servers and web services, and TPC-H for decision support systems. These benchmarks measure performance in terms of how many operations or transactions a given system can execute per unit of time.

The **Standard Performance Evaluation Corporation (SPEC)** is a non-profit organization that establishes and maintains a set of benchmarks in several domains. SPEC develops suites of benchmarks and reviews and publishes submitted results. SPEC is an organization made of three different groups (detailed and updated information on SPEC organization, groups, and benchmarks, can be obtained from SPEC web-site [2]): the Open Systems Group (OSG), which focus on component-level and systems-level benchmarks for desktop systems, workstations and servers running open operating system environments; the High Performance Group (HPG), which establishes, maintains and supports a set of performance benchmarks for high performance system architectures, such as symmetric multiprocessor systems, workstation clusters, distributed memory parallel systems, and traditional vector and vector parallel supercomputers; and the Graphics & Workstation Performance Group (PEC/GWPG), which is the umbrella organization for autonomous groups that develop graphics and workstation benchmarks and performance reporting procedures.

A performance benchmark is typically provided as a computer program ready to be executed (as is the case of SPEC benchmarks) or as a document that specifies how the benchmark should be implemented and run (this is the case of TPC benchmarks) and is normally composed by three main elements: workload, measures, and rules. The **workload** defines the set of tasks that the system under benchmarking has to perform during the benchmark execution. The **measures** portray the time needed to execute the workload or, alternatively, the number of operations executed per unit of time. The purpose of the **rules** is to assure that the results from different executions of the benchmark are valid and comparable.

4 Dependability Benchmarking: A Recent Research Field

The notion of dependability and its terminology have been established by the International Federation for Information Processing (IFIP) Working Group 10.4 [6]. IFIP WG 10.4 defines dependability as *"the trustworthiness of a computing system which allows reliance to be justifiably placed on the service it delivers"*. Dependability is an integrative concept that includes the following attributes [7]: availability (readiness for correct service), reliability (continuity of correct service), safety (absence of catastrophic consequences on the user(s) and the environment), confidentiality (absence of unauthorized disclosure of information), integrity (absence of improper system state alterations), and maintainability (ability to undergo repairs and modifications).

The main problem in measuring the dependability of a given computer system or component is that it is very dependent on many factors, either internal to the system (hardware and software) or external (environment or human made). Assessing system dependability is in fact a very difficult problem and has been addressed by using both model-based and measurement-based techniques. The former include analytical [8] and simulation [9] models and the latter include field measurement [10], fault injection [11],[12] and robustness testing [13],[14].

Dependability benchmarking is mainly inspired on measurement-based techniques. This way, a dependability benchmark can be defined as a specification of a standard procedure to assess dependability related measures of a computer system or computer component. The main components of a dependability benchmark are: **measures** (characterize the performance and dependability of the system), **workload** (work that the system must perform during the benchmark run), **faultload** (set of faults that emulate real faults experienced in the field), **benchmark procedure and rules** (description of the procedures and rules that must be followed to run the benchmark), and **experimental setup** (setup required to run the benchmark).

We propose the following general steps to specify a dependability benchmark:

1. The first step is the identification of the **application area**. The division of the application spectrum into well-defined application areas is necessary to cope with the huge diversity of systems and applications and to make it possible to make choices on the definition of benchmark components.
2. The second step is the **characterization of the SUB** in terms of typical functionalities and features. Obviously, this characterization is of utmost importance to define the benchmark component.

3. The third step is the definition of the dependability **benchmark measures**, which is the first dependability benchmark component to be specified (because the definition of the other components is very dependent on what is being measured).

4. The **remaining components** are defined in the last step.

Two classes of **measures** can be considered in a dependability benchmark:

- **Conditional measures**: measures that characterize the system in a relative fashion (i.e., measures that are directly related to the conditions disclosed in the benchmark report) and are mainly meant to compare alternative systems.
- **Unconditional measures on dependability attributes**: measures that characterize the system in a global fashion taking into account the occurrence of the various events impacting its behavior. Some examples of dependability attributes include: reliability, availability, maintainability and safety [7].

The conditional measures are directly obtained as results of the benchmark experiments. The unconditional measures on dependability attributes have to be calculated using modeling techniques with the help of external data, such as fault rates, MTBF, etc. This external data could be provided from field data or based on past experience considering similar systems. Note that, models of complex systems may be very difficult to define and the external data difficult to obtain.

Our proposal is to focus on direct measures (conditional measures), following the traditional benchmarking philosophy based on a pure experimental approach. These measures are related to the conditions disclosed in the benchmark report and can be used for comparison or for system/component improvement and tuning. This is similar to what happens with performance benchmark results, as the performance measures do not represent an absolute measure of system performance and cannot be used for capacity planning or to predict the actual performance of the system in field.

The measures of a dependability benchmark should:

- Be based on the service provided by the system during the benchmarking process and should be independent from the system structure (to allow comparison).
- Focus on an end-to-end perspective (e.g., the point-of-view of the users).
- Allow the characterization of both dependability and performance features.
- Be easy to understand by users and administrators.
- Not be extrapolated or inferred: measures must be directly computed based on the information collected during the benchmark execution.

The **faultload** represents a set of faults that emulates real faults experienced by systems in the field. Among the main components needed to define a benchmark, the faultload is clearly the most obscure one due to the complex nature of faults. A faultload can be based on three major classes of faults:

- **Operator faults:** operator faults are human mistakes. The great complexity of administration tasks in some systems and the need of tuning and administration in a daily basis, clearly explains why human faults (i.e., wrong human actions) should be considered in a dependability benchmark.
- **Software faults:** software faults (i.e., program defects or bugs) are recognized as an important source of system outages, and given the huge complexity of today's software the weight of software faults tends to increase.

– **Hardware faults:** includes traditional hardware faults, such as bit-flips and stuck-at, and high-level hardware failures, such as hard disk failures or failures of the interconnection network. Hardware faults are especially relevant in systems prone to electrical interferences.

Concerning the definition of the **workload**, the job is considerably simplified by the existence of workloads from performance benchmarks. Obviously, these already established workloads are the natural choice for a dependability benchmark. However, when adopting an existing workload some changes may be required in order to target specific system features. An important aspect to keep in mind when choosing a workload is that the goal is not only to evaluate the performance but also assess specific dependability features.

The **procedures and rules** define the correct steps to run a benchmark and obtain the measures. These rules are, of course, dependent on the specific benchmark but the following points give some guidelines on specific aspects needed in most of the cases:

– Procedures for "translating" the workload and faultload defined in the benchmark specification into the actual workload and faultload that will apply to the system.
– Uniform conditions to build the setup and run the dependability benchmark.
– Rules related to the collection of the experimental results.
– Rules for the production of the final measures from the direct experimental results.
– Scaling rules to adapt the same benchmark to systems of very different sizes.
– System configuration disclosures required for interpreting the benchmark results.
– Rules to avoid optimistic or biased results.

In the following sections we present previous work on dependability benchmarking to demonstrate the relevance of the field. The works presented clearly support our claim that standardization bodies should start including dependability in their benchmarking initiatives. In fact, it is clear that both academia and industry regard dependability benchmarking as a mandatory path for research and practice.

4.1 Special Interest Group on Dependability Benchmarking (SIGDeB)

The Special Interest Group on Dependability Benchmarking (SIGDeB) was created by the International Federation for Information Processing (IFIP) Working Group 10.4 [6] in 1999 to promote the research, practice, and adoption of benchmarks for computer-related systems dependability. The work carried out in the context of the SIGDeB is particularly relevant and merges contributions from both industry and academia.

A preliminary proposal issued by the SIGDeB was in the form of a set of standardized classes for characterizing the dependability of computer systems [15]. The goal of the proposed classification was to allow the comparison among computer systems concerning four different dimensions: availability, data integrity, disaster recovery, and security. The authors have specifically developed the details of the proposal for transaction processing applications. This work proposes that the evaluation of a system should be done by answering a set of standardized questions or performing tests that validate the evaluation criteria.

A very relevant effort in the context of SIGDeB is a book on dependability benchmarking of computer systems [16]. This book presents several relevant benchmarking initiatives carried out by different organizations, ranging from academia to large industrial companies.

4.2 The DBench Project

The DBench project [17] was funded by the European Commission, under the Information Society Technologies Programme (IST), Fifth Framework Programme (FP5). The main goal was to devise benchmarks to evaluate and compare the dependability of COTS and COTS-based systems, in embedded, real time, and transactional systems. The following paragraphs summarize the work carried out in the project.

The work presented in [18] and [19] address the problem of **dependability benchmarking for general purpose operating systems** (OS), focusing mainly on the robustness of the OS (in particular of the OS kernel) with respect to faulty applications. The measures provided are: 1) OS robustness in the presence of faulty system calls; 2) OS reaction time for faulty system calls; and 3) OS restart time after the activation of faulty system calls. Three workloads are considered: 1) a realistic application that implements the driver system of the TPC-C performance benchmark [20]; 2) the PostMark file system performance benchmark for operating systems; and 3) the Java Virtual Machine (JVM) middleware. The faultload is based on the corruption of systems call parameters.

The work presented in [21] is a preliminary proposal of a **dependability benchmark for real time kernels for onboard space systems**. This benchmark, called DBench-RTK, focuses mainly on the assessment of the predictability of response time of service calls in a Real-Time Kernel (RTK). The DBench-RTK benchmark provides a single measure that represents the predictability of response time of the service calls of RTKs used at space domain systems. The workload consists in an Onboard Scheduler (OBS). The faultload consists of faults injected into kernel functions calls by corrupting parameter values.

The work presented in [22] represents a preliminary proposal of a **dependability benchmark for engine control applications for automotive systems**. This benchmark focuses the robustness of the control applications running inside the Electronic Control Units (ECU) with respect to transient hardware faults. This dependability benchmark provides a set of measures that allows the comparison of the safety of different engine control systems. The workload is based on the standards used in Europe for the emission certification of light duty vehicles. The faultload consists in transient hardware faults that affect the cells of the memory holding the software used in the engine control.

The DBench-OLTP dependability benchmark [23] is a **dependability benchmark for on-line transaction processing systems**. The DBench-OLTP is presented in more detail in Section 5.

In [24] it is presented a preliminary proposal of another dependability benchmark for on-line transaction processing systems. The measures provided by this dependability benchmark are the system availability and the total cost of failures. These measures are based in both measurements obtained from experimentation (e.g., percentages of the various failure modes) and external data (e.g., the failure rates and the repair rates). The benchmark user must provide the external data used to calculate the measures. The workload was adopted from the TPC-C performance benchmark [20] and the faultload includes exclusively hardware faults, such as faults in the storage hardware and in the network.

In [25] it is proposed a **dependability benchmark for web-servers** (the WEB-DB dependability benchmark). This dependability benchmark uses the basic experimental setup, the workload, and the performance measures specified in the SPECWeb99 performance benchmark [26]. The measures reported by WEB-DB are grouped into three categories: baseline performance measures, performance measures in the presence of the faultload, and dependability measures. The WEB-DB benchmark uses two different faultloads: one based on software faults and another based on operational faults that emulate the effects of hardware and operator faults.

4.3 Berkeley University

The work developed at Berkeley University has highly contributed for the progress of research on dependability benchmarking in the last few years, principally in what concerns to benchmarking the dependability of human-assisted recovery processes.

In [27] is introduced a general methodology for benchmarking the availability of computer systems. The workload and performance measures are adopted from existing performance benchmarks and the measure of availability of the system under test is defined in terms of the service provided by the system. The faultload (called fault workload by the authors) may be composed by a single-fault (single-fault workload) or by several faults (multi-fault workload).

In [28] the human error is addressed as an important aspect in system dependability, and proposes that human behavior must be considered in dependability benchmarks and system designs. In [29] is proposed a technique to develop dependability benchmarks that capture the impact of human operators on the tested system. The workload and measures are adopted from existing performance benchmarks and the dependability of the system can be characterized by examining how the performance measures deviate from their normal as the system is perturbed by injected faults. In addition to faults injected using traditional fault injection, perturbations are generated by actions of human operators that actually participate in the procedure.

In [30] are presented the first steps towards the development of a dependability benchmark for human assisted recovery processes and tools. This work proposes a methodology to evaluate human-assisted failure recovery tools and processes in server systems. This methodology can be used to both quantify the dependability of single recovery systems and compare different recovery approaches, and combines dependability benchmarking with human user studies.

4.4 Sun Microsystems

Research at Sun Microsystems has defined a high-level framework [31] specifically dedicated to availability benchmarking of computer systems. The proposed framework follows a hierarchical approach that decomposes availability into three key components: fault/maintenance rate, robustness, and recovery. The goal was to develop a suite of benchmarks, each one measuring an aspect of the availability of the system. Within this framework, two benchmarks have already been developed.

In [32] is proposed a benchmark for measuring a system's robustness (degree of protection against outage events) in handling maintenance events, such as the replacement of a failed hardware component or the installation of a software patch.

In [33] it is proposed a benchmark for measuring system recovery in a non-clustered standalone system. This benchmark measures three specific system events; clean system shutdown (provides a baseline metric), clean system bootstrap (corresponds to rebooting a system following a clean shutdown), and a system reboot after a fatal fault event (provides a metric that represents the time between the injection of a fault and the moment then system returns to a useful state).

Another effort at Sun Microsystems is the Analytical RAS Benchmarks [34], which consists of three analytical benchmarks that examine the Reliability, Availability, and Serviceability (RAS) characteristics of computer systems: the Fault Robustness Benchmark (FRB-A) allows assessing techniques used to enhance resiliency, including redundancy and automatic fault correction; the Maintenance Robustness Benchmark (MRB-A) assesses how maintenance activities affect the ability of the system to provide a continuous service; and the Service Complexity Benchmark (SCB-A) examines the complexity of mechanical components replacement.

4.5 Intel Corporation

The work at Intel Corporation has focused on benchmarking semiconductor technology. The work in [35] shows the impact of semiconductor technology scaling on neutron induced SER (soft error rate) and presents an experimental methodology and results of accelerated measurements carried out on Intel Itanium® microprocessors. The proposed approach can be used as a dependability-benchmarking tool and does not require proprietary information about the microprocessor under benchmarking.

Another study [36] presents a set of benchmarks that rely on environmental test tools to benchmark undetected computational errors, also known as silent data corruption (SDC). In this work, a temperature and voltage operating test (known as the four corners test) is performed on several prototype systems.

4.6 IBM Autonomic Computing Initiative

At IBM, the Autonomic Computing initiative [37] is developing benchmarks to quantify a system's level of autonomic capability, which is defined as the capacity of the system to react autonomously to problems and changes in the environment. The goal is to produce a suite of benchmarks covering the four autonomic capabilities: self-configuration, self-healing, self-optimization, and self-protection.

In [38] are described the first steps towards a benchmark for autonomic computing. The benchmark addresses the four attributes of autonomic computing and is able to test systems at different levels of autonomic maturity.

In [39] are identified the challenges and pitfalls that must be taken into account in the development of benchmarks for autonomic computing capabilities. This paper proposes the use of the workload and driver system from performance benchmarks and the introduction of changes into benchmarking environment in order to characterize a given autonomic capability of the system. Authors propose that autonomic benchmarks must quantify the level of the response, the quality of the response, the impact of the response on the users, and the cost of any extra resources needed to support the autonomic response.

5   A Dependability Benchmark Example: DBench-OLTP

To demonstrate the dependability benchmarking concept, in this section we present an example of a dependability benchmark for On-Line Transaction Processing (OLTP) systems. The DBench-OLTP dependability benchmark [23] was proposed in 2003 and was the first dependability benchmark for transactional systems known. It uses the basic setup, the workload, and the performance measures specified in TPC-C [20] and introduces two new components: **measures related to dependability** and the **faultload**. This section presents a short overview of the benchmark (see [23] for details).

The main elements of the DBench-OLTP experimental setup are the System Under Benchmarking (SUB) and the benchmark management system (BMS). The SUB can be any system able to run the workload (a Database Management System (DBMS) in practice). The BMS emulates the client applications, inserts the faults, and control all the aspects of the benchmark run.

The DBench-OLTP measures are divided in three groups:

- The **baseline performance measures** are inherited from the TPC-C benchmark and are obtained during Phase 1 (see Fig. 1). Measures include the number of transactions executed per minute (**tpmC**) and price-per-transaction (**$/tpmC**).
- The **performance measures in the presence of the faultload**, obtained during Phase 2 (see Fig. 1), include the number of transactions executed per minute (**Tf**) and the price-per-transaction (**$/Tf**) in the presence of faults.
- The **dependability measures** (also obtained during Phase 2) consist of the number of data integrity errors detected by consistency tests and metadata tests (**Ne**), the availability from the SUB point-of-view (**AvtS**), and the availability from the end-users (terminals) point-of-view (**AvtC**). Note that, AvtS and AvtC are given as a ratio between the amount of time the system is available and the Phase 2 duration.

The benchmark includes three faultloads, each one based on a different class of faults, namely (see [23] for details): 1) **operator faults** (i.e., database administrator mistakes, such has dropping table, dropping user, deleting data file, shutting down the server); 2) **software faults** (i.e., software bugs at the operating system level); or 3) **high-level hardware failures** (e.g., hard disk failures, power failures, etc).

DBench-OLTP has been used to compare a set of systems that represent quite realistic alternatives for small and medium size OLTP applications. Table 1 shows the systems under benchmarking. Two different versions of a leading commercial DBMS (DB-1 and DB-2), three different operating systems, and two different hardware

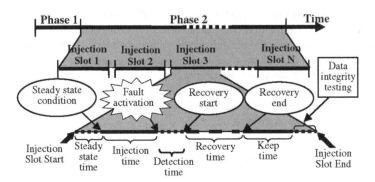

Fig. 1. The benchmark run includes two main phases. In Phase 1, which corresponds to a normal TPC-C execution (see [20]), the TPC-C workload is run without any faults, and the goal is to collect baseline performance measures. During Phase 2, the TPC-C workload is run in the presence of the faultload to measure the impact of faults on specific aspects of the target system dependability. As shown, several independent fault injection slots compose Phase 2.

platforms have been used. We decided to keep as anonym the brand and the versions of the DBMS to assure neutrality and because commercial DBMS licenses do not allow in general the publication of performance results. Both DB-1 and DB-2 were used in two different configurations: Config. A and Config. B.

Figure 2 presents a summary of the DBench-OLTP results (see [23] for the detailed analysis). As we can see, the baseline performance and the performance in the presence of faults are strongly dependent on the hardware platform and DBMS configuration used. The DBMS and operating system have a lower impact. An interesting result is that availability depends mainly on the DBMS configuration. In fact, systems with the same DBMS configuration present a similar level of availability, independently of the hardware platform, operating system and DBMS used. Another interesting result is that the availability from the clients point-of-view (AvtC) is always much lower than the availability from the server point-of-view (AvtS), which seems to be normal because some types of faults affect the system in a partial way.

Table 1. Systems under benchmarking

System	OS	DBMS	Config.	Hardware
A	Win 2000 Prof. SP 3	DB-1	Config. A	
B	Win 2000 Prof. SP 3	DB-2	Config. A	
C	Win Xp Prof. SP 1	DB-1	Config. A	Processor: Intel Pentium III 800 MHz
D	Win Xp Prof. SP 1	DB-2	Config. A	Memory: 256MB
E	Win 2000 Prof. SP 3	DB-1	Config. B	Hard Disks: Four 20GB / 7200 rpm
F	Win 2000 Prof. SP 3	DB-2	Config. B	Network: Fast Ethernet
G	SuSE Linux 7.3	DB-1	Config. A	
H	SuSE Linux 7.3	DB-2	Config. A	
I	Win 2000 Prof. SP 3	DB-1	Config. A	Processor: Intel Pentium IV 2 GHz
				Memory: 512MB
J	Win 2000 Prof. SP 3	DB-2	Config. A	Hard Disks: Four 20GB / 7200 rpm
				Network: Fast Ethernet

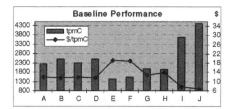
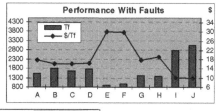
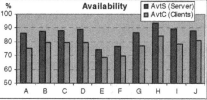

Fig. 2. DBench-OLTP results summary

Table 2. Systems under benchmarking

Criteria	System Ranking (best to worst)
Baseline performance (tpmC)	J, I, D, B, C, A, G, H, F, E
Performance with faults (Tf)	J, I, B, D, C, A, G, H, F, E
Availability (AvtS and AvtC)	H, I, D, J, C, B, G, A, F, E

Table 2 summarizes the ranking proposed according to several criteria. Concerning a global ranking, the analysis of Table 5 and all the results presented before allow us to propose the following order (from the best to the worst): I, J, D, B, C, H, G, A, F, and E. It is important to note that the global ranking always depends on the benchmark performer point-of-view (i.e., depends on what he is looking for).

The results presented show clearly that it is possible to apply dependability benchmarks in complex systems, such as transactional systems, in a very successful way.

6 Dependability Benchmarking Research Needs and Challenges

Although many works have been conducted in the area of dependability benchmarking, it is clear that some key issues remain open. In this section we present the set of research needs and challenges we believed must be accomplished for the establishment of real dependability benchmarks. Among the main issues, we identify:

- Availability of agreed dependability benchmarking measures.
- Elaboration of adaptable benchmarking processes.
- Development of benchmarking frameworks (reusable components and tools).
- Integration of benchmarking with the design methodologies.
- Proper maintenance of benchmarks to avoid negative effects.
- Support from a standardization body or industry.

Table 3. Dependability benchmarking research needs and challenges

Needs
1. Agreed, cost effective, easy to use, fast and representative enough dependability benchmarks for well defined domains.
2. Benchmark frameworks (components and tools) able to be reused to create benchmarks in different benchmarking domains.
3. Inclusion of adequate design methodologies to facilitate benchmark implementation and configuration in future components, systems, and infrastructures.
4. Uniform (standardized) benchmarking process that can be applied by independent organizations to offer certification of the dependability of COTS products (like in the case of standards compliance testing).
Challenges
1. Defining benchmark domains (components, systems, application domains) in order to divide the problem space in adequate/tractable segments.
2. Defining key benchmark elements such as measures, workload, faultload, attackload, models, to ensure the necessary properties (e.g., representativeness, portability, scalability, repeatability) that allow agreement on benchmark proposals.
3. Coping with highly complex, adaptable and evolving benchmark targets (components, systems and services).
4. Coping with human factors in the definition and execution of benchmarks.
5. Assuring proper validation of dependability benchmarks in order to achieve the necessary agreement to establish benchmarks. This implies the validation of the different benchmark properties.
6. Assuring reusability of benchmark frameworks (components & tools) to create benchmarks in different benchmarking domains.
7. Defining and agreeing on a domain-specific dependability benchmarking process that can be accepted by the parties concerned (supplier, customer and certifier) and can be adapted to different products in the domain (e.g., in a product line).

Due to space constraints, Table 3 just outlines the needs and challenges. Details can be found in [40], along with the actions to be conducted to tackle each challenge.

7   Conclusions

In this paper we have presented an overview of the state-of-the art on dependability benchmarking and defined the set of needs and challenges that have to be addressed for the acceptance of dependability benchmarks by researchers and practitioners.

Unlike performance benchmarking, which is a well-established field, dependability benchmarking is a recent research field. However, as the many works conducted by academia and industry show, dependability benchmarking is a mandatory path. In fact, it is of utmost importance to shift the focus from measuring pure performance to the measurement of both performance and dependability. Only this way we will be able to make comparisons among systems in a more realistic manner.

In this paper we argued that standardization bodies like TPC and SPEC must start paying attention to dependability assessment and comparison. This is a key step for the establishment of real dependability benchmarks, which will for sure contribute to improve the dependability characteristics of future generations of systems.

References

1. Transaction Processing Performance Council, http://www.tpc.org/
2. Standard Performance Evaluation Corporation, http://www.spec.org/
3. Curnow, H.J., Wichmann, B.A.: A synthetic benchmark. Computer Journal 19(1), 43–49 (1976)
4. Bitton, D., DeWitt, D.J., Turbyfill, C.: Benchmarking Database Systems – A Systematic Approach. In: 9th Intl. Conf. on Very Large Data Bases. VLDB Endowment (1983)
5. Anon, et al: A Measure of Transaction Processing Power: Datamat (April 1, 1985)
6. IFIP WG10.4 on Dependable Computing And Fault Tolerance, http://www.dependability.org/wg10.4/
7. Laprie, J.-C.: Dependable Computing: Concepts, Limits, Challenges. In: 25th Int. Symp. on Fault-Tolerant Computing, FTCS-25. IEEE Press, Los Alamitos (1995)
8. Trivedi, K.S., Haverkort, B.R., Rindos, A., Mainkar, V.: Methods and Tools for Reliability and Performability: Problems and Perspectives. In: Haring, G., Kotsis, G. (eds.) TOOLS 1994. LNCS, vol. 794, pp. 1–24. Springer, Heidelberg (1994)
9. Jenn, E., Arlat, J., Rimén, M., Ohlsson, J., Karlsson, J.: Fault Injection into VHDL Models: The MEFISTO Tool. In: Randell, B., Laprie, J.-C., Kopetz, H., Littlewood, B. (eds.) Predictably Dependable Computing Systems. LNCS, pp. 329–346. Springer, Berlin (1995)
10. Gray, J.: A Census of Tandem System Availability Between 1985 and 1990. IEEE Transactions on Reliability R-39(4), 409–418 (1990)
11. Hsueh, M.-C., Tsai, T.K., Iyer, R.K.: Fault Injection Techniques and Tools. IEEE Computer 30(4), 75–82 (1997)
12. Carreira, J., Madeira, H., Silva, J.G.: Xception: A Technique for the Experimental Evaluation of Dependability in Modern Computers. IEEE Trans. on Software Engineering 24(2), 125–136 (1998)
13. Koopman, P., DeVale, J.: Comparing the Robustness of POSIX Operating Systems. In: 29th International Symposium on Fault-Tolerant Computing, FTCS-29, pp. 30–37 (1999)
14. Arlat, J., Fabre, J.-C., Rodríguez, M., Salles, F.: Dependability of COTS Microkernel-based Systems. IEEE Transactions on Computers 51(2) (2002)
15. Wilson, D., Murphy, B., Spainhower, L.: Progress on Defining Standardized Classes of Computing the Dependability of Computer Systems. In: DSN 2002 Workshop on Dependability Benchmarking, pp. F1–5 (2002)
16. Kanoun, K., Spainhower, L. (eds.): Dependability Benchmarking for Computer Systems. Wiley, Chichester (2008)
17. DBench Project, Project funded by the European Community under the "Information Society Technology" Programme (1998-2002), http://www.dbench.org/
18. Kalakech, A., Kanoun, K., Crouzet, Y., Arlat, A.: Benchmarking the Dependability of Windows NT, 2000 and XP. In: International Conference on Dependable Systems and Networks, DSN 2004. IEEE Press, Los Alamitos (2004)
19. Kanoun, K., Crouret, Y.: Dependability Benchmarking for Operating Systems. International Journal of Performance Engineering 2(3), 275–287 (2006)
20. Transaction Processing Performance Council: TPC Benchmark C, Standard Specification, Version 5.9. Transaction Processing Performance Council (2007)

21. Moreira, F., Maia, R., Costa, D., Duro, N., Rodríguez-Dapena, P., Hjortnaes, K.: Static and Dynamic Verification of Critical Software for Space Applications. In: Data Systems In Aerospace, DASIA 2003 (2003)

22. Ruiz, J.-C., Yuste, P., Gil, P., Lemus, L.: On Benchmarking the Dependability of Automotive Engine Control Applications. In: IEEE/IFIP International Conference on Dependable Systems and Networks, DSN 2004. IEEE Press, Los Alamitos (2004)

23. Vieira, M., Madeira, H.: A Dependability Benchmark for OLTP Application Environments. In: 29th Intl. Conf. on Very Large Data Bases, VLDB 2003. VLDB Endowment (2003)

24. Buchacker, K., Dal Cin, M., Hoxer, H.-J., Karch, R., Sieh, V., Tschache, O.: Reproducible Dependability Benchmarking Experiments Based on Unambiguous Benchmark Setup Descriptions. In: IEEE/IFIP International Conference on Dependable Systems and Networks, DSN 2003. IEEE Press, Los Alamitos (2003)

25. Durães, J., Vieira, M., Madeira, H.: Dependability Benchmarking of Web-Servers. In: The 23rd International Conference on Computer Safety, Reliability and Security, SAFECOMP 2004. IEEE Press, Los Alamitos (2004)

26. Standard Performance Evaluation Corporation: SPECweb99 Release 1.02 (Design Document. Standard Performance Evaluation Corporation (2000)

27. Brown, A., Patterson, D.A.: Towards Availability Benchmarks: A Cases Study of Software RAID Systems. In: 2000 USENIX Annual Technical Conf. USENIX Association (2000)

28. Brown, A., Patterson, D.A.: To Err is Human. In: First Workshop on Evaluating and Architecting System Dependability, EASY (2001)

29. Brown, A., Chung, L.C., Patterson, D.A.: Including the Human Factor in Dependability Benchmarks. In: DSN 2002 Workshop on Dependability Benchmarking (2002)

30. Brown, A., Chung, L., Kakes, W., Ling, C., Patterson, D.A.: Dependability Benchmarking of Human-Assisted Recovery Processes. In: IEEE/IFIP International Conference on Dependable Systems and Networks, DSN 2004. IEEE Press, Los Alamitos (2004)

31. Zhu, J., Mauro, J., Pramanick, I.: R3 - A Framework for Availability Benchmarking. In: IEEE/IFIP International Conference on Dependable Systems and Networks, DSN 2003, pp. B-86–87. IEEE Press, Los Alamitos (2003)

32. Zhu, J., Mauro, J., Pramanick, I.: Robustness Benchmarking for Hardware Maintenance Events. In: IEEE/IFIP International Conference on Dependable Systems and Networks, DSN 2003, pp. 115–122. IEEE Press, Los Alamitos (2003)

33. Mauro, J., Zhu, J., Pramanick, I.: The System Recovery Benchmark. In: 2004 Pacific Rim International Symposium on Dependable Computing, PRDC 2004. IEEE Press, Los Alamitos (2004)

34. Elling, R., Pramanick, I., Mauro, J., Bryson, W., Tang, D.: Analytical RAS Benchmarks. In: Kanoun, K., Spainhower, L. (eds.) Dependability Benchmarking for Computer Systems. Wiley, Chichester (2008)

35. Constantinescu, C.: Neutron SER characterization of microprocessors. In: IEEE Dependable Systems and Networks Conference, pp. 754–759. IEEE Press, Los Alamitos (2005)

36. Constantinescu, C.: Dependability benchmarking using environmental tools. In: IEEE Annual Reliability and Maintanability Symposium, pp. 567–571. IEEE Press, Los Alamitos (2005)

37. IBM Autonomic Computing Initiative,
    http://www.research.ibm.com/autonomic/

38. Lightstone, S., Hellerstein, J., Tetzlaff, W., Janson, P., Lassettre, E., Norton, C., Rajaraman, B., Spainhower, L.: Towards Benchmarking Autonomic Computing Maturity. In: First IEEE Conference on Industrial Automatics, INDIN-2003. IEEE Press, Los Alamitos (2003)
39. Brown, A., Hellerstein, J., Hogstrom, M., Lau, T., Lightstone, S., Shum, P., Yost, M.P.: Benchmarking Autonomic Capabilities: Promises and Pitfalls. In: 1st International Conference on Autonomic Computing, ICAC 2004 (2004)
40. Bondavalli, A., Ceccarelli, A., Falai, L., Karlsson, J., Kocsis, I., Lollini, P., Madeira, H., Majzik, I., Montecchi, L., van Moorsel, A., Strigini, L., Vadursi, M., Vieira, M.: Preliminary Research Roadmap. AMBER Project – Assessing, Measuring and Benchmarking Resilience, IST – 216295 AMBER. AMBER Project (2008), http://www.amber-project.eu/

Overview of TPC Benchmark E: The Next Generation of OLTP Benchmarks

Trish Hogan

IBM
3039 Cornwallis Road,
Research Triangle Park
NC 27709
thogan@us.ibm.com

Abstract. Set to replace the aging TPC-C, the TPC Benchmark E is the next generation OLTP benchmark, which more accurately models client database usage. TPC-E addresses the shortcomings of TPC-C. It has a much more complex workload, requires the use of RAID-protected storage, generates much less I/O, and is much cheaper and easier to set up, run, and audit. After a period of overlap, it is expected that TPC-E will become the de facto OLTP benchmark.

Keywords: TPC-E, TPC-C, OLTP, database performance, benchmark.

1 Introduction

TPC Benchmark^{TM} E (TPC-E) is a database server benchmark that measures OLTP performance. The benchmark is one of several that have been produced by the Transaction Processing Performance Council (TPC), a non-profit corporation founded to define transaction processing and database benchmarks and to disseminate objective, verifiable TPC performance data to the industry. The TPC has many member companies such as IBM, Dell, HP, Intel, Oracle, Microsoft and AMD.

The TPC-E benchmark uses a database to model a brokerage firm with customers who generate transactions related to trades, account inquiries, and market research. The brokerage firm in turn interacts with financial markets to execute orders on behalf of the customers and updates relevant account information.

The benchmark is "scalable," meaning that the number of customers defined for the brokerage firm can be varied to represent the workloads of different-size businesses. The benchmark defines the required mix of transactions the benchmark must maintain. The TPC-E metric is given in transactions per second E (tpsE). It specifically refers to the number of Trade-Result transactions the server can sustain over a period of time.

The first section of this paper, "Why do we need a new OLTP benchmark?" compares and contrasts TPC-E and TPC-C, and discusses the benefits of the new benchmark. The second section, "Overview of TPC-E," provides more detailed information about the benchmark, including a description of the business model used

R. Nambiar and M. Poess (Eds.): TPCTC 2009, LNCS 5895, pp. 84–98, 2009.

for the benchmark, the kind of information stored in the database, and the types of transactions performed. The final section, "Transition to TPC-E," briefly addresses the coexistence of the TPC-C and the TPC-E and the eventual sun setting of the TPC-C benchmark once TPC members begin to publish results for the new benchmark.

The overall goal is to introduce the audience to the new TPC-E benchmark. Some knowledge and understanding of the TPC-C benchmark on the reader's part is assumed. Another goal is to help the audience understand how to use TPC-E benchmark results to evaluate the performance of database servers.

For more detailed information about the TPC and the TPC-E benchmark, visit the TPC Web site at www.tpc.org.

2 Why Do We Need a New OLTP Benchmark?

Why TPC-E rather than TPC-C? Benchmarks have a life time. Good benchmarks drive industry and technology forward. At some point, all reasonable advances have been made using a particular benchmark. When that happens, benchmarks can become counterproductive by encouraging artificial optimizations. So, even good benchmarks become obsolete over time. The TPC-C Specification was approved July 23, 1992. Since then, it has become the de facto industry-standard OLTP benchmark, but now TPC-C is roughly 17 years old. In "dog years" that's 119. In "computer years," it's basically ancient!

2.1 TPC-C: An Aging Benchmark Losing Relevance

Static Transaction Profiles
The benchmark is running the same workload today as when it was introduced in 1992. TPC-C's transactions are too "lightweight" by today's standards, but it is not practical to modify the existing workload because that would break comparability. (The companies that published the benchmark results don't want to lose their investment by losing comparability.) Those who run the benchmark have a very good understanding of the workload and how to super-tune it.

Unbalanced System Configurations
Over the years, with the advance of technology, we've seen that:

- CPU performance has grown according to Moore's Law.
- Disk drive latencies have not improved substantially.
- Memory has grown disproportionately to I/Os per system.
- The TPC-C workload has not changed.
- Ongoing improvements to software have led to increasingly higher TPC-C scores.

As a result of these factors, running the benchmark requires larger and larger I/O subsystems, which in turn, increases the cost, which is borne entirely by the benchmark sponsor. For example, a recent TPC-C result on an IBM System x3850 M2 used four processors, 256GB of memory, and 1,360 disk drives for the database.

Compare that to the results published in October 2000 for the IBM Netfinity 7600 with four processors, 8GB of memory, and 236 drives.[1]

Today the workload and configurations are less representative of clients' environments than when the benchmark was first introduced. Because of the amount of hardware required, the benchmark has become too expensive and requires too much time to run and audit.

2.2 TPC-E: A Benchmark More Relevant to Today's Application Environment

What is needed and what TPC-E delivers is a new OLTP database-centric benchmark that:

- Provides comparable results (i.e., results from different vendors can be compared)
- Represents a familiar business model that is easy to understand
- Reduces the cost and complexity of running the benchmark
- Enhances the complexity of the database schema
- Encourages database uses that are more representative of client environments

More Realistic Benchmark Configurations

Configurations used to run the new benchmark should be more like actual client configurations. This means that the software and hardware configuration used in the benchmark should be similar or the same as what a client would use. The configuration should not have a large I/O subsystem if clients would not have a similarly large I/O subsystem. Having a benchmark configuration that more closely reflects the client's application environment makes it easier to use benchmark results for capacity planning. Any improvements made to the hardware or software to improve the benchmark result would also benefit the client. This is not always the case now because TPC-C configurations do not reflect typical client configurations. The following table shows that TPC-E configurations more closely resemble client configurations.

Table 1. Comparison of TPC-C and TPC-E

Feature	TPC-C	Client	TPC-E
Drives/core	50 to 150	5 to 10	10 to 50
Database layout	Simple	Complex	Complex
Database transactions	Simple	Complex	Complex
Database constraints	None	Enforced	Enforced
RAID-protected data	No	Yes	Yes

---

[1] IBM System x3850 M2 with the Intel Xeon Processor X7460 2.66GHz (4 processors/24 cores/24 threads), 684,508 tpmC, $2.58 USD / tpmC, total solution availability of October 31, 2008. Results referenced are current as of May 22, 2009. IBM Netfinity 7600 with Intel Pentium® III Xeon (4 processors/4 cores), 32,377 tpmC, $13.70 USD / tpmC, availability of October 25, 2000 (withdrawn).

2.3   TPC-E and TPC-C: Comparison of Key Features

The following table shows the key characteristics of TPC-C and TPC-E side-by-side.

Table 2. Comparison of TPC-C and TPC-E characteristics

Characteristics	TPC-C	TPC-E
Business model	Wholesale supplier	Brokerage house
Number of database tables	9	33
Number of database columns	92	188
Minimum columns per table	3	2
Maximum columns per table	21	24
Datatype count	4	Many
Primary keys	8	33
Foreign keys	9	50
Tables with foreign keys	7	27
Check constraints	0	22
Referential integrity	No	Yes
Database content	Unrealistic	Realistic
Ease of partitioning	Unrealistically easy	Realistic
Database roundtrips per transaction	One	One or many
Number of transactions	5	10
Number of physical I/Os	3x to 5x	x
Client machines needed	Many	Fewer
RAID requirements	Database log only	Everything
Timed database recovery	No	Yes
TPC-provided code	No	Yes

Different Business Model
The TPC-C business model is that of a wholesale supplier, and the database is organized by Warehouses, Districts and Customers. The TPC-E business model is a brokerage house, and the database is organized by Customers, Accounts and Securities.

RAID Protection
A common complaint about TPC-C is that it does not require RAID protection of the disk subsystem that contains the database. In the real world, clients cannot run their databases without some protection against drive failure. TPC-E requires RAID protection and tests how performance is affected when a drive is rebuilding.

Timed Database Recovery
TPC-E requires test sponsors to report how long it takes after a catastrophic failure to get the database back up and running at 95% of the reported throughput. This requirement means that test sponsors can no longer take shortcuts to improve performance while ignoring reliability.

Richer Database Schema and Transactions

TPC-C has nine database tables and five transactions. TPC-E has 33 tables and 10 transactions. TPC-E has many different data types, many primary keys, foreign keys, check constraints, and has referential integrity. TPC-C was very easy to partition because everything was keyed off of the warehouse ID. TPC-E is not unrealistically easy to partition, reflecting the issues clients see when they try to partition their data.

When clients implement transactions in their applications, they often do many roundtrips to the database; that is, they get some data from the database, send the data back to the application, process the data in the application, and then go to the database again for some more data. In TPC-C, the application has been so tuned that all the processing is done in one roundtrip to the database because all the processing is done in a stored procedure in the database. In TPC-E some transactions have rules that the transaction cannot be implemented as a single stored procedure in the database. The rules force more roundtrips to the database.

TPC-E has stricter database isolation requirements than TPC-C. This means that database vendors will have to work on improving database locking performance. Clients will see this performance improvement when they run their applications.

The database schema and transactions for TPC-E are much richer than those of TPC-C. The richer schema means that there are lots of possible ways to optimize performance. Over the life of the benchmark, test sponsors will find ways to use secondary indexes to improve transaction performance. TPC-C has been around so long that all the SQL tuning has been found and done.

Constraint Checking

When TPC-C came out, database constraint checking was not a standard feature for all Database Management Systems; now it is, so constraint checking is enforced in TPC-E.

Configuration Requirements

The transactions in TPC-E are designed to do more logical fetches and consume more CPU time than the TPC-C transactions. Logical fetches are the number of rows a transaction has to read. The rows may already be in memory or they may be out on disk. If the rows are already in memory, then no physical I/O to the disk is required.

During development, extensive prototyping was done to ensure that the TPC-E transactions used a lot of CPU and did some, but not too much, physical I/O. Too much physical I/O requires many more disk drives to ensure that the processor is never idle waiting for physical I/O. The result of this prototyping is that TPC-E does between three to five times less physical I/O than TPC-C. So even though TPC-E requires the disk drives to be RAID-protected, the benchmark still uses significantly fewer disk drives than a TPC-C configuration for the same server with the same number of processors and memory. This is good news for test sponsors. The disk I/O subsystem for TPC-C is incredibly expensive, which means that some hardware vendors cannot afford to run the TPC-C benchmark. TPC-E will be much less expensive to configure and run, so more hardware vendors will be able to publish results. Clients will benefit because they will be able to compare benchmark results from several vendors before deciding which vendor's products they want to buy.

Table 3. Comparison of TPC-C and TPC-E configurations

	TPC-C	**TPC-E**
System	HP ProLiant DL370 G6	IBM System x3650 M2
Total price	$678,231	$302,146
Score	631,766 tpmC	798.00 tpsE
Price/performance	$1.08/tpmC	$378.63/tpsE
Availability date	3/30/09	6/30/09
Processors/cores/threads	2/8/16	2/8/16
Database server memory	144GB	96GB
Disks	1210 (RAID-0)	450 (RAID-10)
RTEs	18	0 (N/A)
Clients	8	2
Total systems to setup and tune	27	3

Another factor that makes TPC-E less expensive to run is that it requires fewer front-end systems because it focuses on benchmarking the database server. In contrast, TPC-C uses a Web page-based front-end, which emulates users keying in the Web page, and thinking. Here is a comparison of the TPC-C and TPC-E configurations for two very similar database servers.

More Realistic Database Content

TPC-C uses random numbers to pick string fragments and then concatenates the string fragments. TPC-E is populated with pseudo-real data. The distributions are based on:

- 2000 U.S. and Canada census data[2]

  - Used for generating name, address, gender, etc.
  - Introduces natural data skew

- Actual listings on the NYSE and NASDAQ

The benefits of using pseudo-real data are that TPC-E has realistic-looking data that is compressible and can be used for backup testing. The data is closer match to the kind of data found in clients' databases.

Table 4. Sample data from TPC-C CUSTOMER table

C_FIRST	**C_MIDDLE**	**C_LAST**	**C_STREET1**
RONpTGcv5ZBZO8Q	OE	BARBARABLE	bR7QLfDBhZPHlyDXs
e8u6FMxFLtt6p Q	OE	BARBARPRI	eEbgKxoIzx99ZTD S
bTUkSuVQGdXLjGe	OE	BARBARPRES	QCGLjWnsqSQPN DS
18AEf3ObueKvubUX	OE	BARBARESE	JnBSg4RtZbALYu S
mFFsJYeYE6AR bUX	OE	BARBARANTI	MLEwwdy3dXfqngFcE

---

[2] Only names from the 2000 census have been used—all other data are fictional and any similarities are purely coincidental.

Table 5. Sample data from TPC-E CUSTOMER table

C_TAX_ID	C_L_NAME	C_F_NAME	C_M_NAME	C_DOB
757FI2006HD923	Mexicano	Courtney	T	1997-11-30
922SN3775RQ823	Udley	Judith	F	1954-09-27
006GT3444BE624	Buchanan	John	R	1971-06-13
181UZ4114LR434	Soloman	Clinton	D	1938-02-27
355IE4773VF335	Orner	Harry	P	1974-11-15

Provided Code

TPC does not provide code for the TPC-C benchmark, but it does provide code for the TPC-E benchmark. The code provided is used to generate the data that is loaded into the database and to generate the transactions and the data for the transactions. By providing code, the TPC hopes that it will be easier for more member companies to set up and run the benchmark. The TPC's intent is that test sponsors will spend time optimizing their products rather than coding and optimizing the driver for the benchmark.

Similarities to TPC-C

TPC-E is similar to TPC-C in these ways:

- The primary metrics for TPC-E are tpsE, $/tpsE and availability date. These metrics correspond to those of TPC-C: tpmC, $/tpmC, and availability date. Also, neither TPC-C nor TPC-E uses a scale factor, as TPC-H does.
- TPC-E and TPC-C both use an OLTP workload, although each is based on a different business model.
- Portions of the database scale in a linear fashion in both benchmarks.
- The transaction profile is held constant.

3   Overview of TPC-E

3.1 Brokerage Firm Model

As Figure 1 illustrates, customers generate transactions related to trade requests, account inquiries and market research. The brokerage firm sends trades to the market. The market returns the results of the trades and also sends a constant stream of the latest price for each security being traded. The brokerage firm returns the results of transactions to the customers.

Several models were considered for the workload. The brokerage firm model, which is based on input received from industry experts, such as Merrill-Lynch and Fidelity, was selected. This model met the volume/scaling and market relevance criteria for the benchmark. Industry analysts have mentioned that TPC-C, the current leading benchmark for database servers, is no longer as relevant to client OLTP workloads. One example of this lack of relevance is that for the current number one TPC-C result the database supported more customers than there are people on the planet. TPC-E needed to be able to have a meaningful number of customers in comparison to the performance of the database server being measured.

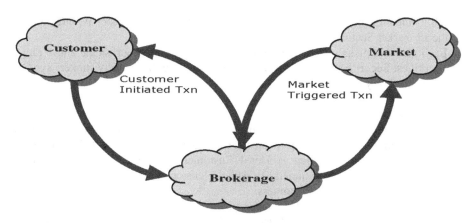

Fig. 1. TPC-E model – A Brokerage Firm

Another criticism leveled at TPC-C is that it has too few transaction types and that the transactions are too simple compared to the type of transactions clients do now. As processing power has increased, clients have added complexity to their transactions. The brokerage firm model is rich enough to enable the TPC-E benchmark to have more transaction types and more database tables than used in TPC-C.

There have been many technological advances since the TPC-C benchmark first came out roughly 17 years ago. The TPC-E workload is defined so that it can exercise some of these technological advances and features. The brokerage firm model lets us exercise features such as rich text from news articles about the companies whose securities are traded. Database Management System (DBMS) features (e.g., integrity constraints) that are commonly used today are also incorporated in the workload.

3.2 TPC-E Database Information

When loading the database for TPC-E, the benchmark sponsor chooses the number of customers based on the tpsE they are aiming for, keeping in mind that there are 500 customers per single tpsE. Customers can be loaded only in blocks of 1,000. Some of the other TPC-E tables scale based on the number of customers chosen.

The TPC provides code to generate the data for the TPC-E database. The TPC-E data generator uses names from a U.S. census and information from the New York Stock Exchange to generate people's names and company information. This makes TPC-E data look like normal data. TPC-C data concatenates "foo," "bar," and so on to generate names, resulting in "unnatural" looking names.

Trading in TPC-E is done by Accounts. Accounts belong to Customers. Customers are serviced by Brokers. Accounts trade Securities that are issued by Companies.

The total set of Securities that can be traded and the total set of Companies that issue Securities scales along with the number of Customers. For each unit of 1,000 Customers, there are 685 Securities and 500 Companies (with Companies issuing one to five Securities, mostly common shares, but some preferred as well).

All Companies belong to one of the 102 Industries. Each Industry belongs to one of the 12 market Sectors.

Each Account picks its average 10 Securities to trade from across the entire range of Securities. Securities to be traded can be identified by the security (ticker) symbol or by the company name and security issue.

Differences between Customer Tiers

The basic scaling unit of a TPC-E database is a set of 1,000 Customers. For each set of 1,000 Customers, 20% belong to Tier 1, 60% to Tier 2, and 20% to Tier 3. Tier 2 Customers trade twice as often as Tier 1 Customers. Tier 3 Customers trade three times as often as Tier 1 Customers. In general, customer trading is non-uniform by tier within each set of 1,000 Customers.

Tier 1 Customers have 1 to 4 Accounts (average 2.5). Tier 2 Customers have 2 to 8 Accounts (average 5.0). Tier 3 Customers have 5 to 10 Accounts (average 7.5). Overall, there is an average of five Accounts per Customer.

The minimum and maximum number of Securities traded by each Account varies by Customer Tier and by the number of Accounts for each Customer. The average number of Securities traded per Account is 10 (so the average number of Securities traded per Customer is 50). For each Account, the same set of Securities is traded for both the initial database population and for any benchmark run.

Customer Partitioning

TPC-E scales with Customers. It is conceivable that Customer information could be partitioned into groups of related Customers. This is called Customer Partitioning. The advantage of Customer Partitioning is that it increases locality of reference within each sub-group of Customers. Transactions relating to a particular set of Customers are directed to that set of Customers rather than to all Customers.

Trade Types

Trade requests are either Buy (50%) or Sell (50%). These are further broken down into Trade Types, depending on whether the request was a Market Order (60%) or a Limit Order (40%).

For Market Orders, the two trade types are Market-Buy (30%) and Market-Sell (30%). For Limit Orders, the three trade types are Limit-Buy (20%), Limit-Sell (10%) and Stop-Loss (10%).

Market-Buy and Market-Sell are trade requests to buy and sell immediately at the current market price, whatever price that may be. Limit-Buy is a request to buy only when the market price is at or below the specified limit price. Limit-Sell is a request to sell only when the market price is at or above the specified limit price. Stop-Loss is a request to sell only when (or if) the market price drops to or below the specified limit price.

If the specified limit price has not been reached when the Limit Order is requested, it is considered an Out-of-the-Money request and remains "Pending" until the specified limit price is reached. Reaching the limit price is guaranteed to occur within 15 minutes based on benchmark implementation details. The act of noticing that a "Pending" limit request has reached or exceeded its specified limit price and submitting it to the market exchange to be traded is known as "triggering" of the pending limit order.

Effects of Trading on Holdings

For a given account and security, holdings will be either all long (positive quantities) or all short (negative quantities).

Long positions represent shares of the security that were bought (purchased and paid for) by the customer for the account. The customer owns the shares of the security and may sell them at a later time (hopefully, for a higher price).

Short positions represent shares of the security that were borrowed from the broker (or Brokerage) and were sold by the customer for the account. In the short-sale case, the customer has received the funds from that sell, but still has to cover the sell by later purchasing an equal number of shares (hopefully at a lower price) from the market and returning those shares to the broker.

Before the database is loaded, there are no trades and no positions in any security for any account. The TPC provides code to generate the data for the database. This data generation code simulates running the benchmark for 300 business days of initial trading, so that the initial database will be ready for benchmark execution. The data-generation code also generates data for daily market closing price information for five years of five-day work weeks, and five years' worth of quarterly report data for all the companies.

If the first trade for a security in an account is a buy, a long position will be established (positive quantity in HOLDING row). Subsequent buys in the same account for the same security will add holding rows with positive quantities. Subsequent sells will reduce holding quantities or delete holding rows to satisfy the sell trade. All holdings may be eliminated, in which case the position becomes empty. If the sell quantity still is not satisfied, the position changes from long to short (see above).

If the first trade for a security in an account is a sell, a short position will be established (negative quantity in HOLDING row). Subsequent sells in the same account for the same security will add holding rows with negative quantities. Subsequent buys will reduce holding quantities (toward zero) or delete holding rows to satisfy the buy trade. All holdings may be eliminated, in which case the position becomes empty. If the buy quantity still is not satisfied, the position changes from short to long.

Database Tables

TPC-C had only nine database tables. Most client databases have more than nine tables. TPC-E has many more tables than TPC-C. The TPC-E database tables can be grouped into four categories:

- Customer – tables containing customer-related information
- Broker – tables containing data related to the brokerage firm and brokers
- Market – tables containing data related to the exchanges, companies, and securities that create the financial market
- Dimension – tables containing generic information that is referenced by multiple fact tables

Table 6. Customer tables

Customer Tables	
ACCOUNT_PERMISSION	Who can execute trades for accounts
CUSTOMER	Customer information
CUSTOMER_ACCOUNT	Accounts for each customer
CUSTOMER_TAXRATE	Tax rates each customer pays
HOLDING	Customer account's security holdings
HOLDING_HISTORY	History of how trades changed holding positions
HOLDING_SUMMARY	Aggregate of customer account's security holdings
WATCH_ITEM	List of securities customers are tracking on their watch lists
WATCH_LIST	Customer's security watch lists

Table 7. Broker tables

Broker Tables	
BROKER	Broker information
CASH_TRANSACTION	Cash transaction information
CHARGE	Information about trade charges
COMMISSION_RATE	Commission rate information
SETTLEMENT	Trade settlement information
TRADE	Trade information
TRADE_HISTORY	History of each trade through various stages
TRADE_REQUEST	Pending limit trades
TRADE_TYPE	Valid trade types

During the benchmark run:

- All customer tables are read.
- CUSTOMER_ACCOUNT balance is updated.
- HOLDING_SUMMARY table is updated.
- Records are appended to the HOLDING_HISTORY table.
- Records are updated, deleted from and inserted in the HOLDING table.

During the benchmark run:

- All broker tables are read.
- BROKER table is updated with the number of trades a broker has executed and the commission the broker has earned so far.
- Records are appended to CASH_TRANSACTION, SETTLEMENT and TRADE_HISTORY tables.
- Records are appended and updated in the TRADE table.
- Records are inserted in and deleted from the TRADE_REQUEST table.

During the benchmark run:

- All market tables are read.
- The LAST_TRADE table is updated many times a second.

Table 8. Market tables

Market Tables	
COMPANY	Information about companies with publicly traded securities
COMPANY_COMPETITOR	Information for the competitors of a given company and the industry in which the company competes
DAILY_MARKET	Daily market statistics for each security
EXCHANGE	Financial exchange information
FINANCIAL	Information about a company's quarterly financial reports
INDUSTRY	Industry information
LAST_TRADE	Latest price and trading volume for each security
NEWS_ITEM	News items of interest
NEWS_XREF	Cross-reference of the news items to companies mentioned in the news item
SECTOR	Market sector information
SECURITY	Information about each security traded on any of the exchanges

During the benchmark run, all the dimension tables are read.

Table 9. Dimension tables

Dimension Tables	
ADDRESS	Address information
STATUS_TYPE	Status values
TAXRATE	Tax rate information
ZIP_CODE	Zip code information

3.3 TPC-E Transactions

TPC-C had only five transactions: New-Order (45% of the transaction mix), Payment (43%), Delivery (4%), Stock-Level (4%), and Order-Status (4%). The tpmC metric equaled the number of New-Order transactions done per minute. Because almost half of the transaction mix was New-Orders, configuration optimizations could change the metric significantly.

TPC-E has 10 transactions that are part of the maintained transaction mix, and two other transactions. Trade-Result is the transaction that is counted for the tpsE metric. Trade-Result is only 10% of the transaction mix. The Data-Maintenance transaction, which runs once per minute, is not part of the maintained transaction mix. The Trade-Cleanup transaction is only run once before starting a benchmark run. The following sections provide a short description of each transaction.

Broker-Volume (4.9% of the Transaction Mix)
The Broker-Volume transaction is designed to emulate a brokerage house's "up-to-the-minute" internal business processing. An example of a Broker-Volume transaction would be a manager generating a report on the current performance potential of various brokers. The transaction is a business intelligence type of query that only does reads and is CPU-heavy.

Customer-Position (13%)
The Customer-Position transaction is designed to emulate the process of retrieving the customer's profile and summarizing their overall standing based on current market values for all assets. This is representative of the work performed when a customer asks the question "What am I worth today?" The transaction is a read-only transaction.

Market-Feed (1%)
The Market-Feed transaction is designed to emulate the process of tracking the current market activity. This is representative of the brokerage house processing the "ticker-tape" from the market exchange. The transaction is a read/write transaction.

Market-Watch (18%)
The Market-Watch transaction is designed to emulate the process of monitoring the overall performance of the market by allowing a customer to track the current daily trend (up or down) of a collection of securities. The collection of securities being monitored may be based upon a customer's current holdings, a customer's watch list of prospective securities, or a particular industry. The transaction is a read-only transaction.

Security-Detail (14%)
The Security-Detail transaction is designed to emulate the process of accessing detailed information on a particular security. This is representative of a customer doing research on a security prior to making a decision about whether to execute a trade. The transaction is a read-only transaction.

Trade-Lookup (8%)
The Trade-Lookup transaction is designed to emulate information retrieval by either a customer or a broker to satisfy their questions regarding a set of trades. The various sets of trades are chosen such that the work is representative of:

- Performing general market analysis
- Reviewing trades for a period of time prior to the most recent account statement
- Analyzing past performance of a particular security
- Analyzing the history of a particular customer holding

The transaction is a read-only transaction. This transaction generates a lot of disk IO because it looks for older records that don't tend to be in memory because they were not used recently.

Trade-Order (10.1%)
The Trade-Order transaction is designed to emulate the process of buying or selling a security by a Customer, Broker, or authorized third-party. If the person executing the trade order is not the account owner, the transaction will verify that the person has the appropriate authorization to perform the trade order. The transaction allows the person trading to execute buys at the current market price, sells at the current market

price, or limit buys and sells at a requested price. The transaction also provides an estimate of the financial impact of the proposed trade by providing profit/loss data, tax implications, and anticipated commission fees. This allows the trader to evaluate the desirability of the proposed security trade before either submitting or canceling the trade. The transaction is a read/write transaction.

Trade-Result (10%)
The Trade-Result transaction is designed to emulate the process of completing a stock market trade. This is representative of a brokerage house receiving from the market exchange the final confirmation and price for the trade. The customer's holdings are updated to reflect that the trade has completed. Estimates generated when the trade was ordered for the broker commission and other similar quantities are replaced with the actual numbers, and historical information about the trade is recorded for later reference. The transaction is a read/write transaction and is counted as the tpsE metric.

Trade-Status (19%)
The Trade-Status transaction is designed to emulate the process of providing an update on the status of a particular set of trades. It is representative of a customer reviewing a summary of the recent trading activity for one of their accounts. The transaction is a read-only transaction.

Trade-Update (2%)
The Trade-Update transaction is designed to emulate the process of making minor corrections or updates to a set of trades. This is analogous to a customer or broker reviewing a set of trades, and discovering that some minor editorial corrections are required. The various sets of trades are chosen such that the work is representative of reviewing:

- General market trends
- Trades for a period of time prior to the most recent account statement
- Past performance of a particular security

The transaction is a read/write transaction. This transaction generates a lot of disk I/O because it looks for older records that don't tend to be in memory because they were not used recently.

Data-Maintenance (Runs Once per Minute)
The Data-Maintenance transaction is designed to emulate the periodic modifications to data that is mainly static and used for reference. This is analogous to updating a customer's e-mail address or other data that seldom changes. The transaction is a read/write transaction.

Trade-Cleanup (Runs Only One Time Before the Benchmark is Started)
The Trade-Cleanup transaction is used to cancel any pending or submitted trades from the database. The transaction is a read/write transaction.

4 Transition to TPC-E

4.1 Current Landscape

The momentum for TPC-E is increasing. To date, 26 TPC-E results have been published from six hardware vendors on systems ranging from 1 to 16 processors. During the year 2008, 17 TPC-C results were published from 7 different hardware vendors compared to 14 TPC-E results from 6 vendors- fairly even. So far in 2009, there are 4 TPC-C publishes from 2 vendors compared to 6 TPC-E publishes from 5 vendors. And TPC-E so far only has publishes on Microsoft Windows and SQL Server. Once the other database vendors get up to speed with TPC-E, the publications should really take off.

4.2 Next Steps

As expected, TPC-C and TPC-E results are coexisting. With the clear benefits of TPC-E, especially the much lower cost of benchmarking in this economy, it has good traction and is expected to supplant TPC-C. However, before that can happen, some non-SQL Server TPC-E publications are needed. This will take time. Even with the TPC-supplied benchmarking code, it takes quite some time to develop and test a benchmark kit and then use it to tune the hardware and software to get a good result. But this is exactly why TPC-E was developed. The hardware and software vendors are using it to help optimize their products for uses that more closely mimic those of typical clients. It may be a while, but the results of this work will be seen. Once results are published using other database products, expect to see back and forth result leadership as the hardware and software become more tuned for the benchmark.

In the meantime, it may be tempting to try to compare TPC-C and TPC-E results. However, TPC-C and TPC-E results are not directly comparable. They are different workloads, and they each scale slightly differently. For instance, with TPC-C, greater performance gains are realized when memory is doubled—not so with TPC-E. But TPC-E does realize greater performance gains from increasing processor frequency or adding processors than does TPC-C. There is no magic formula to translate a database server's TPC-E score to a TPC-C score or vice versa.

References and Additional Information

1. TPC-E Specification, http://www.tpc.org
2. TPC-PR TPC-E presentation, available from members-only side,
    http://www.tpc.org

Converting TPC-H Query Templates to Use DSQGEN for Easy Extensibility

John M. Stephens Jr.[1] and Meikel Poess[2]

[1] Gradient Systems, 643 Bair Island Road #103, Redwood City, CA-94063
jms@gradientsystems.com
[2] Oracle Corporation, 500 Oracle Parkway, Redwood Shores, CA-94107
meikel.poess@oracle.com

Abstract. The ability to automatically generate queries that are not known a-priory is crucial for ad-hoc benchmarks. TPC-H solves this problem with a query generator, QGEN, which utilizes query templates to generate SQL queries. QGEN's architecture makes it difficult to maintain, change or adapt to new types of query templates since every modification requires code changes. DSQGEN, a generic query generator, originally written for the TPC-DS benchmark, uses a query template language, which allows for easy modification and extension of existing query templates. In this paper we show how the current set of TPC-H query templates can be migrated to the template language of DSQGEN without any change to comparability of published TPC-H results. The resulting query template model provides opportunities for easier enhancement and extension of the TPC-H workload, which we demonstrate.

Keywords: Benchmark Development, Databases, Performance Analysis.

1 Introduction

TPC-H [4][6]has been a very successful benchmark for the Transaction Processing Performance Council (TPC), with 147 results published as of June 2009. It relies on a pair of executables for data and query generation (DBGEN and QGEN, respectively) that were originally developed for its predecessor, TPC-D [5], which was released in 1994. QGEN is a command-line utility that uses pattern matching to expand the 22 query templates defined in TPC-H into fully qualified Structured Query Language (SQL). While the substitutions defined in the TPC-H query set have proven adequate, they have not been updated since five new templates were added in 1999, when TPC-D morphed into TPC-H. Further, the substitutions are hard-coded into the QGEN executable. As a result, any refinement or expansion of the query set requires additional software development. The required costs for code modifications and code testing have hindered further evolution of the benchmark.

The underlying design of QGEN remains valid. Its template-based query model and common and well-understood business questions provide TPC-H with a high degree of comparability between benchmark executions. At the same time the precise values or targets of a given instance of a query are random, assuring appropriate

R. Nambiar and M. Poess (Eds.): TPCTC 2009, LNCS 5895, pp. 99–115, 2009.

variability and limiting the amount of foreknowledge that a test sponsor can employ. The result is a query set that provides consistent and meaningful results, while mimicking ad-hoc queries. However, the TPC-H query model has two inherent problems: The query substitutions are hard coded into the query generator and cannot be modified without additional software development and the query templates themselves use a narrow range of syntax and substitution types, and no longer capture the breadth of common decision support systems.

This paper details the migration of the QGEN query template model to the DSQGEN query template model without any changes to TPC-H's current query template set. This preserves the investment that test sponsors have made in TPC-H, and, simultaneously provides the opportunity for an updated query set which employs a richer set of query operations and syntax. In addition, it leaves further enhancement in the hands of the benchmark designers, without requiring further software development.

The remainder of this paper is organized as follows: Section 2 gives a brief overview of TPC-H focusing on how queries are currently generated with QGEN; section 3 introduces the essential syntax of DSQGEN, including both functions needed to write current TPC-H query templates in DSQGEN's query template language and additional functionality that exceeds the current needs of TPC-H; section 4 demonstrates the changes required to migrate the current set of 22 TPC-H queries to DSQGEN's query template language; section 5 shows how the TPC-H query set can be extended using DSQGEN.

2 TPC-H

Since its introduction in 1999 by the Transaction Performance Council, TPC-H has been the industry standard benchmark for data warehouse applications. This section briefly introduces those elements of TPC-H, which are necessary for the understanding the next sections.

2.1 Background

TPC-H models the activity of any industry, which manages, sells, and distributes products worldwide (e.g., car rental, food distribution, parts, suppliers, etc.). It uses a 3rd normal form schema consisting of eight base tables. They are populated with synthetic data, scaled to an aggregate volume or scale factor (SF). For example, in a database with SF=100, the base tables hold 100 gigabytes of generated data. Fig. 1 illustrates the entity relationship (ER) diagram of the TPC-H schema. The two largest tables, Lineitem and Orders contain about 83 percent of the data. Sizes of all tables, except for nation and region scale linearly with the scale factor.

The TPC-H workload consists of database load, execution of 22 read-only queries in both single and multi-user mode and two refresh functions. The queries are intended to test the most common query capabilities of a typical decision support system. In order to facilitate the understanding of TPC-H queries and the mapping of the benchmark queries to real world situations, each query is described in terms of a business question. This business question is formulated in English explaining the

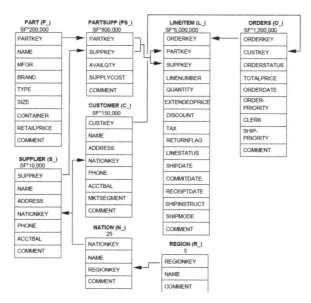

Fig. 1. TPC-H Entity Relationship Diagram (Source: TPC-H Version 2.8.0)

result of the query in context of TPC-H's business model. The business questions are translated into functional query definitions that define the queries using the SQL-92 query language. TPC-H queries are chosen to perform operations that are relevant to common data warehouse applications. Accordingly, the demands a query places on the hardware (processor, IO-subsystem) and software (Operating System, Database Management System) of the tested system varies from query to query. To assure that the benchmark remains dynamic, each TPC-H query contains substitution parameters that are randomly chosen by the benchmark driver immediately before its execution, to mimic ad-hoc workloads.

One TPC-H performance run consists of one execution of a Power Test (see Clause 6.3.3 of [6]), followed by one execution of a Throughput Test described (see Clause 6.3.4. of [6]). The Power Test measures single-user performance. Single-user performance measures a systems ability to parallelize queries across all available resources (memory, CPU, I/O) in order to deliver the result in the least amount of time. In TPC-H's Power Test the single-user performance measurement is implemented as one stream of queries. This stream contains all 22 queries in a pre-defined order (see Appendix A in [6]): The Throughput Test measures multi-user performance. A multi-user test measures a system's ability to execute multiple concurrent queries, allocate resources efficiently across all users to maximize query throughput. In TPC-H's throughput test multi-user measurement is implemented with n concurrent streams. Each stream contains all 22 queries ordered in a different permutation.

2.2 TPC-H Data Generator QGEN

QGEN produces the query streams required by TPC-H. The templates each contain between one and five substitution tokens, each with a static set of possible values.

Query Template

```
:x
:o
SELECT
  l_returnflag,
  l_linestatus,
  sum(l_quantity) as sum_qty,
  sum(l_extendedprice) as sum_base_price,
  sum(l_extendedprice * (1 - l_discount)) as sum_disc_price,
  sum(l_extendedprice * (1 - l_discount) * (1 + l_tax)) as sum_charge,
  avg(l_quantity) as avg_qty,
  avg(l_extendedprice) as avg_price,
  avg(l_discount) as avg_disc,
  count(*) as count_order
FROM
  lineitem
WHERE
  l_shipdate <= date '1998-12-01' - interval ':1' day (3)
GROUP BY
  l_returnflag,
  l_linestatus
ORDER BY
  l_returnflag,
  l_linestatus;
```

Query template is generated with qgen using the following command line:
```
qgen -s 1 1
```

Executable Query Text

```
SELECT
  l_returnflag,
  l_linestatus,
  sum(l_quantity) as sum_qty,
  sum(l_extendedprice) as sum_base_price,
  sum(l_extendedprice * (1 - l_discount)) as sum_disc_price,
  sum(l_extendedprice * (1 - l_discount) * (1 + l_tax)) as sum_charge,
  avg(l_quantity) as avg_qty,
  avg(l_extendedprice) as avg_price,
  avg(l_discount) as avg_disc,
  count(*) as count_order
FROM
  lineitem
WHERE
  l_shipdate <= date '1998-12-01' - interval '120' day (3)
GROUP BY
  l_returnflag,
  l_linestatus
ORDER BY
  l_returnflag,
  l_linestatus;
```

Fig. 2. Sample QGEN Template Usage

QGEN replaces the substitution token with a randomly selected value from the permissible domain to produce fully qualified SQL. Fig. 2 illustrates the transformation of the query template of query 2 to a valid entry in a query stream.

Clearly, QGEN depends heavily on the underlying data set defined for TPC-H. A query generator can only exploit data relationships that exist in its target data population. In QGEN, these relationships are captured in the source code of the query generator itself. This means that the query set cannot be modified without modifying the query generator, and that the relationships and domains employed by the queries can only be discovered by referring to the benchmark specification or to the source code of the query generator. Similarly, the query template permutations that define the benchmark's query streams are hard-coded into QGEN itself, and rely on a static, hand-cobbled query ordering which cannot be extended without source code changes to QGEN.

3 Query Generator DSQGEN

DSQGEN (a.k.a. QGEN2 see [6]) was developed by the TPC for a proposed decision support benchmark. It is a command-line utility that translates an arbitrary set of query templates into streams of valid SQL statements. Query templates are defined in a template language, and parsed using an LALR(1) grammar. DSQGEN provides a rich set of query template translation semantics that go far beyond what is required to support the TPC-H query set. For example, if DSQGEN is used in combination with DSDGEN (a.k.a. MUDD see [1][3]), distribution-based predicate substitutions can be defined. The distribution-related substitutions allow a template to use arbitrary distributions, encoded as ASCII histograms. The result is a tight linkage between data generation and query generation without requiring the template designer to know the specifics of the data distributions. For a detailed description of DSQGEN's functionality, including its sophisticated template language, refer to [2]. The following sections only address those parts of the template language that are relevant to this paper.

3.1 Query Template Grammar

A query template is divided into two parts: substitution definitions and SQL Text. The substitution definitions specify the substitution rules for a query as a list of substitution tags. These tags control the translation of the SQL Text portion of the template into a valid SQL query. Once defined, a substitution tag can be used throughout the query template. Each occurrence of the substitution tag is replaced by values generated according to the tag's definition. Multiple occurrences of the same tag are replaced with the same value. If a substitution tag is post-fixed with a number, then each unique tag/number combination receives a unique value. A simplified grammar for substitution tag, limited to the <random> and <text> substitution types used in Section 4, is outlined in Fig. 3.

```
<tag>= <exp>|
       string[30]|
       <substitution type>|
       list(<substitution type>,<exp>)|
       ulist(<substitution type>,<exp>);
<substitution type>=<random> | <text>
<random> = (<min>,<max>,uniform)
<exp> = <exp>-<exp>|<exp>+<exp>|<exp>/<exp>|
        <exp>*<exp>|<exp>%<exp>|<number>|<const>
<number>=<number>|0|1|2|3|4|5|6|7|8|9
<const>=_SCALE|_SEED|_QUERY|_TEMPLATE|_STREAM|_LIMIT
```

Fig. 3. Basic Substitution Declaration Grammar

The Random substitution type allows defining tags to use randomly-generated integers in an inclusive range [min, max] using a uniform distribution. The specific grammar for a <random> substitution tag is:

```
<random> = random(<exp>,<exp>,uniform);
```

Let's call the first expression min and the second expression max. The likelihood P_i of each value to be picked by DSQGEN is identical:

$$P_i = \frac{1}{max - min} \qquad (1)$$

The location parameter *min* and the scale parameter *max* must be picked such that *min<max*. The designer of a query template must assure that the values picked for *min* and *max* fall within the range of the data distribution of the targeted column. The following examples show how the random substitution tag can be used:

Example 1   `order_quantity = random (1, 10, uniform);`
Example 2   `price_int=random(1,1000,uniform;`
                  `price_frac=random(1,100,uniform);`
Example 3   `birthday=random("1929-01-01"`
                  `,"2009-05-31",uniform);`

Example 1 defines a tag, which randomly chooses a value between 1 and 10. This can be used as a projection predicate on a quantity column. Example 2 defines two tags, one to generate the integer portion of a price (price_int) and a second (price_frac) to generate the fraction of a price. The price can then be combined in the SQL text as: [price_int]+1/[price_frac]. Example 3 selects a random date between 2009 and 2029, with appropriate allowances for leap years.

The TEXT substitution, which uses the grammar shown in Fig. 4, replaces a particular tag with one of a weighted set of ASCII strings. This substitution type can be employed in many different ways. In its basic form, this can be employed in a projection predicate such as: `column_name = "<string>"`, providing a crude form of text searching. The elements of a TEXT substitution tag must be distinct. The empty string is permissible.

```
<text> =({<subelem>, <weight>}<subelem_weight>);
<subelem_weight>=,{<subelem>, <weight>}|NULL
<subelem> = string[100];
<weight>  = integer;
```

Fig. 4. TEXT Substitution Type

The likelihood of a particular "subelem" to be picked as a substitution parameter depends on the ratio of its weight (<subelem_weight>) to the sum of all weights. The probability of S_i for the following definition with n elements tag=TEXT({"S_1", W_1},...,{"S_1", W_1}) is defined as :

$$P_{S_i} = \frac{W_i}{\sum_{j=1}^{n} W_j} : 0 \leq i \leq n : W_i > 0 \qquad (2)$$

Table 1. DSQGEN Build-In Functions

Keyword	Value
_SCALE	Scale factor in GB, as set with -scale command line option
_SEED	Current random-number-generator seed
_QUERY	Sequence number within a query set
_TEMPLATE	Template ID
_STREAM	Query stream ID
_LIMITA,_LIMITB,_LIMITC	Used for vendor specific syntax to limit the number of rows
_LIMIT	Maximum number of rows to be returned by the query

Example 4   `dog=TEXT({"German`
`sheppard",1},{"poodle",1},{"pug",1});`

Example 5   `dog_color=TEXT({"brown",6},{"black",3},{"gre`
`y",1});`

Example 4 defines the tag dog, which generates values German Sheppard, poodle and pug with the same likelihood. Example 5 defines dog colors to be brown, back or grey. However, in this example the color brown gets picked six out of ten times, while back gets picked three out of ten times and grey gets only picked one out of ten times.

By default, substitution tags produce singleton values. When combined with the LIST or ULIST operators, each tag produces a list of <number> values that can be referred to by adding a ".<n>", suffix to the substitution tag. ULIST guarantees uniqueness within the list of values, while the LIST operator does not. There are some limitations to the ULIST operator. If the domain from which the ULIST operator picks its value set is smaller than or equal to the size of the requested list (i.e., <number>), the ULIST operator behaves like the LIST operator.

DSQGEN recognizes some keywords and built-in functions as integer constants. Table 1 summarizes some commonly used keyword substitutions and their values. These constants are commonly used to instrument the query stream, provide unique names for temporary table or view definitions, or to access vendor-specific syntax to constrain the size of a result set. For instance, a vendor might need to define a temporary view if they didn't support SQL's common-sub-expression syntax. In order to distinguish the view name between streams, a unique identifier needs to be assigned to it. The _STREAM keyword fulfills this requirement, and can be used in the rewrite of Query 15 of TPC-H. Another example creates a predicate based on the scale factor, which is used in Query 11 of TPC-H. Example 6 prints the number of rows in the part table together with the scale factor.

Example 6   `SELECT 'part count at scale factor`
`[_SCALE]'|count(*)`
`FROM PART;`

The built-in functions can also be used to access vendor-specific syntax to limit the number of rows returned by a query. Vendors have dialect-specific extensions to SQL that control the number of rows returned by a query, and require those syntactic changes at different points in the query. DSQGEN defines three possible additions (_LIMITA, _LIMITB, and _LIMITC) that, in conjunction with a global limit to the number of rows to be returned (_LIMIT) and vendor specific definitions, allow a single query template to satisfy the requirements of all supported database dialects (currently, ANSI, Oracle, DB2, Netezza, SqlServer). Example 7 shows a sample usage of the LIMIT tags to return the 100 most frequent last names from a customer table. Vendor-specific substitutions (__LIMITA, __LIMITB and __LIMITC) are defined to limit the number of rows returned by a query (Example 7a). The query template (Example 7b) needs only define the desired number of rows (via _LIMIT) and include the potential syntax substitutions (_LIMITA, _LIMITB, _LIMITC). The result is a single query template that can produce appropriate SQL for all defined dialect, as illustrated for ANSI SQL (Example 7c). The call to generate the query is shown in Example 7d.

Example 7   Implementation of the ANSI specific dialect to limit the number of rows returned by a query

7a: ansi.tpl

```
DEFINE __LIMITA = "";
DEFINE __LIMITB = "top %d";
DEFINE __LIMITC = "";
```

7b: query.tpl

```
DEFINE LIMIT=100;
[_LIMITA]
SELECT [_LIMITB] last_name, count(*) as name_count
FROM customer
GROUP BY name_count, order by name_count
[_LIMITC];
```

7c: query_0.sql

```
SELECT top 100 last_name, count(*) as name_count
FROM customer
GROUP BY name_count, order by name_count;
```

7d: Command line call to DSQEN for generating vendor specific syntax

```
DSQGEN -scale 1 -template query.tpl -dialect ansi.tpl
```

3.2 Generating Query Workloads

DSQGEN is capable of generating three different kinds of workload: Single-Template, Single-Stream, and Multi-Stream. Each type of workload requires a set of query templates to be defined. Each template must be stored in a separate file (e.g. T_1.tpl, T_2.tpl,…,T_n.tpl). While a template can contain more than one SQL statement, there can only be one set of substitution tag declarations for all queries included in a given template, and they must occur before the first SQL statement. Having multiple

SQL queries in one template allows for the implementation of business questions that usually occur in the same sequence, such as drill down queries.

The *Single-Template Workload* generates one or multiple versions of the same query. It can be used to stress test the execution of a single query with multiple substitution parameters. This is especially useful to test the query optimizer's ability to generate the most optimal execution plan for every query that can be generated from one template. The syntax to generate 500 queries for scale factor 100 using query template T1 in the ANSI SQL syntax is:

```
DSQGEN -scale 100 -template T1.tpl
       -count 500 -dialect ansi.tpl
```

For the *Single-Stream Workload,* fully qualified paths to a set of template files are listed in an ASCII meta-file (e.g. MF.txt). This workload generates one query for every template included in the meta-file. The Single-Stream query workload is identical to the workload used in TPC-H's Power-Test.

The *Multi-Stream Workload* simulates n users, each running a unique permutation of the query templates defined in a meta-file. The following command line generates n files, query_0.sql through query_<n-1>.sql, each containing a different permutation of the queries defined in M.tpl according to the vendor-specific dialect defined in dialect.tpl:

```
DSQGEN -input M.tpl -stream <n> -dialect <dialect.tpl>
```

4   Modeling Existing TPC-H Queries with DSQGEN

4.1 Substitution Analysis

The 22 TPC-H queries use the substitution parameters listed in Table 2. After eliminating duplicates, we are able to classify all substitutions into the 10 types as listed in the third column.

The **Type 1** substitution type randomly selects one or more numbers from a dense interval. Most queries use substitutions of integer numbers, a straightforward use of the RANDOM function. Query 16 concatenates two independently selected values in [1..5] to identify a value for P_BRAND (Type 1a). Query 6 requires random floating value between 0.02 and 0.09 to build a selectivity predicate on L_DISCOUNT (Type 1b). Another variant of Type 1 is used in Query 16, which applies an in-list predicate on P_SIZE.

The **Type 2** substitution type randomly selects one or more strings from a list of possible items.

The **Type 3** substitution type randomly selects a date. The desired value may be a random day in a static month and year (Type 3a), a static day of a random month and year (Type 3b), a static day of a random month between the January of a static year and October of a static year (Type 3c), or the first of January of a random year (Type 3d).

The **Type 4** substitution type selects the scale factor of the database being queried.

The **Type 5** substitution type selects the number of rows to be returned by the top most SQL statement.

Table 2. TPC-H parameter substitutions and their characterization into types

Table Column	Substitution Domain	Type	Query
P_BRAND	'Brand#MN' where MN is a two character string representing two numbers randomly and independently selected within [1...5]	1a	16
N/A	Randomly selected within [60 ... 120]	1a	16
C_PHONE	Randomly selected within [11 ... 35]	1a	16
L_QUANTITY	Randomly selected within [312 ... 315]	1a	16
L_DISCOUNT	Randomly selected within [0.02 ... 0.09]	1b	6
P_SIZE	Randomly selected within [1 ... 50]	1a	16
P_SIZE	8 numbers randomly selected within [1 ... 50] (no duplicates)	1c	16
P_NAME	Randomly selected from the list of P_NAMEs	2	16
P_CONTAINER	Randomly selected from the list defined for P_CONTAINER	2	16
N_NAME	Randomly selected within the list of N_NAME	2	16
R_NAME	Randomly selected within the list of R_NAME	2	16
C_MKT_SEGMENT	Randomly selected within the list of Segments	2	16,3
L_SHIPMODE	Randomly selected within the list of values defined for Modes	2	16
P_TYPE	Made of the first 2 syllables of a string randomly selected within the list of 3-syllable strings defined for Types	2	16
P_TYPE	Randomly selected within the list Syllable 3 defined for Types	2	16
O_COMMENT	Randomly selected of "special", "pending", "unusual", "express"	2	16
DATE	Randomly selected day [1995-03-01 ... 1995-03-31].	3a	3
DATE	The first day of a random month of years [1993 ... 1997].	3b	
DATE	The first day of a random month between the first month of 1993 and the 10th month of 1997.	3c	4
DATE	The first of January of a random year within [1993 ... 1997].	3d	6
N/A	Chosen as 0.0001 / SF.	4	11
N/A	Limit the number of rows to <n>	5	3

In the following sections, we will use these query substitution types to translate representative TPC-H query templates into the DSQGEN syntax. The accompanying figures outline the QGEN syntax for a given query include the substitution definitions used for that query, but it is worth noting that the substitution definition is not included in the template in the actual QGEN template. The substitution definitions would only be clear to a user who was able to access and understand the source code of QGEN itself. While this paper does not illustrate the translation of the entire TPC-H query set, the process outlined here can be applied to all queries defined for TPC-H.

4.2 Query 16

Query 16 finds out how many suppliers can supply parts with given attributes. It might be used, for example, to determine whether there are a sufficient number of suppliers for heavily ordered parts. Query 16 is an example that uses the substitution types: 1, 1c and 2 (see Table 2).

```
SELECT p_brand ,p_type ,p_size
       ,count(distinct ps_suppkey) as supplier_cnt
FROM partsupp, part
WHERE p_partkey = ps_partkey
  AND p_brand <> ':1'
  AND p_type not like ':2%'
  AND p_size in (:3, :4, :5, :6, :7, :8, :9, :10)
```

Fig. 5. Query 16 of TPC-H in QGEN Syntax

```
AND ps_suppkey not in (SELECT s_suppkey
                       FROM supplier
                       WHERE s_comment like
                              '%Customer%Complaints%')
GROUP BY p_brand ,p_type, p_size
ORDER BY supplier_cnt desc, p_brand, p_type, p_size;
```

Fig. 5. (*continued*)

:1 (p_brand) is substituted as Brand#MN, where M and N are two single character strings representing two numbers randomly and independently selected within [1 .. 5];

:2 (p_type) is made of the first 2 syllables of a string randomly selected within the list of 3-syllable strings "STANDARD", "ANODIZED", "TIN", "SMALL", "BURNISHED", "NICKEL", "MEDIUM", "PLATED", "BRASS", "LARGE", "POLISHED", "STEEL", "ECONOMY", "BRUSHED", "COPPER", "PROMO"

:3 to :10 (p_size) are eight randomly selected as a set of different values of [1...50];

Query 16 can be rewritten in DSQGEN syntax by utilizing the RANDOM and TEXT substitution types and the ULIST operator as follows.

```
DEFINE PBRAND_A = RANDOM(1,5,uniform);
DEFINE PBRAND_B = RANDOM(1,5,uniform);
DEFINE PTYPE = LIST(TEXT({"STANDARD",1},{"ANODIZED",1}
                        ,{"TIN",1},{"SMALL",1}
                        ,{"BURNISHED",1},{"NICKEL",1}
                        ,{"MEDIUM",1},{"PLATED",1}
                        ,{"BRASS",1},{"LARGE",1}
                        ,{"POLISHED",1},{"STEEL",1}
                        ,{"ECONOMY",1},{"BRUSHED",1}
                        {"COPPER",1},{"PROMO",1}),8);
DEFINE SIZE = ULIST(RANDOM(1,50,uniform),8);

SELECT p_brand ,p_type ,p_size
      ,count(distinct ps_suppkey) as supplier_cnt
FROM partsupp ,part
WHERE p_partkey = ps_partkey
  AND p_brand <> '[PBRAND_A][PBRAND_B]'
  AND p_type not like '[PTYPE]%'
  AND p_size in ([SIZE.1],[SIZE.2],[SIZE.3],[SIZE.4]
                ,[SIZE.5],[SIZE.6],[SIZE.7],[SIZE.8])
  AND ps_suppkey not in (SELECT s_suppkey
                         FROM supplier
                         WHERE s_comment like
                                '%Customer%Complaints%')
GROUP BY p_brand ,p_type ,p_size
ORDER BY supplier_cnt desc ,p_brand ,p_type, p_size;
```

Fig. 6. Query 16 of TPC-H in DSQGEN Syntax

The substitution parameter for P_BRAND is essentially a two-digit number, each digit from the domain of [1,5]. It can be constructed from the two independent substitution tags PBRAND_A and PBRAND_B, each defined with the RANDOM substitution type as an integer between 1 and 5. The substitution parameter for P_TYPE is a random string from a list of 16 elements (see above). It can be implemented as a TEXT substitution of 16 elements, each with the same weight. P_SIZE requires 8 substitution parameters, each from the domain of [1,50]. Additionally the set of 8 parameters has to be unique. Hence, we implement the substitution parameter using a combination of the RANDOM substitution and the ULIST operator.

4.3 Query 6

Query 6 quantifies the amount of revenue increase for a given year that would have resulted from eliminating discounts. Query 6 is an example that uses the substitution types: 1b and 3d (see Table 2).

```
SELECT sum(l_extendedprice * l_discount) as revenue
FROM    lineitem
WHERE  l_shipdate>= date ':1'
   AND l_shipdate<add_months(date':1'+ interval '1' year
   AND l_discount between :2 - 0.01 and :2 + 0.01
   AND l_quantity < :3;
```

Fig. 7. Query 6 of TPC-H with QGEN Syntax

:1 DATE is the first of January of a randomly selected year within [1993 .. 1997];
:2 DISCOUNT is randomly selected within [0.02 .. 0.09];
:3 QUANTITY is randomly selected within [24 .. 25].

Query 6 can be implemented solely with the RANDOM substitution type. The substitution tag on L_SHIPDATE, S_YEAR is implemented as a random number between 1993 and 1997. The month and day portion of the date are statically set to 01. The substitution tag for L_DISCOUNT requires a fraction [0.02,0.09]. Since the RANDOM substitution type only allows for integer values, we use a random number tag between 2 and 9 and build the fraction by prefixing the number with "0.0". The substitution tag for L_QUANTITY is a simple random substitution of [24,25].

```
DEFINE SYEAR     = random(1993,1997,normal);
DEFINE DF        = random(2,9,normal);
DEFINE LQUANTITY = random(24,25,normal);
SELECT sum(l_extendedprice * l_discount) as revenue
FROM   lineitem
WHERE  l_shipdate>= date'[SYEAR]-01-01'
   AND l_shipdate< date'[SYEAR]-01-01'+interval '1' year
   AND l_discount between 0.0[DF]-0.01 and 0.0[DF]+0.01
   AND l_quantity < [LQUANTITY];
```

Fig. 8. Query 6 of TPC-H with QGEN Syntax

4.4   Query 3

Query 3 retrieves the ten unshipped orders with the highest value. It is an example that uses the substitution types: 2, 3a and 5 (see Table 2).

```
SELECT  l_orderkey
        ,sum(l_extendedprice*(1-l_discount)) as revenue
        ,o_orderdate ,o_shippriority
FROM customer ,orders, lineitem
WHERE c_mktsegment = ':1'
  AND c_custkey = o_custkey
  AND l_orderkey = o_orderkey
  AND o_orderdate < date ':2'
  AND l_shipdate > date ':2'
GROUP BY l_orderkey, o_orderdate, o_shippriority
ORDER BY revenue desc, o_orderdate;
:n
```

Fig. 9. Query 3 in TPC-H qgen sytax

:1 is randomly selected within the list of values defined for Segments
:2 is a randomly selected day within [1995-03-01 .. 1995-03-31].
:n defines the maximum number of rows returned by the query (top)

Query 3 uses the TEXT substitution type, the RANDOM substitution type and the build-in functions to limit the number of rows returned by the query. As in the P_TYPE substitution of Query 16, this query implements the substitution parameter for C_MKTSEGMENT using the TEXT substitution type with a four item list, each with the same likelihood. The substitution parameters O_ORDERDATE and L_SHIPDATE are implemented with the RANDOM substitution. Since both

```
DEFINE  SEGMENT=text({"AUTOMOBILE",1},{"BUILDING",1}
                    ,{"FURNITURE",1},{"MACHINERY",1}
                    ,{"HOUSEHOLD"});
DEFINE  SHIPDAY = random(1,31,uniform);
DEFINE _LIMIT=10;
[_LIMITA] select [_LIMITB] l_orderkey
        ,sum(l_extendedprice*(1-l_discount)) as revenue
        ,o_orderdate, o_shippriority
FROM customer, orders, lineitem
WHERE c_mktsegment = '[SEGMENT]'
  AND c_custkey = o_custkey
  AND l_orderkey = o_orderkey
  AND o_orderdate < date '1995-03-[SHIPDAY]'
  AND l_shipdate > date '1995-03-[SHIPDAY]'
GROUP BY l_orderkey, o_orderdate, o_shippriority
ORDER BY revenue desc, o_orderdate
[_LIMITC];
```

Fig. 10. Query 3 in TPC-H DSQGEN syntax

substitution parameters are the same they can be implemented with the same substitution tag, SHIPDAY, which picks a day between 1 and 31 prefixed with the static string "'1995-03-". This query also needs to limit the number of rows to be returned to ten. This is done with three substitution tags, _LIMITA, _LIMITB and _LIMITC. _LIMITA, _LIMITB and _LIMITC are defined in the vendor specific template _LIMIT is defined as 10.

4.5 Query 4

Query 4 determines how well the order priority system is working and gives an assessment of customer satisfaction. It is an example using the substitution type 3c.

```
SELECT o_orderpriority, count(*) as order_count
FROM orders
WHERE o_orderdate >= date ':1'
  AND o_orderdate < date ':1' + interval '3' month
  AND exists (SELECT * FROM lineitem
              WHERE l_orderkey = o_orderkey
                AND l_commitdate < l_receiptdate)
GROUP BY o_orderpriority ORDER BY o_orderpriority;
```

Fig. 11. Query 4 in TPC-H QGEN syntax

:1 is the first day of a randomly selected month between the first month of 1993 and the 10th month of 1997.

Query 4 uses the RANDOM substitution type in combination with the build-in arithmetic capability of DSQGEN. There are 58 months between January 1993 and October 1997. In order to choose a random month between those dates, we first generate a random number between 0 and 58 (SEQMO). Then we divide that number by 12 to generate the year (YR). Please note that the result of the division is an integer. In order to generate the months, we take that number modulo 12 (MO). In the query we build the date by concatenating these numbers into: [YR]-[MO]-01

```
DEFINE SEQMO = random(0,57,uniform);
DEFINE YR    = ([SEQMO] / 12) + 1;
DEFINE MO    = ([SEQMO] % 12) + 1;
SELECT o_orderpriority,
       count(*) as order_count
FROM orders
WHERE o_orderdate>=date'[YR]-[MO]-01'
  AND o_orderdate<date'[YR]-[MO]-01'+interval '3' month
  AND exists (SELECT *
              FROM lineitem
              WHERE l_orderkey = o_orderkey
                AND l_commitdate < l_receiptdate)
GROUP BY o_orderpriority
ORDER BY o_orderpriority;
```

Fig. 12. Query 4 in TPC-H DSQGEN syntax

5 Scope of Possible Expansions to the TPC-H Query Set

Section 4, identified the substitution types that are found in the TPC-H query set. We have also shown that DSQGEN's current functionality is sufficient to generate queries for all 22 TPC-H query templates. It is also possible to extend the TPC-H query set very elegantly using DSQGEN, well beyond the identified substitution types. Since DSQGEN uses textual substitutions, we are able to introduce aggregation substitutions, column substitutions and full date substitutions. In the following sections we will illustrate how new queries can be introduced into TPC-H, creating a new query using the existing substitution types, followed by examples using new substitution types: aggregation substitution, and column substitution. Please note, we are not proposing new queries to TPC-H, but merely illustrating how new queries could be added to TPC-H's query set without any modifications to the query generator.

5.1 Query Using Existing Substitution Types

The following query retrieves unshipped orders with the highest value for customers with specific account balances and located in specific nations. This query uses the SQL ROLLUP operator, grouping by any combination of customer name, customer nation, order date and ship priority. The query uses three substitutions. The ABAL substitution tag, used in a *between predicate*, is defined using the RANDOM

```
DEFINE ABAL=random(0,9000,uniform);
DEFINE NT=text({"ALGERIA",1},{"ARGENTINA",1},{"IRAQ",1}
            ,{"BRAZIL",1},{"CANADA",1},{"RUSSIA",1}
            ,{"ETHIOPIA",1},{"FRANCE",1},{"INDIA",1}
            ,{"GERMANY",1},{"JORDAN",1},{"KENYA",1}
            ,{"INDONESIA",1},{"IRAN",1},{"EGYPT",1}
            ,{"JAPAN",1},{"MOROCCO",1},{"ROMANIA",1}
            ,{"MOZAMBIQUE",1},{"PERU",1},{"CHINA",1}
            ,{"ROMANIA",1},{"SAUDI ARABIA",1}
            ,{"VIETNAM",1},{"UNITED KINGDOM",1});
DEFINE _LIMIT=10;
[_LIMITA] select [_LIMITB] c_name, c_nation
      ,sum(l_extendedprice*(1-l_discount)) as revenue
      ,o_orderdate, o_shippriority
FROM customer, orders, lineitem, nation
WHERE c_acctbal between [ABAL]-999.99 and [ABAL]
  AND c_nationkey = n_nationkey
  AND c_custkey = o_custkey
  AND n_name = '[NT]'
  AND l_orderkey = o_orderkey
GROUP BY ROLLUP (c_name, c_nation
                ,o_orderdate, o_shippriority)
ORDER BY revenue desc, o_orderdate, c_name, c_nation
[_LIMITC];
```

Fig. 13. Query Using Existing Substitution Types

substitution type. It chooses the upper boundary of the account balance from the interval [0..9000]. The lower boundary of the between predicate is computed by subtracting 999.99 from ABAL. The second tag (NT) is used to choose a nation from a text list rather than the nation key. The last tag, _LIMIT, caps the number of rows returned to 10.

5.2 Query Using Aggregate Substitutions

The following query is based on Query 11 of TPC-H. It lists the most important subset of suppliers' stock in a given nation. In this context "importance" is based on the total, largest or smallest stocking cost. It uses the random substitution type for the NK substitution tag to implement a predicate on nation key. It uses the text substitution type to implement the AGG substitution tag, which chooses between the aggregation functions sum, min and max for calculating a supplier's stock.

```
DEFINE NK = random (0,31, uniform);
DEFINE AGG= text({"sum",1},{"min",1},{"max",1});

SELECT ps_partkey
       ,[AGG](ps_supplycost * ps_availqty) as value
FROM partsupp,supplier
WHERE ps_suppkey = s_suppkey
  AND s_nationkey = [NK]
GROUP BY ps_partkey;
```

Fig. 14. Query using aggregate substitution

5.3 Query Column Substitutions and Full Date Substitution

The final example query is based on Query 3 from TPC-H. It employs column substitution to randomly select the target of an aggregation from a set of statistically equivalent columns. The resulting queries generated by DSQGEN would exercise similar selectivity and computational load, but would increase the cost and complexity of maintaining summary tables or other auxiliary data structure, by increasing the randomness of the eventual SQL.

```
DEFINE SHIPDATE = random(1,31,uniform);
DEFINE LIMIT=10;
DEFINE COL=text({"l_quantity",1},{"l_discount",1}
                ,{"l_extendedprice",1},{"l_tax",1});

[_LIMITA] select [_LIMITB] l_orderkey
       ,sum([COL]), o_orderdate, o_shippriority
FROM customer, orders, lineitem
WHERE c_custkey = o_custkey
  AND l_orderkey = o_orderkey
  AND o_orderdate < date '1995-03-[SHIPDAY]'
  AND l_shipdate > date '1995-03-[SHIPDAY]'
GROUP BY l_orderkey, o_orderdate, o_shippriority
ORDER BY [COL] desc, o_orderdate
[_LIMITC];
```

Fig. 15. Query using Column Substitutions

6 Conclusion

This paper has demonstrated how the enhanced syntax available with the query generator developed for the proposed TPCDS benchmark, DSQGEN, can be used to express the queries defined for TPC-H, which currently uses the older, simpler query generator, QGEN. The migration from one query dialect to the other has no impact on the syntactic formulation of the queries, the selectivity of their predicates, the work they present to the system under test or the answer sets that will be returned. As such, the migration from the old query dialect to the new dialect can be accomplished without any impact on the viability or comparability of existing TPC-H results.

At the same time, moving the TPC-H query set from the existing syntax to that provided by DSQGEN presents the TPC with a two-fold opportunity that could enrich the existing benchmark and extend its useful life. The rephrased queries would reduce the support burden borne by the TPC, since the query templates could be revised or corrected without the need to fund additional software development. The migration would also provide the TPC with the opportunity to explore, and potentially adopt, additional queries that broaden the scope of the functions tested by the TPC's only decision support benchmark, expand the relevance of the workload to modern decision support customers, and increase the relevance of TPC-H results to customers faced with the complex and costly process of selecting a decision support solution, whether in hardware or software.

References

1. Stephens Jr., J.M., Poess, M.: MUDD: a multi-dimensional data generator. In: WOSP 2004, pp. 104–109 (2004)
2. Poess, M., Stephens Jr., J.M.: Generating Thousand Benchmark Queries in Seconds. In: VLDB 2004, pp. 1045–1053 (2004)
3. Poess, M.: Controlled SQL query evolution for decision support benchmarks. In: WOSP 2007, pp. 38–41 (2007)
4. Poess, M., Floyd, C.: New TPC Benchmarks for Decision Support and Web Commerce. ACM SIGMOD RECORD 29(4) (2000)
5. TPC-D Version 2.1: http://www.tpc.org/tpcd/default.asp
6. TPC-H specification 2.8.0, http://www.tpc.org/tpch/spec/tpch2.8.0.pdf
7. Transaction Processing Performance Council Policies Version 5.17, http://www.tpc.org/information/about/documentation/spec/TPC_Policies_v5.17.pdf

Generating Shifting Workloads to Benchmark Adaptability in Relational Database Systems

Tilmann Rabl[1], Andreas Lang[1], Thomas Hackl[2], Bernhard Sick[3],
and Harald Kosch[1]

[1] Chair of Distributed Information Systems
[2] InteLeC-Zentrum
[3] Computationally Intelligent Systems Group
University of Passau,
Germany
{rabl,langa,hackl,sick,kosch}@fim.uni-passau.de
http://www.fim.uni-passau.de

Abstract. A large body of research concerns the adaptability of database systems. Many commercial systems already contain autonomic processes that adapt configurations as well as data structures and data organization. Yet there is virtually no possibility for a just measurement of the quality of such optimizations. While standard benchmarks have been developed that simulate real-world database applications very precisely, none of them considers variations in workloads produced by human factors. Today's benchmarks test the performance of database systems by measuring peak performance on homogeneous request streams. Nevertheless, in systems with user interaction access patterns are constantly shifting. We present a benchmark that simulates a web information system with interaction of large user groups. It is based on the analysis of a real online eLearning management system with 15,000 users. The benchmark considers the temporal dependency of user interaction. Main focus is to measure the adaptability of a database management system according to shifting workloads. We will give details on our design approach that uses sophisticated pattern analysis and data mining techniques.

Keywords: Benchmarking, Adaptability, Polynomial Approximation, Time Series Generation.

1 Introduction

More and more database systems feature autonomic processes for optimization and adaptation. Nearly all major database vendors offer offline database design advisors [1,2,3] and recent research considers the online tuning of database systems [4,5]. Certainly the query workload is the most important variable for physical tuning during runtime. New developments in database benchmarks start to face this trend. For example, TPC-DS [6] features a new query generator that allows to generate a large set of queries which are syntactically different but semantically similar [7]. Still synthetic query streams are usually homogeneous in

R. Nambiar and M. Poess (Eds.): TPCTC 2009, LNCS 5895, pp. 116–131, 2009.

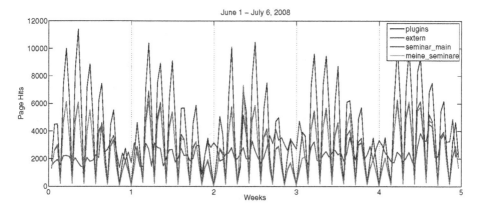

Fig. 1. Most accessed web sites in June 2008 per 6 hours

the frequency of queries and the ratio between different query types, while real database workloads tend to be bursty [8]. Traditionally the workload is seen as a set of SQL query classes and the physical design is tuned accordingly. However, new approaches define it as a sequence [9] or chain [10] of statements. This offers new opportunities to adapt the database system. Nevertheless, there is only little research on how to analyze the efficiency of such systems. To the best of our knowledge there is only one publication that introduces a benchmark for autonomic database tuning [11], yet this benchmark also only features homogeneous workloads.

Even though database access in most cases is triggered by human interaction, programs generate the actual SQL code. Therefore most queries are very similar and can be divided in relatively few distinct classes. Within these classes usually only simple parameters, like predicates change. Due to user interaction the occurrence of the classes depends on timetables. The most important examples are the day and night rhythm and the week cycle. In figure 1 this can be seen clearly for the accesses of an online eLearning portal (see section 2 for more details). It is easy to see that there is a daily and a weekly period. Each of the website accesses displayed will generate at least one and in most cases a sequence of SQL queries. For one website the queries will only differ in form of variables. Apart from the workload difference between day and night and workday and weekend, shifts in the workload between the single classes can also be seen. In figure 2 an average of the days in the data above is pictured. Not all websites are accessed in the same pattern. Thus, depending on the time of day the database will have different access rates and different access patterns.

Similar access patterns can be seen for any user accessed information system, see for example the access rates at the Wikimedia clusters[1] in figure 3. This periodic behavior gives chances for optimizations. On the one hand peak loads

---

[1] The Wikimedia foundation is a non-profit organization that hosts various websites, most notably the online encyclopedia Wikipedia.

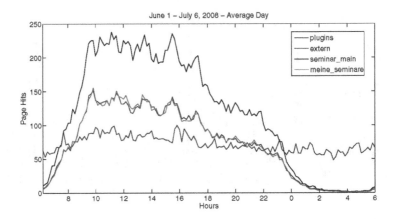

Fig. 2. Most accessed websites in June 2008, average day per 10 minutes

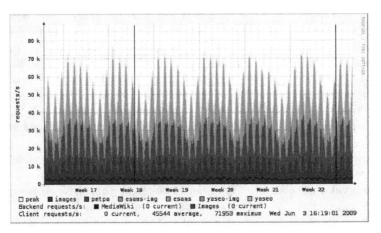

Fig. 3. Requests per second at the Wikimedia clusters in April 2009 in Europe (green) and the USA (blue) (image source: http://en.wikipedia.org/wiki/Most_viewed_article)

get more predictable and in times of low access the database can be prepared for the higher load. Such preparations could be index tuning or data restructuring. On the other hand clusters can be scaled according the access rates, in order to save energy or use the free capacity for other time-independent tasks.

In this paper we introduce a benchmark that is based on a real online information system. We designed it to test our dynamic allocation algorithms for cluster databases [12]. The main design focus was to build a realistic workload model that reflects user dependent workload patterns. The implemented query generator is able to simulate realistic workloads that shift in quantity and ratio of the statements. Another focus lay on the data generation. To generate datasets in arbitrary sizes, we analyzed the value and reference distributions in the original database and built an data generator that supports different probability distributions.

The rest of the paper is organized as follows, in section 2 we will give details about the eLearning information system which is the basis of our benchmark model. After that we will describe the benchmark database layout, query set and workload definition. In section 4, we will show possible benchmarking objectives, like measuring the adaptability of a database system, before concluding with future work in section 5.

2   Application Domain

As the focus of the benchmark lies on changing workloads, online information systems are a promising application domain. Usually it is very hard to get any detailed information about the structure and especially the workload of such systems, since they are treated as industrial secrets. We are in the fortunate position to have access to a sufficiently large online eLearning platform that is used at the University of Passau, which is therefore the basis of our benchmark.

Stud.IP[2] is a popular eLearning management system. It started as a simple forum and evolved into a full-featured Course and Campus Management System over the years. The system supports the complete course life cycle, beginning with creating the course, filling it with data, assigning times and rooms, specifying application procedures and exporting the data into PDF or HTML. Online communication and cooperation are encouraged by providing a forum for each course, wiki, messaging system, chat and online material. Today, 38 universities and 16 other institutes, are using Stud.IP[3], one of them is the University of Passau.

Stud.IP is written in PHP and uses a MySQL database. New functions can easily be added by using the provided plug-in interface. The database schema consists of 198 tables.

On a normal day during the semester, between 50 and 100 parallel users are online at any given time. At the beginning of a new semester, this number is drastically higher, normally there are about 200-300 users online at the same time. The normal MySQL load is at about 1,200 database requests per second as each PHP page generates several database requests.

In the spring semester of 2009, there are 1,734 courses with a total of 15,047 registered users of which 1,374 have a teacher role. Among those users, 672 teachers and 7,072 users in student role logged in at least once during the semester. 6,921 of those student role users are registered in courses with a total of 63,895 course registrations.

Since the launch of Stud.IP in fall 2006, 8,907 courses were entered, 222,349 course registrations processed, 52,017 documents uploaded and 178,070 internal messages sent. The database has 7,688,642 entries and is 1.3 GB in size.

---

[2] Stud.IP - http://www.studip.de

[3] http://www.studip.de/nbu.php?page_id=9cd4b3aac2bfe40abc26fcc0ba6254ce

3 Benchmark

The basic benchmark design is generic, so that a variety of database systems could be modeled. The current implementation is based on the Stud.IP eLearning platform. The database schema is a reduction of the original schema to the core functionality. The data generation is hard coded to this database layout, but it supports various database sizes. To generate realistic data the attribute value and reference distributions were analyzed and modeled with probability distributions.

The main contribution of the benchmark is the query generation. Since the goal of the benchmark is to represent temporal dependencies in the database access, attention was especially paid to modeling query streams. The benchmark emulates the access behavior of students on Stud.IP based on web server logs from the University of Passau. In the following we will detail on the analysis of the original system and the according realization in the benchmark.

3.1 Database Design

The database schema is only a fraction of the Stud.IP schema as it is used at the University of Passau. For simplicity reasons it is reduced to the core functionality, thus it only consists of 25 tables compared to the nearly 200 tables in the production system. The schema can be seen in figure 4. In the following, we will give a brief explanation of the main tables and the relationship between them.

The tables **users** and **user_info** store all information about the users, which may be students, teaching staff or employees. **seminar** contains information about seminars, which may be lectures, tutorials or seminars. Which user is registered in which seminars is stored in **seminar_user**.

Each seminar has one or more courses, which are stored in **courses**. Each course has one or more lecturers which are stored in **course_lecturer**. In a course students can work in teams, for example for assignments. Each team is stored in **teams**. The relation **courses_user** stores in which course and team a student is.

The tables **dokumente** and **folder** represent all existing documents. These documents and folders are linked to each other via **eigeneDateien_links**. This relation links seminars to their root folder, folders to subfolders and folders to documents. The table **permissions** manages and stores user permissions to documents and folders.

Each user has an **inbox** and an **outbox** which stores references to all messages he has received or sent. The messages themselves are stored in the table **messages**.

All objects a user can visit, i.e. a document, a course, etc., are modeled in the table **objects**. The last visits for each user are stored in **object_user_visits**.

The table **user_studiengang** references the users to the table **studiengaenge** in which all degree programs are stored. Therefore, it describes which user is enrolled in which degree program.

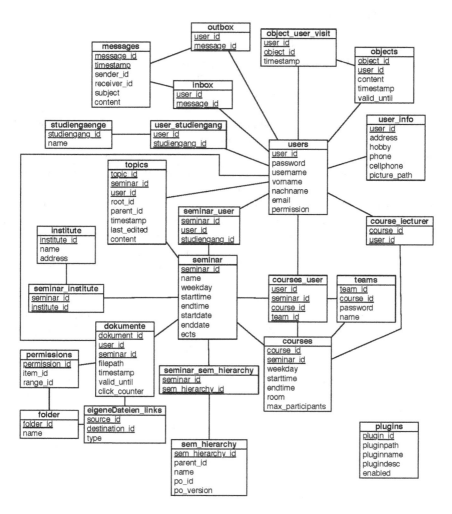

Fig. 4. The database schema of the benchmark

institute stores all institutions of the university. Each seminar belongs to an institute and this association is stored in **seminar_institute**.

A seminar can be credited for different degree programs, each of which can have different versions of examination rules. These connections are stored in the **sem_hierarchy** table. The seminars are linked to this table via **seminar-_sem_hierarchy** in order to define which seminar can be credited for which degree program and which examination rule.

Additionally, there is a table which stores all information about Stud.IP plug-ins called **plugins**. It contains the path of each plug-in, the name, if it is enabled and an unique id.

3.2   Data Generation

To populate the schema above a generator for arbitrary sized data was implemented. Different scaling factors can be specified for each table, to enable non-linear scaling. The generated data has similar distribution properties to the original data. To achieve this, we have analyzed the value and reference distributions between the tables. For the table `seminar_users` a reference distribution can be seen in figure 5. As described above this table stores the relationship between users and seminars. We use maximum likelihood estimation to fit standard probability distributions to the data. For now our data generator only supports normal and log-normal distributions, since they model most distributions sufficiently (for a discussion about log-normal distribution see [13]). Figure 6 shows that the distribution of the number of seminars a user is registered for can be modeled by a log-normal distribution, even though a gamma distribution would produce a better fit. The distribution of the number of users per seminar does not match the log-normal distribution very good, but still sufficiently. This can be seen in figure 7. Similar observations about reference distributions were made by Hsu et al. in [8]. They used the Hill equation to model the references, which is related to the log-logistic distribution.

Our data generation differentiates between entity and relationship tables according to the entity-relationship modeling [14]. Entity tables can be generated directly by the given distributions, while relationship tables are generated with knowledge of the according entity tables. The basic entity data generation works similar to dbgen or MUDD [15]. For each attribute we specify a domain and a distribution. Whenever possible we use real data from the Stud.IP database or other sources. Table `user` is for example defined as follows.

Each user gets a unique, consecutively numbered id first. The name of a user is generated by selecting a first name and a last name randomly. These names can

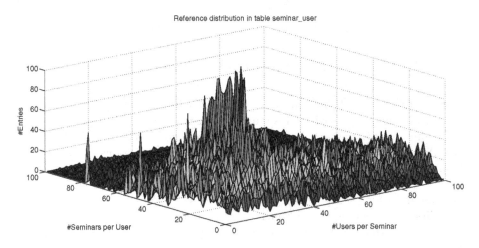

Fig. 5. Distribution of the references in table *seminar_users*

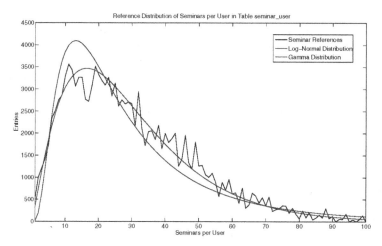

Fig. 6. Distribution of seminars per user in table *seminar_user*

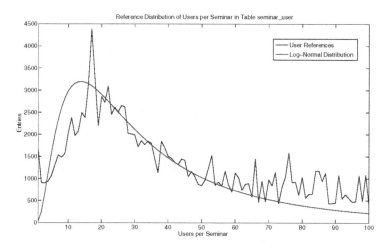

Fig. 7. Distribution of users per seminar in table *seminar_user*

be listed in a separate configuration file. Additionally, each user gets a unique username, which consists of his last name and a serial number. For his email address, a domain is added to the username. A password is also generated for every user by calculating the MD5 hash of the unique username. For a seminar, the process is similar.

Relationship tables are generated based on the entity tables. Thus for each referenced entity table the references are copied according to the modeled distribution. Additional attributes are generated in the same way as for entity tables.

3.3 Query Set

We extracted a set of 30 common queries from the original system. The queries are different in their characteristics and workload. Yet all queries must be processed within seconds. We changed the query syntax to comply with the SQL 92 standard. In the following we will give some examples of possible queries. The first example selects information about a user. This is usually done at the login for the users start page or if a user homepage is visited:

```
SELECT s.name, u.vorname, u.nachname, ui.address, ui.phone,
    u.email
  FROM users u, user_info ui, user_studiengang us,
      studiengaenge s
 WHERE u.user_id = ui.user_id
   AND us.user_id = u.user_id
   AND us.studiengang_id = s.studiengang_id
   AND u.user_id = $user_id;
```

The next query is executed, if a user browses the seminars he is registered for. This is one of the most common actions in Stud.IP. The query is rather expensive.

```
SELECT seminar.name, courses.weekday, courses.starttime,
    course.endtime, user.vorname, user.nachname
  FROM seminar_user, seminare, object_user_vists,
      seminar_sem_tree
 WHERE seminar_user.seminar_id = seminare.seminar_id
   AND object_user_vists.object_id = seminar_user.seminar_id
   AND object_user_vists.user_id = serminar_user.user_id
   AND seminar_sem_tree.seminar_id = seminar_user.seminar_id
   AND seminar_user.user_id = $user_id
UNION
SELECT seminar.name, courses.weekday, courses.starttime,
    course.endtime, user.vorname, user.nachname
  FROM course_lecturer, courses, seminare, object_user_vists,
      seminar_sem_tree
 WHERE course_lecturer.course_id = courses.course_id
   AND seminare.seminar_id = courses.seminar_id
   AND object_user_vists.object_id = seminar_user.seminar_id
   AND object_user_vists.user_id = serminar_user.user_id
   AND seminar_sem_tree.seminar_id = seminar_user.seminar_id;
   AND course_lecturer.user_id = $user.id;
```

Additionally there are update queries, which are executed whenever an object, i.e. a seminar, a document etc. is visited. As well as inserts, when new courses or users are created. An example is the following query which is executed when a user accesses an object.

```
UPDATE object_user_visits
   SET last_access = NOW()
 WHERE user_id = $user_id
   AND object_id = $object_id;
```

3.4   Query Generation

To benchmark our adaptation techniques we will generate sample query streams that are artificial but reflect a realistic user behavior. For that purpose we propose a new kind of random generator for time series.

We start from the assumption that the essential shape of a time series can be modeled by means of an approximating polynomial. Here, a time series describes the aggregated user behavior over one day, for instance, with values each reflecting the number of accesses in a time interval of 60 minutes. Thus, we have time series with 24 measurements starting at 5 am in the morning, for instance, when the number of accesses is lowest (close to zero). That is, we are given a time series consisting of $N + 1 = 24$ observations y_n at points in time x_n with $n \in \{0, \ldots, N\}$. These points are assumed to be equidistant in time. In general, an optimally (in the least-squares sense) approximating polynomial p_a of degree K can be represented by a linear combination of $K + 1$ basis polynomials p_k:

$$p_a(x) = \sum_{k=0}^{K} a_k p_k(x),\tag{1}$$

with a weight vector $a \in \mathbb{R}^{K+1}$, $a = (a_0, a_1, \ldots, a_K)^{\mathrm{T}}$, where T denotes the transposition of the parameter vector.

In principle, the basis polynomials $p_k(x)$ ($k \in \{0, \ldots, K\}$) could be *monomials*. Here, however, we claim that they must have the following properties:

1. They must have different and ascending degrees $0, \ldots, K$.
2. The leading coefficient (coefficient of the monomial with the highest degree) of each basis polynomial must be one.
3. Each pair of basis polynomials p_{k_1} and p_{k_2} (with $k_1 \neq k_2$) must be *orthogonal* with respect to the inner product

$$\langle p_{k_1} | p_{k_2} \rangle = \sum_{n=0}^{N} p_{k_1}(x_n) p_{k_2}(x_n).\tag{2}$$

That is, $\langle p_{k_1} | p_{k_2} \rangle = 0$ for all $k_1 \neq k_2$.

It must be mentioned that the choice of these basis polynomials depends on the points in time when samples are observed. If the observations were made at equidistant points in time, the choice depends only on their number $N + 1$ if we assume—without loss of generality—that the first observation is made at time 0—otherwise we simply shift the time series to this point.

In the context of a representation with orthogonal basis polynomials, the a_k are called *orthogonal expansion coefficients*. Each time series—or the polynomial representing this time series, to be precise—can now be regarded as one point in a particular space (we call it *shape space*) which is spanned by the orthogonal expansion coefficients. Due to the particular representation of the approximating polynomial sketched above, these orthogonal expansion coefficient can be interpreted as optimal (in the least-squares sense) estimators of *average* (a_0), *slope* (a_1), *curve* (a_2), *change of curve* (a_3), etc. of the time series.

The description of appropriate techniques for the determination of orthogonal basis polynomials and the efficient computation of the orthogonal expansion coefficients for a given time series is out of the scope of this article. We refer to our previous work published in [16,17] which is based on mathematical background outlined in [18,19].

Assume now, we want to construct a random generator for time series describing the user behavior on Mondays which are working days. Then, a set of sample time series is needed to build this generator (ideally, about 25 or more). The time series are all approximated as described above (e.g., with polynomials of degree 6). In our experiments it turned out that the representations of the sample time series all originating from a particular kind of day (e.g., public holiday, working Friday, etc.) can be regarded as being nearly *normally distributed* in the shape space. More precisely, to model this distribution we need the functional form of a *multivariate Gaussian distribution*

$$\mathcal{N}(a|\mu, \Sigma) = \frac{1}{(2\pi)^{(K+1)/2}} \frac{1}{|\Sigma|^{1/2}} \exp\left\{-\frac{1}{2}(a - \mu)^{\mathrm{T}} \Sigma^{-1}(a - \mu)\right\} \qquad (3)$$

with a $(K+1)$-dimensional center (or mean) μ and a $(K+1)\times(K+1)$-dimensional matrix Σ. To find the model parameters μ and Σ from a sample data set, we assume that the points in the shape space are independent and identically distributed and apply a standard *maximum likelihood* technique (cf., e.g., [20]) to determine their values.

A model for a specific set of time series can then be used as a random generator for time series in the following way:

1. A random number generator parameterized by means of the multivariate Gaussian is used to generate random numbers which are points in the shape space distributed according to Eq. 3.
2. Using the (known) orthogonal basis polynomials, these points can be transformed into the respective polynomials.
3. The polynomials can be evaluated at the desired points in time (e.g., at points corresponding to time intervals of 60 minutes).
4. Random noise can be added, e.g., white noise with a standard deviation corresponding to the average approximation error for the set of sample time series.

Altogether, we obtain an arbitrarily large set of artificial time series which all have an essential shape that is similar to the shapes of the time series contained in the set of (real) samples which has been used to build the random generator. An example of an polynomial approximation for Mondays during the lecture period can be seen in figure 8.

Each day of the week has different access rates, which can be seen in figure 1. We therefore build single models for every day of the week. This way we can also easily simulate holidays and outliers with anomalous accesses.

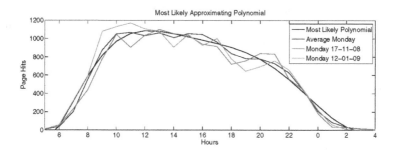

Fig. 8. The most likely approximating polynomial for Mondays during the lecture period

3.5 Scaling Time

An important factor for the usability of a benchmark is its runtime [21]. The smallest unit of time that has periodical access rates is usually one day. To test adaptability several periods have to be processed. Since this is too long for most benchmarking purposes, we propose to scale time. With a scaling factor of 1/7 a complete week can be simulated within 24 hours. Depending on the application under test, even smaller factors could be reasonable. An other possibility to shorten runtime is to use a reduced week that only consists of three days.

Of course the system under test should be aware of the time scaling factor. Since daily and weekly periods are usual in information systems, good tuning processes will use this previous knowledge for periodical tasks.

4 Benchmarking Objectives

Depending on the benchmark objective, different test cases can be built. Shifting workloads give lots of opportunities to test automatic and autonomic systems. Usually the metric is *transactions per second* or *average response time* for a given database size, depending on the optimization goal (e.g. the *QphDS@SF* metric in TPC-DS [6]). It has to be mentioned that whichever is used, the other should also be monitored. In the following we will give four examples on how we use the benchmark.

4.1 Basic Performance

The most common benchmarking objective in database systems is to test the speed, i.e. transactions per second or similar. A good baseline for such a test is the peak performance of the system without any automatic tuning and without any workload shifts. We concur with Bruno, who argues that only primary indexes should be used for a reasonable baseline [22].

To test if the system can automatically produce a better throughput in a real time environment, alternating workloads can be used. This way the system has phases of high load, which can be used to measure the peak performance. In phases of low load, the system has time to optimize its table structure, scale itself or tune the indices without risking serious performance bottlenecks. Throughout the test the ratio of different query classes stay constant. After some periods the peak performance should increase and should be better than the baseline performance.

4.2   Adaptivity

As stated in the introduction a major goal was to measure adaptability. The idea is to test how well a system can adjust itself to the workload. Partially this is already tested by the throughput test above. But as we have shown before, the rates of query classes change within a single day. This can be simulated by shifting workloads. So different query sets are defined and for each set a separate time series is generated. Also the workload is different for each day of the week. Either a complete week can be simulated, or only a reduced week consisting only of two working days and one weekend day, which should suffice in most cases. With this test, a system under test that is aware of the temporal dependencies in the workload, should get a better performance than a system that is not.

Changes in the workload behavior can be introduced to further test the adaptivity. In figure 9 the most frequently accessed websites in Stud.IP between October 08 and May 09 can be seen. It is easy to see that there are sections with very different characteristics. The diagram starts shortly after the beginning of the lecture period, which lasts until the first week of February. The next lecture period started at April 20. Additionally the Christmas break from December 24 until January 06 can be seen. So for an eLearning system at a university a week can be classified in one of the three classes, lecture period, free period and holidays. All three of these sections are well-defined and their limits are previous knowledge. This form of test is in some respects already implemented in current benchmarks, TPC-DS for example consists of four consecutive phases with very different characteristics (i.e. load, query run, data maintenance, query run - cf.

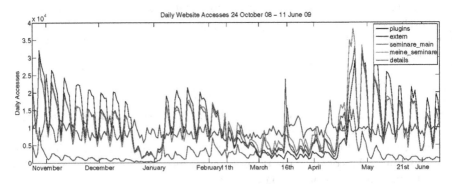

Fig. 9. Most accessed websites in Stud.IP between October 24, 2008 and June 10, 2009 per day

[23]). However, our form of query generation also makes it possible to model the trends within one phase. Such a trend can be seen in the fall term 2008 where the workload constantly decreases and then slightly increases at the end of the term.

4.3 Robustness

To test the robustness of an autonomic system outliers can be introduced. In figure 9 these can be seen in form of legal holidays on May 21 and June 1 and in form of unpredictable outliers for example on February 11 (server maintenance) or March 16 (unexpected user behavior). An autonomic system should be able to identify such outliers and handle them correctly. So, it should not change its configuration completely based on the single day. Yet it also must not have a serious performance collapse. For legal holidays this could also be supported by previous knowledge. Outliers can be modeled like other days and either triggered randomly (maintenance) or at previously defined points in time. To test robustness the performance before and after an outlier can be compared and the time until the original performance is reached again. To find out if a system is *over adapted*, the performance during an outlier day can be used.

4.4 Energy and Space Efficiency

The shifting workloads can of course be used to test the energy and space efficiency of a system. An autonomic system might be able to reduce its space and energy consumption in phases of low load. To measure the energy efficiency an *transaction per watt* metric, as introduced in [24], can be used.

5 Conclusion

Autonomic tuning is an ongoing field of research in the database community, new evaluation methods are therefore needed. The benchmark introduced in this paper features a new way to model database workloads. With the polynomial representation of every week-day a good compromise between realistic access rates and comparable patterns is found. This opens new possibilities to test automatic and autonomic tuning. The benchmark is based on an online eLearning application that was analyzed extensively.

For future work we will first examine and tune the benchmark. We will improve our eLearning benchmark and analyze how our techniques can be used in other benchmarks as well (e.g. TPC-C, TPC-H). To ease the adaptation of our benchmark we will implement more generic query and data generators. These generators will be controlled by configuration files that make adoption of the schema or value domains and distributions more easy. As online information systems are usually evolving over their life time, an interesting extension will be the introduction of schema evolution. We will include possibilities to alter the current table definitions and add new tables. This will add further challenges to physical design tuning. To learn about realistic schema evolution, we will further monitor the development of the Stud.IP installation at the University of Passau.

Acknowledgments

The authors would like to thank Marco Sitzberger and Yang Chen for their help on analyzing the Apache logs and Thiemo Gruber for his help with the implementation of the polynomial approximation.

References

1. Zilio, D.C., Rao, J., Lightstone, S., Lohman, G.M., Storm, A.J., Garcia-Arellano, C., Fadden, S.: Db2 design advisor: Integrated automatic physical database design. In: VLDB 2004: Proceedings of the Thirtieth International Conference on Very Large Data Bases, pp. 1087–1097. Morgan Kaufmann, San Francisco (2004)
2. Dageville, B., Das, D., Dias, K., Yagoub, K., Zaït, M., Ziauddin, M.: Automatic sql tuning in oracle 10g. In: VDLB 2004: Proceedings of the Thirtieth International Conference on Very Large Data Bases, pp. 1098–1109. Morgan Kaufmann, San Francisco (2004)
3. Agrawal, S., Chaudhuri, S., Kollár, L., Marathe, A.P., Narasayya, V.R., Syamala, M.: Database tuning advisor for microsoft sql server 2005. In: VDLB 2004: Proceedings of the Thirtieth International Conference on Very Large Data Bases, pp. 1110–1121. Morgan Kaufmann, San Francisco (2004)
4. Bruno, N., Chaudhuri, S.: An online approach to physical design tuning. In: ICDE 2007: Proceedings of the 23rd International Conference on Data Engineering, pp. 826–835. IEEE, Los Alamitos (2007)
5. Wiese, D., Rabinovitch, G., Reichert, M., Arenswald, S.: Autonomic tuning expert: a framework for best-practice oriented autonomic database tuning. In: CASCON 2008: Proceedings of the 2008 conference of the center for advanced studies on collaborative research, pp. 27–41. ACM, New York (2008)
6. Nambiar, R.O., Poess, M.: The making of tpc-ds. In: VLDB 2006: Proceedings of the 32nd international conference on Very large data bases, pp. 1049–1058 (2006)
7. Poess, M.: Controlled sql query evolution for decision support benchmarks. In: WSOP 2007: Proceedings of the 6th International Workshop on Software and Performance, pp. 38–41. ACM, New York (2007)
8. Hsu, W.W., Smith, A.J., Young, H.C.: Characteristics of production database workloads and the tpc benchmarks. IBM Systems Journal 40(3), 781–802 (2001)
9. Agrawal, S., Chu, E., Narasayya, V.: Automatic physical design tuning: Workload as a sequence. In: SIGMOD 2006: Proceedings of the 2006 ACM SIGMOD international conference on Management of data, pp. 683–694. ACM, New York (2006)
10. Holze, M., Ritter, N.: Autonomic databases: Detection of workload shifts with n-gram-models. In: Atzeni, P., Caplinskas, A., Jaakkola, H. (eds.) ADBIS 2008. LNCS, vol. 5207, pp. 127–142. Springer, Heidelberg (2008)
11. Consens, M.P., Barbosa, D., Teisanu, A.M., Mignet, L.: Goals and benchmarks for autonomic configuration recommenders. In: SIGMOD 2005: Proceedings of the 2005 ACM SIGMOD International Conference on Management of Data, pp. 239–250. ACM, New York (2005)
12. Rabl, T., Pfeffer, M., Kosch, H.: Dynamic allocation in a self-scaling cluster database. Concurrency and Computation: Practice and Experience 20(17), 2025–2038 (2007)

13. Mitzenmacher, M.: A brief history of generative models for power law and lognormal distributions. Internet Mathematics 1(2), 226–251 (2004)
14. Chen, P.P.S.: The entity-relationship model — toward a unified view of data. ACM Transactions on Database Systems 1(1), 9–36 (1976)
15. Stephens, J.M., Poess, M.: Mudd: a multi-dimensional data generator. In: WOSP 2004: Proceedings of the 4th international workshop on Software and performance, pp. 104–109. ACM, New York (2004)
16. Fuchs, E., Gruber, C., Reitmaier, T., Sick, B.: Processing short-term and long-term information with a combination of polynomial approximation techniques and time-delay neural networks. IEEE Transactions on Neural Networks (2009) (accepted – to appear)
17. Fuchs, E., Gruber, T., Nitschke, J., Sick, B.: On-line motif detection in time series with SwiftMotif. Pattern Recognition 42(11), 3015–3031 (2009)
18. Elhay, S., Golub, G.H., Kautsky, J.: Updating and downdating of orthogonal polynomials with data fitting applications. SIAM Journal on Matrix Analysis and Applications 12(2), 327–353 (1991)
19. Fuchs, E.: On discrete polynomial least-squares approximation in moving time windows. In: Gautschi, W., Golub, G., Opfer, G. (eds.) Applications and Computation of Orthogonal Polynomials. International Series of Numerical Mathematics, vol. 131, pp. 93–107. Birkhäuser, Basel (1999); (Proceedings of the Conference at the Mathematical Research Institute Oberwolfach, Germany, March 22-28 1998)
20. Bishop, C.M.: Pattern Recognition and Machine Learning. Springer, New York (2006)
21. Blackburn, S.M., McKinley, K.S., Garner, R., Hoffmann, C., Khan, A.M., Bentzur, R., Diwan, A., Feinberg, D., Frampton, D., Guyer, S.Z., Hirzel, M., Hosking, A.L., Jump, M., Lee, H., Moss, J.E.B., Phansalkar, A., Stefanovic, D., Van Drunen, T., von Dincklage, D., Wiedermann, B.: Wake up and smell the coffee: evaluation methodology for the 21st century. Communications of the ACM 51(8), 83–89 (2008)
22. Bruno, N.: A critical look at the tab benchmark for physical design tools. SIGMOD Record 36(4), 7–12 (2007)
23. Poess, M., Nambiar, R.O., Walrath, D.: Why you should run tpc-ds: A workload analysis. In: VLDB 2007: Proceedings of the 33rd international conference on Very large data bases, pp. 1138–1149. VLDB Endowment (2007)
24. Poess, M., Nambiar, R.O.: Energy cost, the key challenge of today's data centers: A power consumption analysis of tpc-c results. Proceedings of VLDB Endowment 1(2), 1229–1240 (2008)

Measuring Database Performance in Online Services:
A Trace-Based Approach

Swaroop Kavalanekar[1], Dushyanth Narayanan[2], Sriram Sankar[1], Eno Thereska[2], Kushagra Vaid[1], and Bruce Worthington[1]

[1] Microsoft Corporation, 1 Microsoft Way, Redmond WA 98052, USA
[2] Microsoft Research Ltd., 7 J J Thomson Avenue, Cambridge CB3 0FB, United Kingdom
{swaroopk,dnarayan,srsankar,etheres,kvaid,bworth}@microsoft.com

Abstract. Many large-scale online services use structured storage to persist metadata and sometimes data. The structured storage is typically provided by standard database servers such as Microsoft's SQL Server. It is important to understand the workloads seen by these servers, both for provisioning server hardware as well as to exploit opportunities for energy savings and server consolidation. In this paper we analyze disk I/O traces from production servers in four internet services as well as servers running TPC benchmarks. We show using a range of load metrics that the services differ substantially from each other and from standard TPC benchmarks. Online services also show significant diurnal patterns in load that can be exploited for energy savings or consolidation. We argue that TPC benchmarks do not capture these important characteristics and argue for developing benchmarks that can be parameterized with workload features extracted from live production workload traces.

Keywords: online services, TPC, benchmarks, storage traces, storage performance, data centers, capacity planning.

1 Introduction

Companies such as Microsoft host a variety of large-scale online services in mega-scale data centers. These services have unique workload attributes that need to be taken into account for optimal service scalability. Provisioning compute and storage resources to provide a seamless user experience is challenging, since customer traffic loads vary widely across time and geographies, and the servers hosting these applications have to be right-sized to provide performance both within the box and across the services cluster.

These online services typically have a tiered architecture, with stateless higher tiers above structured and unstructured storage tiers. For the structured storage, Microsoft's data centers use *SQL Server* since it provides a well-understood data model and a mature server engine. All the tiers present different provisioning and partitioning challenges: in this paper we focus on analyzing the structured storage tier. In this tier the most important resource for provisioning is usually I/O, and hence the I/O load at the structured storage tier is the focus of this paper.

R. Nambiar and M. Poess (Eds.): TPCTC 2009, LNCS 5895, pp. 132–145, 2009.
© Springer-Verlag Berlin Heidelberg 2009

We address the question: what are the I/O characteristics at the structured storage tier in production environments? We analyze I/O traces from live production servers in different online services, and compare them to each other and to standard TPC benchmarks. We compare a range of I/O metrics such as I/O rate, read/write ratio, and access locality. In addition we also examine the time variation in the online services workloads on a diurnal time scale. User-facing services often have strong diurnal patterns since users are not evenly distributed across time zones [1]. It is important to understand these patterns to improve performance, efficiency and responsiveness. Other opportunities include server consolidation, e.g., consolidating servers within a service or across services that have uncorrelated or even anti-correlated patterns.

Based on our analyses, we observe that:

1. When characterized using standard I/O metrics (e.g. IOPS/GB ratio, read/write ratios), online services workloads differ by orders of magnitude from TPC benchmarks even during phases of sustained peak activity.
2. Online services workloads also differ from each other on many metrics, again by orders of magnitude.
3. Some online services show distinct diurnal patterns in load level.

These observations imply that standard TPC benchmarks are not well-suited to characterizing performance in these environments since they do not match the I/O characteristics of individual workloads; they do not capture the range and diversity of these workloads; and they do not model diurnal patterns of variation in load. Production server traces, on the other hand, accurately capture these workload-specific features. In previous research[2, 3, 4], we have also seen that a trace-based approach allows evaluation of system designs and performance metrics that benchmarks alone do not allow. Based on these experiences we advocate widespread use of tracing to drive server performance evaluation. We also argue for the development of parameterized benchmarks that combine the advantages of benchmarks with the realism of live traces.

The rest of the paper is organized as follows. Section 2 presents an analysis of four online services workloads, and a comparison of these workloads with TPC benchmarks.

Section 3 briefly summarizes our previous research using I/O traces in the form of three case studies, each of which highlights a different advantage of traces *vis-à-vis* benchmarks. Section 4 provides practical guidelines to follow in tracing live production servers, based on our experiences. Section 5 discusses the challenges and limitations of traces, and directions for future research including hybrid approaches that could combine the advantages of traces and benchmarks. Section 6 completes the paper with some conclusions and recommendations.

2   Online Services Workload Analysis

In this section we analyze and visualize storage workloads from four online services within Microsoft, comparing the production storage workloads against the storage workloads from three TPC benchmarks. We first provide some background and motivation for the core problem: that of right-sizing storage in online services. We then describe the online services that we analyze in the paper and the low-overhead tracing technology used to trace production servers. We then present the results of our analysis.

2.1 Right-Sizing Storage in Online Services

Online services scale by partitioning and replicating data over a large number of commodity servers. It is important to optimize both the server design and the number of servers, since capital acquisition and power costs can quickly add up across a large server base. Increasingly, the aim is also to consolidate many different services onto a single infrastructure to improve utilization. Sets of consolidated services must scale across large deployments measured in hundreds of thousands of servers. Server design and right-sizing strategies for such environments present a whole new set of challenges in optimizing performance per dollar and per watt. To implement a data-driven methodology for server design, we have to ensure that applications are duly characterized and that the implications for various platform subsystems are well understood.

While CPU processing power continues to increase at a tremendous rate, disk bandwidth and latency have not kept pace. To bridge this gap, typical enterprise server solutions are designed with large storage arrays that account for a major portion of server capital acquisition costs and consume significant power, even when idle. Emerging technologies such as Solid State Devices (SSDs) can bridge the performance gap, but are still too expensive (per byte) for broad deployments at datacenter scale[4]. Hence, the first optimizations for server right-sizing need to focus on the storage subsystem, to ensure optimal overall performance for a given design. Additionally, customer datasets in online services environments are usually partitionable. Therefore, it is possible to design each service tier using commodity single- or dual-CPU socket platforms and then load-balance the traffic across multiple servers in the service cluster. In such scenarios, the approach is to disaggregate the customer dataset into small subsets, and to determine the right amount of capacity and I/O for hosting each subset. Ideally, identical self-contained server building blocks are used (e.g., a cluster of 2U servers with up to perhaps 24 drives each). This methodology enables a simpler storage subsystem design for optimal $/GB and $/IOPS. This also highlights a key difference in the service deployment strategy in an online services environment versus a typical enterprise where the dataset may be hosted on a single large server using scale-up platform technologies.

2.2 Workloads Traced

We chose four different web services for this analysis. Traces were captured from one representative database server from the structured storage tier of each service:

1. **IM-DB (Windows Live Messenger Database Server):** Address Book Database machines store user profiles and instant messenger buddy lists. They are essential to several online services related to social networking and interactions.
2. **MSN-DB (MSN Content Aggregation Database Server):** This database hosts a content publishing system for the online portal front page and is updated by mainly editorial tools and feed management systems via web services. Most of

the stored data is actually unstructured in nature, consisting of either raw content or links to content on other partner sites.

3. **EMAIL-DB (Windows Live Email Database Server):** This database hosts mail message metadata which maps online users to file stores. Incoming messages goes through a lookup process to determine which file server is hosting the receiving user's email message store. The message is then deposited in the appropriate message store, and other metadata corresponding to the user account is updated.

4. **BLOB-DB (Windows Live Blob Metadata Server):** These metadata lookup servers hold user account mappings for various blob storage services such as online photos, videos, social networking updates, etc. Each incoming request is looked up in this database to determine which back-end file server is hosting the appropriate content, and the user request is routed to that server for either storage or lookup of the content.

In addition we also ran and traced the TPC-C, TPC-E, and TPC-H benchmarks. In this paper neither the online services nor the benchmarks correspond to "e-commerce" browsing/shopping applications; although e-commerce is certainly important it is only one of many possible applications. We are currently looking for block I/O traces from e-commerce deployments and the corresponding benchmarks (TPC-W and TPC-App).

Table 1. Workloads traced

Workload	Trace start (PDT)	Trace length	RAID arrays	Disks
IM-DB	03 Oct 2008, 12:47	25 min	5 x RAID-10	34
MSN-DB	10 Mar 2009, 17:21	24 hrs	10 x RAID-10	46
EMAIL-DB	04 Apr 2008, 00:00	2 hrs	4 x RAID-10	34
BLOB-DB	26 Nov 2008, 14:00	24 hrs	10 x RAID-10	46
TPC-C	19 Oct 2007, 15:52	6 min	14 x RAID-0	392
TPC-E	18 Oct 2007, 17:46	17 min	12 x RAID-0	336
TPC-H	20 May 2009, 17: 31	1.5 hrs	4 x RAID-0	36

Table 1 summarizes the traces and the storage hardware on the traced servers. All the servers are configured with multiple RAID arrays, with multiple partitions on each array. The data and log files are then balanced across these partitions. The traces include both data and log file I/Os: generally the data file I/Os dominate the load. Log I/Os were 11%—12% of the total for BLOB-DB and MSN-DB, and less than 2% for the others.

2.3 Block-Level I/O Tracing

Windows operating systems have included a built-in tracing capability called Event Tracing for Windows (ETW) since Windows 2000. Each subsequent Windows release has increased the breadth and depth of system instrumentation, including instrumentation in the Windows kernel. ETW provides a high performance, low overhead, and highly scalable tracing framework. It uses efficient buffering and non-blocking logging mechanisms with per-CPU buffers written to stable storage by a separate thread. ETW tracing is extensible and can also be extended to applications by application developers. Since Windows 2003, ETW tracing can be dynamically enabled or disabled without requiring a system reboot or an application restart. Typical ETW events are discrete time-stamped trace points, but sampling and statistical data captures are also possible. Storage related instrumentation includes, but is not limited to: initiation and completion disk events for reads, writes, and flushes; and file events for creates, deletes, reads, writes, and attribute queries and updates.

There are several tools that can use ETW events to capture and correlate information about system activity. Since Windows 2008, the performance monitor built into Windows (PerfMon.exe) can capture ETW events. Another powerful tool designed specifically for system analysis using ETW is the Windows Performance Tools kit (WPT), which is an extensible performance analysis toolset that provides high level control and decoding of ETW events. It provides a controller that can be used to enable and disable ETW event capture. It understands the relationship between different ETW events in the system and presents a comprehensive visual representation of captured events. This allows detailed analyses of a wide range of system activities. WPT provides powerful interactive summary tables and graphs with dynamic grouping, sorting, and aggregation capabilities. WPT can also dump a trace in a text format that other analysis tools can consume.

The ETW traces referenced in this paper contain "Disk I/O" ETW events from the Windows kernel. The traces were broken into intervals to reduce the size of individual traces as well as to make analysis and visualization easier. The interval size was determined heuristically based on the storage activity of the workload. A post-processing script library was used to extract the workload characteristics and metrics reported in this paper. The traces analyzed for this paper contain only events related to the disk subsystem and do not have any information that can be related to the end-user; i.e., the disk traces used for our analysis are by definition anonymized from an end-user standpoint.

2.4 Trace Analysis Results

Given a block-level I/O trace, we summarize the trace by computing a number of standard metrics. Table 2 shows the most important summary metrics for the different workloads. The main load metric is **IOPS**: I/Os per second issued by the workload. IOPS is computed for each 1-second interval in the trace; we then show the mean over all the intervals, as well as the peak, defined as the 99th percentile of load seen during the trace. In general we use the peak IOPS value to compare workloads, since servers are provisioned for this load. Further, unlike TPC benchmarks, online services have high peak-to-mean ratios and hence comparing them to benchmarks using mean IOPS would be misleading.

R/W is the read/write ratio of the I/Os seen in the workload. **Seq** is the fraction of I/Os that were considered sequential, i.e., the logical blocks read or written were contiguous to the immediately previous I/O. Finally **GB** is the size of the data set accessed by the workload, which we estimate as the highest logical block number accessed expressed in units of GB. Capacity usage (GB) is important because, unlike benchmarks, provisioning for some online services can be capacity-bound rather than I/O-bound. Further, these services are scaled out and load-balanced over many

Table 2. Summary of workload metrics

Workload	Mean IOPS	Peak IOPS	R/W	Seq	GB
IM-DB	3386	4038	6.19	0.02	101
EMAIL-DB	59	610	0.69	0.00	2608
BLOB-DB	299	1030	1.67	0.11	265
MSN-DB	1056	3830	1.91	0.11	399
TPC-C	49757	52800	1.80	0.02	873
TPC-E	112654	186568	8.34	0.02	321
TPC-H	2228	11801	29.94	0.35	260

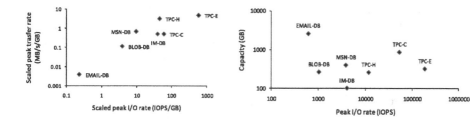

Fig. 1. Peak IOPS and capacity   **Fig. 2.** Scaled IOPS and MB/s

servers, and different services have different provisioning (e.g. number of spindles) per server as well as different numbers of servers. Hence, we cannot directly compare the raw IOPS rate across these servers. Instead, we use capacity as scaling factor, i.e., we compare "IOPS per GB of data" instead of "IOPS per server".

In addition to I/O rate we also measured the mean and peak transfer rate (measured in MB/s). However as we will see later transfer rate is in general highly correlated to I/O rate due to the fixed transfer sizes used by SQL Server. For simplicity we do not show the transfer rate in Table 2.

From Table 2, we can already see that the online services workloads differ widely both among themselves and from the TPC benchmarks. We now show this visually by plotting the workloads as points in two dimensions, using two workload metrics at a time. Note that all the graphs use log-log scales to capture the wide variation across workloads.

Figure 1 shows the workloads along the axes of capacity and peak I/O rate. We see that TPC-C and TPC-E do have much higher I/O rates relative to capacity than the other workloads, and in general there are order-of-magnitude differences between workloads. However, the absolute value of I/O rate is affected by the provisioning of the specific server; as we saw in Table 1, the different servers are provisioned with different numbers of disks. Hence when a server is part of a scale-out configuration, it is more useful to look at a scaled metric of load, i.e., I/O rate relative to the amount of data stored on that server. Figure 2 shows the I/O rate and transfer rate metrics scaled by the data size, i.e. the capacity in GB. We see here that there is indeed a very wide

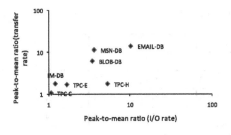 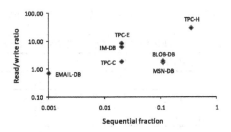

Fig. 3. Peak-to-mean ratios   **Fig. 4.** Sequentiality and R/W ratio

variation between the online services workloads, and that they also differ substantially from TPC benchmarks. Thus for a server storing a given amount of data, for example, IM-DB sees an order of magnitude less I/O load than TPC-E. We also see that the ratio of transfer rate and I/O rate is similar for most of the workloads, with the exception of TPC-H. This ratio is just the most common transfer size used by SQL Server for its I/O request, i.e. 8 KB; for TPC-H large sequential scans also result in larger transfer sizes for some I/Os.

Figure 3 shows the peak-to-mean ratio for I/O rate and transfer rate. We see that in general the TPC benchmarks and IM-DB have far lower variability than the other three. Interestingly BLOB-DB and MSN-DB have much higher variability in transfer rate than in I/O rate.

Figure 4 shows the metrics Seq (fraction of I/Os that are sequential) and R/W (read/write ratio). Here again we see a wide variation, with most workloads being read-dominated except EMAIL-DB which is write-dominated. EMAIL-DB stores e-mail metadata and thus issues several write I/Os for each metadata update. We also see a wide variation in sequentiality: ranging from TPC-H (35% sequential) to EMAIL-DB. The latter is 0% sequential (shown as 0.1% sequential to accommodate the data point on a log scale).

Finally, we are interested in diurnal patterns shown by our workloads, since these are important for server consolidation and energy savings. Clearly the notion of diurnal variation is not meaningful for TPC benchmarks, since the benchmarks do not specify any such variation. However, for two of our online services workloads — BLOB-DB and MSN-DB — we have 24-hour traces and hence can examine them for diurnal patterns.

Figures 5 and 6 show load over time for BLOB-DB and MSN-DB. We see that BLOB-DB shows a clear variation over a 24-hour period, indicating the concentration of users in different time zones. It also shows a second periodic behavior with a 1-hour period. For MSN-DB although there is substantial variation, i.e., burstiness, it is harder to identify any clear periodic behavior.

2.5 Trace Analysis Summary

In this section we compared online services workloads with TPC benchmarks across a range of I/O related metrics. We showed that they workloads vary widely among themselves — by orders of magnitude in many cases — and also differ from the TPC

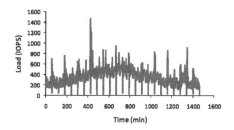

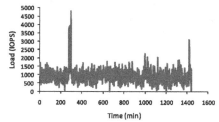

Fig. 5. Load over time (BLOB-DB)   **Fig. 6.** Load over time (MSN-DB)

benchmarks. We also showed that some workloads have periodic variations in load, and these are not captured by today's benchmarks.

3 Research Case Studies

In the previous section we analyzed I/O traces from live productions servers supporting online services. These traces were key to understanding these workloads, which differ considerably from standard benchmark workloads. In addition, traces also allow us to evaluate new designs, features, and research systems with more realistic workloads. In this section we summarize briefly the results from three different research projects[2, 3, 4] at Microsoft Research Cambridge. In each case we highlight how production workload traces allowed us to evaluate metrics and test hypotheses where benchmark-based evaluation would not have sufficed.

The research described in this section predates the traces described in Section 2, and was not specifically focused on online services. It was based on a previously collected set of traces from small and medium enterprise servers[2, 5]. The traces are ETW disk I/O traces as described in Section 2.3.

3.1 Disk Spin-Down for Energy Savings

In this study we examined the potential for saving energy in enterprise storage by powering down storage hardware during periods of idleness[2]. Previous work had claimed that there was little scope for power savings in enterprise storage since server I/O workloads had little idle time[6]. However, based on I/O traces from a range of small/medium enterprise servers, there is substantial idle time, mostly at night. This diurnal pattern reflects the user-driven load on the servers.

During periods of low load, idle times are further lengthened by *write off-loading*[2]: temporarily logging writes from several spun-down storage volumes to a single spun-up volume. With write off-loading, spinning disks down during idle periods saves 45-60% of the disk power. However, there is a response time penalty for requests to a powered-down volume, which must be spun up to service read requests. This happens rarely in the traces, but the penalty is large.

Both the costs and benefits of write off-loading depend on the variation in I/O load over time, specifically the existence of large amounts of idle time. Standard benchmarks do not capture this property and would not tell us anything about potential energy savings for real workloads. For example, TPC-C is a saturation benchmark and hence by design has little idle time at the storage level[6] (TPC-C's successor, TPC-E, has a similar, albeit lighter, steady-state I/O load).

3.2 Burst Absorption

Write off-loading can also be used during periods of high load, i.e. bursts[3]. Here the aim is not energy savings but reducing the high I/O response times seen during such bursts. A volume under heavy load can temporarily off-load writes to lightly loaded volumes: this improves performance both for writes (since they are redirected) and for reads (since they see less contention from writes. When the volume's load level subsides, the off-loaded data is reclaimed and subsequently deleted from the remote volumes. If bursts are short and have sufficient idle time in between, only a small amount of capacity is used on the remote volumes, and only for a small amount of time.

An evaluation of this technique using disk I/O traces from a large Exchange server with over 100 spindles, showed a 1.4 to 70 times reduction in response times at peak load. Note that the evaluation is only meaningful when both bursts in I/O load as well as the idle periods following them, are correctly captured. Further, the performance benefits depend on the read/write mix and the access locality of I/O during the burst. Thus the performance is strongly tied to workload-specific behavior, which is best captured by a trace.

3.3 Evaluating Solid-State Disks (SSDs)

We have also used disk I/O traces to drive a cost-benefit analysis of the potential uses of SSDs in enterprise storage[4]. The analysis is based on a tool that computes the cheapest storage configuration that will satisfy all the requirements for a given workload: capacity, random-access I/O, sequential I/O, and fault-tolerance. It considers disk-only configurations, SSD-only configurations, and hybrid configurations where SSDs are used as an intermediate tier.

To adequately provision storage for a workload, we must satisfy several requirements: capacity, random-access I/O rate, and sequential bandwidth. The best configuration is the one that satisfies all workload requirements at the lowest cost. SSDs score much higher than disks on some metrics (e.g. IOPS/$) but much lower on others (GB/$). Thus the provisioning decision depends on the demand for the different metrics, which we estimated from production workload traces. Thus while a TPC-C benchmark is always configured to be "IOPS-bound", we found that most real workloads become capacity-bound when using SSDs, due to the very high cost per GB of SSDs. Overall, we found that few workloads had a sufficiently high IOPS/GB ratio to warrant replacing disks by SSDs at current prices.

In this research we also observed one disadvantage of evaluation based on disk I/O traces. Trace replay relies on an "open loop" assumption, i.e., an assumption that the rate of I/O requests would be the same no matter what storage was used. From an open-loop I/O model we cannot compute the effect of alternate storage configurations on higher-level application performance metrics such as transaction rate. Benchmarks, on the other hand, can give these higher-level performance metrics, but do not realistically model the application. Thus we need a hybrid approach that combines the realism of traces with the "end-to-end" measurement given by benchmarks. We will explore this idea further in Section 5.

4 Tracing Guidelines

The value of tracing production servers is that they provide a very realistic picture of real user-driven workloads. However this also presents a challenge: the tracing must be done without impacting the efficient operation of the service. This section provides some recommended techniques and processes that can be used for collecting traces from production servers.

The first step in tracing production servers is establishing communication with the people who can authorize trace collection, demonstrating the value of tracing to them, and convince them of low impact on the operations team. Also one needs to find a sponsor with sufficient influence to get past the inevitable initial negative reaction, and convince the legal group that the rewards outweigh the risks. The primary legal concerns will be safeguarding company IP and anonymizing any personally identifiable information (PII). For ETW traces of storage activity, we have already convinced Microsoft Legal that traces can be sufficiently sanitized to remove PII, and thus have a very useful precedent for others to reference. Once collection has been authorized, the people gathering the actual traces must be provided with sufficient detail about the "How-To" and logistics of tracing (e.g., where to store traces, how to sanitize and transfer them). Having a clear set of guidelines and instructions as well having an automated process for tracing goes a long way to smooth this process.

Once you have one or more precedents of successful tracing efforts, convincing the next set of participants is much easier. However, it takes only one instance of a negative impact from tracing to make it extremely difficult to obtain future traces. Thus, it is wise to be very conservative during the initial phases of collecting traces – e.g., by collecting traces for shorter durations or at lower rates, by directly monitoring the performance impact of tracing, and by providing precise guidelines to the operations team. Production environments often run "stress" benchmarks for testing their deployments. Sample traces from the stress environment can help to estimate the worst case impact of tracing. Also make sure to be sensitive and responsive to the concerns expressed by the operations staff. At least initially, tracing is an imposition on their work schedule, perhaps with no proven upside and a nontrivial potential for a job-threatening downside.

When actually collecting traces there are several factors to consider: here we describe the most important ones and some guidelines to address each.

Performance Impact
Typically, the runtime tracing overhead as well as logistics such as trace size and available space need to be considered. It is a recommended best practice to take a sample trace on any production server before deployment. It is also recommended to store the trace on a separate disk or network share, if available, so tracing activity does not impact the storage I/O traffic of the real workload. In cases where this is not possible, the tracing-related I/Os can be filtered out during post processing.

For the worst case scenario, factors to consider include the maximum peak workload, the possibility of system failures, and the ability to stop trace collection in case of a real or perceived emergency. For example, ETW tracing can be stopped either programmatically or from the command line at any time during the trace collection process.

Operations Impact

Providing automated scripts for capturing traces and setting up a process for transferring the traces from the production environment reduces the actual time an operations engineer has to spend collecting the traces. The operations engineers will also need to provide information about the system configuration, especially the storage subsystem hardware, which may not be available directly to the operating system (e.g., any hardware RAID configuration, storage cache configuration, and the number of physical spindles). It is useful to know if a backup, replication, or rebalancing operation is in progress during the trace capture, or if the workload has innate periodic or phased behavior that can be tagged during trace post-processing. Long enough traces should be captured since periodic activity can have a significant impact on the characteristics of the workload.

Security and Access

The security of the production servers as well as the trace content must be considered. Typically kernel level trace collection tools need administrator privileges on servers, and they should come from a trusted source (e.g. via digital signatures). The traces may contain personally identifiable information (PII) in the form of filenames, directory paths, or process names. These same fields could also expose confidential application or hardware configuration detail. All information captured by the trace events should be disclosed beforehand and cleared by the appropriate parties. Post processing tools can sanitize and encrypt the traces or selected portions after they are captured.

Most production servers are insulated from the other systems on the corporate network. They can be accessed only from dedicated systems such as boundary servers that have additional access restrictions. If any of the servers along this chain do not have enough space to store the traces, then transferring them becomes more difficult. In one case we encountered, a boundary server had no available permanent storage space at all. This was by design, for security. The transfer of traces had to be done serially from the temporary drive of the boundary server via an automated script to iteratively check available space and transfer files one at a time. If systems along the path are under the control of different administrators with different access rights, coordinating trace transfers can be challenging.

Excessive Tracing

Sometimes trace providers can be too aggressive in collecting traces. We encountered one case where the operations team collected day-long traces from a large number of servers, exhausting the space on the trace storage server. This experience taught us to carefully select representative servers to avoid the storage and processing overhead of tracing servers with basically identical workloads.

5 Challenges

Although block I/O tracing is a very valuable tool for understanding workload performance as well as server provisioning, it is not a panacea. Here we discuss several challenges, limitations, and directions for future research.

5.1 End-to-End Tracing

Trace replay at the block I/O level is generally performed *open-loop*. This ignores feedback effects, e.g., a faster storage system could have higher overall throughput and as a result receive a higher request rate. Thus while I/O tracing can help to size the storage layer to avoid overload and give good response times, it cannot predict overall server throughput. Depending on the provisioning task, traces from other components, such as the main memory buffer cache, CPU scheduler, and network stack may also be required. Ideally, all the individual resource utilizations of each request (e.g., SQL statement) are captured, from the moment the request enters the system until it exits. Such *end-to-end* tracing is very useful for holistic system analysis. For example, we built a Resource Advisor prototype for SQL Server that, given an end-to-end trace, can answer "what-if" questions about upgrading system resources[7]. E.g., "What would be the throughput of transaction type X if the amount of memory in the system were doubled?"

In general, the idea of end-to-end tracing is that traces be collected simultaneously from multiple levels of the system. This allows maximum flexibility in characterizing the workload and its use of different system resources such as CPU, memory, network, and disk I/O. For example:

1. Traces at the SQL statement level can be used to evaluate the overall throughput of a proposed configuration.
2. Correlated traces of CPU, network, and disk usage can be used to find out which of the resources dominates throughput and latency, as well as evaluate "what-if" questions about bottleneck shifts for entire workload or a part of the workload.
3. SQL buffer cache traces can address "what-if" questions about memory sizing.

Our experience indicates that the overhead of collecting large amount of traces varies widely based on the number of events captured, the hardware configuration, the specific type of workload, and the workload intensity. The overhead can be reduced arbitrarily through sampling, i.e. selective enabling of events at runtime.

Much, though not all, of the support for end-to-end tracing on a single machine already exists today. For example, both Windows and SQL Server can post thread context switch events to ETS to enable tracking of CPU usage and control flow of concurrent threads. True end-to-end tracing would also track requests as they move across different tiers and machines on the network. This could require modification of standard network protocols to enable matching requests and events across systems, or perhaps a new layer in the network driver stack to communicate end-to-end metadata for individual requests.

5.2 Scaling and Sampling

A second limitation of trace-based evaluation is the difficulty of scaling trace replay up or down. This limitation is shared by most benchmarks. For example, in the evaluation of Everest (Section 3.2), our test bed was too small to accommodate the traces from all volumes collected. Hence, we had to "scale down" the tracing by making a decision as to which traces to incorporate (three of the volumes were chosen). Scaling up is similarly difficult. For example, if one collects traces from three volumes and has a testbed of 1000 machines, one might use some mixture or permutation of the traces from the three volumes and duplicate it 997 times. It is unclear that such scaling reflects reality.

Large-scale online services have a single application that is load-balanced across a large number of servers. Thus a good approach to scaling would be to apply statistical tests to capture similarities between traces from many servers. This would ensure that the traces remain representative. The challenge is to devise the appropriate tests for any given purpose, e.g., provisioning, simulation of new system design, etc.

5.3 Workload Model Extraction

Trace replay and simulation is more effective for capturing workload specifics than benchmarks. However, benchmarks are standardized, simple, and scalable (although typically only linearly along one dimension). To ideally represent a workload class, we would extract key features of workloads and use them to construct a parameterized workload model and hence a representative custom benchmark. The parameter values may be based actual trace characteristics, or on hypothetical workloads.

A production workload typically contains a variety of asynchronous and synchronous activities occurring in parallel. Thus a key component of modeling this complex activity is identifying the *sub-workloads*. As an example, a workload may consist of periods of heavy as well as light activity. These may be further divided into regions of read-heavy versus write-heavy activity, which may be further divided into sequential and random activity. Time-varying characteristics include not only the well-known concept of burstiness (i.e., workload intensity variations at short time scales) but also periodicity at different time scales, e.g. diurnal patterns.

Finer granularity leads to better simulation but also increases the complexity of the benchmark. It is essential to identify the point of diminishing returns, where the simulated benchmark is "close enough" to the real workload and provide the necessary level of accuracy. Tools can be written to automatically extract sub-workloads based on heuristics; to simulate these workloads through a I/O request generator; and, to compare and contrast various load metrics produced by the simulated workload against the original trace[8].

6   Conclusion

We analyzed I/O workload trace from the structured storage tier in four online services. Our analysis shows that real-world workloads have very different characteristics from TPC benchmarks in terms of basic metrics such as IOPS/GB and read/write ratios, as well as in time-varying characteristics such as peak-to-mean ratios and diurnal patterns.

We believe there is a need for greater use of traces when designing benchmarks and also when designing systems for deployment. Benchmarks should derive burstiness metrics, request mixes, and think times from real traces. They should also mimic the periodic load variations found in real workloads. This calls for more flexible and tunable benchmarks. In addition, it would be advantageous for the research community to have access not only to more realistic benchmarks, but also to the traces upon which such benchmarks are based. For example, the TPC could create and maintain a database trace repository similar to that maintained by the Storage Networking Industry Association (SNIA)[9]]. The traces used for the research described in Section 3 have been contributed to the SNIA repository. Hence, we call on the TPC to create such a repository and encourage enterprises to trace their productions systems and to make the traces (suitably anonymized and obfuscated) available for research purposes.

References

[1] Hamilton, J.: Internet-scale service efficiency (September 2008), http://mvdirona.com/jrh/TalksAndPapers/JamesRH_Ladis2008.pdf
[2] Narayanan, D., Donnelly, A., Rowstron, A.: Write off-loading: Practical power management for enterprise storage. In: Proc. USENIX Conference on File and Storage Technologies (FAST), San Jose, CA, February 2008, pp. 256–267 (2008)
[3] Narayanan, D., Donnelly, A., Thereska, E., Elnikety, S., Rowstron, A.: Everest: Scaling down peak loads through I/O off-loading. In: Proc. Symposium on Operating Systems Design and Implementation (OSDI), San Diego, CA, December 2008, pp. 15–28 (2008)
[4] Narayanan, D., Thereska, E., Donnelly, A., Elnikety, S., Rowstron, A.: Migrating enterprise storage to SSDs: analysis of tradeoffs. In: Proceedings of EuroSys 2009, Nuremberg, Germany. ACM, New York (2009)
[5] Kavalanekar, S., Worthington, B., Zhang, Q., Sharda, V.: Characterization of storage workload traces from production Windows servers. In: Proc. IEEE International Symposium on Workload Characterization (IISWC), Austin, TX, October 2008, pp. 119–128 (2008)
[6] Zhu, Q., Chen, Z., Tan, L., Zhou, Y., Keeton, K., Wilkes, J.: Hibernator: Helping disk arrays sleep through the winter. In: Proceedings of the ACM Symposium on Operating Systems Principles (SOSP 2005), Brighton, United Kingdom (October 2005)
[7] Narayanan, D., Thereska, E., Ailamaki, A.: Continuous resource monitoring for self-predicting DBMS. In: Proceedings of IEEE International Symposium on Modeling, Analysis, and Simulation of Computer and Telecommunication Systems (MASCOTS 2005), Atlanta, GA. IEEE, Los Alamitos (2005)
[8] Sankar, S., Vaid, K.: Storage characterization for unstructured data in online services applications. In: Proc. IEEE International Symposium on Workload Characterization (IISWC) (to appear)
[9] SNIA: IOTTA repository (January 2009), http://iotta.snia.org/

Issues in Benchmark Metric Selection

Alain Crolotte

Teradata Corporation, 100 N Sepulveda Blvd.
El Segundo, Ca. 90045
alain.crolotte@teradata.com

Abstract. It is true that a metric can influence a benchmark but will esoteric metrics create more problems than they will solve? We answer this question affirmatively by examining the case of the TPC-D metric which used the much debated geometric mean for the single-stream test. We will show how a simple choice influenced the benchmark and its conduct and, to some extent, DBMS development. After examining other alternatives our conclusion is that the "real" measure for a decision-support benchmark is the arithmetic mean.

1 Introduction

The purpose of this paper is to examine a basic problem facing benchmark designers when selecting a metric in the context of a decision-support benchmark. Once the database has been populated and the queries defined comes the apparently simple task to define a metric i.e. a single number that will summarize the elapsed times. The most natural way to accomplish that is to use the arithmetic mean. But, since no benchmark participant has run all the queries at this stage of the game, the usual nagging question comes up: "What if one query dominates the entire set?" To solve the outlier problem, although it has not appeared yet, a potential solution would be to define a rule such as "throw away one" by which benchmark participants would be allowed to remove their worst query time from the final result set.

Another approach to the problem of aggregating highly skewed observations could be to select a different metric that would hopefully use all the queries without being dominated. In this paper we examine potential ways to define *a priori* a metric to summarize a set of raw observations when potentially large discrepancies could occur in the value set as is potentially the case in a decision-support benchmark. In particular we will look into the choice made by the subcommittee who designed the TPC-D benchmark in tackling with this problem. We will also show that the only valid *a priori* metric for a decision-support benchmark is the arithmetic mean.

The paper is organized in 6 sections including this introduction. In section 2 we provide background information on the problem of choosing a metric. Section 3 examines potential solutions to the general problem while section 4 looks at the actual metric used by the TPC-D and examines some of the consequences of this choice. In section 5 we make the case for the arithmetic mean being the only valid alternative for a single-stream decision-support metric. Finally, a short section summarizing the conclusions of this study is provided.

R. Nambiar and M. Poess (Eds.): TPCTC 2009, LNCS 5895, pp. 146–152, 2009.
© Springer-Verlag Berlin Heidelberg 2009

2 Background

In the case of TPC-D, the subcommittee in charge of defining the benchmark chose an interesting approach for the definition of the single-stream metric based on the geometric mean but with a twist. The TPC-D benchmark specification including the metric is described in [1]. The TPC-D benchmark (now obsolete and replaced by the TPC-H benchmark) was defined in the early nineties and, at this time, the geometric mean enjoyed a deserved popularity as a metric in benchmarks. This popularity can be traced to a paper in which the authors showed that the only correct metric to summarize normalized benchmark results is the geometric mean [2]. The key here is "normalized". The numbers to be summarized in the case of a single-steam decision-support benchmark such as TPC-D are elapsed times i.e. raw numbers and therefore not normalized. In [5] for instance, it is argued that the arithmetic mean should be used when averaging times. Therefore the use of the geometric mean in this case cannot be justified on this basis unlike for the Spec benchmark (see [3] for a discussion on the relative merits of the arithmetic mean, geometric mean and harmonic mean in this context).

Aside for the so-called lack of sensitivity to outliers the geometric mean has an interesting property established in section 3. It treats all relative changes in the same way – for instance, if an observation varies by 10% the relative change in the geometric mean is the same whether the observation is large or small. The arithmetic mean has the same property but only for "absolute" improvements.

The subject of finding a single measure of performance has been debated for quite a while in the area of computer performance (see [2], [6], [7] and [8]) but the issue is eventually resolved by paying attention at the type of data is under review. The particular subject of decision-support metrics has been examined in [4].

3 Characteristics of Central Tendency

There are three basic metrics that are commonly used, (1) the arithmetic mean or simple average, (2) the geometric mean and (3), the harmonic mean – they are usually associated with basic operations namely addition, multiplication and division In this paper we will place things in a more general context. First we start with a set of n positive numbers (elapsed times) x_1, x_2, up to x_n. We assume that these observations will be weighted equally in all cases. We usually denote the arithmetic mean as m, the geometric mean as g and the harmonic mean as h. The usual formulas for these metrics are

$$m = \frac{1}{n}\sum x_i \qquad (1)$$

$$g = \left(\prod x_i\right)^{1/n} \qquad (2)$$

$$h = \frac{1}{\frac{1}{n}\sum\frac{1}{x_i}} \tag{3}$$

Given a monotonic function ϕ one can define a measure of central tendency associated with this function as follows (see also [4] and [9]) called phi-average:

$$\phi(M_\phi) = \frac{1}{n}\sum\nolimits_{i=1}^{n}\phi(x_i) \tag{4}$$

The formulas for the usual metrics can be represented this way using the function $\phi(x)=x^r$ hence we will name the phi-average associated with r-th power function the r-th power average. The arithmetic mean is obtained for r=1, the harmonic mean for r=-1 and the geometric mean is obtained as a limit case for r=0. Taking the logarithm in both sides of equation 2 we obtain an equivalent expression for the geometric mean;

$$\log g = \frac{1}{n}\sum\log x_i \tag{5}$$

To see how this formula is a limit case of equation 4 with $\phi(x)$ being x to the power r when r tends toward zero use the fact that

$$x^r = e^{r\log x} = 1 + r\log x + o(r) \tag{6}$$

Assume that all observations in (5) are constant except say x_k and take the derivative on both sides. We get dg/g=(1/n)(dx$_k$/x$_k$) and the results still holds approximately when the differentials dg and dx$_k$ are replaced by finite quantities. This establishes the geometric mean property mentioned in section 2 that a relative variation in an observation will result in the same overall variation of the geometric mean whether the observation is small or large.

Also, it can readily be established that the r-th power average is an increasing function of r so that the geometric mean is always lower than the arithmetic mean [2]. Whether we look at formula 2 or formula 5 we see that there is a very undesirable property of the geometric mean. If just one observation is equal to zero the geometric average of all the quantities is equal to zero. In other words the geometric mean puts overwhelming emphasis on small observations in cases where large or regular values are mixed with very small values. In order to solve the problem and as suggested in [4] we could use any r-th power average with r between 0 and 1 – for instance r=1/2. The corresponding formula for the one-half power average s is

$$s = \left(\sqrt{x_1} + \sqrt{x_2} + ...\sqrt{x_n}\right)^2 \tag{7}$$

While s avoids the pitfall of the discontinuity for small values exhibited by the geometric mean and reduces the influence of outliers in the high end, it is not familiar like the harmonic mean, the geometric mean, the arithmetic mean or even the 2-nd power or square power average which is so popular in Statistics. Also, it does not have meaning in terms of the problem at hand since it has the dimension of a time (like the geometric mean) but it is not a time (also like the geometric mean).

Another way to deal with the basic problem exhibited by the geometric mean with observations close to zero is to avoid those observations by adding a small positive quantity to all observations e.g. 1/1000 or 1/100. We can define a log-based mean within the framework of the ϕ-average by using the function $\phi(x) = \log(x+a)$ where a is a fixed positive integer. This new measure of central tendency g_a is called the a-displaced geometric mean and is given by the formula:

$$\log(g_a + a) = \frac{1}{n}\sum \log(x_i + a) \tag{8}$$

If a is very small, this new average has "almost" all the interesting properties of the geometric mean and avoids its unpleasant pitfall. In [4] we have shown that, for a given set of observations, the a-displaced geometric mean is an increasing function of a. So for any positive a it will be always larger than the geometric mean g. Also the arithmetic mean is a limit case for the a-displaced average when a becomes very large. Factoring a out of all quantities under the log in equation 8 and remembering that, when x is small $\log(1+x)$ is equivalent to x leads to (9) when a tends toward infinity:

$$\log a + \log(1 + \frac{g_a}{a}) = \log a + \frac{1}{n}\sum \log(1 + \frac{x_i}{a}) = \log a + \frac{1}{a}\frac{1}{n}\sum x_i + o(\frac{1}{a}) \tag{9}$$

Therefore ga/a tends towards 0 and

$$\log(1 + \frac{g_a}{a}) = \frac{g_a}{a} + o(\frac{1}{a}) = \frac{m}{a} + o(\frac{1}{a}) \tag{10}$$

Therefore, when a becomes large, the a-displaced average tends toward the arithmetic mean. In summary the a-displaced mean is an increasing function of a and is always between the geometric mean and the arithmetic mean. This makes this metric a perfect alternative among log-based measures.

4 The TPC-D Single-Stream Metric

The TPC-D benchmark consisted of 17 queries numbered Q1 through Q17 and two refresh functions UF1 and UF2. The single-stream metric is a "query per hour" rate using the inverse of the geometric mean of the query times. However, the TPC subcommittee in charge of developing the benchmark realized that very small query times would pose a problem opted for the following solution: the minimum query elapsed time that can be reported cannot be less than the largest observed query time divided by 1000. The a-displaced geometric mean was considered but not retained because it used values that were not observed ("measured" plus the displacement would be actually used instead of the "measured" values).

Very soon after the TPC-D benchmark became official, vendors started noticing that it was more advantageous to get better performance from the small queries. As a result, to get a good number one would need to have a lot of very small elapsed times in order to boost the power number based on the geometric mean. In order to increase TPC-D power stream results, a number of techniques were developed such as semantic query optimization, materialized join structures and finally aggregated single table and aggregated join structures. The use of materialized aggregated structures eventually made the benchmark useless and it was retired in 1999 leading to the TPC-H benchmark that prevents the use of materialized structures. Even though the "minimum query time" rule is still in vigor in the TPC-H benchmark it never applied since the inception of the benchmark.

Both the a-displaced average and the TPC-D single-stream metric are geometric-based and provide undue advantage to very small query times although they avoid the main pitfall. The TPC-D metric gives extra incentive to lowering the largest query but either one would be very harmful in the following case. Let us consider a real-life case of an optimization of TPC-D benchmark query 1, a full scan of the lineitem table with a large aggregation. With an easily defined pre-aggregated structure the query is reduced to scan of the structure. At scale factor 100 the size of the table is about 600 million rows while the structure is only a few thousand rows. As a result, the elapsed time goes from minutes to less than a second while the updating of the small structure has virtually no impact on the inserts (UF1) and deletes (UF2). To illustrate the impact of the approach assume for the sake of argument that all query times are 100 seconds. With query 1 time going to 0.2 second the arithmetic mean goes from 100 second to 95 seconds – a 5% improvement - while the geometric mean goes from 100 seconds to 72 seconds – a 28% improvement. Had the arithmetic mean been used, the hyper-inflation in single-stream metric may not have occurred and it is even possible that the relative rankings of the results would have been the same – this point is made in a different context in [5].

5   The Case for the Arithmetic Mean

In addition to its hyper-sensitivity to small values the geometric mean is difficult to "sell" especially in the context of a decision-support benchmark. The first difficulty is its relatively complicated formula. But the main problem is that it does not relate to a physical quantity that can be readily understood by users. In the context of decision-support, elapsed times are what a system is measured against. In a single-stream context where a number of queries are run back to back only the total elapsed time and the average query elapsed time have physical meaning. Elapsed times are absolute numbers and the only operations that make sense for users in this context are additions. In the sequel we show that under these conditions the only valid metric is the arithmetic mean.

In [2] the authors demonstrated that the geometric mean was the only valid metric to summarize normalized numbers. Using a similar argument we will show here that the only valid metric to summarize single-stream elapsed times in the context of a decision-support benchmark is the arithmetic mean. We will first establish properties that such a metric $f(x_1,x_2,..,x_n)$ should have.

If all observations are equal to some value a then the metric itself must be equal to a. In other words, whatever the value of a

$$f(a,a,...,a) = a \tag{11}$$

Since all queries must be treated equally then any permutation of the values $x_1, x_2,..,x_n$ must provide the same value, i.e. for all permutations $a_{i1}, a_{i2}, .. a_{in}$.

$$f(a_{i1}, a_{i2},.., a_{in}) = f(a_1, a_2,.., a_n) \tag{12}$$

Finally, we want the metric to have meaning in the context of absolute elapsed times i.e. we want an additive property. Indeed, if we were to run the same benchmark on two machines, then, to aggregate the results we should be able to add the individual metrics obtained on the individual machines, i.e.

$$f(a_1 + b_1, a_2 + b_2,..., a_n + b_n) = f(a_1, a_2,.., a_n) + f(b_1, b_2,..., b_n) \tag{13}$$

Using the properties above it is very easy to see that

$$a = f(a,a,...,a) = f(a,0,..,0) + f(0,a,0,..,0) + ... + f(0,0,...,a) \tag{14}$$

Hence

$$a = nf(a,0,0,...) \text{ and } f(a,0,..,0) = \frac{a}{n} \tag{15}$$

Similarly

$$f(0,b,0,..,0) = \frac{b}{n} \text{ and}$$

$$f(a,b,...) = f(a,0,...,0) + f(0,b,0,...0) + ... = \frac{a}{n} + \frac{b}{n} + .. \tag{16}$$

and consequently, the metric is equal to the arithmetic mean.

6 Conclusion

In this paper we have summarized the arguments for and against the arithmetic mean and the geometric mean. We have also provided esoteric metrics similar to the geometric mean – some new - but we made the case for simplicity and meaning. In the context of decision-support we have shown through the example of the TPC-D single stream metric that a choice made a priori due to the nature of industry standard benchmarks led to unexpected results. Finally, we hope to have shown that the best way to handle a metric for a decision-support benchmark is the arithmetic mean.

References

1. TPC BENCHMARK D (Decision Support), Transaction Processing Council,
   `http://www.tpc.org`
2. Fleming, P., Wallace, J.: How Not to Lie With Statistics: The Correct Way to Summarize Benchmarks. Comm. ACM 29(3), 218–221 (1986)
3. Licea-Kane, B.: `http://www.spec.org/gwpg/gpc.static/geometric.html`
4. Crolotte, A.: Issues in Metric Selection and the TPC-D Single Stream Power,
   `http://www.tpc.org`
5. Smith, J.: Characterizing Computer Performance with a Single Number. Communications of of the ACM 31(10) (October 1988)
6. Kurian John, L.: More on Finding a Single Number to indicate Overall Performance of a Benchmark Suite. ACM SIGARCH Computer Architecture News 32 (March 2004)
7. Citron, D., Hurani, D., Gnadrey, A.: The Harmonic or Geometric Mean: Does it Really Matter? ACM SIGARCH Computer Architecture News 34(4) (September 2006)
8. Mashey, J.: War of the benchmark Means: Time for a Truce. ACM SIGARCH Computer Architecture News 32(4) (September 2004)
9. Calot, G.: Cours de Statistique Descriptive, Dunod, Paris (1964)

Benchmarking Query Execution Robustness

Janet L. Wiener, Harumi Kuno, and Goetz Graefe

Hewlett-Packard Labs, Palo Alto, CA 94304, USA
{janet.wiener,harumi.kuno,goetz.graefe}@hp.com

Abstract. Benchmarks that focus on running queries on a well-tuned database system ignore a long-standing problem: adverse runtime conditions can cause database system performance to vary widely and unexpectedly. When the query execution engine does not exhibit resilience to these adverse conditions, addressing the resultant performance problems can contribute significantly to the total cost of ownership for a database system in over-provisioning, lost efficiency, and increased human administrative costs. For example, focused human effort may be needed to manually invoke workload management actions or fine-tune the optimization of specific queries.

We believe a benchmark is needed to measure query execution robustness, that is, how adverse or unexpected conditions impact the performance of a database system. We offer a preliminary analysis of barriers to query execution robustness and propose some metrics for quantifying the impact of those barriers. We present and analyze results from preliminary tests on four real database systems and discuss how these results could be used to increase the robustness of query processing in each case. Finally, we outline how our efforts could be expanded into a benchmark to quantify query execution robustness.

Keywords: robust query processing, robust query execution, data warehouses, operational business intelligence.

1 Introduction

Database system performance may vary widely and unexpectedly in response to runtime conditions. We understand *robustness* as the ability of the database to perform well under a variety of conditions, including adverse runtime conditions such as unexpected data skew or resource contention. While traditional benchmarks run specific queries on well-tuned databases and measure their raw performance, we believe that measuring robustness is as or more important: it is seldom possible to tune a database for all of the runtime conditions that will be encountered. Quantifying how performance degrades across a wide variety of conditions highlights situations where a small increase in adversity results in an inordinate impact on performance.

We distinguish three types of robustness. Query optimizer robustness is the ability of the optimizer to choose a good plan as expected conditions change, for example, as statistics change to reflect a growing database. Query execution

R. Nambiar and M. Poess (Eds.): TPCTC 2009, LNCS 5895, pp. 153–166, 2009.

robustness is the ability of the query execution engine to process a given plan efficiently under different runtime conditions. It can be used to examine a single plan or operator or to compare different algorithms for the same logical operator, such as join or sort, and identify opportunities for algorithmic improvements. Workload management robustness characterizes how vulnerable database system performance is to unexpected query performance. For example, if skew causes a query to use a thousand times more resources than expected, what is the impact on the system as a whole? In this paper, we focus on how to test for query execution robustness.

Encountering unexpected and adverse conditions has become more and more common recently. Anecdotal reports from multiple database vendors and customers indicate that the same query often performs differently when run at different times: different times of day, concurrently with different other queries, or sometimes even when conditions appear to be the same. The varying performance usually comes as an unexpected and often unpleasant surprise. As data warehouses become more operational, mixing transactions, report queries, maintenance, and ad hoc queries in increasing numbers, the number of surprises is increasing, too. The goal of robustness testing is to get a handle on these surprises — and eliminate as many as possible.

Database software developers who measure the impact of adverse conditions can focus on making their algorithms more robust and on containing the severity of performance problems. They can use robustness tests to motivate, track, and protect algorithmic improvements. Database hardware vendors can use robustness tests to improve their sizing and provisioning tools: by gauging the cost of not having enough resources, they can make intelligent decisions about how much hardware is needed for a given workload. Finally, customers can use robustness results to choose databases with *reliable* performance, knowing that they will be able to add or change their workloads at will without significantly increasing their total cost of ownership.

Measuring robustness is difficult. To evaluate robustness, we need to run the same query using the same physical implementation under many different sets of conditions.

Traditional performance measures focus on the impact that a system configuration has on performance. For example, potential customers might use TPC benchmark results in order to derive a performance per dollar spent on software and hardware metric for comparing the performance of databases from various vendors. Our intent is to consider the administrative price for performance — to develop a metric that captures the relationship between cost of ownership and database performance. Our hope is that future database benchmarks include measures of query robustness.

The rest of the paper is structured as follows. In Section 2, we describe existing benchmarks and how they differ from a robustness benchmark, as well as other work in robustness. In Section 3, we identify the different types of adverse conditions that can affect query execution robustness and how to vary them together to measure robustness. We present several metrics for quantifying robustness in

Section 4. We then present robustness results for sort queries on three different database systems in Section 5. Finally, in Section 6, we offer our conclusions about the importance of measuring and achieving robust query processing. We hope that future benchmarks will include measures of robustness.

2   Related Work

2.1   Current Benchmarks

We want to measure how database execution is impacted by adverse conditions. Current benchmarks measure how fast a database can complete some well-defined mix of queries under a single set of conditions. For example, the TPC suite of commercial database benchmarks specifies standard workloads and scenarios that can be used to provide relative price/performance comparisons of database systems [14,15]. However, by reporting the speed for compiling and running each query, these benchmarks do not isolate query processing performance: they combine the effects of the query optimizer, the query execution engine, and the hardware into a single number. We control for the effects of the query optimizer by forcing a particular plan. Although the hardware affects the performance, we are more concerned with the shape of the performance curve than the actual speed numbers. Different scale factors of these benchmarks can be used to control the amount of data processed, but there are no controls for resource availability, e.g., the mount of memory or I/O contention.

2.2   Query Processing Robustness

A number of researchers evaluate the runtime performance of implementations of individual operators but do not attempt to use this information to compare how performance degrades as conditions change. For example, Schneider and DeWitt analyze and compare four parallel join algorithms under a variety of conditions, including a comparison of how their performance changes with varying amounts of available memory [18]. Gupta et al. compare the performance of property map and bitmap indexing techniques, including a discussion of how parameters such as block size, selectivity, and cardinality impact performance [7]. Cole and Graefe define primitives that enable dynamic plans to be constructed at compile-time while postponing certain decisions until run-time so as to accommodate errors in selectivity estimation, unknown run-time bindings for host variables in embedded queries, and unpredictable availability of resources [3,5]. However, the focus of such efforts is entirely on the run-time behavior of the operators themselves, as opposed to our own goal of enabling the evaluation and comparison of the robustness characteristics of different operator implementations.

2.3   Query Optimizer Robustness

Many researchers focus on the query optimizers compile-time choices and propose methods by which the query optimizer can detect and compensate for errors in cardinality estimation. Systems like COMET and the IBM LEO (LEarning Optimizer) and, more recently, Microsoft SQL Server use monitoring and feedback to repair incorrect cardinality estimates and statistics [12,19,20]. Babu, Bizarro, Kabra, Markl, and their co-authors propose different ways to recover from bad cardinality estimates by dynamically re-optimizing or otherwise dynamically changing the query's plan [1,2,13]. Similarly, Ioannidis et al. propose parametric query optimization methods whereby multiple alternative plans are identified at compile-time, after which an actual plan is selected at run-time when the actual parameter values are known [10].

2.4   Database System Robustness

There are also related efforts to achieve database system robustness that treat query processing internals as a black box. Robust physical design endeavors to make good physical design decisions despite uncertain information about workload characteristics [4]. Workload management creates policies to cope with unpredictable queries while still meeting service level objectives, but does not modify the database engine [11].

2.5   Visualizing Robustness

Haritsa et al. [9,8,16,17] visualize query optimizer robustness. Their papers graph the compile-time choices of database query optimizers over the relational selectivity space. They then examine the area each query plan covers as well as the estimated cost of those plans. In [9], they explore how to identify "robust" plans, by which they mean a single plan whose estimated cost is within a certain threshold (e.g., 20%) of all of the "best" plans across the entire selectivity space. If no single plan meets that threshold, then they would "fail" to find a robust plan and stick with the original plan.

Our interest, on the other hand, started with capturing and visualizing query execution robustness. In [6] we graph runtime measurements of how a simple selection query plans performance degrades as work increases or resources decrease. In this paper, we extend the work to more formal metrics to evaluate the robustness of a plan and to more types of queries.

3   Adverse Runtime Conditions

Robustness tries to quantify how algorithms degrade under adverse runtime conditions. In this section, we spell out the different kinds of adverse conditions. We then consider how to vary these conditions individually and together to understand their impact on an algorithm's performance.

3.1   What Are They?

Adverse conditions fall into three broad categories. The first, the size of the input, stems solely from the database contents. The other two occur when multiple queries are run simultaneously. Any two queries (or any other programs run on the same machine as the database system) may create resource contention. Concurrency conflicts occur only when two simultaneous queries require the same data. We discuss each category in turn.

Different Input Sizes. Some algorithms are reputed to run in $O(n)$ (or $O(n\log n)$ or $O(n^2)$) time, where n is the number of rows in the input data. Testing for robustness aims to confirm that the algorithm's actual performance curve is linear (or logarithmic, etc) — and if not, where it deviates from linear and by how much. We therefore need to run the algorithm for multiple values of n.

Scan is an example of an algorithm whose behavior is usually, but not necessarily always, linear. Read-ahead or sharing among concurrent scans might break down depending on table or index sizes. Such break-downs might lead to very surprising query performance. Its input size can be controlled either by changing the size of the scanned table or by controlling the fraction of the table that is read (using query selectivity). Note that varying selectivity to control the amount of data needs to be done carefully: if non-contiguous rows are required or an index is used, the effect is different than that of simply scanning a smaller table. In our experiments in Section 5.2, we use tables of different scale factors to vary the input size.

To test the robustness of an operator with two inputs, such as join, it is necessary to vary both input sizes, preferably independently.

Resource Contention. Resource contention also affects the execution time of an algorithm. For example, a sort algorithm that has enough memory to hold all of its input will run much faster than the same algorithm given half as much memory as input data. The amount of memory available for an operator to use, the number of pages in the buffer pool that it can use, and the available I/O bandwidth may all be constrained by other queries executing concurrently. (They may also be affected by other processes on the same machine(s) as the database system.) To test robustness against resource availability, it is necessary to contrain artificially the amount of the resource available. For example, in some databases, we can constrain the total size of the buffer pool. We therefore run the query in isolation multiple times, each time with a different size buffer pool.

Concurrency Conflicts. Concurrency conflicts occur when a query prevents another query from making progress. Lock conflicts are the most common example, other than resource conflicts, which are covered above. In read only scenarios, lock conflicts are not an issue. However, even data warehouses are moving toward continuous incremental appending and updating of data. So far, we have been concentrating on measuring the robustness of queries run in isolation. We therefore do not discuss how to measure lock conflicts here.

3.2   How to Explore Their Impact?

Ideally, we would like to acquire a full picture of how the operators implemented by the query executor perform across the full spectrum of possible runtime conditions. To do this, one could run the same individual test query many times, systematically varying each potentially adverse condition in turn. In reality, a benchmark can include only a finite number of queries, and these must complete in a determinate amount of time. Also, with some database systems, it may be difficult to control certain runtime conditions.

Our approach is to identify the regions of the space of possible runtime adverse conditions that are likely to contain features of interest, and to focus our queries in those regions, while also providing enough coverage over the rest of the space to acquire a baseline for assessing performance degradation.

In the experiments we present here, we have thus far focused on the relationship between input size and memory contention. Our hypothesis is that memory contention and disk usage are both heavily influenced by this relationship.

4   Robustness Metrics

We argue that future TPC benchmarks should include "robustness" in their characterizations of database performance. In the previous section, we discussed barriers to query execution robustness. In this section, we propose metrics to characterize how resilient database systems are to these barriers and discuss how to interpret them.

Traditional performance measures focus on the impact that a system configuration has on performance. For example, potential customers sometimes use TPC benchmark results in order to derive a performance per dollar metric for comparing the performance of databases from various vendors. Analyzing performance per dollar can yield a marginal utility function that indicates how much additional performance another dollar will purchase for any given price point. For example, if the data accessed by a set of queries fits into 200 MB of memory, then the first 200 MB of memory allocated to the workload will result in a much bigger performance payoff than the second.

Our intent is to develop similar trade-offs for decisions that lead to query execution robustness. In particular, we focus on how to measure the following characteristics of query execution robustness:

- *Optimality.* How much does performance vary between the algorithms used to implement a given function or plan fragment? How does the cost function of the implementation being evaluated compare to that of the best known implementation for any given set of data and runtime resource availability conditions?
- *Consistency.* How much does performance of a given implementation of a function or plan fragment vary across widely differing runtime conditions? Are there regions of runtime conditions where performance is markedly sub-optimal?
- *Graceful degradation.* To what degree can minor differences in runtime conditions significantly impact performance? For example, is it difficult to make resource allocation decisions based on performance expectations because there are regions where a small change in input cardinality will have an inordinately large impact on performance?

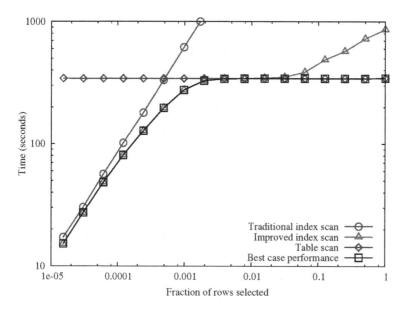

Fig. 1. Elapsed execution times for three methods of selecting rows from a table. The amount of memory is fixed. If it were not, we would plot (number of rows) / (amount of memory) on the x axis.

In order to evaluate these characteristics, we create a set of database query plans and run each plan repeatedly while varying input sizes and runtime conditions and collecting performance statistics. We then plot absolute performance against runtime conditions for each plan (e.g., elapsed time against work done and resources used).

For example, the graph in Figure 1 shows execution times for selecting rows from a table (TPC-H line items, about 60M rows) for a variety of selectivities (result sizes) on a well-known database system. Selectivities and execution times both use logarithmic scales. Query result sizes differ by a factor of 2 between data points. We will use this experiment as a running example through the rest of this section.

The performance of three query execution plans is shown. One plan is a traditional table scan. Its performance is constant across the entire range of selectivities but for small result sizes it is unacceptably slow compared to the index scans, which touch only a few pages rather than the whole table. The traditional index scan, retrieves each row (in random order) as soon as it retrieves its row id from the index. It is unacceptably slow for moderate and large result sizes because it needs so many random reads. Its cost is so high that it is not even shown across the entire range of selectivities. The "improved" index scan algorithm first retrieves all of the row ids from the index, then sorts them, then retrieves the rows in sequential order. The cost of the improved index scan remains competitive with the table scan for much longer, as long as the set of row ids retrieved from the index fits in memory. When that set does not fit in memory, which happens at the 1/12 selectivity point on the x axis in this experiment, the sort spills to disk and the elapsed time rises with the amount of data retrieved.

4.1   Optimality

To measure optimality, we plot the best performance of all known algorithms at each point in the search space. Then, for each algorithm, we calculate the geometric mean of the algorithm's performance divided by the best seen performance for each measurement point. For example, Figure 2 shows the geometric mean computed for three query execution plans shown in Figure 1.

Figure 2 shows that traditional index scan performs about ten times worse than optimal, when averaged over the search space. The improved index scan and table scan are both, on average, about double the best time (averaged using geometric mean). This factor of two indicates that there is still significant room for improvement in the existing algorithms. The improved index scan appears better than the table scan. However, had we experimented with much larger input sizes, it is likely that the improved index scan's performance would have degraded rapidly as its sort spilled to disk.

4.2   Consistency

To measure consistency, we calculate the variance of the performance of each algorithm and compare it to the variance of the best case performance. For example, Figure 3 shows the variance of the three execution plans shown previously.

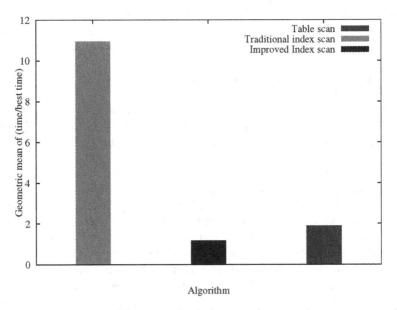

Fig. 2. Geometric mean of ($measured time / best time$) across the entire range of selectivities for the algorithms shown in Figure 1

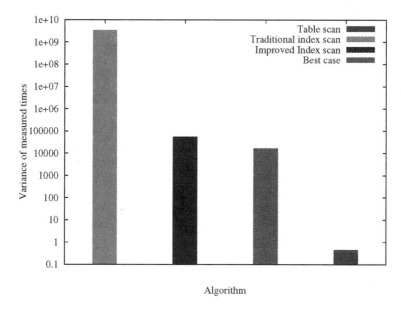

Fig. 3. Variance of times for each algorithm across the entire range of selectivities

4.3   Graceful Degradation

In order to evaluate how gracefully performance is impacted as conditions degrade, we calculate the marginal utility function, which measures the curvature of the performance graph. Marginal utility lets us answer the question: how much would a given change in runtime conditions impact performance for various starting system conditions?

We calculate the first and second derivative of each algorithm's performance curve to get its marginal utility. The first derivative captures the impact of changes in runtime conditions on performance. The second derivative indicates the rate at which performance changes across runtime conditions. A monotonically non-increasing marginal utility function indicates a steady rate of change. However, an ill-shaped (e.g., convex) utility function or an increasing marginal utility function can indicate an irregularly-spaced search space with local minima that can be expensive to explore. Ill-shaped functions increase the chances that the query optimizer will select an inappropriate implementation for runtime conditions.

5   Experiments

To develop our approach, we ran experiments testing the query execution robustness of operator implementations on four instances of three different database systems. In earlier work [6], we reported on the robustness of selection queries that used the scan and index-scan operators (and sometimes forms of join to combine multiple index scans) of these same database systems. In this paper, we report briefly on the robustness of sort operators.

The most important factor for the performance of any sort operator is the ratio of input size to memory. If input data completely fits in memory, then quicksort can be used; if not, then an external sort incurs I/O costs.

The metrics we described in Section 4 were chosen to answer questions such as:

- How *optimal* is performance in various regions? How does each implementation's performance compare to that of other implementations in similar circumstances? How much better could the execution be under a set of given runtime conditions with a different implementation of sort?
- How *consistent* is performance across runtime conditions? How does the number of rows sorted per second vary with input size?
- How *gracefully* does the sort implementation's performance degrade as input data size exceeds allocated memory? If the input data size contains just a few more rows than fit into memory, does performance plunge?

5.1   Set Up

We wanted to run each query on each system while tightly controlling input sizes and resource availability. However, it was difficult to control memory allocation: in one system, the "knob" for memory did not work properly, and in another, the file system buffered the database I/O, so that the effects of restricting the database memory where shielded. We therefore held the memory and buffer pool sizes constant as best we could and cleared the buffer pools (both database and file system) between queries.

For each system, we ran each query in isolation so that there was no resource contention. We varied the input sizes such that the smallest input size fit in the operator's allocated memory and the maximum size input tested was bigger than the total memory for the machine. For systems where we could dictate how much memory was available to sort, we ran each query in isolation while systematically varying input sizes and allocated memory.

For the first system tested, our data was the TPC-H *lineitem* table, which we created at scale factors 0.001, 0.003, 0.01, 0.03, 0.1, 0.3, 1, 3, and 10. The scale factor 1 table is approximately 1 GB in each database system.

We ran the query *select * from lineitem_$sf order by $skey asc* for each scale factor *sf* and for the two sort keys *L_partkey* and *L_comment*, an integer and a string, respectively. We used each database's variant of *last* with the queries to avoid trying to write or store in memory the entire output of sort.

For the second system we wanted to use the same tables and queries (and will have done so by the time this paper is published). However, we did not have the opportunity to load those tables. Instead, we ran queries of the form *select * from facttable where facttable.clusteredindexcolumn < constant order by facttable.nonindexedcolumn* against a custom fact table that was designed to facilitate testing of this nature. We used the selectivity of the clustered index column to control the amount of data being sorted.

5.2   Results for Sort Operator

Figure 4 shows the sort performance on one system as we vary the table size. The two curves show sorting on the integer vs. string sort keys. Memory was held constant at 4 MB and the sort implementation spills all of the data to external runs as soon as the data does not fit in memory. We expected to see a sharp increase in elapsed time between the approximately 3 and 10 MB tables (scale factors 0.003 and 0.01). However, the performance curve clearly appears linear. Why? The answer lies in the file system buffering. Although we were able to restrict the memory used by the database, the database runs on top of the file system. The file system automatically used as much of the machine's 8 GB of memory as it could to buffer the sort runs. The file system's buffering degrades gracefully, spilling just one more page to disk as the runs overflow its buffer pool, which causes the linear performance curve.

Figure 5 shows the sort performance for a different sort implementation on a different database system and with a different data schema. For this system, note the dramatic drop in performance when the data no longer fits in memory. This cliff indicates that there is a great risk in underestimating the amount of data and hence amount of memory that the sort needs: being wrong by only a few rows could cause the sort operation to take nearly five times longer than expected. Furthermore, while the query optimizer can anticipate such a cliff, its exact location depends on the amount of memory, which is not known until runtime, and the amount of data, which is subject to errors in cardinality estimation. Resource contention can reduce the amount of available memory to a small

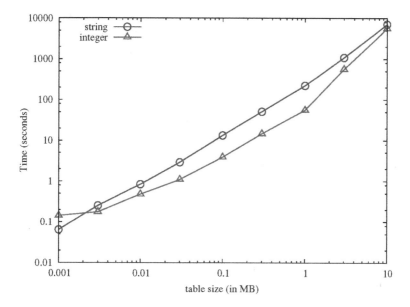

Fig. 4. Performance vs. data size for a sort implementation that appears to degrade gracefully

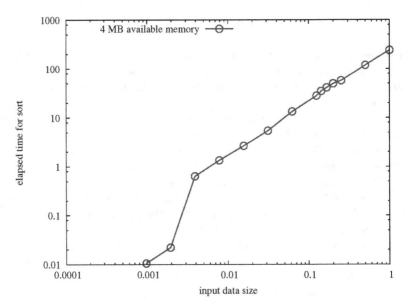

Fig. 5. Performance to data size graph for a sort implementation that does not degrade gracefully

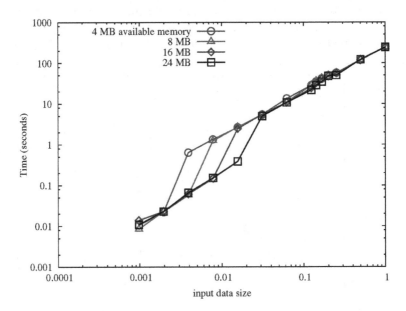

Fig. 6. The point at which the sort input spills to disk and performance degrades suddenly depends on the amount of available memory

fraction of what was anticipated and multiple levels of intermediate results can compound cardinality estimation errors.

Since we could control memory allocation on this system, we also ran the sort queries with different memory allocations. Figure 6 shows how performance degrades as available memory decreases. It illustrates how memory contention changes the location of the critical point where a small increase in data size causes a major drop in performance.

6   Conclusions and Future Work

Database administrators today spend a significant amount of time and effort resolving problems caused by adverse runtime conditions. We propose that future database benchmarks should consider including robustness in their performance measures.

Fundamentally, we identify three types of robustness: query optimizer robustness, query execution robustness, and workload managment robustness. Our focus here is on how to measure and evaluate query execution robustness, which we define as the ability of the query execution engine to process a given plan efficiently under a spectrum of runtime conditions.

We have run preliminary tests on a number of different systems, and present results and initial conclusions. We discuss how to use our measures to evaluate various aspects of robustness. For example, if you care about how predictable performance is (e.g., can a small error in estimated cardinality have a large impact on performance?), look at the curvature of the degradation function. If you care about the degree to which performance depends on conditions (e.g., does performance change dramatically with resource availability?) look at the slope of the function. If you care about the degree to which performance depends on the optimizer's plan choices, compare the performance curves of various plans for the same query.

We intend that database software developers should be able to use query execution robustness measures to motivate, track, and protect algorithmic improvements, and that database hardware vendors will be able to use robustness tests to improve their sizing and provisioning tools. We also believe that execution robustness measures can inform workload management systems. Last, but not least, we hope that customers will eventually be able to use robustness measures to gain an understanding of the total cost of ownership that their workloads will incur on various database systems.

References

1. Babu, S., Bizarro, P., DeWitt, D.: Proactive re-optimization with rio. In: SIG-MOD 2005: Proceedings of the 2005 ACM SIGMOD international conference on Management of data, pp. 936–938. ACM, New York (2005)
2. Bizarro, P., Babu, S., DeWitt, D., Widom, J.: Content-based routing: different plans for different data. In: VLDB 2005: Proceedings of the 31st international conference on Very large data bases, pp. 757–768. VLDB Endowment (2005)

3. Cole, R.L., Graefe, G.: Optimization of dynamic query evaluation plans. In: SIG-MOD 1994: Proceedings of the 1994 ACM SIGMOD international conference on Management of data, pp. 150–160. ACM, New York (1994)
4. El Gebaly, K., Aboulnaga, A.: Robustness in automatic physical database design. In: EDBT (2008)
5. Graefe, G.: Query evaluation techniques for large databases. ACM Comput. Surv. 25(2), 73–169 (1993)
6. Graefe, G., Kuno, H.A., Wiener, J.L.: Visualizing the robustness of query execution. In: CIDR (2009)
7. Gupta, A., Davis, K.C., Grommon-Litton, J.: Performance comparison of property map and bitmap indexing. In: DOLAP 2002: Proceedings of the 5th ACM international workshop on Data Warehousing and OLAP, pp. 65–71. ACM, New York (2002)
8. Harish, D., Darera, P.N., Haritsa, J.R.: On the production of anorexic plan diagrams. In: VLDB 2007: Proceedings of the 33rd international conference on Very large data bases, pp. 1081–1092. VLDB Endowment (2007)
9. Harish, D., Darera, P.N., Haritsa, J.R.: Identifying robust plans through plan diagram reduction. In: VLDB, pp. 1124–1140 (2008)
10. Ioannidis, Y.E., Ng, R.T., Shim, K., Sellis, T.K.: Parametric query optimization. VLDB Journal 6(2), 132–151 (1997)
11. Krompass, S., Kuno, H., Dayal, U., Kemper, A.: Dynamic workload management for very large data warehouses: Juggling feathers and bowling balls. In: VLDB (2007)
12. Markl, V., Lohman, G.: Learning table access cardinalities with LEO. In: SIG-MOD 2002: Proceedings of the 2002 ACM SIGMOD international conference on Management of data, pp. 613–613. ACM, New York (2002)
13. Markl, V., Raman, V., Simmen, D., Lohman, G., Pirahesh, H., Cilimdzic, M.: Robust query processing through progressive optimization. In: SIGMOD 2004: Proceedings of the 2004 ACM SIGMOD international conference on Management of data, pp. 659–670. ACM, New York (2004)
14. Othayoth, R., Poess, M.: The Making of TPC-DS. In: Proc. of the 32nd Intl. Conf. on Very Large Data Bases (VLDB), pp. 1049–1058 (2006)
15. Poess, M., Floyd, C.: New tpc benchmarks for decision support and web commerce. SIGMOD Rec. 29(4) (2000)
16. Reddy, N., Haritsa, J.R.: Analyzing plan diagrams of database query optimizers. In: VLDB 2005: Proceedings of the 31st international conference on Very large data bases, pp. 1228–1239. VLDB Endowment (2005)
17. Sarda, P., Haritsa, J.R.: Green query optimization: taming query optimization overheads through plan recycling. In: VLDB 2004: Proceedings of the Thirtieth international conference on Very large data bases, pp. 1333–1336. VLDB Endowment (2004)
18. Schneider, D.A., DeWitt, D.J.: A performance evaluation of four parallel join algorithms in a shared-nothing multiprocessor environment. SIGMOD Rec. 18(2), 110–121 (1989)
19. Stillger, M., Lohman, G.M., Markl, V., Kandil, M.: LEO - db2's learning optimizer. In: VLDB 2001: Proceedings of the 27th International Conference on Very Large Data Bases, pp. 19–28. Morgan Kaufmann Publishers Inc., San Francisco (2001)
20. Zhang, N., Haas, P.J., Josifovski, V., Lohman, G.M., Zhang, C.: Statistical learning techniques for costing XML queries. In: VLDB 2005: Proceedings of the 31st international conference on Very large data bases, pp. 289–300. VLDB Endowment (2005)

Benchmarking Database Performance in a Virtual Environment

Sharada Bose[1], Priti Mishra[2], Priya Sethuraman[2], and Reza Taheri[2]

[1] Hewlett-Packard, Cupertino
[2] VMware Inc., Palo Alto
sharada_bose@hp.com, {pmishra, psethuraman, rtaheri}@vmware.com

Abstract. Data center consolidation, for power and space conservation, has driven the steady development and adoption of virtualization technologies. This in turn has lead to customer demands for better metrics to compare virtualization technologies. The technology industry has responded with standardized methods and measures for benchmarking hardware and software performance with virtualization. This paper compares the virtualization technologies available today and existing benchmarks to measure them. We describe some real-life data center scenarios that are not addressed by current benchmarks and highlight the need for virtualization workloads that incorporate database-heavy computing needs. We present data from experiments running existing TPC database workloads in a virtualized environment and demonstrate that virtualization technologies are available today to meet the demands of the most resource–intensive database application. We conclude with ideas to the TPC for a benchmark that can effectively measure database performance in a virtual environment.

Keywords: virtualization technology, virtual machines, virtual machine monitors, server consolidation, software systems, performance, benchmarking.

1 Introduction

Data centers are adopting virtualization technologies for the many benefits they offer: power and space consolidation, live migration, high availability, and fault tolerance. A growing number of users are running resource-intensive database applications inside virtual machines (VM). Not surprisingly, there is now a critical need for benchmarks to evaluate the database performance in a virtual environment.

In this paper, we explore how virtualization has evolved from being a platform to host multiple operating environments on proprietary hardware into a technology which supports vendor-independent operating systems on generic x86 servers. We show how virtualization technologies are used and how this in turn has triggered innovations in hardware, operating system and application software technology.

We present an overview of benchmarks available for evaluating virtualized performance and highlight what is needed to effectively benchmark databases in a virtual environment. We present results that show that current virtualization technologies can provide excellent performance to VMs running intensive database

R. Nambiar and M. Poess (Eds.): TPCTC 2009, LNCS 5895, pp. 167–182, 2009.
© Springer-Verlag Berlin Heidelberg 2009

workloads. Based on this experience, we conclude with ideas to the Transaction Processing Council (TPC) for databases benchmarks for virtual environments.

2   Evolution of Virtualization

IBM's VM operating system [4] permitted the execution of a variety of IBM operating systems in multiple virtual machines on a single hardware platform. Virtualization on the Intel x86 architecture was introduced in the late 1990s [5, 9, 12]. What started out as a means of allowing multiple Linux and Windows operating systems to execute simultaneously on a single PC has evolved into the availability of enterprise-class *hypervisor* operating systems from multiple vendors, including VMware, Microsoft, Xen, KVM, Virtual Iron, etc., enabling users to serve multiple operating environments on a single enterprise-class server.

2.1   Virtualization Technologies

Virtualization technologies available today vary in how they exploit the virtualization-specific hardware features in the latest generation of x86 processors and non-x86-based processors, their reliance on paravirtualization (see section 2.3), the number of supported guest operating systems, and the richness of the ecosystems around the hypervisor. In this paper, we will limit ourselves to x86-based virtualization technologies and solutions.

2.2   How Virtualization Is Used Today

Originally x86 virtualization allowed a computing enthusiast to run multiple operating systems concurrently on a single PC. Virtualization has now grown into an indispensible technology and is used to gain improved business efficiencies such as:

- Consolidating multiple operating environments onto one server. Each VM utilizes a fraction of the computing resources of a server, drastically reducing capital expenditure. Power, cooling, and space costs are a major concern and reducing the number of physical servers also results in lower operating expenses.
- The ability to migrate a VM [10] to a new physical server while the applications on the VM continue to be in use, freeing the original server for maintenance operations
- The ability to migrate VMs live between hosts allows for a rich set of load balancing and resource management features. Virtualization is the fundamental enabling technology behind cloud computing.
- Achieving high availability (HA) by allowing a VM to be restarted on a new server if the server running the VM fails [14]. Virtualization-enabled HA allows a few generic servers to act as the backup for a large number of active servers because the properties of the operating environment are captured in the VM.
- Fault-tolerance on generic servers without hardware fault-tolerance features [17]. Two VMs are run in lockstep as is done in traditional hardware fault-tolerant architectures. The Virtual Machine Monitor (VMM) ensures externally-visible output, e.g., network packets, are sent out from only one VM, but all VMs receive copies of incoming external stimuli, e.g., reads from disk.

2.3 Virtualization-Motivated Technology Development

The x86 architecture was not designed with virtualization in mind. Thus, the earliest virtualization technologies relied exclusively on *Binary Translation (BT)*. Later advances in the x86 architecture have introduced hardware features that provide significant performance improvements over binary translation for many workloads.

2.3.1 Binary Translation

VMware's Binary Translation technology (BT) [2,6], pioneered in 1998, runs the guest instructions through a just-in-time binary translator in the VMM. To optimize performance, the VMM enables direct execution of the guest's user mode instructions by the processor. User mode instructions should run as fast as they would on native hardware. Kernel mode instructions have to be inspected and translated by the VMM before execution. Although the term binary translation might suggest a low-performance, interpretive execution mode, in practice most guest instructions are executed without intervention from the VMM. Performance can be well over 90% of native performance for guest applications that execute mostly in user mode.

2.3.2 Hardware Support for Instruction Set Virtualization

As the popularity of virtualization increased, x86 vendors introduced virtualization support features. VT-x from Intel and AMD-V from AMD increased the number of guest operating system instructions that can be executed without VMM intervention. With VT-x and AMD-V, the processor runs the guest's instructions without an initial inspection by the VMM. When one of the privileged instructions is encountered, the execution stops, and control is passed to the VMM to emulate the instruction against the VM state, then the processor resumes executing the guest instructions directly.

Hardware assist is not only a great contributor to performance, it can simplify the implementation of the virtualization infrastructure. However, HV mode has not replaced BT completely. One reason is that HV mode is not always faster than binary translation. Switching from direct execution mode to giving the control back to the VMM (a *VM exit*) is an expensive operation [1]. So for certain applications, binary translation may be faster than HV. Also, on some older hardware platforms, binary translation is the only available option.

2.3.3 Hardware Support for Memory Virtualization

The dependence of DBMS workload performance on good memory management is well understood and accounted for in DBMS software design. Adding the hypervisor in the software stack has a significant impact in this area: the guest OS no longer directly controls physical machine memory and the hypervisor is responsible for managing how this memory is shared by several VMs [18,21]. This has lead to the evolution of hardware support for memory features in current processors.

Operating systems translate virtual addresses to physical addresses (VA to PA) using page tables. But the guest VM's PAs have to further be translated to the host system's Machine Addresses (MA). To facilitate this additional step without hardware support, traditional VMMs maintain a set of *shadow page tables* that map the VA directly to MA. The VMM loads the VA-MA translation into the TLB such that when the guest is running, a TLB hit on a memory access will result in the direct generation of the MA, and the correct host memory location is accessed. This is done without the intervention of the VMM except for certain manipulations of the guest page tables. However, handling of these rare cases by the VMM is expensive.

Intel's EPT and AMD's RVI allow the VMM to maintain a *nested page table* of PA to MA mappings, and expose that to the hardware. On a TLB miss, the processor uses both the guest VM's page table and the VMM's nested page table to service the miss. This drastically reduces the need for the VMM to intervene in the manipulation of page tables. The need to walk two page tables increases the cost of TLB miss processing. For most application, the net is a positive gain in performance [16].

2.3.4 Paravirtualization

While it is possible to run an unmodified guest operating system in a VM, it may not always have the best performance. Modification of the guest operating system for better performance is called *paravirtualization*.

A common use of paravirtualization is in the design and implementation of virtualization-aware device drivers. In VMware ESX environments, for example, users typically load paravirtualized drivers for the mouse, keyboard, screen, and the networking interface card [19]. There is also a paravirtualized HBA driver available within VMware vSphere 4. Microsoft Hyper-V features *Integrations Components* such as VMBUS (transport for Synthetic devices), Time Sync (used to keep VM clocks in sync with the root partition sometimes called the host), Video Driver, Network Driver, and Storage Driver [8].

Another use of paravirtualization is modifying the guest kernel to insert *hypercalls* to pass critical information to the VMM. Microsoft Windows Server 2008, as a guest, has Enlightenment features that allow it to use hypercalls to optimize its performance on top of the Hyper-V hypervisor. VMI for Linux SLES 10 from VMware is a similar feature. The Xen hypervisor also uses paravirtualization for high performance [22].

Paravirtualized guests enable virtualization of a guest in the absence of hardware support for instruction execution, and can have better performance. This requires that the guest operating system be available in paravirtualized form for the hypervisor.

3 Benchmarking Virtualization Technologies

The popularity of virtualized systems has engendered a need for benchmarks designed specifically to measure performance in such environments. Traditional benchmarks are typically not good choices to measure the performance of a virtual server. To see why, consider what makes virtual servers useful. A typical server in a virtual environment runs multiple applications, under a variety of operating systems, with none of the applications fully utilizing the server. In contrast, traditional benchmarks aim to maximize the performance of the server by fully utilizing the server under a single operating system, typically with a single application. A virtualization system benchmark needs to provide a measure of how well the system performs in the environment that makes a virtual server valuable.

3.1 What's Available Today?

Server consolidation typically collects several diverse workloads onto a single physical server. This approach ensures that all system resources such as CPU, network, and disk are more efficiently utilized. In fact, virtual environments tend to function more smoothly when resource demands are balanced across multiple resources. Several benchmarks have been developed or proposed for virtual systems. Below is a survey of these benchmarks, and their strengths and weaknesses.

3.1.1 VMmark

VMware's VMmark was developed and launched in 2007 [13] and is designed to benchmark the performance of virtualization software and hardware. It is not designed as a benchmark of any other software component. The strength of VMmark is its public acceptance, and its ability to capture some important benefits of visualization technology: consolidation of applications, and the ability to measure the performance of a heterogeneous environment.

The unit of work for a benchmark of virtualized consolidation environments can be naturally defined as a collection of VMs executing a set of diverse workloads. The VMmark Benchmark refers to this unit of work as a tile. The total number of tiles that a physical system can accommodate gives a coarse-grain measure of that system's consolidation capacity. This concept is similar to some server benchmarks, such as TPC-C, which scale the workload in a step-wise fashion to increase the system load.

Tiles are relatively heavyweight objects that cannot by themselves capture small variations in system performance. To address this, both the number of tiles and the performance of each individual workload determine the overall benchmark score.

When a tile is added, workloads in existing tiles might measure lower performance, but if the system has not been overcommitted, the aggregate score, including the new tile, should increase. The result is a flexible benchmark metric that provides a measure of the total number of workloads that can be supported by a particular system as well as the overall performance level within the VMs.

Table 1. VMmark Workload Summary

Workload	Application	Virtual Machine Platform
Mail server	Exchange 2003	Windows 2003, 2 CPU, 1GB RAM, 24GB disk
Java server	SPECjbb®2005-based	Windows 2003, 2 CPU, 1GB RAM, 8GB disk
Standby server	None	Windows 2003,1 CPU, 256MB RAM, 4GB disk
Web server	SPECweb®2005-based	SLES 10, 2 CPU, 512MB RAM, 8GB disk
Database server	MySQL	SLES 10, 2 CPU, 2GB RAM, 10GB disk
File server	dbench	SLES 10, 1 CPU, 256MB RAM, 8GB disk

3.1.2 SPECvirt

SPECvirt, a virtualization benchmark, is under development by the Standard Performance Evaluation Corporation (SPEC), a standards organization established in 1988. SPEC is a successful standards body publishing hundreds of results annually with their various benchmarks. SPEC is quick to respond with the development and launch of new benchmarks as new technologies have emerged. Some examples are SPECweb, SPECjAppserver and SPECpower.

SPECvirt is SPEC's latest endeavor to address the need for a virtual benchmark. SPECvirt aims to be a benchmark that will model server consolidation of commonly virtualized systems such as mail servers, database servers, application servers, web servers, and file servers, providing a means to fairly compare server performance while running a number of VMs, producing a benchmark designed to scale across a wide range of systems and supporting hardware virtualization, operating system virtualization, and hardware partitioning schemes for server consolidation scenarios.

Though the details of the SPECvirt specification aren't public, information has been presented that shows SPECvirt will use a tile concept similar to VMmark. SPECvirt has some clear advantages over VMmark – it is developed and governed under a standards body. Since it is being based on SPEC workloads that use open standards it may address scenarios not covered by the current VMmark benchmark. SPECvirt is expected to launch in the second half of 2009.

3.1.3 vConsolidate

IBM and Intel developed vConsolidate [3] in 2007 as a benchmark for virtualization users. vConsolidate runs multiple instances of consolidated database, mail, Web and JAVA workloads in multiple virtual CPU (vCPU) partitions on Intel-based System x servers. A fifth, idle VM is also present during test. vConsolidate refers to a single collection of these five VMs as a consolidate stack unit (CSU). Depending on the type of server and its available resources, testers can choose to run one or more CSUs.

The typical goal, as in VMmark also, is to run enough CSUs to push the server under test to its maximum capacity by consuming 100 percent of the CPU capacity or very close to it. The vConsolidate workload comes with four sets of VM specification, which it calls profiles. These profiles define key factors for each workload VM including virtual CPUs, virtual RAM, etc.

3.1.4 Other

vApus Mark I developed and introduced earlier this year by Sizing Server Lab is run internally only by the developer and another collaborating company and not available to the general public. With one OLAP workload, one DSS workload and two heavy website workloads combined in one tile, vApus Mark attempts to focus on heavier service oriented applications. Also worth mentioning is vServCon developed for internal use by Fujitsu Siemens Computers. vServCon uses a framework that is similar to vConsolidate and consolidates already established benchmarks in order to simulate the load of a virtualized consolidated server environment. Three proven benchmarks are used, which cover database, application server and web server application scenarios.

3.2 TPC's Role in Benchmarking

The TPC has been in existence since 1988. Over the last 20 years the TPC has been successful in creating benchmarks that have been primarily focused on the performance of computer systems and databases. Its online transaction processing (OLTP) benchmarks and Decision Support benchmarks (TPC-C and TPC-H being the most popular) have been successfully used by top computer system and database vendors to showcase the steady development of technology in various areas. These benchmarks have a performance component and a price component as part of the end result which are two key data points that help customers make an objective decision when purchasing these systems.

The first TPC-C result published in September, 1992 measured 54 tpmC (transactions per minute for the C benchmark) with a cost per tpmC of $188,562. As of June 2009 the top result is 6,085,166 tpmC at $2.81 per tpmC. These results demonstrate the technological advances in computer systems and databases in terms of real world performance and the cost improvements of these systems. A similar explosion can also be seen in the number of results for the TPC-H benchmark. The intelligent and well thought-out design of these benchmarks supports the scaling of workloads as servers grow in power. The scaling factors built into these benchmarks, such as number of users and the size of the database tables, increase proportionally with the increasing power of the system to produce higher transaction rates.

Both TPC-C and TPC-H have gained widespread acceptance as the industry's premier benchmarks in their respective fields (OLTP and Decision Support). But as the challenges in the industry take a turn from a demand for higher performance to consolidation of power and space, computer vendors have responded with newer technologies like virtualization. Once again the TPC has an opportunity to formulate a workload to address benchmarking needs in the virtualized environment.

3.3 What's Missing?

Benchmarks and workloads must continually be enhanced to keep them relevant to real world environments, which today include virtual environments. Most virtual benchmarks today cover consolidation cases; none are aimed at transaction processing or decision support applications, the traditional areas addressed by TPC benchmarks. These areas are a large segment of the application space being virtualized today. The challenge is no longer successful consolidation of a set of applications running on lightly loaded physical servers. The new frontier is virtualization of resource-intensive workloads, including those which are distributed across multiple physical servers. None of the above virtual benchmarks available today measure the database-centric properties that have made TPC benchmarks the industry standard that they are today.

4 Benchmarking Database Workloads

Ideas and possibilities for benchmarking database-heavy workloads in a virtualized environment abound. In DBMS intensive applications, Business Intelligence (BI) and On Line Transaction Processing (OLTP) workloads lead the list in IT spend value. BI is a broad category of applications and technologies for gathering, storing, analyzing, and providing access to data to help enterprise users make better business decisions. BI applications include the activities of decision support systems, query and reporting, online analytical processing (OLAP), statistical analysis, forecasting, and data mining.

Similarly in a classic 2-tier data warehouse architecture, the source data warehouse is on an enterprise-class server and the many less demanding data marts, specific snapshots of the data warehouse, are on smaller servers. As these configurations move towards server consolidation, virtualization of all data marts on a single virtualized system is often an option. Consolidation of the source data warehouse with a selection of data marts on a single server, based on locality requirements, is another option.

Given the volatility of data in data warehouses, Operational Business Intelligence (OBI) is now a much needed capability for many businesses. OBI is the ability to perform action on data that makes sense to the business, when it makes sense to perform that action. This involves technology that assures right-time data arrival, coupled with neural nets to put the current transaction into "context", and then produce an actionable result for the business to operate from. Research and innovation in the area of dynamic creation of VMs [7] makes it possible for data marts to be created on VMs dynamically on an as-needed basis.

A large percentage of database applications have a multi-tiered structure. TPC-App models one such class of applications. When each tier is mapped to a single VM this results in great flexibility with respect to the physical location of the entire application. To generalize further, this applies to any application or workflow with multiple distinct and serial steps. For example, data is periodically pulled from operational databases and piped to warehouses. Operational data may simply be rolled up into summary form for storage in the warehouse but often undergoes other, more complex, transformation. The operational and warehouse databases are most likely to be on different servers. When run within VMs, each tier or phase in a workflow can be isolated and yet run on the same physical server. This is a special case of consolidation: the difference is presence of the data traffic between VMs. Current virtualization benchmarks do not take this aspect of virtualization into account.

5   Performance Evaluation of Database Workloads

This section presents results from benchmarking database applications at VMware. We used workloads derived from TPC benchmarks to compare the performance of virtual systems to physical machines, and to showcase the consolidation benefits of virtualization. We used non-comparable implementations of the TPC-C[1] and TPC-E[1] benchmarks that we refer to as the *order entry* workload and the *brokerage* workload.

The test cases are classified based on the number of VMs run on the server (single vs. multiple VMs) and the total resources consumed by the VMs (under committed vs. fully committed). Table 2 summarizes the test environments (For detailed descriptions of the test environment, see [15,20]):

The following metrics were used as indicators of VM performance

- Ratio-to-native: throughput of a single VM as a percentage of the throughput on a physical environment

---

[1] The Order-Entry benchmark is a non-comparable implementation of the TPC-C business model; our results are not TPC-C compliant, and not comparable to official TPC-C results. TPC requires that we disclose deviations from the benchmark specification. The deviations from the specification are: batch implementation and an undersized database for the observed throughput. The Brokerage benchmark is a non-comparable implementation of the TPC-E business model; our results are not TPC-E compliant, and not comparable to official TPC-E results. Deviations from the TPC-E specification: an undersized database for the observed throughput in the multi-VM experiments.

Table 2. Configuration used for order entry and brokerage workload experiments

Order entry workload	8-core server with Intel processors
	Oracle 11g R1 DBMS; RHEL 5.1; VMware ESX 4.0
Brokerage workload	8-core server with AMD processors
	MS Windows Server 2008; MS SQL Server 2008; VMware ESX 4.0

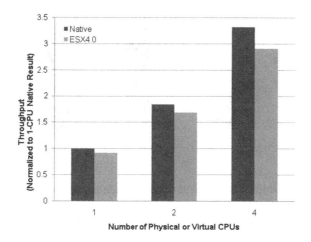

Fig. 1. Brokerage workload throughput of under committed single VM

- Fairness: throughput distribution for individual VMs in a multi-VM test
- Scale-out performance: cumulative throughput of VMs in a multi-VM test

5.1 Under-Committed Single VM

Hypervisors can offload the processing of tasks such as networking and storage I/O to idle processors. Running an under-committed single VM highlights this capability.

As an example, running the order entry benchmark on a 4 vCPU VM delivers ~8% higher throughput than in the fully-committed case. The brokerage workload running on a 2 vCPU (virtual CPU) VM on an 8 pCPU (physical CPU) host performs at 92% of physical machine performance. Figure1 shows the performance relative to native for 1,2 and 4 vCPU VMs running the brokerage workload on an 8 pCPU server.

5.2 Fully Committed Single VM

In this section, we describe results from a fully committed VM containing 8 vCPUs. On an 8 vCPU virtual running the order entry workload, we achieved 85% of native performance. Similarly an 8 vCPU VM using the brokerage workload performed at 86% of native performance. Figure 2 represents the performance relative to native for a 1, 2 and 4 vCPU VM running the order entry workload on a physical system booted with 1 , 2 and 4 pCPUs.

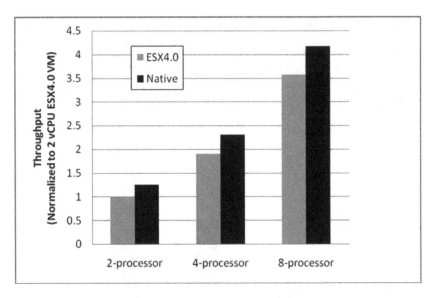

Fig. 2. Order Entry workload throughput of fully committed single VM

Table 3. Native and VM *order entry* workload profiles in the 8 CPU configuration

Metric	Physical Machine	Virtual Machine
Throughput in business transactions per minute	293K	250K
Disk IOPS	71K	60K
Disk bandwidth	305MB/s	258MB/s
Network packets/s	12K/s receive; 19K/s send	10K/s receive; 17 K/s send
Network bandwidth	25 Mb/s receive; 66 Mb/s send	21 Mb/s receive; 56 Mb/s send

Table 4. Native and VM *brokerage* workload profiles in the 8 CPU configuration

Metric	Physical Machine	Virtual Machine
Throughput in transactions per second*	3557	3060
Average response time of all transactions**	234 ms	255 ms
Disk I/O throughput (IOPS)	29 K	25.5 K
Disk I/O latencies	9 ms	8 ms
Network packets/s receive	10 K/sec	8.5 K/sec
Network packets/s send	16K/sec	8 K/sec
Network bandwidth	11.8 Mb/sec receive 123 Mb/sec send	10 Mb/sec receive 105 Mb/sec send

* Workload consists of a mix of 10 transactions. Metric reported is the aggregate of all transactions.
** Average of the response times of all 10 transactions in the workload.

System metrics from the two environments in Table 3 and Table 4 demonstrate that current VM software can handle the needs of these resource intensive workloads.

5.3   Under Committed Multiple VMs

We simulated multiple backend database servers being consolidated onto VMs on the same host by running the brokerage workload on multiple homogenous VMs and report the aggregate throughput metric. We also report the throughput of individual VMs and their contribution to the overall metric (See Figure 3). The under committed host uses the spare cycles to run more VMs or perform other tasks.

Each VM uses 15% of the physical CPU; the aggregate throughput scales linearly with the number of VMs. Figure 4 shows resources are distributed fairly across VMs.

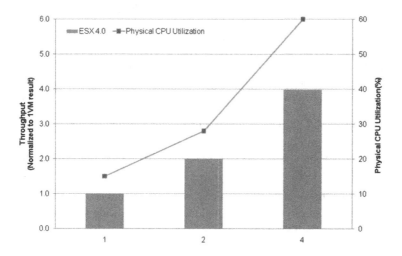

Fig. 3. Consolidation of Multiple SQLServer VMs

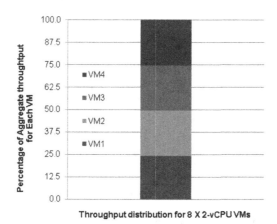

Fig. 4. Throughput distribution for under committed VMs

5.4   Over Committed Multiple VMs

Virtualization platforms have the ability to run VMs where the total number of vCPUs exceeds the number of pCPUs. This is called "Over commitment".

Table 5 highlights the resource intensive nature of the 8 VMs.

Table 5. Aggregate System metrics for 8 SQLServer VMs

Aggregate throughput in transactions per second	Host CPU Utilization	Disk I/O throughput (IOPS)	Network packet rate	Network bandwidth
2760	100%	23K	8K/s receive 7.5K/s send	9Mb/s receive 98Mb/s send

As the graph in Figure 5 shows, throughput increases linearly as we add up to 4 VMs (8 vCPUs). As we overcommit the physical cpus by increasing the number of VMs from 4 to 6 (factor of 1.5), the aggregate throughput increases by a factor of 1.4 at 90% physical CPU utilization. Adding 8 VMs to this saturates the physical CPUs on this host. ESX 4.0 now schedules 16 vCPUs onto 8 pCPUs yet the benchmark aggregate throughput increases a further 5%.

The throughput contribution of each VM is approximating 12.5% of the aggregate throughput as shown in Figure 6.

Based on our benchmarking experience, we have found the following factors to be reliable indicators of virtualized performance:

- the degree to which CPU resources are over or under committed
- comparison of physical and virtual machine using scale-up data, based on the # of CPUs configured

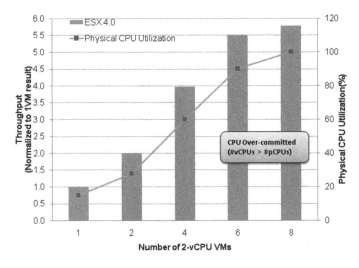

Fig. 5. Consolidation of Multiple SQLServer Virtual Machines

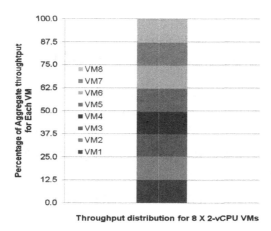

Fig. 6. Over-commit fairness for 8VMs

- fair sharing of resources among VMs using scale-out experiments, based on the individual and cumulative performance of a number of VMs

6 Proposals

Many scenarios of virtualization of database-intensive applications exist and some of them have been discussed in this paper. Data from experiments conducted on VMware running OLTP workloads show that virtualization technology today is ready to be challenged with database-intensive workloads.

In developing a new virtualization benchmark that emphasizes database and server performance what should we consider? We recommend that the following scenarios be considered in any benchmark designed to evaluate virtualized database performance. They specify broad rules for the software configurations of such a benchmark as well as some practical considerations that the TPC might view as strengths and weaknesses of each approach.

6.1 Scenario 1: Comprehensive Database Virtualization Benchmark

- Virtual machine Configuration:
    - o System should contain a mix of at least two multi-way CPU configurations, for example an 8-way server result might contain 2x2 vCPU and 1x4 vCPU VMs.
    - o Measure the cpu overcommitment capabilities in hypervisors by providing an overcommitted result along with a fully committed result.
    - o Both results should report throughput of individual VMs.
- Workloads used
    - o Each VM runs homogenous or heterogeneous workloads of a mix of database benchmarks, e.g., TPC-C, TPC-H and TPC-E.
    - o Consider running a mix of operating systems and databases.

- Run rules and reporting

  o Throughput of individual VMs.
  o Virtual results can only be compared against each other and not with physical machine results.
- Advantages

  o Comprehensive database consolidation benchmark
- Disadvantages

  o Complex benchmark rules may be too feature-rich for an industry standard workload.

6.2 Scenario 2: Virtualization Extension of an Existing Database Benchmark

- Virtual Machine configuration:

  o System contains a mix of homogenous VMs, for example an 8-way server might contain 4x2 vCPU VMs.
  o The number of vCPUs in a VM would be based on the total number of cores and the cores/socket on a given host.
  o The benchmark specification would prescribe the number of VMs and number of vCPUs in each VM for a given number of cores.
- Workloads used

  o Homogeneous database workload, e.g., TPC-E, in each VM
- Run rules and reporting

  o Aggregate throughput from all VMs.
  o Individual throughput for a fairness comparison across VMs.
  o Virtual results can only be compared against each other and not with physical machine results.
- Advantages

  o Simple approach provides the audience of the benchmark result with a wealth of information about virtualized environments that they do not have currently.
  o The simplicity of the extension will make it possible to develop a new benchmark in a short amount of time, which is critical if the benchmark is to gain acceptance.
- Disadvantages

  o Unlike Scenario 1, this approach does not have consolidation scenarios.
  o Features of virtual environments such as over-commitment not part of the benchmark definition.

6.3 Scenario 3 Benchmarking Multi-tier/Multi-phase Applications

The basic premise is to map each step in a workflow (or, each tier in a multi-tier application) to a VM. (For large-scale implementations, the mapping may instead be to a set of identical/homogeneous VMs.) From a benchmark design perspective, this would be a challenging exercise and there are a number of open questions, e.g.:

- Does the benchmark specify strict boundaries between the tiers?
- Are the size and number of VMs in each layer parts of the benchmark spec?
- Does the entire application have to be virtualized? Or, would benchmark sponsors have freedom in choosing the components that are virtualized? This question arises due to the fact that support and licensing restrictions often lead to parts not being virtualized.

In the near term, Scenarios 1 & 2 have the most potential to result in a viable and useful benchmark. Scenario 3 has interesting possibilities and could form the basis for future virtualization-aware benchmarks.

7 Conclusion

The objective of this paper is to show that virtualization technology is fairly mature today and is capable of handling database-intensive workloads. Today's benchmarks in general don't facilitate the development of future efficient architectural design of systems for the common–case usage [11]. However, TPC benchmarks have in the past not only provided a means of objectively comparing products across computer systems and databases, but have also proven to drive system-level technology further. The authors of this paper urge the TPC to respond to the growth in virtualization technology and capture some of the common-case usage of virtualization with database workloads, in a well-designed benchmark for the virtual environment.

References

1. Adams, K., Agesen, O.: A Comparison of Software and Hardware Techniques for x86 Virtualization. In: Proceedings of ASPLOS 2006 (2006)
2. Agesen, O.: Software and Hardware Techniques for x86 Virtualization (2009), http://www.vmware.com/files/pdf/ software_hardware_tech_x86_virt.pdf
3. Casazza, J., Greenfield, M., Shi, K.: Redefining Server Performance Characterization for Virtualization Benchmarking. Intel® Technology Journal (August 2006), http://www.intel.com/technology/itj/2006/v10i3/
4. Creasy, R.J.: The Origin of the VM/370 Time-Sharing System. IBM Journal of Research and Development 25(5), 483
5. Figueiredo, R., Dinda, P.A., Fortes, J.A.B.: Guest Editors' Introduction: Resource Virtualization Renaissance. Computer 38(5), 28–31 (2005), http://www2.computer.org/portal/web/csdl/doi/10.1109/ MC.2005.159
6. Goldberg, R.P.: A Survey of Virtual Machine Research. Computer, 34–45 (June 1974)
7. Lin, B., Dinda, P.A.: Towards Scheduling Virtual Machines Based on Direct User Input. In: First International Workshop on Virtualization Technology in Distributed Computing (2006)

8. Microsoft, Hyper-V Integration Components and Enlightenment,
   `http://blogs.msdn.com/tvoellm/archive/2008/01/02/hyper-v-integration-components-and-enlightenments.aspx`
9. Nanda, S., Chiueh, T.-c.: A Survey on Virtualization Technologies. Technical Report ECSL-TR-179, SUNY at Stony Brook (February 2005),
   `http://www.ecsl.cs.sunysb.edu/tr/TR179.pdf`
10. Nelson, M., Lim, B.-H., Hutchins, G.: Fast Transparent Migration for Virtual Machines. In: USENIX 2005, April 2005, pp. 391–394 (2005)
11. Ranganathan, P., Jouppi, N.: Enterprise IT Trends and Implications for Architectural Research. In: Proceedings of the 11th International Symposium on High Performance Computer Architecture (2005)
12. Rosenblum, M., Garfinkel, T.: Virtual Machine Monitors: Current Technology and Future Trends. Computer 38(5), 39–47 (2005)
13. VMware Inc. VMmark: A Scalable Benchmark for Virtualized Systems,
   `http://www.vmware.com/pdf/vmmark_intro.pdf`
14. VMware Inc., VMware High Availability, Concepts, Implementation, and Best Practices (2007), `http://www.vmware.com/files/pdf/VMwareHA_twp.pdf`
15. VMware Inc., Performance and Scalability of Microsoft® SQL Server® on VMware vSphere™ 4,
   `http://www.vmware.com/pdf/perf_vsphere_sql_scalability.pdf`
16. VMware Inc., Performance Evaluation of AMD RVI Hardware Assist,
   `http://www.vmware.com/pdf/RVI_performance.pdf`
17. VMware Inc., Protecting Mission-Critical Workloads with VMware Fault Tolerance (2009),
   `http://www.vmware.com/files/pdf/resources/ft_virtualization_wp.pdf`
18. VMware Inc. and Kingston Technology, The Role of Memory in VMware ESX Server 3 (2006), `http://www.vmware.com/pdf/esx3_memory.pdf`
19. VMware Inc., Transparent Virtualization (2006),
   `http://www.vmware.com/interfaces/paravirtualization.html`
20. VMware Inc., Virtualizing Performance-Critical Database Applications in VMware® vSphere™, `http://www.vmware.com/pdf/Perf_ESX40_Oracle-eval.pdf`
21. Waldspurger, C.: Memory Resource Management in VMware ESX Server. In: USENIX Symposium on Operating Systems Design and Implementation (2002)
22. Xen Wiki page, HVM compatible Motherboards,
   `http://wiki.xensource.com/xenwiki/HVM_Compatible_Motherboards`

Principles for an ETL Benchmark

Len Wyatt[1], Brian Caufield[2], and Daniel Pol[3]

[1] Microsoft Corporation
1 Microsoft Way
Redmond, WA 98052 USA
lenwy@microsoft.com
[2] IBM Corporation
555 Bailey Ave.
San Jose, CA 95141 USA
bcaufiel@us.ibm.com
[3] Hewlett-Packard Company
11445 Compaq Center Dr W
Houston, TX, 77070, USA
daniel.pol@hp.com

Abstract. Conditions in the marketplace for ETL tools suggest that an industry standard benchmark is needed. The benchmark should provide useful data for comparing the performance of ETL systems, be based on a meaningful scenario, and be scalable over a wide range of data set sizes. This paper gives a general scoping of the proposed benchmark and outlines some key decision points. The Transaction Processing Performance Council (TPC) has formed a development subcommittee to define and produce such a benchmark.

Keywords: ETL, ELT, extract, transform, load, data integration, TPC, benchmark, database, data warehouse, performance, transformations, reliability, metric.

1 Introduction

ETL is an acronym for Extract, Transform, Load [1]. It is a process of obtaining data from one or more data sources, performing various manipulations on the data, and placing it in one or more destination locations. Most commonly – but certainly not exclusively – ETL is used to extract data from data sources, perform data integration functions, and load a data warehouse. Some people consider "Data Integration" to be a broader term that encompasses ETL [2]. While ETL as a discipline lacks the shared conceptual framework that relational databases benefit from, there is an increasing amount of common understanding in the industry [3].

Sometimes ETL functionality is created simply by developing programs or database procedures to read and transform data, but there is also a significant market for ETL tools which can make the job easier or more efficient. The most common reason for choosing specialized ETL tools is that they enhance developer productivity and ease maintenance, by expressing data manipulation tasks in a form that is easier

R. Nambiar and M. Poess (Eds.): TPCTC 2009, LNCS 5895, pp. 183–198, 2009.

to express and visualize. However, ETL tools can often also increase the speed of such operations by providing facilities that would be difficult for developers to reproduce. Obviously it is theoretically possible for developers to write specialized code that would outperform general purpose ETL tools, but consider that it's also theoretically true that a machine-language developer can write code that outperforms compiler-generated code. Just as compilers are better suited for most programming tasks, ETL tools often are better suited for data transformation and integration.

The last 10 years have seen significant evolution of ETL tools and growth of the market. Section 2 shows some of the competition and performance claims that have resulted from this market. An amazing number of "world record" claims have been made, but while they provide good marketing material for the vendors, there has been little of real value for customers to evaluate. In April of 2008 the TPC formed a Working Group to assess the purpose and scope of an ETL benchmark. As a result of this assessment, the TPC formed an ETL Benchmark Development Subcommittee in November of 2008 to undertake the definition and implementation of a standard ETL benchmark.

This paper relates the work of the subcommittee so far. There are aspects of the work where the subcommittee believes it has a consensus, and aspects of the work that are still under consideration. Where it appears that a consensus exists, the paper will describe our understanding at this time. It must be noted that as a work in progress, nothing about the benchmark is actually final until the benchmark is ratified by the TPC as a whole. For areas that are still under consideration, and there are significant ones, the main alternatives will be presented.

The authors represent three companies that are members of the ETL Benchmark Development Subcommittee, but we acknowledge that the paper builds on work by all thirteen member companies, and we thank them for their support. We hope they feel this paper does their work justice.

2   Market/Industry Conditions

The existence of performance claims from many vendors suggests that there is competition in a market, and the lack of a meaningful way to compare the claims suggests a need for a standard benchmark. For example, in the 1980s significant competition evolved between vendors in the emerging relational database market, and from that, benchmarks like DebitCredit led to the immensely successful Transaction Processing Performance Council (TPC) benchmarks. There are significant parallels between the developing market for OLTP systems in the 1980s and the ETL market in the 2000s. Table 1 illustrates these parallels, where the 1980s information is excerpted from "The History Of DebitCredit and the TPC" by Omri Serlin [4]. Table 2 provides evidence of the diverse ETL vendor claims made in the 2000s.

These tables show vendors competing aggressively in an area that lacks common ground rules for evaluating the performance of the products. The lack of a standard benchmark allows vendors to make almost any claim they wish, and market pressures drive them to make the biggest claim they can. This may be good for marketing purposes, but it is not very helpful to customers.

Table 1. Parallels between the 1980s OLTP market and the 2000s ETL market

	1980s	2000s
Interest	Interest in characterizing the performance of OLTP systems	Interest in characterizing the performance of ETL systems
Driving Factor	Driven by … increased demand for very high performance	Driven by increased demand for performance with high data volumes
Measures	No agreement on exactly how TPS ratings were to be derived	No agreement on how to measure ETL performance
Comparability	While plenty of TPS claims were being unleashed, it wasn't at all clear whether any of the published TPS ratings were in any sense comparable	While plenty of ETL claims are being unleashed, it is clear that they are not comparable
Vendor Claims	[Before the TPC] vendors … claim performance under the "industry standard benchmark"	Vendors claim "record performance" under different conditions

Table 2. Examples of ETL vendor claims

Date	Claim
May 2001	Informatica demonstrates massive scalability, powerful performance of its data integration platform on HP servers… three complex data mappings representing typical business scenarios [5].
Feb. 2002	Ascential shatters data integration performance record; outperforms competitors' published benchmark results by more than 500 percent … working under the same parameters of prior benchmarks announced by competitors [6].
March 2005	New release of SAS® Enterprise ETL Server sets performance world record [7].
April 2005	Unisys and SAS deliver record-breaking ETL benchmark result [8].
June 2005	Informatica and Sun achieve record-setting results In data integration performance and scalability test … Data sets for the tests were generated by the industry-standard TPC-H utility dbgen [9]
April 2006	Sunopsis Data Conductor demonstrates indisputable superiority for high volumes, complex transformations [10].
May 2006	SAS, Sun Microsystems establish new data integration performance world record [11].
Aug. 2006	Informatica sets world record data integration performance [12].
Jan. 2007	Jaspersoft launches Jasperetl…Performance tests indicate performance up to 50% faster than other leading commercial ETL tools [13].

Table 2. (*continued*)

April 2007	SAS smashes ETL world record while establishing new, real-world benchmarks [14].
Feb. 2008	ETL World Record ... SSIS ... Over 1 TB of TPC-H data was loaded in under 30 minutes [15].
Dec. 2008	Syncsort and Vertica Shatter Database ETL World Record [16]

3 Purpose and Benefits of an ETL Benchmark

A well designed benchmark is beneficial to customers evaluating systems and also to the vendors of those systems. Once there is a common basis for comparing ETL tools, vendors will improve their products to compete on the basis of the benchmark.

An ETL benchmark will give customers reliable, comparable performance information based on a meaningful scenario. Following the model of all TPC benchmarks, the ETL benchmark will present a realistic business task for the tools to implement. While a single scenario cannot represent all applications of ETL technology, a well chosen scenario will be sufficiently meaningful so that many customers can learn from the benchmark results.

Also following the model of all TPC benchmarks, a "Full Disclosure Report" will be required for every benchmark result. This will allow customers to understand how a certain result was achieved, so they can use the same methods if desired. Full disclosure also provides transparency in case vendors might create unrealistic implementations solely for the sake of benchmarking.

In addition to creating better performing products, vendors will also benefit from greater credibility of the ETL market, as a result of a recognized industry organization setting the ground rules.

3.1 ETL vs. ELT

For purposes of this benchmark, we take the term ETL to define a business task, namely the obtaining of data from multiple sources, integrating it together in a way appropriate to the business, and placing it in a data warehouse. We specifically do not mean to suggest that the term ETL requires a certain order of doing things (extract, transform and then load). There are some tools in the market that prefer to define themselves as ELT tools, because they load data into the destination database and then use database functionality to perform the transformations. The ELT model is explicitly allowed in the benchmark.

4 Providing the Benchmark with a Business Context

Each TPC benchmark has an underlying scenario which provides a foundation for the requirements of the benchmark. TPC-C models an order-entry environment. The most recent benchmark, TPC-E, models the OLTP system operated by a brokerage house [17]. The TPC-E schema represents a schema such as a brokerage OLTP system might use, the transactions are units of work similar to those in a brokerage, and the data sets are similar to financial data. As a whole the benchmark gains credibility and understandability by having a coherent underlying model.

Similarly, an ETL benchmark should have an underlying scenario to provide coherence and credibility. This inherently means that the benchmark does not represent all usage models – no benchmark can do that – but the model it does follow must have enough characteristics of real-world systems so that it is credible. The scenario that is being developed by the ETL Benchmark Development Subcommittee is based on loading data into the data warehouse of a brokerage company. The data is modeled as coming from multiple sources, including the brokerage OLTP system, a human resources (HR) database, and an external source with marketing information on prospective clients. This scenario was chosen because integrating and loading data from operational systems into a data warehouse is one very common usage pattern for ETL tools. Data from these sources is initially stored in a staging area, and from the staging area it must be integrated together according to rules appropriate to the business, transformed according to defined business rules, and loaded into the data warehouse. The benchmark measures the performance of the system while reading from the staging area, doing transformations, and writing to the data warehouse, as illustrated in Figure 1.

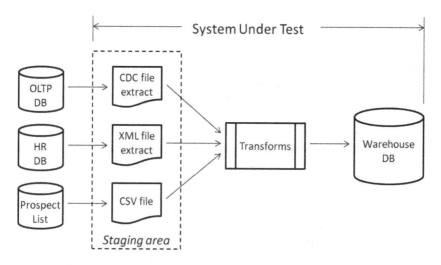

Fig. 1. Logical flow of the ETL benchmark

The availability of the TPC-E schema provided one source of data for the ETL benchmark. This does not mean that running the ETL benchmark requires running TPC-E, only that the schema was used as a starting point. In fact, the ETL benchmark is expected to model the presence of a Change Data Capture (CDC) system [18] [19] [20] used in conjunction with the OLTP database, which is not part of the TPC-E benchmark. When regular updates are being made to the data warehouse from the OLTP system, CDC allows the ETL process to begin with only the data that was altered since the last update. The model is that the output of the CDC system will be text files that are read by the ETL process.

The ETL benchmark scenario will also model data sourced from a human resources (HR) database and an external source of marketing data. The HR database is used to obtain supplemental information on brokers, data that was not in the OLTP system. The HR database does not support CDC, so for each incremental update the ETL process must determine what changes have occurred since the last update. Extracts from the HR database are in an XML format. The marketing data source contains names, addresses and demographic data for prospective customers, such as a company might purchase from a syndicated data provider. This data arrives in a comma separated value (CSV) file format, this being the lowest common denominator of information exchange. The prospect list is updated with each incremental update.

When the data sources are determined there are still many possibilities for the data warehouse schema and the types of transformations to be carried out in the ETL process. To give the benchmark realism, the committee hypothesized the kinds of business questions a relational data warehouse might be used to answer, and designed the data warehouse schema accordingly. The design process was analogous to one that a "real" data warehouse design team might follow. A dimensional data warehouse design approach [21] was followed.

In a dimensional model, dimension tables describe entities of interest to the business. Examples include the broker dimension table, which lists all the brokers and their attributes of interest, the customer dimension, the security dimension, etc. Fact tables describe events of interest, such as a trades table recording all stock purchases and sales, or a security history table which lists the closing prices and trade volumes of all the securities. Foreign key relationships provide the connection between events and the entities involved in the events. For example a trade is executed by a particular broker on behalf of a particular customer, involving a particular security. The ETL Benchmark Development Subcommittee is considering a schema using approximately eight dimension tables and about six fact tables, plus potentially a small number of additional special purpose tables.

Once the data warehouse schema was determined, the remaining design task is to specify the data mappings and transformations that occur as data is integrated from the data sources and placed in the data warehouse. Here the subcommittee is considering variations in the design, because one goal is to represent a diverse set of typical operations. For example, the HR database is modeled as not having a business key in common with the broker table from the OLTP database. In order to match broker information with the corresponding HR data, the records must be matched on the broker name – requiring a string comparison. At the time of writing this paper, the complete set of transformation rules is still being determined.

Another aspect of the benchmark related to the business context is the frequency with which the data warehouse is updated. The ETL system must provide for both historical loads and incremental updates. A historical load occurs when a "full" load of all data into the data warehouse is needed; this is required when the data warehouse is initially created or when a major change is made, such as an incompatible schema change. Incremental updates occur when new data is added to the data warehouse.

Typically this is at some regular interval which can vary widely between businesses. There are businesses that update their warehouses only weekly or monthly; others require near-real-time data streams. Daily updates are common in businesses today. Since this fits well with the daily closing cycles that are common in a brokerage, it seems likely that daily incremental updates will be the model for the ETL benchmark.

The authors have noted feedback from some parties that near-real-time updates are very important, and recognize that this is an increasingly common business requirement. However, the technologies commonly used for near-real-time data integration are somewhat different than the more batch-oriented tools typically thought of as ETL tools. We believe that a different, but possibly similar, benchmark is needed for continuous data integration.

5   Scope of the System under Test (SUT)

While the application of ETL technologies has extended beyond its origins in data warehousing into more general data integration applications, the fundamental elements of its roots -- Extract, Transform, and Load – are still the pillars of the ETL industry. The data that an ETL tool transforms comes from somewhere and goes somewhere, and it is within the scope of the ETL tool to get this data from the source and put this data into the target. The benchmark must take each of these aspects into consideration as they are integral parts of the work performed by ETL tools.

5.1   Extract: Scope of the Source

There are a wide variety of data sources for ETL applications. These sources range from general purpose and specialty databases to various types of data files, including binary and text, fixed and variable length, hierarchical and flat, to message queues and web services. A common task of an ETL application is to combine data from different sources as part of the transformation process.

While it is desirable to extract data from widely varied sources in the ETL benchmark, there are complications in doing so. Simply including database sources presents several issues. First, it is not practical to require benchmark sponsors to run databases from multiple vendors to serve as data sources for the benchmark. The potential costs involved with acquiring, configuring, and tuning multiple databases appropriately may be prohibitive for some sponsors. Second, using multiple database vendors complicates the evaluation of test results. If one sponsor uses a different set of databases than another sponsor, it is difficult to determine what performance differences are due to the ETL tools, since the source databases can greatly affect the overall result. One way to establish comparability would be to require the same set of database products for all benchmark tests, but no single set of database choices will be acceptable to all database and ETL tool vendors. Lastly, using any database as the source is also not desirable because it could allow ETL tools to "cheat" the benchmark by passing work off to the source database. While this practice can be useful in the real world in certain situations, the intent of the benchmark should be to test the ETL tool's performance, not the source database.

One solution to the source database issue is to extract data from files instead of databases. The ability of an ETL tool to obtain, interpret, and operate on varied source data can still be exercised, without the complications introduced by source databases. Given the variety of possible file formats and data representations, reading source files can pose significant challenges. The ETL benchmark will use file data sources, and use different formats to represent data obtained from different data sources that must be combined in the ETL process.

A common practice in data warehousing applications is to extract data from OLTP systems into a staging area. This staging area serves to isolate the OLTP system from the ETL processing. The extract can be done at a time that is most convenient for the OLTP system, and the ETL processing can work on the data when it needs, without affecting the performance of the online system. The extract also provides a backup of the data and a starting point in the event the ETL process needs to be restarted.

Following this practice, the benchmark will use the source files to represent a staging area. Some files will be representative of the output of a change data capture system on the OLTP database. Additional files will be included in the staging area to represent other sources of data. The system under test will begin with the staging area. The data generator provided for the benchmark will generate these source data files. Any movement, modification, or processing of the data in these files is part of the SUT, and therefore must be measured as part of the benchmark.

5.2 Transform: Scope of the Transformations

One of the problems with many of the non-standard ETL benchmarks that have been used by vendors in the past is that there were few or no transformations involved. An ETL benchmark must include actual data transformations in order to truly evaluate an ETL tool's performance. Certain functionality, such as lookups and joins, as well as string and date manipulations, are extremely common and must play a prominent role.

Since the benchmark scenario is based on realistic source and target data models, simply mapping the source schema to the target schema results in some reasonable approximation of the transformations involved in real world ETL workloads. At the current time, the complete set of source to target mappings has not been defined. It is likely that adjustments will need to be made to the initial source or target schemas to refine the transformations required in the benchmark. However, rooting the benchmark in realistic sources, targets, and methodologies provides a solid basis to build upon.

The benchmark scenario includes both the historical loading and incremental updating of the warehouse. In the historical load, the data warehouse is initially empty and it is common to have a relatively large data volume because the data represents a long time period. In the incremental update scenario, ETL tools are used to perform ongoing updates to the warehouse tables. While some of the transformations are the same as in the initial load, the interaction with the target database is more complicated and requires additional transformations because the target tables may require updates, inserts, or deletes. Data volumes for incremental updates tend to be relatively smaller than for historical loads.

5.3 Load: Scope of Target

The ultimate destination in most ETL scenarios is a target database. In many applications, the target database also plays a role in the transformation process. Data that has already been loaded will often serve as reference data that is required to load other related tables. Star schema fact and dimension tables are a good example. Dimension data must first be loaded into a target table. In order to load an associated fact table, the dimension table must be used as a reference to obtain the surrogate keys. It is also common that target tables need to be updated, not just appended.

Some tools operate by first loading data into the target, then performing the data transformations using the target database. In an environment like this, it is virtually impossible to separate transformation workload from database workload. It is the intent of the ETL benchmark committee to define the benchmark in such a way as to allow these "ELT" style tools to participate.

For both of these reasons, the benchmark will include the target database in the system under test. In some respects, including the database target in the benchmark carries some of the same complications for a benchmark sponsor as including source databases. However, given the interdependency between the target database and the transformation process, it is not practical to exclude it without trivializing the benchmark scenario and possibly excluding "ELT" style vendors.

6 Functionality to Be Measured

The ETL benchmark being defined is a performance benchmark. It is not meant to test the ease of use of the development environment of the ETL tools, or every possible feature and function. Further, it is the intent of the benchmark subcommittee not to exclude ETL tools by requiring specialized functionality that would not be common to most tools. Instead, the transformations involved will be representative of common ETL tasks which are assumed to be achievable by a majority of ETL tools.

6.1 Common Transformations

The committee has not defined the complete set of transformations for the benchmark at this time. However, it is expected that the following types of transformations will be part of the workload:

- Parse and validate input data. The source data will be in files. A record structure will be defined for each file that describes what the data in the file represents. Each record type will contain of variety of data types, including string, numeric, date, and time. More than one basic file format will be used (e.g. XML, CSV). The ETL tools must read and validate data from these various file types.

- <u>String, date, time and numeric transformations</u>. The source data will contain fields using a variety of data types. The transformation process will require a wide range of operations to be performed, including string manipulations, date and time processing, numeric calculations, and data type conversions.
- <u>Lookups and joins</u>. Lookups and joins are functionally similar in that they are both means of combining sets of data. There are some differences in behavior, particularly in the handling of duplicate matches and non-matched records, and may vary from one tool to another. The benchmark will require that source and target data be combined for various purposes, but will not specify how this must be accomplished. It is expected that implementations will use the technique that is most appropriate for the ETL tool in use. One characteristic of a star schema data model, such as the one created for the target of the benchmark, is the use of surrogate keys to identify and reference dimension records. Surrogate keys do not exist in the source data; they are generated during the ETL process and stored in the warehouse tables. In order to transform a source record, the ETL process often needs to determine if a record already exists in the warehouse, and if so, obtain its surrogate key. This is typically done via a key lookup. Since surrogate keys are required for most operations on the warehouse, this will result in benchmark implementations making extensive use of key lookups as part of the transformation process.
- <u>Conditional processing</u>. It is a common element of ETL processing that some aspect of the source to target transformation varies, depending on the data. This may include performing the same basic transformation on all rows of the data, but only performing certain transformations in specific cases. For example, products could be obtained from suppliers or be developed in-house, and require different steps to obtain supplier information. Transformations may also vary when splitting source records to populate different targets, performing error handling, on field level transformations, and so on. The benchmark will include a variety of source to target mappings and business rules that will require conditional processing.
- <u>Aggregations</u>. An aggregation is essentially a grouping of records based on some condition, with a function to be applied to the group. SQL uses aggregate functions (e.g SUM) and GROUP BY clauses to specify aggregations on database tables. ETL tools are often used to aggregate data in order to pre-compute results for common warehouse queries. In some cases, ETL tools are used to calculate aggregations that go beyond what can be done in a single SQL statement. For example, sales transaction amounts might need to be summarized by month, quarter, and year. The ETL benchmark will include aggregations as part of the transformations.
- <u>Data cleansing</u>. Data cleansing includes a broad range of functionality, so much so that an entire market exists for tools that specialize in just data quality and cleansing. These tools typically specialize in very complex data cleansing processes such as name or address validation, matching, and standardization. While some ETL tools have integrated these capabilities or have relationships with vendors of these tools, the benchmark committee does not want

complicate the benchmark by requiring the sort of data cleansing that would require the use of a data quality tool. However, it is common practice for ETL tools to handle more straightforward data cleansing. This would include fixing 'dirty' data and standardizing values. For example, a simple one-character gender field could contain M,F,m,f,0,1. The ETL tool could standardize this data, so in the data warehouse the values are all 'FEMALE' and 'MALE'. The data generator for the benchmark will generate 'dirty' data in certain source fields. The business rules specified in the benchmark will define how this data should be handled by the ETL process.

- Database load, update, insert, and delete. An important element of the ETL process is the interaction with the target base. Initially, the transformed data must be put into the data warehouse. Then the ETL tool must be able to maintain the warehouse by performing subsequent lookups, inserts, updates, and deletes of the target database tables. The ETL benchmark specifies both an historical load scenario and an incremental update scenario to cover these cases.

6.2 Error Processing

There are many types of data inconsistencies and anomalies that can arise in the transformation process. In some cases, these are handled directly in the course of the transformation – these cases fall into the 'data cleansing' class of transformation described above. Cases that are not handled by the transformation logic become error conditions.

In the ETL benchmark, error conditions represent cases the ETL process does not resolve automatically (via transformation). These may be cases that are unaccounted for in the transformation (e.g. Gender field contains 'U') or other cases that would require human intervention to reconcile.

The benchmark will define the error conditions that can arise, and a standard behavior for processing the error records. The data generator for the benchmark will generate data that matches these error conditions, but the ratio of "good" data to "bad" data is not yet determined.

7   Reliability Requirements

ETL has become an integral part of the day to day operations of IT departments. In order for an ETL implementation to be considered a legitimate alternative, it must operate at a certain level of reliability. The exact requirements for reliability differ from one application to another, and therefore can be somewhat elusive to define in a general way. Despite the difficulty of defining ETL reliability, it is still an important aspect of the ETL processing and must be considered in the benchmark.

The development subcommittee intends to include some aspect of reliability into the benchmark. Beyond that, no substantive decisions have been reached at this time.

This section reflects the thoughts and opinions of the authors, not the subcommittee as whole.

Fundamentally, reliability relates to the correctness and predictability of the ETL implementation in both normal operation and failure conditions. The ETL tools and benchmark implementations should demonstrate these properties in both situations.

Under normal conditions, the ETL implementation should complete successfully with correct results. Given the same initial state and same set of inputs, two runs of the ETL process should produce the same result, with the caveats that the order of the rows in the result set may be different, and values generated by the ETL process itself may differ, provided the integrity of the results is maintained. For example, generated surrogate key values may be different, as long as they still uniquely identify rows in the result set, and references to those rows are set correctly. It should be possible to perform a standard series of checks to ensure the correctness of the results at the completion of each run.

Failure conditions may unexpectedly interrupt the ETL process. These are situations that are beyond the control of the ETL process, but cause an abnormal termination of the ETL process. Examples of failure conditions would be the user terminating the process, loss of connectivity to the target database, or a power failure. Note that this differs from data error handling. The benchmark specification will define the error handling behavior for data errors, and these will not cause the ETL process to abort. When an ETL process is interrupted, it should be able to be completed later, or restored to the starting point and re-run in its entirety. This implies that the original source data must remain intact, and the target database must not be left in an unusable or unrecoverable state. There are many approaches that can be taken to meet these reliability requirements; some may be automated and some may require manual intervention. It is not necessary for the benchmark to define the exact approach for implementations to follow, only the requirement that an interrupted run must ultimately be able to be completed with correct results.

The existence of the target database in the system under test raises additional questions about the reliability aspect of the benchmark. Should the benchmark also define reliability conditions for the target database to demonstrate? Being an ETL benchmark, this does not seem necessary. The benchmark should focus on aspects that are specific to the ETL process. In most cases, the ETL implementations will rely on the ACID properties of the database to meet the reliability requirements, and so these features will be indirectly demonstrated to some extent.

There are different approaches to incorporating reliability into the benchmark. It could be included as part of the overall metric, or simply demonstrated during the execution of the benchmark as a basic requirement, but not included in the actual measurements. However this is handled, the benchmark should at least require that the reliability requirements be met, and require disclosure of how the reliability of the ETL implementation was achieved.

8 Measuring ETL Performance

An ETL performance metric should be reflective of ETL processes and report parameters that are relevant for a prospective ETL customer. Ideally it would be a metric similar to what many customers already use to evaluate system performance. The metric should be simple to understand and explain.

As an industry-standard benchmark the metric must provide an easy and reliable way to compare system performance. Like other TPC benchmarks we expect to provide a single primary performance metric which will represent all aspects of the performance of a system. Multiple performance metrics would make the results difficult to compare. As a result the performance metric must measure overall system performance rather than individual components.

The metric must be able to appropriately reflect the performance of a wide range of systems from an entry-level single processor machine to a high-end multi-processor system and from a single node machine to a multi-node cluster. The metric must continue to be valid as system architectures evolve over time.

The business context section noted that the benchmark will involve a historical load ETL process and an incremental update ETL process. The performance metric must account for both processes.

There are two primary ways of measuring system performance, which we refer to as "time-based" and "workload-based." TPC-C [22] and TPC-E [17] are examples of time-based workloads. Using a time-based method, the timeframe to measure a system's performance is chosen and the measurement is based on how many operations the system is able to process in that timeframe. Higher performing systems will process a higher number of operations. This type of measurement is similar to situations where a limited time is available to execute the ETL process. Time-based measurements also provide predictability for benchmark sponsors since the time to run the benchmark is the same regardless of the size and performance of system under test.

TPC-H [23] and TPC-DS [24] are examples of workload-based benchmarks. Using this method the workload is fixed – for example a known set of operations against a known size of database – and the time to execute the workload is measured. Higher performing systems will process the same workload faster. This approach is similar to situations where the data warehouse must be completely updated and other work will be delayed until ETL process finishes. The need to use different workload sizes in order to properly exercise faster systems can provide a challenge when comparing results across differing systems. Results using different workload sizes cannot properly be compared.

There could be other measurement options, including a blend of the time-based and workload-based approaches. At this time the ETL benchmark development subcommittee has not chosen a method.

TPC benchmarks provide added value to customers by including a price-performance metric in addition to the pure performance metric, and soon an energy metric will be included as well. The price-performance metric is the ratio between the three year total cost of ownership (TCO) of the system and the primary performance metric. TPC pricing guidelines [25] apply to all TPC benchmarks and include the cost for hardware, software and maintenance. The definition of the energy metric for TPC benchmarks is nearing completion and will provide information about power consumption in relation to system performance in addition to other useful power usage information [26].

9   Scaling the Benchmark

As data volumes increase in databases everywhere, data volumes that must be handled by ETL processes are increasing as well. This is one of the key concerns that ETL customers have, so the method of scaling the ETL benchmark is a critical design point. The benchmark must be highly scalable to have a reasonable lifespan. At the same time, benchmark scaling is highly interconnected with the measurement method. As seen in the previous section a workload-based metric would result in a fundamentally different scaling approach compared to a time-based metric.

Workload-based metrics could present some interesting challenges in order to make all results comparable. For example, a workload that is appropriate for a small server might fit entirely in the cache of a much larger server, resulting in an unrealistic comparison. On the other hand, creating multiple sizes of workloads leads to non-comparable results, as happens with TPC-H results today, where results at different scale points cannot be compared.

Regardless of the approach taken to measure the performance, there are certain aspects of reality to observe in designing the scaling method. For example a country field should not scale to such a size that it exceeds the number of countries that exist. Likewise, dimension tables generally grow more slowly than fact tables, and this behavior should be modeled. The same principle applies to historical load versus incremental load: While the historical load will probably contain data spanning years, the incremental load would contain data representing a shorter period.

Scaling increment granularity should be chosen with care to allow for linear performance scaling. For example, setting the scaling granularity too big can lead to clusters of results grouped around certain scale increments. The usual approach is to focus on a dimension table that expresses a key component of the business process – for example the Customer table – and assign cardinality to the other tables in relation to this main table. There are a few dimension tables, such as a table of dates, which contain static information and will not scale with the rest of the tables.

10   Conclusion

Much work remains to complete the ETL benchmark. This paper has examined the need for and benefits of the benchmark, outlined what the ETL Benchmark Development Subcommittee has in place, and shown the areas that are still under discussion. The areas of apparent consensus include: the need for an ETL benchmark, the general scoping of the benchmark and the System Under Test, the scenario on which the benchmark will be based, the definitions of the source and destination data models, the general types of transformations, and the idea that the benchmark must include both a historical load and incremental updates. The areas still under discussion include: the reliability requirements to be specified, the definition of the benchmark metrics, and the method of scaling the benchmark. When these issues are settled, the data generator needs to be developed and the benchmark needs to be tested before it can be ratified.

Since ETL is a new area for the TPC, it is likely that some readers will have comments or feedback. Comments may be directed to the subcommittee chair at this address: LenWy@Microsoft.com. To follow the progress of the benchmark, check the TPC web site http://www.tpc.org.

The authors would like to thank the members of the subcommittee for their efforts and we look forward to working with them to complete the ETL benchmark.

References

1. Wikipedia article,
   `http://en.wikipedia.org/wiki/Extract,_transform,_load`
2. Wikipedia article, `http://en.wikipedia.org/wiki/Data_integration`
3. Kimball, R., Caserta, J.: The Data Warehouse ETL Toolkit. Wiley, Chichester (2004)
4. Serlin, O.: The History Of DebitCredit and the TPC,
   `http://research.microsoft.com/en-us/um/people/gray/`
   `benchmarkhandbook/chapter2.pdf`
5. Press release,
   `https://www.informatica.com/news/press_releases/2001/`
   `default.htm`
6. Press release quoted,`http://www.kid.co.za/content/company/`
   `product_announcements.asp#58`
7. Press release, `http://www.tmcnet.com/usubmit/2005/mar/1126716.htm`
8. Press release quoted,
   `http://www.crm2day.com/content/`
   `t6_librarynews_1.php?news_id=114041`
9. Press release,
   `http://www.informatica.com/news_events/press_releases/2005/`
   `06062005d_sun.aspx`
10. Press release, `http://www.biosmagazine.co.uk/`
    `press-release.php?id=7959`
11. Press release,`http://www.sas.com/news/preleases/051706/news8.html`
12. Press release,
    `http://www.informatica.com/news_events/press_releases/2006/`
    `08142006a_hp_server.aspx`
13. Press release, `https://www.jaspersoft.com/`
    `nw_press_jaspersoft_etl_talend.html`
14. Press release,
    `http://www.sas.com/news/preleases/041707/news9SASSUN.html`

15. Web log, http://blogs.msdn.com/sqlperf/archive/2008/02/27/etl-world-record.aspx
16. Press release, http://www.vertica.com/company/news_and_events/Syncsort-and-Vertica-Shatter-Database-ETL-World-Record-Using-HP-BladeSystem-c-Class
17. Transaction Processing Performance Council, http://tpc.org/tpce/
18. IBM Corporation, IBM InfoSphere Change Data Capture, http://www-01.ibm.com/software/data/infosphere/change-data-capture/
19. Oracle Corporation, Asynchronous Change Data Capture Cookbook, http://www.oracle.com/technology/products/bi/db/10g/pdf/twp_cdc_cookbook_0206.pdf
20. Microsoft Corporation, Change Data Capture, http://msdn.microsoft.com/en-us/library/bb522489.aspx
21. Kimball, R.: A Dimensional Modeling Manifesto, http://www.dbmsmag.com/9708d15.html
22. Transaction Processing Performance Council, http://www.tpc.org/tpcc/default.asp
23. Transaction Processing Performance Council, http://www.tpc.org/tpch/default.asp
24. Transaction Processing Performance Council, http://www.tpc.org/tpcds/The_Making_of_TPCDS.pdf
25. Transaction Processing Performance Council, http://www.tpc.org/pricing/default.asp
26. Transaction Processing Performance Council, http://www.tpc.org/information/TPC-PR-Webcast-Energy.wmv

Benchmarking ETL Workflows

Alkis Simitsis[1], Panos Vassiliadis[2], Umeshwar Dayal[1],
Anastasios Karagiannis[2], and Vasiliki Tziovara[2]

[1] HP Labs, Palo Alto, CA, USA
{alkis, Umeshwar.Dayal}@hp.com
[2] University of Ioannina, Dept. of Computer Science, Ioannina, Hellas
{pvassil, ktasos, vickit}@cs.uoi.gr

Abstract. Extraction–Transform–Load (ETL) processes comprise complex data workflows, which are responsible for the maintenance of a Data Warehouse. A plethora of ETL tools is currently available constituting a multi-million dollar market. Each ETL tool uses its own technique for the design and implementation of an ETL workflow, making the task of assessing ETL tools extremely difficult. In this paper, we identify common characteristics of ETL workflows in an effort of proposing a unified evaluation method for ETL. We also identify the main points of interest in designing, implementing, and maintaining ETL workflows. Finally, we propose a principled organization of test suites based on the TPC-H schema for the problem of experimenting with ETL workflows.

Keywords: Data Warehouses, ETL, benchmark.

1 Introduction

Data warehousing is a technology that enables decision-making and data analysis in large organizations. Several products are available in the market and for their evaluation, the TPC-H benchmark has been proposed as a decision support benchmark [16]. TPC-H focuses on OLAP (On-Line Analytical Processing) queries and it mainly deals with the data warehouse site. Another version termed TPC-DS has been around for the last few years, but this version is still in a draft form [11, 15]. TPC-DS considers a broader picture than TPC-H including the whole flow from the sources to the target data warehouse. However, it partially covers the data warehouse maintenance part, considering only simple mechanisms for inserting and deleting tuples.

To populate a data warehouse with up-to-date records extracted from operational sources, special tools are employed, called *Extraction – Transform – Load* (ETL) tools, which organize the steps of the whole process as a workflow. To give a general idea of the functionality of these workflows we mention their most prominent tasks, which include: (a) the *identification* of relevant information at the source side; (b) the *extraction* of this information; (c) the *transportation* of this information to the Data Staging Area (DSA), where most of the transformation usually take place; (d) the *transformation*, (i.e., customization and integration) of the information coming from

R. Nambiar and M. Poess (Eds.): TPCTC 2009, LNCS 5895, pp. 199–220, 2009.
© Springer-Verlag Berlin Heidelberg 2009

multiple sources into a common format; (e) the *cleansing* of the resulting data set, on the basis of database and business rules; and (f) the *propagation* and loading of the data to the data warehouse and the refreshment of data marts.

Due to their importance and complexity (see [2, 12] for relevant discussions and case studies), ETL tools constitute a multi-million dollar market. There is a plethora of commercial ETL tools available. The traditional database vendors provide ETL solutions along with the DBMS's: IBM with InfoSphere Information Server [7], Microsoft with SQL Server Integration Services (SSIS) [9], and Oracle with Oracle Warehouse Builder [10]. There also exist independent vendors that cover a large part of the market (e.g., Informatica with Powercenter [8] and Ab Initio [1]). Nevertheless, an in-house development of the ETL workflow is preferred in many data warehouse projects, due to the significant cost of purchasing and maintaining an ETL tool. The spread of existing solutions comes with a major drawback. Each one of them follows a different design approach, offers a different set of transformations, and provides a different internal language to represent essentially similar functions.

Although Extract-Transform-Load (ETL) tools are available in the market for more than a decade, only in the last few years have researchers and practitioners started to realize the importance that the integration process has in the success of a data warehouse project. There have been several efforts towards (a) modeling tasks and the automation of the design process, (b) individual operations (with duplicate detection being the area with most of the research activity) and (c) some first results towards the optimization of the ETL workflow as a whole (as opposed to optimal algorithms for their individual components). For lack of space, we refer the interested reader to [12] for a detailed survey on research efforts in the area of ETL tools.

The wide spread of industrial and ad-hoc solutions combined with the absence of a mature body of knowledge from the research community is responsible for the absence of a principled foundation of the fundamental characteristics of ETL workflows and their management. A small list of shortages concerning such characteristics include: no principled taxonomy of individual activities exists, few efforts have been made towards the optimization of ETL workflows as a whole, and practical problems like recovering from failures and handling evolution have mostly been ignored. Thus, *a commonly accepted, realistic framework for experimentation is also absent.*

Contributions. In this paper, we aim at providing a principled categorization of test suites for the problem of experimenting with a broad range of ETL workflows. First, we provide a principled way for constructing ETL workflows (Section 2). We identify the main functionality provided by representative commercial ETL tools and categorize the ETL operations into abstract logical activities. Based on that, we propose a categorization of ETL workflows, which covers frequent design cases. Then, we describe the main configuration parameters and a set of measures to be monitored for capturing the generic functionality of ETL tools (Section 3). Finally, we provide specific ETL scenarios based on the aforementioned analysis, which can be used as an experimental testbed for the evaluation of ETL design methods or tools (Section 4).

2 Problem Formulation

In this section, we introduce ETL workflows as graphs. Then, we zoom in the *micro-level* of ETL workflows inspecting each individual activity in isolation and then, we return at the *macro-level*, inspecting how individual activities are "tied" altogether to compose an ETL workflow. Finally, we discuss the characteristics of ETL execution and we tie them to the goals of the proposed benchmark.

2.1 ETL Workflows

An ETL workflow is a design blueprint for the ETL process. The designer constructs a workflow of activities (or operations), usually in the form of a graph, to specify the order of cleansing and transformation operations that should be applied to the source data, before being loaded to the data warehouse. In what follows, we use the term *recordsets* to refer to any data store that obeys a schema (such as relational tables and record files) and the term *activity* to refer to any software module that processes the incoming data, either by performing any schema transformation over the data or by applying data cleansing procedures. Activities and recordsets are *logical abstractions* of physical entities. At the logical level, we are interested in their schemata, semantics, and input-output relationships; however, we do not deal with the actual algorithm or program that implements the logical activity or with the storage properties of a recordset. When in a later stage, the logical-level workflow is refined at the physical level a combination of executable programs/scripts that perform the ETL workflow is devised. Then, each activity of the workflow is physically implemented using various algorithmic methods, each with different cost in terms of time requirements or system resources (e.g., CPU, memory, disk space, and disk I/O).

Formally, we model an ETL workflow as a directed acyclic graph $G(V,E)$. Each node $v \in V$ is either an activity a or a recordset r. An edge $(a,b) \in E$ is a *provider relationship* denoting that b receives data from node a for further processing. Nodes a and b are the data *provider* and data *consumer*, respectively. The following well-formedness constraints determine the interconnection of nodes in ETL workflows:

- Each recordset r is a pair (*r.name, r.schema*), with the schema being a finite list of attribute names.
- Each activity a is a tuple (N,I,O,S,A). N is the activity's name. I is a finite set of input schemata. O is a finite set of output schemata. S is a declarative description of the relationship of its output schema with its input schema in an appropriate language (without delving into algorithmic or implementation issues). A is the algorithm chosen for activity's execution.
- The data consumer of a recordset cannot be another recordset. Still, more than one consumer is allowed for recordsets.
- Each activity must have at least one provider, either another activity or a recordset. When an activity has more than one data providers, these providers can be other activities or activities combined with recordsets.
- The data consumer of an activity cannot be the same activity.

2.2 Micro-level Activities

At a micro level, we consider three broad categories of ETL activities: (a) *extraction* activities, (b) *transformation* and *cleansing* activities, and (c) *loading* activities.

Extraction activities extract the relevant data from the sources and transport them to the ETL area of the warehouse for further processing (possibly including operations like ftp, compress, etc.). The extraction involves either differential data sets with respect to the previous load, or full snapshots of the source. Loading activities have to deal with the population of the warehouse with clean and appropriately transformed data. This is typically done through a bulk loader program; nevertheless the process also includes the maintenance of indexes, materialized views, reports, and so on. Transformation and cleansing activities can be coarsely categorized with respect to the result of their application to data and the prerequisites, which some of them should fulfill. In this context, we discriminate the following categories of operations:

- *Row-level* operations, which are locally applied to a single row.
- *Router* operations, which locally decide, for each row, which of the many (output) destinations it should be sent to.
- *Unary Grouper* operations, which transform a set of rows to a single row.
- *Unary Holistic* operations, which perform a transformation to the entire data set. These are usually blocking operations.
- *Binary* or *N-ary* operations, which combine many inputs into one output.

All frequently built-in transformations in the majority of commercial solutions fall into our classification (see for example Figure A3 – in the appendix).

2.3 Macro Level Workflows

The macro level deals with the way individual activities and recordsets are combined together in a large workflow. The possibilities of such combinations are infinite. Nevertheless, our experience suggests that most ETL workflows follow several high-level patterns, which we present in a principled fashion in this section.

We introduce a broad category of workflows, called *Butterflies*. A butterfly (see also Figure 1) is an ETL workflow that consists of three distinct components: (a) the left wing, (b) the body, and (c) the right wing of the butterfly. The left and right wings (separated from the body with dashed lines in Figure 1) are two non-overlapping groups of nodes which are attached to the body of the butterfly. Specifically:

- The left wing of the butterfly includes one or more sources, activities and auxiliary data stores used to store intermediate results. This part of the butterfly performs the extraction, cleaning and transformation part of the workflow and loads the processed data to the body of the butterfly.
- The body of the butterfly is a central, detailed point of persistence that is populated with the data produced by the left wing. Typically, the body is a detailed *fact* or *dimension* table; still, other variants are also possible.
- The right wing gets the data stored at the body and utilizes them to support reporting and analysis activity. The right wing consists of materialized views, reports, spreadsheets, as well as the activities that populate them. In our setting, we abstract all the aforementioned static artifacts as materialized views.

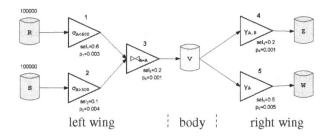

left wing   body   right wing

Fig. 1. Butterfly configuration

Balanced Butterflies. A butterfly that includes medium-sized left and right wings is called a *Balanced butterfly* and stands for an ETL scenario where incoming source data are merged to populate a warehouse table along with several views or reports defined over it. Figure 1 is an example of this class of butterflies. This variant represents a symmetric workflow (there is symmetry between the left and right wings). However, this is not always the practice in real-world cases. For instance, the butterfly's triangle wings are distorted in the presence of a router activity that involves multiple outputs (e.g., copy, splitter, switch, and so on). In general, the two fundamental wing components can be either *lines* or *combinations*. In the sequel, we discuss these basic patterns for ETL workflows that can be further used to construct more complex butterfly structures. Figure 2 depicts example cases of these variants.

Lines. Lines are sequences of activities and recordsets such that all activities have exactly one input (unary activities) and one output. Lines form single data flows.

Combinations. A combinator activity is a join variant (a binary activity) that merges parallel data flows through some variant of a join (e.g., a relational join, diff, merge, lookup or any similar operation) or a union (e.g., the overall sorting of two independently sorted recordsets). A combination is built around a combinator with lines or other combinations as its inputs. We differentiate combinations as left-wing and right-wing combinations.

Left-wing combinations are constructed by lines and combinations forming the left wing of the butterfly. The left wing contains at least one combination. The inputs of the combination can be:

- *Two lines.* Two parallel data flows are unified into a single flow using a combination. These workflows are shaped like the letter '*Y*' and we call them *Wishbones*.
- *A line and a recordset.* This refers to the practical case where data are processed through a line of operations, some of which require a lookup to persistent relations. In this setting, the *Primary Flow* of data is the line part of the workflow.
- *Two or more combinations.* The recursive usage of combinations leads to many parallel data flows. These workflows are called *Trees*.

Observe that in the cases of trees and primary flows, the target warehouse acts as the body of the butterfly (i.e., there is no right wing). This is a practical situation that covers (a) fact tables without materialized views and (b) the case of dimension tables that also need to be populated through an ETL workflow. In some cases, the body of the butterfly is not necessarily a recordset, but an activity with many outputs (see last example of Figure 2). Then, the main goal of the scenario is to distribute data to the appropriate flows; this task is performed by an activity serving as the butterfly's body.

Right-wing combinations are created by lines and combinations on the right wing of the butterfly. These lines and combinations form either a flat or a deep hierarchy.

- *Flat Hierarchies.* These configurations have small depth (usually 2) and large fan-out. An example of such a workflow is a *Fork*, where data are propagated from the fact table to the materialized views in two or more parallel data flows.
- *Right - Deep Hierarchies.* We also employ configurations with *right-deep hierarchies.* These configurations have significant depth and medium fan-out.

A more detailed description of the above structures is given in Section 4.2.

Butterflies are important for benchmarking at least in the following ways. Since such constructs are based on the classification of ETL activities discussed before, they form a taxonomy as aid for designing or understanding complex ETL workflows. In particular, we can use them for constructing more complex ETL workflows in a principle way. For example, if we need a memory intensive workflow, we should consider using tree or fork flows, which include routers/joins and a significant number of sorting or aggregating operations. If we wish to examine pipelining as well, we may consider extending these flows with line workflows (we need to tune the distribution of blocking and non-blocking operations in these flows too). In addition, to further enrich our workflows, we may also consider having multiple "bodies" in our design, which can represent not necessarily data warehouse tables, but ETL activities as well.

Moreover, having in hand such categorization one may decompose existing complex ETL workflows into sets of primitive constructs for getting insight into their functionality. This decomposition can be used for optimization purposes too. We can study the behavior of the abovementioned ETL patterns in isolation, and then, we can use our findings for optimizing and tuning the whole workflow for performance, maintainability or some other quality. For example, the performance of a complex workflow can be derived from the performance of the component primitive ones.

2.4 Goals of the Benchmark

The design of a benchmark should be based upon a clear understanding of the characteristics of the inspected systems that do matter. Therefore, we propose a configuration that covers a broad range of possible workflows (i.e., a large set of configurable parameters) and a limited set of monitored measures.

The goal of this benchmark is to provide the experimental testbed to be used for the assessment of ETL engines and design methods concerning their basic behavioral properties (measures) over a broad range of ETL workflows.

This benchmark's goal is to study and evaluate workflows as a whole. Here, we are not interested in providing *specialized performance measures for very specific tasks* in the overall process. We are not interested either, in exhaustively enumerating *all the possible alternatives for specific operations.* For example, this benchmark is not intended to facilitate the comparison of alternative methods for duplicate detection in a data set, since it does not take the tuning of all the possible parameters for this task under consideration. On the contrary, this benchmark can be used for the assessment of the integration of such methods in complex ETL workflows, assuming that all the necessary knobs have been appropriately tuned.

There are two modes of operation for ETL workflows: off-line (batch) and active (or continuous or real-time) modes. In the *off-line mode*, the workflow is executed during a specific time window (typically at night), when the systems are not servicing their end-users. Due to the low load of both the source and warehouse systems, the refreshment of data and any other administrative activities (cleanups, auditing, and so on) are easier to complete. In the *active mode*, the sources continuously try to send new data to the warehouse. This is not necessarily done instantly; rather, small groups of data are collected and sent to the warehouse for further processing. The two modes do not differ only on the frequency of the workflow execution, but also on how the workflow execution affects the load of the systems too.

Independently of the mode under which the ETL workflow operates, the two fundamental goals that should be reached are *effectiveness* and *efficiency*. Hence, given an ETL engine or a specific design method to be assessed over one or more ETL workflows, these fundamental goals should be evaluated.

Effectiveness. Our extensive discussions with ETL practitioners and experts have verified that in real-life ETL projects performance is not the only objective. On the contrary, other optimization qualities are of interest as well. We refer to these collectively as QoX [6]. The QoX metric suite is incorporated at all stages of the design process, from high-level specifications to implementation. A non-exhaustive list of metrics that can be used to guide optimization include: performance, recoverability, reliability, freshness, maintainability, scalability, availability, flexibility, robustness, affordability, consistency, traceability, and auditability. Some metrics are quantitative (e.g., reliability, freshness, cost) while other metrics may be difficult to quantify (e.g., maintainability, flexibility). Also, there are significant tradeoffs that should be taken under consideration, since an effort for improving one objective may hurt another one [13]. For example, improving freshness typically hurts recoverability, since considering recovery points on the way to the warehouse may be prohibitive in this case; on the other hand, having redundancy may be an interesting solution for achieving fault-tolerance. Due to space consideration, we do not elaborate on all the abovementioned measures (for a more detailed discussion we refer to [13]).

However, the main objective is to have data respect both database and business rules. We believe that the following (non-exhaustive) list of questions should be considered in the creation of an ETL benchmark:

Q1. Does the workflow execution reach the maximum possible level of data *freshness*, *completeness*, and *consistency* in the warehouse within the necessary time (or resource) constraints?

Q2. Is the workflow execution *resilient to* occasional *failures*?

Q3. Is the workflow easily *maintainable*?

Freshness. A clear business rule is the need to have data as fresh as possible in the warehouse. Also, we need all of the source data to be eventually loaded at the warehouse; the update latency depends on the freshness requirements. Nevertheless, the sources and the warehouse must be consistent at least at a certain frequency (e.g., at the end of a day).

Missing changes at the source. Depending on what kind of change detector we have at the source, it is possible that some changes are lost (e.g., if we have a log sniffer, bulk updates not passing from the log file are lost). Also, in an active warehouse, if the active ETL engine needs to shed some incoming data in order to be able to process the rest of the incoming data stream successfully, it is imperative that these left-over tuples need to be processed later.

Recovery from failures. If some data are lost from the ETL process due to failures, then, we need to synchronize sources and warehouse and compensate the missing data. Of course, tuples from aborted transactions that have been sent to the warehouse (or they are on their way to it) should be undone.

Maintainability. In addition, keeping the ETL workflow maintainable is crucial for the cost of ETL lifecycle. A number of parameters may affect the maintainability of the system. Here, we focus on parameters indicating the cost of handling evolution events during the ETL lifecycle. Ideally, a simple ETL design is more maintainable, whereas in a complex one it is more difficult to keep track of a change.

Efficiency. Efficiency is an important aspect of ETL design. Since typically ETL processes should run within strict time windows, performance does matter. In fact, achieving high performance is not only important per se, it can also serve as a means for enabling (or achieving) other qualities as well. For example, a typical technique for achieving recoverability is to add recovery points to the ETL workflow. However, this technique is time-consuming (usually, the i/o cost of maintaining recovery points is significant), so in order to meet the execution time requirements, we need to boost ETL performance. Typical questions need to be answered are as follows:

Q4. How *fast* is the workflow executed?

Q5. What degree of *parallelization* is required?

Q6. How much *pipelining* does the workflow use?

Q7. What *resource overheads* does the workflow incur at the source, intermediate (staging), and warehouse sites?

Parallelization. The configuration in terms of parallelism plays an important role for the performance of an ETL process. In general, there exist two broad categories of parallel processing: pipelining and partitioning. In pipeline parallelism, the various activities are operating simultaneously in a system with more than one processor. This scenario performs well for ETL processes that handle a relative small volume of data. For large volumes of data, a different parallelism policy should be devised: the partitioning of the dataset into smaller sets. Then, we use different instances of the ETL process for handling each partition of data. In other words, the same activity of an ETL process would run simultaneously by several processors, each processing a different partition of data. At the end of the process, the data partitions should be merged and loaded to the target recordset(s). Frequently, a combination of the two policies is used to achieve maximum performance. Hence, while an activity is processing partitions of data and feeding pipelines, a subsequent activity may start operating on a certain partition before the previous activity had finished.

Minimal overheads at the sources and the warehouse. The production systems are under continuous load due to the large number of OLTP transactions performed simultaneously. The warehouse system supports a large number of readers executing client applications or decision support queries. In the offline ETL, the overheads incurred are of rather secondary importance, since the contention with such processes is practically non-existent. Still, in active warehousing, the contention is clear.

- *Minimal overhead of the source systems.* It is imperative to impose the minimum additional workload to the source, in the presence of OLTP transactions.
- *Minimal overhead of the DW system.* As the warehouse is populated by loading processes, other processes ask data from it. Then, the desideratum is that the warehouse operates with the lightest possible footprints for the loading processes as well as the minimum possible delay for incoming tuples and user queries.

3 Benchmark Parameters

In this section, we propose a set of configuration parameters along with a set of measures to be monitored in order to assess the fulfillment of the benchmark goals.

Experimental Parameters. The following *problem parameters* are of particular importance to the measurement of ETL workflows:

P1. the *size of the workflow* (i.e., the number of nodes contained in the graph),
P2. the *structure of the workflow* (i.e., the variation of the nature of the involved nodes and their interconnection as the workflow graph),
P3. the *size of input data* originating from the sources,
P4. the *workflow selectivity*, based on the selectivities of the workflow activities,
P5. the values of *probabilities of failure*,
P6. the *latency* of updates at the warehouse (i.e., it captures freshness requirements),
P7. the required *completion time* (i.e., this reflects the maximum tolerated execution time window),
P8. the system *resources* (e.g., memory and processing power), and
P9. the "*ETL workload*" that determines an execution *order* for ETL workflows and the *number* of instances of the workflows that should run concurrently (e.g., for evaluating parallelization in an ETL engine, one may want to run first a complex ETL workload composed of a high number of line workflows that should run in parallel, and then, a smaller set of tree workflows for merging the former ones).

Measured Effects. For each set of experimental measurement, certain *measures* need to be assessed, in order to characterize the fulfillment of the aforementioned goals. In the sequel, we classify these measures according to the assessment question they are employed to answer.

<u>Q1. Measures for data freshness and data consistency</u>. The objective is to have data respect both database and business rules. Also, we need data to be consistent with respect to the source as much as possible. The latter possibly incurs a certain time window for achieving this goal (e.g., once a day), in order to accommodate high refresh rates in the case of active data warehouses or failures in the general case. Concrete measures are:

- (M1.1) Percentage of data that violate business rules.
- (M1.2) Percentage of data that should be present at their appropriate warehouse targets, but they are not.

<u>Q2. Measures for the resilience to failures</u>. The main idea is to perform a set of workflow executions that are intentionally abnormally interrupted at different stages of their execution. The objective is to discover how many of these workflows were successfully compensated within the specified time constraints. For achieving resilience to failures, we consider two strategies or quality objectives: recoverability and redundancy. For the former, the most typical technique is to enrich the ETL process with recovery points (used for intermediate staging of data processed up to that point), so that after a failure the process may resume from the latest recovery point. However, where to put such points is not a straightforward task. Redundancy can be achieved with three techniques: replication, diversity or fail-over. For lack of space, here we refer only to replication, which involves multiple instances of the same process (or of a part of it) that run in parallel. Concrete measures are:

- (M2.1) Percentage of successfully resumed workflow executions.
- (M2.2) MTBF, the mean time between failures.
- (M2.3) MTTR, mean time to repair.
- (M2.4) Number of recovery points used.
- (M2.5) Resumption type: synchronous or asynchronous.
- (M2.6) Number of replicated processes (for replication).
- (M2.7) Uptime of ETL process.

<u>Q3. Measures for maintainability</u>. Maintainability is a qualitative objective and finding measures to evaluate it is more difficult than the other quantitative objectives (e.g, performance or recoverability). An approach to this, is to consider the effort for modifying the process after a change has been occurred either at the SLA's (service level agreements) or the underlying systems (e.g., after adding, renaming or deleting an attribute or a table at a source site). Concrete measures are:

- (M3.1) Length of the workflow or in other words, the length of its longest path (i.e., how far in the process a change should be propagated).
- (M3.2) Complexity of the workflow refers to the amount of relationships that combine its components [3].
- (M3.3) Modularity (or cohesion) refers to the extent to which the workflow components perform exactly one job; thus, a workflow is more modular if it contains less sharable components. Modularity imposes some interesting tradeoffs, for example with parallelization.

- (M3.4) Coupling captures the amount of relationship among different recordsets or activities (i.e., workflow components).

Q4. Measures for the speed of the overall process. The objective is to perform the ETL process as fast as possible. In the case of off-line loading, the objective is to complete the process within the specified time-window. Naturally, the faster this is performed the better (especially, in the context of failure resumption). In the case of active warehouse, where the ETL process is performed very frequently, the objective is to minimize the time that each tuple spends inside the ETL module. Concrete measures are:

- (M4.1) Throughput of regular workflow execution (this may also be measured as total completion time).
- (M4.2) Throughput of workflow execution including a specific percentage of failures and their resumption.
- (M4.3) Average latency per tuple in regular execution.

Q5. Measures for partitioning. The partitioning parallelism is affected by a set of choices. Partitioning a flow is not straightforward, since the splitting and especially, the merging operations required for the partitioning do not come without a cost. Concrete measures are:

- (M5.1) Partition type (e.g., round-robin, hash-based, follow-database-partitioning, and so on), which should be chosen according the characteristics of the workflow. For example, a flow heavy on sort-based operations may consider hash-based partitioning instead of round-robin.
- (M5.2) Number and length of workflow parts that use partitioning.
- (M5.3) Number of partitions.
- (M5.4) Data volume in each partition (this is related to partition type too).

Q6. Measures for pipelining. The pipelining parallelization is affected by parts of the workflow that contain (or not) blocking operations (e.g., transformations based on sort or aggregation). Concrete measures are:
- (M6.1) CPU and memory utilization for pipelining flows or for individual operation run in such flows.
- (M6.2) Min/Max/Avg length of the largest and smaller paths (or subgraphs) containing pipelining operations.
- (M6.3) Min/Max/Avg number of blocking operations.

Q7. Measured Overheads. The overheads at the source and the warehouse can be measured in terms of consumed memory and latency with respect to regular operation. Concrete measures are:

- (M7.1) Min/Max/Avg/ timeline of memory consumed by the ETL process at the source system.
- (M7.2) Time needed to complete the processing of a certain number of OLTP transactions in the presence (as opposed to the absence) of ETL software at the source, in regular source operation.

- (M7.3) The same as 7.2, but in the case of source failure, where ETL tasks are to be performed too, concerning the recovered data.
- (M7.4) Min/Max/Avg/ timeline of memory consumed by the ETL process at the warehouse system.
- (M7.5) (active warehousing) Time needed to complete the processing of a certain number of decision support queries in the presence (as opposed to the absence) of ETL software at the warehouse, in regular operation.
- (M7.6) The same as M7.5, but in the case of any (source or warehouse) failure, where ETL tasks are to be performed too at the warehouse side.

4 Specific Scenarios

A particular problem that arises in designing a test suite for ETL workflows concerns the complexity (structure and size) of the employed workflows. A means to deal with this is to construct a *workflow generator*, based on the aforementioned disciplines. Another means is to come up with an *indicative set of ETL workflows* that serve as the basis for experimentations. For space consideration, here we present the latter and we propose a small, exemplary set of specific ETL flows based on the TPC-H [16].

4.1 Database Schema

The information kept in the warehouse concerns parts and their suppliers as well as orders that customers have along with demographic data for the customers. The scenarios used in the experiments clean and transform the source data into the desired *warehouse schema*. The sources for our experiments are of two kinds, the *storage houses* and *sales points*. Every storage house keeps data for the suppliers and parts, while every sales point keeps data for the customers and the orders. (The schemata of the sources and the data warehouse are depicted in Figure A1 – in the appendix.)

4.2 ETL Scenarios

We consider the butterfly cases discussed in Section 2 to be representative of a large number of ETL scenarios and thus, we propose a specific scenario for each kind. Due to space limitation, here we provide only small-size scenarios indicatively (e.g., a right-deep scenario is not given). However, as we discussed, one may create larger scenarios based on these exemplary structures. The scenarios are depicted in Figure 2 (their detailed descriptions can be found in the appendix of this paper).

The **line** workflow has a simple form since it applies a set of filters, transformations, and aggregations to a single table. This scenario type is used to filter source tables and assure that the data meet the logical constraints of the data warehouse.

A **wishbone** workflow joins two parallel lines into one. This scenario is preferred when two tables in the source database should be joined in order to be loaded to the data warehouse or in the case where we perform similar operations to different data that are later joined. In our exemplary scenario, we track the changes that happen in a

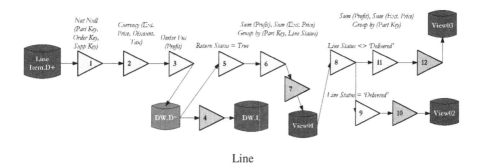

Line

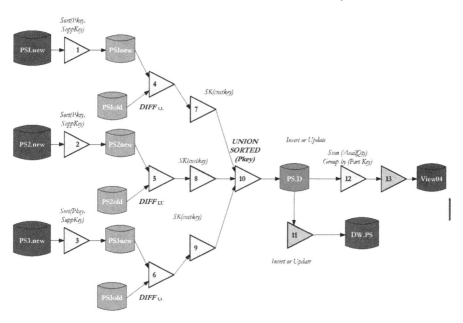

Wishbone   Primary Flow

Tree

Fig. 2. Specific ETL workflows

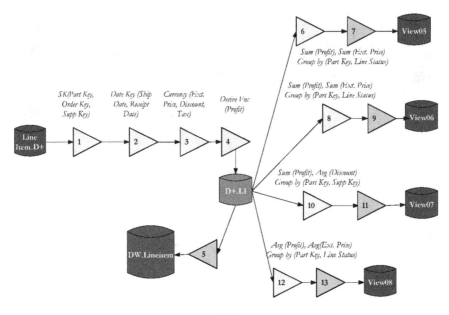

Fork

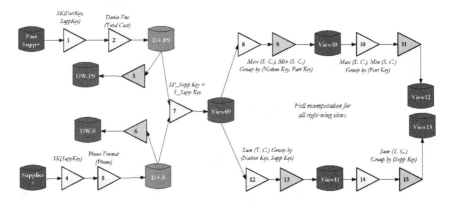

Balanced Butterfly (1)

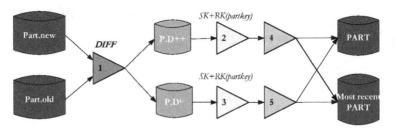

Balanced Butterfly (2)

Fig. 2. (*continued*)

source containing customers. We compare the customers of the previous load to the ones of the current load and search for new customers to be loaded in the warehouse.

The **primary flow** scenario is a common scenario in cases where the source table must be enriched with surrogate keys. This exemplary primary flow that we use has as input the *Orders* table. The scenario is simple: all key-based values ("orderstatus", "custkey", "orderkey") pass through surrogate key filters that lookup (join) the incoming records in the appropriate lookup table. The resulting rows are appended to the relation *DW.Orders*. If incoming records exist in the *DW.Orders* relation and they have changed values then they are overwritten (thus, the Slowly Changing Dimension Type 1 tag in the figure); otherwise, a new entry is inserted in the warehouse relation.

The **tree** scenario joins several source tables and applies aggregations on the result recordset. The join can be performed over either heterogeneous relations, whose contents are combined, either over homogeneous relations, whose contents are integrated into one unified (possible sorted) data set. In our case, the exemplary scenario involves three sources for the warehouse relation *PartSupp*.

The **fork** scenario applies a set of aggregations on a single source table. First the source table is cleaned, just like in a line scenario and the result table is used to create a set of materialized views. Our exemplary scenario uses the *Lineitem* table as the butterfly's body and starts with a set of extracted new records to be loaded.

The most general-purpose scenario type is a **butterfly** scenario. It joins two or more source tables before a set of aggregations is performed on the result of the join. The left wing of the butterfly joins the source tables, while the right wing performs the desired aggregations producing materialized views. Our first exemplary scenario uses new source records concerning *Partsupp* and *Supplier* as its input. A second exemplary scenario introduces a Slowly Changing Dimension plan, populating the dimension table *PART* and retaining its history at the same time.

5 Related Work

Several benchmarks have been proposed in the database literature, in the past. Most of the benchmarks that we have reviewed make careful choices: (a) on the database schema & instance they use, (b) on the type of operations employed and (c) on the measures to be reported. Each benchmark has a guiding goal, and these three parts of the benchmark are employed to implement it.

As an example, we mention two benchmarks mainly coming from the Wisconsin database group. The OO7 benchmark was one of the first attempts to provide a comparative platform for object-oriented DBMS's [4]. The OO7 benchmark had the clear target to test as many aspects as possible of the efficiency of the measured systems (speed of pointer traversal, update efficiency, query efficiency). The BUCKY benchmark had a different viewpoint: the goal was to narrow down the focus only on the aspects of an OODBMS that were object-oriented (or object-relational): queries over inheritance, set-valued attributes, pointer navigation, methods and ADTS [5]. Aspects covered by relational benchmarks were not included in the BUCKY benchmark.

TPC has proposed two benchmarks for the case of decision support. The TPC-H benchmark [16] is a decision support benchmark that consists of a suite of business-oriented ad-hoc queries and concurrent data modifications. The database describes a sales system, keeping information for the parts and the suppliers, and data about orders and the supplier's customers. The relational schema of TPC-H consists of eight separate tables with 5 of them being clearly dimension tables, one being a clear fact table and a couple of them combinations of fact and dimension tables. *Unfortunately, the refreshment operations provided by the benchmark are primitive and not particularly useful as templates for the evaluation of ETL scenarios.*

TPC-DS is a new Decision Support (DS) workload being developed by the TPC [11, 15]. This benchmark models the decision support system of a retail product supplier, including queries and data maintenance. The relational schema of this benchmark is more complex than the schema presented in TPC-H. There are three sales channels: store, catalog and the web. There are two fact tables in each channel, sales and returns, and a total of seven fact tables. In this dataset, the row counts for tables scale differently per table category: specifically, in fact tables the row count grows linearly, while in dimension tables grows sub-linearly. This benchmark also provides refreshment scenarios for the data warehouse. Still, *all these scenarios belong to the category of primary flows*, in which surrogate and global keys are assigned to all tuples. Recently, a new effort has been started driven by the TPC-ETL committee, but so far, concrete results have not been reported [15].

An early version of this paper was presented in [17]; due to lack of formal proceedings, please refer to the online version.

6 Conclusions

In this paper, we have dealt with the challenge of presenting a unified experimental playground for ETL processes. First, we have presented a principled way for constructing ETL workflows and we have identified their most prominent elements. We have classified the most frequent ETL operations based on their special characteristics. We have shown that this classification adheres to the built-in operations of three popular commercial ETL tools; we do not anticipate any major deviations for other tools. Moreover, we have proposed a generic categorization of ETL workflows, namely butterflies, which covers frequent design cases. We have identified the main parameters and measures that are crucial in ETL environment and we have discussed how parallelism affects the execution of an ETL process. Finally, we have proposed specific ETL scenarios based on the aforementioned analysis, which can be used as an experimental testbed for the evaluation of ETL methods or tools.

Open issues involve (a) the handling of non-relational data, the treatment of near real time ETL, (c) the tuning of several parameters of the benchmark with values that reflect real-world applications, (d) the handling of indexes, materialized views and auxiliary data structures at the target side of the warehouse, and (e) the treatment of platform and hardware characteristics. Extra care should be taken also for the control flow part of ETL processes.

The main message from our work is the need for a commonly agreed benchmark that reflects real-world ETL scenarios, both for research purposes and, ultimately, for the comparison of ETL tools. Feedback is necessary for further tuning the benchmark.

References

[1] Ab Initio (2009), http://www.abinitio.com/
[2] Adzic, J., Fiore, V.: Data Warehouse Population Platform. In: DMDW (2003)
[3] Briand, L.C., Morasca, S., Basili, V.R.: Property-Based Software Engineering Measurement. IEEE Trans. on Software Engineering 22(1) (1996)
[4] Carey, M.J., DeWitt, D.J., Naughton, J.F.: The OO7 Benchmark. In: SIGMOD (1993)
[5] Carey, M.J., et al.: The BUCKY Object-Relational Benchmark. In: SIGMOD (1997)
[6] Dayal, U., Castellanos, M., Simitsis, A., Wilkinson, K.: Data Integration Flows for Business Intelligence. In: EDBT (2009)
[7] IBM, IBM InfoSphere Information Server (2009),
   http://www-01.ibm.com/software/data/integration/
   info_server_platform/
[8] Informatica, PowerCenter (2009),
   http://www.informatica.com/products/powercenter/
[9] Microsoft. SQL Server Integration Services (SSIS) (2009),
   http://technet.microsoft.com/en-us/sqlserver/bb331782.aspx
[10] Oracle, Oracle Warehouse Builder 11g (2009),
   http://www.oracle.com/technology/products/warehouse/
[11] Othayoth, R., Poess, M.: The Making of TPC-DS. In: VLDB (2006)
[12] Simitsis, A., Vassiliadis, P., Skiadopoulos, S., Sellis, T.: Data Warehouse Refreshment. In: Data Warehouses and OLAP: Concepts, Architectures and Solutions. IRM Press (2006)
[13] Simitsis, A., Wilkinson, K., Castellanos, M., Dayal, U.: QoX-Driven ETL Design: Reducing the Cost of the ETL Consulting Engagements. In: SIGMOD (2009)
[14] TPC. TPC Benchmark Status. TPC-ETL (2009),
   http://www.tpc.org/reports/status/
[15] TPC. TPC-H benchmark. Transaction Processing Council (2009),
   http://www.tpc.org/
[16] Vassiliadis, P., Karagiannis, A., Tziovara, V., Simitsis, A.: Towards a Benchmark for ETL Workflows. In: QDB (2007),
   http://www.cs.uoi.gr/~pvassil/publications/publications.html

Appendix

The schemata of the sources and the data warehouse are depicted in Figure A1.

```
Data Warehouse:
PART(rkey s_partkey,name,mfgr,brand,type,size,container,comment)
SUPPLIER (s_suppkey, name, address, nationkey, phone, acctbal, comment, totalcost)
PARTSUPP(s_partkey, s_suppkey,availqty,supplycost, comment)
CUSTOMER (s_custkey, name, address, nationkey, phone, acctball, mktsegment, comment)
ORDER (s_orderkey, custkey, orderstatus, totalprice, orderdate, orderpriority, clerk, shippri-
              ority, comment)
LINEITEM (s_orderkey, partkey, suppkey, linenumber, quantity, extendedprice, discount,
              tax, returnflag, linestatus, shipdate, commitdate, receiptdate, shipinstruct, ship-
              mode, comment, profit)
Storage House:
PART (partkey, name,mfgr,brand,type,size,container, comment)
SUPPLIER (suppkey, name, address, nationkey, phone, acctbal, comment)
PARTSUPP (partkey, suppkey, availqty, supplycost, comment)
Sales Point:
CUSTOMER (custkey, name, address, nationkey, phone, acctball, mktsegment, comment)
ORDER (orderkey, custkey, orderstatus, totalprice, orderdate, orderpriority, clerk, shippri-
              ority, comment)
LINEITEM (orderkey, partkey, suppkey, linenumber, quantity, extendedprice, discount, tax,
              returnflag, linestatus, shipdate, commitdate, receiptdate, shipinstruct, shipmode,
              comment)
```

Fig. A1. Database schemata

Detailed Description of Scenarios

Line. In the proposed scenario, we start with an extracted set of new source rows *LineItem.D+* and push them towards the warehouse as follows:

1. First, we check the fields "partkey", "orderkey" and "suppkey" for NULL values. Any NULL values are replaced by appropriate special values.

2. Next, a calculation of a value "profit" takes place. This value is locally derived from other fields in a tuple as the amount of "extendedprice" subtracted by the values of the "tax" and "discount" fields.

3. The third activity changes the fields "extendedprice", "tax", "discount" and "profit" to a different currency.

4. The results of this operation are loaded first into a delta table *DW.D+* and subsequently into the data warehouse *DWH*. The first load simply replaces the respective recordset, whereas the second involves the incremental appending of these rows to the warehouse.

5. The workflow is not stopped after the completion of the left wing, since we would like to create some materialized views. The next operation is a filter that keeps only records whose return status is "False".

6. Next, an aggregation calculates the sum of "extendedprice" and "profit" fields grouped by "partkey" and "linestatus".

7. The results of the aggregation are loaded in view *View01* by (a) updating existing rows and (b) inserting new groups wherever appropriate.

8. The next activity is a router, sending the rows of view *View01* to one of its two outputs, depending on the "linestatus" field has the value "delivered" or not.

9. The rows with value "delivered" are further aggregated for the sum of "profit" and "extendedprice" fields grouped by "partkey".

10. The results are loaded in view *View02* as in the case for view *View01*.

11. The rows with value different than "delivered" are further aggregated for the sum of "profit" and "extendedprice" fields grouped by "partkey".

The results are loaded in view *View03* as in the case for view *View01*.

Wishbone. The scenario evolves as follows:

1. The first activity on the new data set checks for NULL values in the "custkey" field. The problematic rows are kept in an error log file for further off-line processing.

2. Both previous and old data are passed through a surrogate key transformation. We assume a domain size that fits in main memory for this source; therefore, the transformation is not performed as a join with a lookup table, but rather as a lookup function call invoked per row.

3. Moreover, the next activity converts the phone numbers in a numeric format, removing dashes and replacing the '+' character with the "00" equivalent.

4. The transformed recordsets are persistently stored in relational tables or files which are subsequently compared through a difference operator (typically implemented as a join variant) to detect new rows.

5. The new rows are stored in a file $C.D^+$ which is kept for the possibility of failure. Then the rows are appended in the warehouse dimension table *Customer*.

Tree. The scenario evolves as follows:

1. Each new version of the source is sorted by its primary key and checked against its past version for the detection of new or updated records. The $DIFF_{I,U}$ operator checks the two inputs for the combination of pkey, suppkey matches. If a match is not found, then a new record is found. If a match is found and there is a difference in the field "availqty" then an update needs to be performed.

2. These new records are assigned surrogate keys per source

3. The three streams of tuples are united in one flow and they are also sorted by "pkey" since this ordering will be later exploited. Then, a delta file *PS.D* is produced.

4. The contents of the delta file are appended in the warehouse relation *DW.PS*.

At the same time, the materialized view *View04* is refreshed too. The delta rows are summarized for the available quantity per pkey and then, the appropriate rows in the view are either updated (if the group exists) or (inserted if the group is not present).

Fork. The fork scenario evolves as follows:

1. Surrogate keys are assigned to the fields "partkey", "orderkey" and "suppkey".

2. We convert the dates in the "shipdate" and "receiptdate" fields into a "dateId", a unique identifier for every date.

3. The third activity is a calculation of a value "profit". This value is derived from other fields in every tuple as the amount of "extendedprice" subtracted by the values of the "tax" and "discount" fields.
4. This activity changes the fields "extendedprice", "tax", "discount" and "profit" to a different currency. The result of this actvity is stored at a delta table $D^+.LI$. The records are appended to the data warehouse *LineItem* table and they are also reused for a number of aggregations at the right wing of the butterfly. All records pushed towards the views, either update or insert new records in the views, depending on the existence (or not) of the respective groups.
5. The aggregator for *View05* calculates the sum of the "profit" and "extendedprice" fields grouped by the "partkey" and "linestatus" fields.
6. The aggregator for *View06* calculates the sum of the "profit" and "extendedprice" fields grouped by the "linestatus" fields.
7. The aggregator for *View07* calculates the sum of the "profit" field and the average of the "discount" field grouped by the "partkey" and "suppkey" fields.
8. The aggregator for *View08* calculates the average of the "profit" and "extendedprice" fields grouped by the "partkey" and "linestatus" fields.

Butterfly. The first scenario uses *Partsupp* and *Supplier* as its input.

1. Concerning the *Partsupp* source, we generate surrogate key values for the "partkey" and "suppkey" fields. Then, the "totalcost" field is calculated and added to each tuple.
2. Then, the transformed records are saved in a delta file $D+.PS$ and appended to the relation *DW.Partsupp*.
3. Concerning the *Supplier* source, a surrogate key is generated for the "suppkey" field and a second activity transforms the "phone" field.
4. Then, the transformed records are saved in a delta file $D+.S$ and appended to the relation *DW.Supplier*.
5. The delta relations are subsequently joined on the "ps_suppkey" and "s_suppkey" fields and populate the view *View09*, which is augmented with the new records. Then, several views are computed from scratch, as follows.
6. View *View10* calculates the maximum and the minimum value of the "supplycost" field grouped by the "nationkey" and "partkey" fields.
7. *View12* calculates the maximum and the minimum of the "supplycost" field grouped by the "partkey" fields.
8. *View11* calculates the sum of the "totalcost" field grouped by the "nationkey" and "suppkey" fields.
9. *View13* calculates the sum of the "totalcost" field grouped by the "suppkey" field.

The second butterfly scenario concerns Slowly Changing dimensions, populating the dimension table *PART* and retaining its history at the same time. The trick is found in the combination of the "rkey", "s_partkey" attributes. The "s_partkey" assigns a surrogate key to a certain tuple (e.g., assume it assigns 10 to a product X). If the product changes in one or more attributes at the source (e.g., X's "size" changes), then a new record is generated, with the same "s_partkey" and a different "rkey" (which can be a timestamp-based key, or similar). The scenario works as follows:

1. A new and an old version of the source table *Part* are compared for changes. Changes are directed to *P.D++* (for new records) and *P.DU* for updates in the fields "size" and "container"
2. Surrogate and recent keys are assigned to the new records that are propagated to the table *PART* for storage.
3. An auxiliary table *MostRecentPART* holding the most recent "rkey" per "s_partkey" is appropriately updated.

Observe that in this scenario the body of the butterfly is an activity.

Statistics

Figure A2 presents summarized statistics of the constituents of the ETL workflows depicted in Figure 2. Such statistics reveal the functionality (i.e., the nature) of each workflow. (The numbers L+R refer to the left (L) and right (R) wings, respectively.)

	Filters	Functions	Routers	Aggr	Holistic f.	Joins	Diff	Unions	Load Body	Load Views
Line	1+1	2+0	0+1	0+3					INCR	INCR
Wishbone	1+0	4+0				1+0			INCR	-
Pr. Flow						3+0			I/U	-
Tree				0+1	1+0	1+0		1+0	I/U	I/U
Fork		3+0		0+4					INCR	INCR
BB(1)		4+0		0+4		1+0			INCR	FULL
BB(2)		0+2					1		-	I/U
	2+1	13+2	0+1	0+12	1+0	6+0	1	1+0		

Fig. A2. Statistics of the proposed ETL workflows

Taxonomy of Activities

Figure A3 presents a taxonomy of activities at the micro level and similar built-in transformations provided by commercial ETL tools. For each category of activities presented in Section 2.2, a representative set of transformations, which are provided by three popular commercial ETL tools, is presented. The figure is indicative and in many ways incomplete. The goal is not to provide a comparison among the three tools. On the contrary, we would like to stress out the genericity of our classification. For most ETL tools, the set of built-in transformations is enriched by user defined operations and a plethora of functions. Still, as figure A3 shows, all frequently built-in transformations existing in commercial solutions fall into our classification.

	Transformation Category[*]	SQL Server Information Services SSIS	DataStage	Oracle Warehouse Builder
Transformation and Cleansing	**Row-level**: Function that can be applied locally to a single row	– Character Map – Copy Column – Data Conversion – Derived Column – Script Component – OLE DB Command – Other filters (not null, selections, etc.)	– Transformer (A generic representative of a broad range of functions: date and time, logical, mathematical, null handling, number, raw, string, utility, type conversion/casting, routing.) – Remove duplicates – Modify (drop/keeps columns or change their types)	– Deduplicator (distinct) – Filter – Sequence – Constant – Table function (it is applied on a set of rows for increasing the performance) – Data Cleaning Operators (Name and Address, Match-Merge) – Other SQL transformations (Character, Date, Number, XML)
	Routers: Locally decide, for each row, which of the many outputs it should be sent to	– Conditional Split – Multicast	– Copy – Filter – Switch	– Splitter
	Unary Grouper: Transform a set of rows to a single row	– Aggregate – Pivot/Unpivot	– Aggregator – Make/Split subrecord – Combine/Promote records – Make/Split vector	– Aggregator – Pivot/Unpivot
	Unary Holistic: Perform a transformation to the entire data set (blocking)	– Sort – Percentage Sampling – Row Sampling	– Sort (sequential, parallel, total)	– Sorter
	Binary or N-ary: Combine many inputs into one output	Union-like: – Union All – Merge Join-like: – Merge Join (MJ) – Lookup (SKJ) – Import Column (NLJ)	Union-like: – Funnel (continuous, sort, sequence) Join-like: – Join – Merge – Lookup Diff-like: – Change capture/apply – Difference (record-by-record) – Compare (column-by-column)	Union-like: – Set (union, union all, intersect, minus) Join-like: – Joiner – Key Lookup (SKJ)
Extr.		– Import Column Transformation	– Compress/Expand – Column import	– Merge – Import
Load		– Export Column – Slowly Changing Dimension	– Compress/Expand – Column import/export	– Merge – Export – Slowly Changing Dimension

[*] All ETL tools provide a set of physical operations that facilitate either the extraction or the loading phase. Such operations include: extraction from hashed/sequential files, delimited/fixed width/multi-format flat files, file set, ftp, lookup, external sort, compress/uncompress, and so on.

Fig. A3. Taxonomy of ETL activities

A Performance Study of Event Processing Systems

Marcelo R.N. Mendes, Pedro Bizarro, and Paulo Marques

CISUC, University of Coimbra,
Dep. Eng. Informática – Pólo II, 3030-290, Coimbra, Portugal
{mnunes, bizarro, pmarques}@dei.uc.pt

Abstract. Event processing engines are used in diverse mission-critical scenarios such as fraud detection, traffic monitoring, or intensive care units. However, these scenarios have very different operational requirements in terms of, e.g., types of events, queries/patterns complexity, throughput, latency and number of sources and sinks. What are the performance bottlenecks? Will performance degrade gracefully with increasing loads? In this paper we make a first attempt to answer these questions by running several micro-benchmarks on three different engines, while we vary query parameters like window size, window expiration type, predicate selectivity, and data values. We also perform some experiments to assess engines scalability with respect to number of queries and propose ways for evaluating their ability in adapting to changes in load conditions. Lastly, we show that similar queries have widely different performances on the same or different engines and that no engine dominates the other two in all scenarios.

Keywords: Benchmarking, Complex Event Processing, Micro-benchmarks.

1 Introduction

Complex Event Processing (CEP)[1] has emerged as a new paradigm to monitor and react to continuously arriving *events* in (soft-)real time. The wide applicability of event processing has drawn increased attention both from academia and industry, giving rise to many research projects [1, 2, 7, 16] and commercial products. CEP has been used for several purposes, including fraud detection, stock trading, supply-chain monitoring, network management, traffic monitoring or intensive care units control.

Most scenarios where event engines are being deployed are mission-critical situations with demanding performance requirements (e.g., high throughput and/or low latency). Interestingly, the range of scenarios is very broad and presents very different operational requirements in terms of throughput, response time, type of events, patterns, number of sources, number of sinks, scalability, and more. It is unclear what type of requirements demand more from engines, what happens when parameters are varied, or if performance degrades gracefully. To address the lack of event processing performance information, in this paper we make the following contributions:

---

[1] We use the terms "complex event processing", "CEP" and "event processing" interchangeably. Likewise, we also use the terms "CEP system" and "CEP engine" interchangeably.

R. Nambiar and M. Poess (Eds.): TPCTC 2009, LNCS 5895, pp. 221–236, 2009.
© Springer-Verlag Berlin Heidelberg 2009

i. We present a number of micro-benchmarks to stress fundamental operations such as selection, projection, aggregation, join, pattern detection, and windowing (summarized in Section 3).

ii. We perform an extensive experimental evaluation of three different CEP products (two commercial, one open-source), with varying combinations of window type, size, and expiration mode, join and predicate selectivity, tuple width, incoming throughput, reaction to bursts and query sharing (Section 4).

2   Event Processing Overview

Like Data Stream Management Systems (DSMS) [1, 2, 16], CEP systems are designed to handle real time data that arrive constantly in the form of *event streams*. CEP queries are *continuous* in the sense that they are registered once and then run indefinitely, returning updated results as new events arrive. Due to low-latency requirements, CEP engines manipulate events in main memory rather than in secondary storage media. Since it is not possible to keep all events in memory, CEP engines use *moving windows* to keep only a subset (typically the most recent part) of the event streams in memory. In addition to these features shared with DSMS, CEP engines also provide the ability to define reactive rules that fire upon detection of specific patterns. Ideally, CEP engines should be able to *continuously adapt* their execution to cope with variations (e.g., in arrival rate or in data distributions) and should be able to scale by *sharing computation* among similar queries.

Section 2.1 lists the operations typically performed by CEP systems. We use these operations as the basis of the micro-benchmarks of Section 3.

2.1   CEP Characterization

A few event processing uses cases have been recently published [6], but it is still unclear which of them, if any, is representative of the field. There is, however, a core set of operations used in most scenarios and available, in one form or another, in all products:

- *Windowing;*
- *Transformation;*
- *Aggregation/Grouping;*
- *Merging (Union);*

- *Filtering (Selection/Projection);*
- *Sorting/Ranking;*
- *Correlation/Enrichment (Join);*
- *Pattern Detection.*

The performance of a CEP engine depends on: i) the algorithms implementing these basic operations; ii) parameters such as window type and size, and predicate selectivity; and iii) external parameters such as available resources, incoming data, and number and type of queries and rules.

2.2   Window Policies

Moving windows are fundamental structures in CEP engines, being used in many types of queries. Windows with different properties produce different results and have radically different performance behaviors. *Window policies* determine when events are inserted and removed (expired) from moving windows and when to output computations. Three aspects define a policy [12]:

i. **Window Type:** determines how the window is defined. *Physical* or *time-based* windows are defined in terms of time intervals. *Logical*, *count-based*, or *tuple-based* are defined in terms of number of tuples[2].

ii. **Expiration Mode:** determines how the window endpoints change and which tuples are expired from the window. In *sliding* windows endpoints move together and events continuously expire with new events or passing time (e.g., "last 30 seconds"). In *jumping* or *tumbling* windows the head endpoint moves continuously while the tail endpoint moves (jumps) only sporadically (e.g. "current month"). The infrequent jump of the tail endpoint of jumping windows is said to *close or reset the window*, expiring all tuples at once. In a *landmark* window one endpoint is moving, the other is fixed, and events do not expire (e.g., "since 01-01-2000").

iii. **Update Interval (Evaluation Mode):** determines when to output results: every time a new event arrives or expires, only when the window closes (i.e., reaches its maximum capacity/age), or periodically at selected intervals.

In general, commercial engines do not support all the combinations above.

3 Dataset and Micro-benchmarks

In this section we describe the dataset used in our tests and summarize the micro-benchmarks in Table 2 (*a detailed description of the queries appears in Section 4*). We use a synthetic dataset because it allows exploring the parameter and performance space more freely than any single real dataset. The dataset schema is based on sample schemas available at the Stream Query Repository (SQR) [21]. In most application domains of SQR, event records consist in: i) an identifier for the entities in the domain (e.g., stock symbols in trading examples); ii) a set of domain-specific properties (e.g., "price", "speed", or "temperature"), typically represented as floating point numbers; and iii) the time when the event happened or was registered.

Based on these observations, we define the generic dataset schema of Table 1. The ID field identifies the entity being reported in the stream. The number of different entities, MAX_ID (ranges from 10 to 5.000.000), can greatly affect performance in

Table 1. Schema of the dataset used

Field	Type	Domain
ID	int	Equiprobable numbers in the range (1, MAX_ID)
$A_1...A_N$	double	Random values following a uniform distribution U(1,100)
TS	long	Timestamp.

---

[2] There are also *semantic windows* whose contents depend on some property of the data (e.g., all events between events "*login*" and "*logout*"). We do not consider semantic windows in our study as none of the engines we tested implements them.

Table 2. Summary of micro-benchmarks

Query	Factors under analysis	Metrics
Selection and Projection	• Selectivity: [1%, 5%, 25%, 50%] • # attributes: [5, 10, 25, 50, 125]	Throughput
Aggregations and Windows	• Window size (tuples): 500 to 500K • Window expiration: [*sliding, jumping*] • Aggregations: [*SUM, MAX, STDEV*]	Throughput
Joins	• Input Source: [stream, window, in-memory table, external table] • Input Size (# events): 500 to 100M • Join Selectivity: 0.01 to 10	Throughput
Pattern Detection	• Window Size (secs): 10 to 600 • MAX_ID: [100, 1k, 10k, 100k] • Predicate Selectivity: 0.1% to 10%	Throughput
Large Time-Based Windows	• Injection Rate (events/sec): 500 to 100K • Window Size: 10 minutes to 12 hours	Throughput Memory consumption
Adaptability	(See Section 4.8.)	Maximum latency Latency degradation ratio Recovery Time Post-peak latency variation ratio
Multiple queries	• Number of Queries: [1, 4, 16, 64] • Window definition (size: 400k to 500k)	Throughput Memory consumption

joins, pattern matching queries, and aggregations. Tuple width is varied with the number of attributes A_i (from 1 to 125). The TS timestamp field is expressed in milliseconds and assigned by the load generator at runtime.

4 Tests Specification and Results

In this section we discuss the results obtained after running the micro-benchmarks on three CEP engines. We emphasize that it is not our intention to provide an in-depth comparison of existing CEP engines, but rather to give a first insight into the performance of current products as a way to identify bottlenecks and opportunities for improvement. We focus on analyzing general behavior and performance trends of the engines (e.g. variations with respect to window size, tuple width, or selectivity).

4.1 Tests Setup

The tests were performed on a server with two Intel Xeon E5420 (*12M Cache, 2.50 GHz, 1333 MHz FSB*) Quad-Core processors (a total of 8 cores), 16 GB of RAM, and 4 SATA-300 disks, running Windows 2008 x64 Datacenter Edition, SP2.

We ran our queries on three CEP engines, two of which are developer's editions of commercial products and the other is the open-source Esper [11]. Due to licensing restrictions, we are not allowed to reveal the names of the commercial products, and will call engines henceforth as "X", "Y", and "Z". We tried multiple combinations of configuration parameters to tune each engine to its maximum performance (e.g., enabling buffering at client side, or using different event formats and SDK versions).

Figure 1 shows the components involved in the performance tests. Two slightly different architectures were employed. In either case, the load generation component communicates with an intermediary process called Adapter via plain socket, and CSV text messages. The Adapter then converts these messages into the native format of CEP engines and transmits them using their respective application programming interfaces (API). The difference between the two architectures shown in Figure 1 is that engines X and Z are standalone applications (*architecture 1*), while engine Y consists in a .jar file that is embedded into an existing application (*architecture 2*). This means that X and Z, receive/send events/results using inter-process communication, while Y uses lower-latency local method calls.

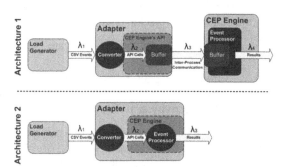

Fig. 1. Architecture of evaluation setup

The input streams data were generated and submitted using the FINCoS framework [15], a set of benchmarking tools we have developed for assessing performance of CEP engines. Both the load generation components and the event processing engines under test ran in a single machine to eliminate network latencies and jitter. CPU's affinity was set to minimize interferences between the load generator, adapters and CEP engines. For all tests, unless otherwise stated, CEP engines ran in a single dedicated CPU core[3], while the load generator and Adapter ran in the remaining ones.

4.2 Methodology

Tests consisted in running a single continuous query at the CEP engine (*except for the multiple-query tests of Section 4.9*). They began with an initial 1 minute warm-up phase, during which the load injection rate increased linearly from 1 event per second to a pre-determined maximum throughput[4]. After warm-up, the tests proceeded for at least 10 minutes in steady state with the load generation and injection rate fixed at the maximum throughput. Tests requiring more time to achieve steady state (*e.g. using long time-based windows*) had a greater duration. All the measures reported represent averages of at least two performance runs after the system reaches a steady state.

4.3 Test 1: Selection and Projection Filters

This micro-benchmark consists in two queries that filter rows (selection) or columns (projection) using query Q1 of Figure 2 (written in CQL [16]):

---

[3] We verified that two of the engines did not automatically benefit from having more cores available. For the third engine, the version we tested was limited to use only one CPU core.

[4] The maximum injection rate was determined by running successive tests with increasing throughputs until CPU utilization was maximized or some other bottleneck was reached.

```
Q1: SELECT  ID, A₁,…,Aₘ, TS
    FROM    stream1
    WHERE   ID <= K
```

Fig. 2. Filtering query

The two data reduction queries vary the values of parameters K, N, and m (results in Figure 3). K is used to force desired selectivity, N is the number of input attributes and m is the number of projected output attributes (m≤N):

i.   Row selection: varies predicate selectivity from 1% to 50%; N=m=5;
ii. Column projection: varies number of input attributes N from 5 to 125; m is fixed at 1 and row selectivity at 100%.

The throughputs achieved in this test series were very high, in millions of events per second. As expected, more selective predicates allow higher throughputs. The acute drop in performance in the projection query as the number of input attributes increases shows that tuple-width greatly affects performance. Notice that in both tests, Engine X was not fully utilizing the available resources (*utilization of its CPU was between 50% and 90%*) when its client API adapter became the bottleneck. Dedicating more CPU-cores to the adapter (*up to 7*) did not solve this issue.

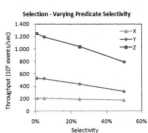

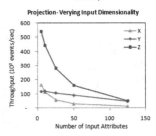

Fig. 3. Filtering tests: Selection and Projection

4.4 Test 2: Aggregation and Window Policy

The second micro-benchmark (query Q2 in Figure 4) evaluates aggregations over different tuple-window configurations. (*Time-based windows are tested in sections 4.6 and 4.7.*)

```
Q2: SELECT  ID, f(A1)
    FROM    stream1 [ROWS R Slide S]
    GROUP   BY ID
```

Fig. 4. Aggregation Query, written in CQL [21]

We vary window size (parameter R from 500 to 500K), window type (parameter S=1 implies sliding window and parameter S=R implies jumping window), and aggregation function (parameter f=MAX, AVG, STDDEV, MEDIAN). Note that some functions can be computed at fixed cost (STDDEV, AVG) while others become more expensive as the window gets larger (MAX on sliding windows, or MEDIAN). Regarding expiration mode, we expected *sliding* windows to be more expensive than *jumping* for two reasons. First, *sliding* windows expire tuples one-by-one while

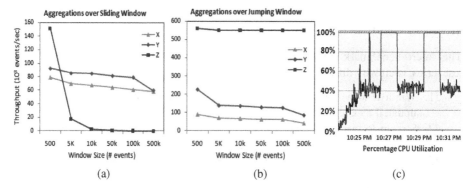

Fig. 5. Aggregations Tests: varying windows sizes and policies on (a) sliding windows and on (b) jumping windows. Graph (c) is the CPU utilization of engine X for jumping windows.

jumping windows expire them in batches. Second, *sliding* windows might need to keep more in-memory state (to deal with tuple-by-tuple expirations) while *jumping* windows may keep only counters and small summary data. Results are summarized in Figure 5.

Oddly, engine X had a worse performance with the *jumping* expiration mode than with *sliding* one. The cause seems to be inefficient batch-expiration of the *jumping* window tuples as shown by the peak CPU utilization coinciding with the periodic batch-expiration (Figure 5c). On engine Z, performance difference between the two expiration modes was surprising: very high throughputs with *jumping* windows (the best of the three engines at around 550K tuples/second) but very low throughputs with *sliding* windows (the worse of the three, reaching only 50 tuples/second for windows of size 500K). For engine Y, results appears

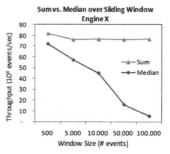

Fig. 6. Median vs. Sum aggregates on engine X

at first to meet our expectations, but in fact these two test cases are not directly comparable since Y's sliding windows output updated results for every tuple while its jumping windows update results only on window reset. Indeed, jumping windows showed a better performance not due to an implementation that benefit from the characteristics of this expiration mode, but rather, to a reduced evaluation/output frequency – *examining Y's open-source code we observed that the MAX aggregation is always computed by keeping the events of the window in a sorted structure; while this is a reasonable approach for sliding windows, it is inefficient for jumping windows, where MAX could be computed at constant cost.* Except for the aforementioned issue regarding computation of MAX on engine Y, varying the aggregation functions between AVG, STDEV and MAX generally had minor effects on performance of all engines. In contrast, all engines achieved considerably lower throughputs in the tests with the MEDIAN function. The MEDIAN function also showed to be more sensitive to window size than the other functions (e.g. see Figure 6).

4.5 Test 3: Joins

This micro-benchmark evaluates join performance of CEP engines. We define three test series, each with different data sources and factors under analysis:

J1. Window-to-window join – joins two windows that are constantly being updated by event arrivals in the corresponding input streams;

J2. Stream-to-in-memory-table – simulates the situation where the content of an input stream must be enriched with static data stored as an in-memory table;

J3. Stream-to-DBMS-relation – table stored in an external database;

J1: Window-to-Window
The window-to-window join query is the following:

```
Q3: SELECT * FROM  stream1 [ROWS S] AS S1,
                   stream2 [ROWS S] AS S2
    WHERE  S1.ID = S2.ID
```

Fig. 7. Window-to-window Equi-Join Query

J1 series is comprised of three different tests as described below:

J1-1 *Varying window size and join selectivity*: parameter S varies from 500 to 500k. MAX_ID is held constant at 50k (i.e., the join is more selective for smaller window sizes);

J1-2 *Varying window size and keeping join selectivity*: parameters S and MAX_ID take the same values, from 500, to 500k, which ensures a fixed 100% join selectivity (each event finds a single match on the other window);

J1-3 *Varying join selectivity and keeping window size fixed*: MAX_ID takes the values 5k, 50k, 500k, and 5M while parameter S is held at 50k (each event finds, on average, 10, 1, 0.1 and 0.01 matching events on the other window).

Figure 8 below shows the results for this test series.

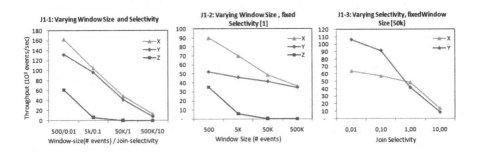

Fig. 8. Tests Join: Window-to-window

In J1-1, the acute drop in throughput was expected (due to increases in join input and selectivity) although the performance of engine Z degraded much faster than the performance of other engines. (*Recall that engine Z showed performance issues on previous tests with aggregations over sliding windows, which seems to indicate that it has some problems with this expiration mode.*)

Tests J1-2 and J1-3 reveal that engine X is more sensitive to window size while engine Y performs very well when join selectivity is low, but degrades more quickly when it gets close to or exceeds 1. For engine Z, we ran a modified version of J1-3, with a smaller window (size 500, not shown) in order to minimize the cost of window maintenance but there were no noticeable performance differences when varying the join selectivity, indicating again that sliding windows are not efficiently handled by Z.

J2/J3: Stream-to-in-Memory-Table and Stream-to-DB-Relation
The queries of tests J2 and J3 have the following format:

```
Q4: SELECT * FROM    stream1 AS S,
                     table1  AS T
    WHERE  S.ID = T.ID
```

Fig. 9. Stream-to-table Join Query

Figure 10 shows the corresponding results. In both tests a stream "S" with 4 fields is joined with a static table with 10 fields. In J2 the CEP engine is responsible for maintaining the table in main memory and for performing the join. In J3 the table is stored in an external database, which becomes responsible for the join (*every new event in stream S fires a parameterized query to the DBMS[5]*). The number of records in the table ranged from 1k to 10M (in-memory) and from 1k to 100M (DB); join selectivity is always 100% (*every event in the stream is matched against one and only one record in the table*).

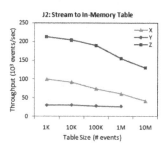

In series J2, engine Y could not complete the test with 10M because it ran out of memory (prolonged garbage collections made it unresponsive). It is also interesting to notice how Z had a better join performance when operating over a table rather than over sliding windows (*see J1-2, in Figure 8*). In J3, two facts are worth mentioning: first, neither the CEP engines nor the DBMS were in their processing limits; the bottleneck was primarily the communication between these two components. Second, the performance was virtually unaffected

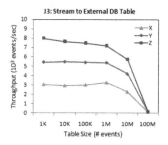

Fig. 10. Tests Join between stream and table (J2) in-memory or (J3) in external database

---

[5] We tested both with MS-SQL Server™ 2005 and Oracle™ 11g, and the results were similar.

from 1k to 1M as the DBMS was able to buffer the entire table into main memory. From this point on, the presence of IO calls, significantly lowered the query throughput.

4.6   Test 4: Pattern Matching and Negative Pattern Matching

We used query Q5 and Q5n below to test pattern matching. Q5 searches for instances of two events with the same ID in a time-based window of size *interval*, where the "A1" attribute of the second event is above some constant *K*. Q5n searches for sequences of an event not followed by a corresponding event within an interval.

```
Q5: PATTERN SEQ(A a1, A a2)      Q5n: PATTERN SEQ(A a1, ~(A a2))
       WHERE a1.id = a2.id AND          WHERE a1.id = a2.id AND
          a2.A1 > K                        a2.A1 > K
       WITHIN interval                 WITHIN interval
```

Fig. 11. Sample Pattern Matching Queries (expressed using the SASE+ language [23])

The purpose of the "a2.A1>K" predicate is to verify that CEP engines indeed benefit of predicates in pattern detection by pushing them earlier in query plan construction. This micro-benchmark exercises three factors:

i.   *Varying Window Size*: parameter *interval* ranges from 10 to 600 seconds. *MAX_ID* is held constant at 10k and *K* ensures a selectivity of 0.1%;

ii. *Varying Cardinality of Attribute ID*: *MAX_ID* ranges from 100 to 100k. *interval* was held constant at *1 minute* and *K* ensures selectivity of 0.1%;

iii. *Varying Predicate selectivity*: the predicate selectivity varied from 0.1% to 10%, while *interval* was held at *1 minute* and *MAX_ID* at 10k.

Figure 12 show the results of Q5. In the first experiment, all the engines had a very similar decrease in throughput as *interval* got larger. We could not determine the performance of engine Z for windows of sizes above 5 minutes because it consumed all available memory before tests could reach steady state (*the edition we tested was limited to address at most 1.5GB of memory*). As expected, increasing the cardinality of the correlation attribute ID *decreases* query cost, since less tuples pairs will have matching IDs. Similarly, more selective predicates (lower percentages) yield better performance as less tuples are considered as potential patterns matches.

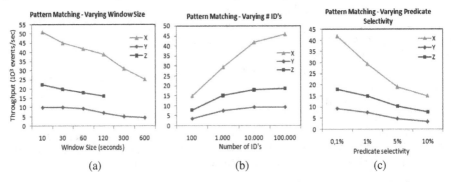

Fig. 12. Pattern matching Tests varying (a) window size; (b) #*ID*s; (c) predicate selectivity

Q5n showed to be less expensive than Q5. This difference has to do with the consumption mode [10] used in these tests (*all-to-all*): in the case of negative patterns a single occurrence of an event "a2" eliminates many potential matches. (*results of tests with negative pattern have been omitted due to space constraints*).

4.7 Test 5: Large Time-Based Windows

Large time-based windows over high throughout sources may quickly drain system resources if all incoming events need to be retained. For example, one hour of 20-byte-size events on a 50k event/sec stream represents around 3.4 GB. Fortunately, certain applications require results to be updated only periodically, say every second, rather than for every new event (see Q6 bellow). In that case, for *distributive* or *algebraic* functions [14], Q6 can be rewritten in the equivalent query Q7.

```
Q6:  SELECT AVG(A1)
     FROM    A [RANGE 1 HOUR]
     OUTPUT EVERY 1 SECOND;

Q7:  SELECT SUM(s1)/SUM(c1)
     FROM (SELECT SUM(A1) AS s1, COUNT(A1) AS c1
           FROM A[RANGE 1 SECOND]
           OUTPUT EVERY 1 SECOND
          ) [RANGE 1 HOUR];
```

Fig. 13. Two versions of aggregation query over time-based window with controlled output

Query Q7 computes 1-second aggregates on the inner query and 1-hour aggregates over the 1-second aggregates with the outer query. The space requirements of Q7 are:

Inner window: (50000 events/second * 20bytes/event) * 1second = 977KB +
Outer window: (1 tuple/second * 20bytes/tuple) * 3600 seconds = 70KB

This micro-benchmark runs Q6 and Q7 for large different window sizes and varying input rates. The goal is to verify if: i) Q6 is internally transformed into Q7; and ii) if not, to quantify the benefits of such transformation. The results of Q6 and Q7 for a 10-minute window appear in Table 3.

Table 3. Memory consumption (in MB) of CEP Engines for Q6 and Q7 (*10-minute window*)

Engine/Query	Input Rate			
	500	5,000	50,000	100,000
X, Q6	187	1,553	Out-of-memory	Out-of-memory
X, Q7	39	40	64	98
Y, Q6	455	3,173	Out-of-memory	Out-of-memory
Y, Q7	139	141	1,610	1,652
Z, Q6	56	64	56	55
Z, Q7	69	68	77	91

Table 4. CEP Engines' memory consumption for very large time-based windows (MB)

Engine/Query	Window Size				
	20 min	1 hr.	2 hrs.	6 hrs.	12 hrs.
X, Q7	114	128	141	146	147
Y, Q7	5,275	5,303	5,232	5,362	5,279
Z, Q7	70	73	55	58	52
Z, Q6	63	58	46	48	48

Observe that in engines X and Y query Q7 indeed reduced memory consumption when compared to Q6. In fact, Q6 showed a near-linear growth with respect to input rate and as such, engines X and Y exhausted memory (more than 13GB) for input rates above 50k events/sec even on small 10-minute windows. Engine Z had its memory consumption virtually unaffected by the input rate and almost identical in both query versions; these results made us suspect at first that Z could be the only engine applying the query transformation automatically.

We then ran a second series of experiments with much larger windows. Input rate was kept at 100k events per second and window size was progressively increased up to 12 hours. The durations of these tests were always 1.5 times the window size. For engines X and Y, we ran the tests with Q7. For engine Z we tested both versions. Table 4 summarizes the results.

This new experiment exposed a behavior of engine Z not revealed in previous tests. While in the first experiments Z was able to keep memory consumption roughly unaffected by the number of events in the window, in this second series of tests, the CPU utilization and consequently maximum throughput were severely affected by the window size. As shown in Figure 14, Q6 had a drastic drop in maximum throughput as window size was increased, while Q7 showed a very steady throughput curve. It is worthy to point out that in the tests with Q6 CPU was pushed to its

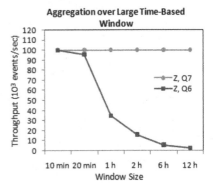

Fig. 14. Q6 and Q7 aggregations over large time-windows (engine Z)

maximum (*for windows of 20 min and beyond*), while with Q7 CPU utilization stayed always around 1%. These numbers indicate that Z also does not perform the transformation mentioned above, but rather has an alternative implementation which sacrifices maximum throughput to keep memory consumption controlled.

4.8 Test 6: Adaptability to Bursts

The objective of this micro-benchmark is to verify how fast and efficiently the CEP engines adapt to changes in the load conditions. Although many factors may cause variations in the execution of continuous queries, here we focus solely on input rate. The tests of this series consist in:

i. An 1-minute warm-up phase during which the injection rate is progressively increased until a maximum value λ that makes CPU utilization around 75%;

ii. A 5-minute steady phase during which the injection rate is kept fixed at λ;

iii. A 10-second "peak" phase during which the injection rate is increased 50% (to 1.5λ), making the system temporarily overloaded;

iv. A 5-minute "recovery" phase in which the injection rate is again fixed at λ;

The query used is Q2, shown in Figure 4. To characterize the adaptability of CEP systems we define the following metrics:

- Maximum peak latency (Max_RT$_{peak}$): maximum latency either during or after the injection of the peak load;

- Peak latency degradation ratio (RT_Degradation$_{peak}$): 99.9th-percentile latency of peak phase with respect to 99.9th-percentile latency of steady phase:

$$99.9\texttt{th\_RT}_{peak}/99.9\texttt{th\_RT}_{steady}$$

In other words, what is the increase in latency caused by the peak?

- Recovery Time (Δτ$_{recovery}$):

$$\tau_{recovery}-\tau_{peak}$$

where τ$_{recovery}$ represents the timestamp of the first output event after peak injection whose latency is less than or equal the average latency of the steady phase and τ$_{peak}$ is the timestamp of the last input event of the peak phase. That is, how long does it take for to return to the same latency levels?

- Post-peak latency variation ratio: Average latency after recovery divided by the average latency during steady phase:

$$\texttt{RT}_{after\_ecovery}/\texttt{RT}_{steady\_phase}$$

That is, what is the state of the system after it recovers from the peak?

Discussion: Blocking/Non-blocking API and Latency Measurement

Recall from Figure 1 that events are sent to engines through API calls. On engine X, those API calls are non-blocking while on engines Y and Z they are blocking. In practice this means that X continues queuing incoming events even if overload while Y and Z prevent clients from submitting events at a higher rate than that they can process. As shown in Figure 15, there are multiple ways of computing latency. In order to properly measure latency for blocking calls, it is necessary to employ the "*creation time*" of input events instead of their "*send time*" – formula (3) in Figure 15. This formula allows accounting for the delays introduced by the blocking mechanism of the client APIs, which otherwise would pass unnoticed if we employed the moment immediately before sending the event.

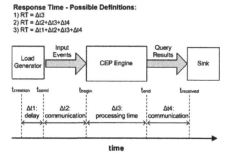

Fig. 15. Latency Measurement

Results

Table 5 and Figure 16 show the results of the adaptability test. Engine X, which adopts a non-blocking posture in the communication with clients, took much longer to recover from the peak and had a higher maximum latency than the two blocking engines, Y and Z. Nonetheless, after recovery, all engines returned to virtually the same latency level as that observed before the peak.

Table 5. Results for Adaptability Tests

	Engine		
Metric	X	Y	Z
Max_RT$_{peak}$ (ms)	4.725,0	1.262,0	1.483,0
RT_Degradation$_{peak}$	82,8	57,4	5,9
$\Delta\tau_{recovery}$ (ms)	43.039,0	1.308,0	1.544,0
RT_Variation$_{post}$	1,0	0,9	1,0

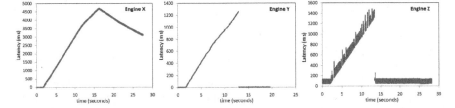

Fig. 16. Adaptability Test: Scatter plot of latency before, during and after the peak

4.9 Test 7: Multiple Queries (Plan Sharing)

The objective of this micro-benchmark is to analyze how the CEP engines scale with respect to the number of simultaneous similar queries. The query used in this experiment is a window-to-window join similar to Q3 (Figure 7). We tested two variations:

- **Test 1: Identical queries.** In this test we focus on computation sharing and the main metric is hence throughput. Window size is fixed in 1000 rows. To keep output rate fixed (*1 output per input event*), all queries have a predicate whose selectivity increases as we add more queries;

- **Test 2: Similar queries with different window sizes.** In this test we focus on memory sharing, so windows are large enough to observe differences when we increase the number of queries (in the range [400k-500k events]) and the injection rate is low so that CPU does not become a bottleneck;

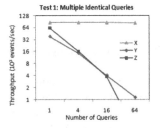

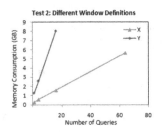

Fig. 17. Multiple Queries Tests

The results of these two tests are shown in Figure 17. Engine X is the only one to implement some kind of query plan sharing: in the first test its throughput remained unaffected when the number of queries was increased. However, in the second test, in which queries were similar but different, it was not able share resources. Results also indicate that engines Y and Z do not implement query plan sharing. In fact, Y and Z could not finish some tests of the second series: Y ran out of memory for 64 queries and Z become unresponsive while the window was being filled.

5 Related Work

Up to now, little previous work focused on the performance evaluation of event processing systems. White et al. [22] present a performance study which shows the latencies of a commercial CEP product while handling large volumes of events. Dekkers [8] carried out some tests for evaluating pattern detection performance in two open-source CEP engines. None of them characterize how query options such as window size and policy, or selectivity affects performance, nor covered more than one or two query type(s) or CEP product(s).

Some benchmarks have been proposed in areas related to CEP such as the BEAST benchmark [5] for active databases, or the *Linear Road* [3] or NEXMark [17] benchmarks for data stream management systems. However, these benchmarks measure only steady state performance for a fixed number of queries, and do not consider issues such as adaptability and query plan sharing. *SPECjms2007* [18] is a benchmark produced and maintained by the Standard Performance Evaluation Corporation (SPEC) aimed at evaluating the performance and scalability of JMS-based messaging middlewares. *SPECjms2007* thus focus on the communication side of event-driven systems rather than on query processing, which distinguishes it from our work.

6 Conclusions and Future Work

In this paper we presented a performance study of event processing systems. We proposed a series of queries to exercise factors such as window size and policy, selectivity, and event dimensionality and then carried out experimental evaluations on three CEP engines. The tests confirmed that very high throughputs can be achieved by CEP engines when performing simple operations such as filtering. In these cases the communication channel – *in our tests, the client API* – tends to be the bottleneck. We also observed that window expiration mode had a significant impact on the cost of queries. In fact, for one of the tested engines the difference in performance between jumping and sliding windows in one test was about 4 orders of magnitude. With respect to joins, tests revealed that accessing data stored in databases can significantly lower the throughput of a system. Pre-loading static data into CEP engine offers good performance and may thus solve this issue, but this approach is feasible only when data do not change often and fit in main memory. The tested engines had disparate adaptability characteristics. We observed that the approach used to receive events from clients – *either blocking or non-blocking* – plays a fundamental role on that aspect, although further investigation is still required to fully understand this topic (*e.g., testing bursts of variable amplitudes and durations or having changes in other parameters such as data distributions*). Finally, the tests with multiple queries showed that plan sharing happened only in one CEP engine and only for identical queries (*we still plan to broaden the investigation of this topic by incorporating tests with other classes of queries*). It was also quite surprising and disappointing to realize that CEP engines were not able to automatically benefit from the multi-core hardware used in our tests. In general terms, we concluded that no CEP engine showed to be superior in all test scenarios, and that there is still room for performance improvements.

References

1. Abadi, D.J., et al.: Aurora. A New Model and Architecture for Data Stream Management. VLDB Journal 12, 120–139 (2003)
2. Arasu, A., et al.: STREAM: The Stanford Stream Data Manager. In: Proc. SIGMOD 2003 (2003)
3. Arasu, A., et al.: Linear Road: A Stream Data Management Benchmark. In: Proc. of VLDB 2004 (2004)
4. Babcock, B., et al.: Models and Issues in Data Stream Systems. In: Proc. of SIGMOD 2002 (2002)
5. Berndtsson, M., et al.: Performance Evaluation of Object-Oriented Active Database Management Systems Using the BEAST Benchmark. Theory and Practice of Object Systems 4(3), 135–149 (1998)
6. Bizarro, P., et al.: Event Processing Use Cases. In: Tutorial, DEBS 2009, Nashville USA (2009)
7. Chandrasekaran, S., et al.: TelegraphCQ: Continuous dataflow processing for an uncertain world. In: Proc. of CIDR 2003 (2003)
8. Dekkers, P.: Master Thesis Computer Science. Complex Event Processing. Radboud University Nijmegen, Thesis number 574 (October 2007)
9. DSAL Real-Time Event Processing Benchmark, http://www.datastreamanalysis.com/images/ Real-Time%20EP%20Benchmark.pdf
10. Chakravarthy, S., Mishra, D.: Snoop: An Expressive Event Specification Language for Active Databases. Data Knowl. Eng. (DKE) 14(1), 1–26 (1994)
11. Esper, http://esper.codehaus.org/
12. Golab, L., Özsu, M.T.: Issues in data stream management. SIGMOD Record 32(2), 5–14 (2003)
13. Gray, J. (ed.): The Benchmark Handbook for Database and Transaction Processing Systems, 2nd edn. Morgan Kaufmann, San Francisco (1993)
14. Gray, J., et al.: Data Cube: A Relational Aggregation Operator Generalizing Group-by, Cross-Tab, and Sub Totals. Data Min. Knowl. Discov. 1(1), 29–53 (1997)
15. Mendes, M.R.N., Bizarro, P., Marques, P.: A Framework for Performance Evaluation of Complex Event Processing Systems. In: Proc. of DEBS 2008 (2008)
16. Motwani, R., et al.: Query Processing, Resource Management, and Approximation in a Data Stream Management System. In: Proc. of CIDR 2003 (2003)
17. NEXMark Benchmark, http://datalab.cs.pdx.edu/niagara/NEXMark/
18. Sachs, K., Kounev, S., Bacon, J.M., Buchmann, A.: Workload Characterization of the SPECjms2007 Benchmark. In: Wolter, K. (ed.) EPEW 2007. LNCS, vol. 4748, pp. 228–244. Springer, Heidelberg (2007)
19. STAC-A1 Benchmark, http://www.stacresearch.com/council
20. STAC Report: Aleri Order Book Consolidation on Intel Tigertown and Solaris 10, http://www.stacresearch.com/node/3844
21. Stream Query Repository, http://infolab.stanford.edu/stream/sqr/
22. White, S., Alves, A., Rorke, D.: WebLogic event server: a lightweight, modular application server for event processing. In: Proc. of DEBS 2008 (2008)
23. Wu, E., Diao, Y., Rizvi, S.: High Performance Complex Event Processing over Streams. In: Proc. of SIGMOD 2006 (2006)

The Star Schema Benchmark and Augmented Fact Table Indexing

Patrick O'Neil, Elizabeth O'Neil, Xuedong Chen, and Stephen Revilak

University of Massachusetts at Boston, Boston, MA 02125-3393, USA
{xuedchen, poneil, eoneil, srevilak}@cs.umb.edu

Abstract. We provide a benchmark measuring star schema queries retrieving data from a fact table with Where clause column restrictions on dimension tables. Clustering is crucial to performance with modern disk technology, since retrievals with filter factors down to 0.0005 are now performed most efficiently by sequential table search rather than by indexed access. DB2's Multi-Dimensional Clustering (MDC) provides methods to "dice" the fact table along a number of orthogonal "dimensions", but only when these dimensions are columns in the fact table. The diced cells cluster fact rows on several of these "dimensions" at once so queries restricting several such columns can access crucially localized data, with much faster query response. Unfortunately, columns of dimension tables of a star schema are not usually represented in the fact table. In this paper, we show a simple way to adjoin physical copies of dimension columns to the fact table, dicing data to effectively cluster query retrieval, and explain how such dicing can be achieved on database products other than DB2. We provide benchmark measurements to show successful use of this methodology on three commercial database products.

Keywords: Benchmark, Star Schema, Data Warehousing, Clustering, Multi-Dimensional Clustering, DB2, Oracle, Vertica.

1 Introduction

Our Star Schema Benchmark (SSB) was developed in 2006 to measure star schema query performance. A Data Warehouse is typically made up of a number of star schemas [7], and star schema queries typically retrieve data from a fact table with Where clause column restrictions on Dimension tables (Figure 1), although occasional restrictions may be on the fact table itself. The SSB is derived from the TPC-H benchmark, and we will show how the method employed illustrates how to turn a (partially) normalized schema into a star schema.

The development of SSB was originally commissioned by Stonebraker's Vertica, which was compared to a number of commercial database systems with results published in [15]. The excellent Vertica performance displayed was achieved by a clever sort-order of columns in the fact table that resulted in a variant form of DB2's Multi-Dimensional Clustering (MDC) [1, 3, 4, 5, 6, 8, 13]. A comparable approach was applied to other database systems that were measured. Clustering data to reduce query access disk coverage has become the major way to improve query performance

R. Nambiar and M. Poess (Eds.): TPCTC 2009, LNCS 5895, pp. 237–252, 2009.

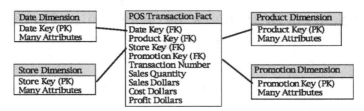

Fig. 1. Point of Sale Star Schema

since fast high-density disks have made regular indexed access inferior to sequential access for all but needle-in-a-haystack queries. The MDC approach uses conceptually orthogonal indexes that slice and dice the fact table into cells so that most SSB queries retrieve from only a small subset of localized cells. Surprisingly, MDC as well as the approach we took doesn't provide the necessary dicing on the fact table without an extra trick of creating a materialized view fact table that adjoins certain dimension columns to the fact table itself. This is necessary because MDC acting on the fact table can only cluster on columns that lie in the fact table, and the foreign keys to the dimensions are generally not sufficient for the necessary dicing. Yet we found no suggestions in DB2 literature to materialize dimension columns in the fact table for this purpose.

We talked with a number of DB2 Universal Database (DB2 UDB) experts who suggested that the DB2 Design Advisor might recommend creating an MQT (Materialized Query Table, DB2's name for a Materialized View) that adjoined the fact table with versions of the dimension columns as we had done to achieve improved performance. But when we tried this, the Advisor materialized aggregated column data with group-by columns to answer each of the thirteen queries in SSB (allowing variation of all possible constants that might take the place of specific constants we used). Of course this solution did not provide answers for any type of drill-down queries that might be suggested by results in ad-hoc querying by knowledge workers.

1.1 Contribution of This Paper

1. In Section 2, we explain the design of a Star Schema benchmark (SSB) and explain some techniques that allow us to derive it from the normalized TPC-H benchmark.

2. In Section 3, we explain why clustering data has become so important for performance and secondary column indexing less important. Then we show how high-level columns in commonly restricted hierarchies of dimension tables can be adjoined to the SSB fact table to speed up queries with predicates on these hierarchies. We refer to this approach as Adjoined Dimension Columns (ADC), and explain how it can be applied on three different commercial database products, with some minor flaws that can be addressed by simple design improvements in each DBMS.

3. In Section 4, we provide experimental results of SSB and show the advantage of ADC on three anonymized database products. Then we discuss our use of the DB2 Design Advisor materializes and what we see as its limitations.

2 Star Schema Benchmark Specification

The SSB is designed to measure performance of database products in support of classical data warehousing applications, and is based on the TPC-H benchmark [18], modified in a number of ways. We list below some of the schema changes we made to change the Normalized TPC-H schema (see Figure 2) to the efficient star schema form of SSB (see Figure 3). Many reasons for these changes are taken from [7], which we recommend. See [11] at http://www.cs.umb.edu/~poneil/StarSchemaB.pdf for a more detailed description of SSB.

1. We combine the TPC-H LINEITEM and ORDERS tables into one sales fact table that we name *LINEORDER*. This denormalization is standard in warehousing, as explained in [7], pg. 121, and makes many joins unnecessary in common queries.

2. We drop the PARTSUPP table since it is actually inappropriate even in TPC-H. The ORDERS and LINEITEM tables have a Transaction Level temporal grain, while the PARTSUPP table has a Periodic Snapshot grain [7]. Even transactions that insert new orders do not modify rows in PARTSUPP, which is frozen in time. Query Q9, which retrieves, for each nation and year, the profits for certain parts ordered that year, calculates profit using l_extendedprice from LINEITEM and ps_supplycost from PARTSUPP. Of course it is impossible that ps_supplycost could have remained constant during all seven years of order history. This problem arises from the temporal grain mismatch. The presence of the PARTSUPP table in TPC-H seems suspicious anyway, as if placed there to require a non-trivial normalized join schema. It is what we would expect in an update transactional design, where in adding an order LINEITEM for some part, we would access PARTSUPP to find the minimal cost supplier in some region, and then correct ps_availqty after filling the order. But ps_availqty is never updated during the Refresh that inserts new ORDERS. In the Star Schema data warehouse, we remove the PARTSUPP table and create a column lo_supplycost for each LINEORDER Fact row to answer queries about profits.

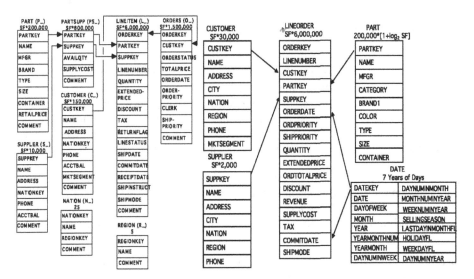

Fig. 2. TPC-H Schema   **Fig. 3.** SSB Star Schema

3. We drop the comment attribute of a LINEITEM (27 chars), the comment for an order (49 chars), and the shipping instructions for a LINEITEM (25 chars), because a warehouse does not store such information in a fact table (it can't be aggregated, and takes significant storage). See [7], pg. 18.

4. We drop the tables, NATION and REGION outboard to the dimensions CUSTOMER and SUPPLIER in TPC-H. Such tables *might be* appropriate in an OLTP system to enforce integrity, but not in a warehouse system where the data is cleaned before being loaded and dimension tables are not so limited in space use as the fact table. We assume Nation and Region are added to the ADDRESS columns.

5. We drop the dates (and attributes) of events added after the orderdate of an item, such as shipdate, receiptdate, and returnflag. Clearly the order information must be queryable after the order, and prior to the shipping event, receipt at destination, and possible return many days later. A sequence of dates such as this is normally handled in data warehousing by a sequence of tables: see [7], pg. 94. We retain the commitdate (commit to ship by given date) in SSB, since it is agreed to at order time.

6. We add the DATE dimension table, as is standard for a warehouse on sales.

7. The growth in size of the Part table for given Scale Factor has been reduced to logarithmic rather than linear, which seems more realistic. (Slower growth is also part of the TPC-DS benchmark [16, 17] proposal.) Also a new column named p_brand1 with cardinality 1000 has been added to the p_mfgr/p_category hierarchy, since an upper bound of 50 on p_category seemed unrealistic for part breakdown.

With changes described above, the SSB database at SF = 10 takes up about 7 GBytes. The type, length and type of columns of SSB listed in Figure 3 is provided in Section 2.2 of [11]. Below, we list columns named in SSB queries and their cardinality.

d_year 7	lo_discount 11	s_region 5	c_region 5	p_mfgr 5
d_yearmonth 84	lo_quantity 50	s_nation 25	c_nation 25	p_category 25
d_weeknuminyear 53		s_city 250	c_city 250	p_brand1 1000

2.1 SSB Queries

As in the Set Query Benchmark [9], we strive in SSB to provide functional coverage (different common types of Star Schema queries) and Selectivity Coverage (varying fractions of the LINEORDER table accessed as in drill-down queries). We only have a small number of flights to use to provide such coverage, but we do our best. Some model queries will be based on the TPC-H query set, but we need to modify these queries to vary the selectivity, resulting in what we call a *Query Flight* below. Other queries that we feel are needed will have no counterpart in TPC-H.

Q1. We start with a query flight (of three queries Q1.1, Q1.2 and Q1.3) with restrictions on only one dimension and restrictions on the Fact table as well, based on TPC-H query TPCQ6. The query calculates the revenue increase that would have resulted by eliminating certain company-wide discounts in a given percentage range for products shipped in a given year.

select sum(lo_extendedprice*lo_discount) as revenue from LINEORDER, date
    where lo_orderdate = d_datekey and d_year = [YEAR] and lo_discount between

[DISCOUNT] - 1 and [DISCOUNT] + 1 and lo_quantity < [QUANTITY];

Q1.1 d_year = 1993, lo_quantity < 25, lo_discount between 1 and 3. The Filter Factor (FF[1]) for this query is $(1/7)(0.5)(3/11) = 0.0194805$.

Q1.2 d_yearmonth = 199401, lo_quantity between 26 and 35, lo_discount between 4 and 6. FF = $(1/84)(3/11)(0.2) = 0.00064935$.

Q1.3 d_weeknuminyear = 6 and d_year = 1994, lo_quantity between 36 and 40, lo_discount between 5 and 7. FF = $(1/364)(3/11)(0.1) = .000075$.

Q2. For a second query flight, we want one with restrictions on two dimensions, not found in TPC-H. Q2 compares revenue for some product classes, for suppliers in a certain region, grouped by more restrictive product classes and all years of orders.

select sum(lo_revenue), d_year, p_brand1 from LINEORDER, date, part, supplier
    where lo_orderdate = d_datekey and lo_partkey = p_partkey and lo_suppkey =
    s_suppkey and p_category = 'MFGR#12' and s_region = 'AMERICA'
        group by d_year, p_brand1 order by d_year, p_brand1;

Q2.1 Q2 as written: p_category = 'MFGR#12', FF = 1/25; s_region, FF=1/5. So FF = $(1/25)(1/5) = 1/125$.

Q2.2 Change p_category = 'MFGR#12' to p_brand1 between 'MFGR#2221' and 'MFGR#2228' (or equivalent in-list) and s_region to 'ASIA'. FF = 1/625.

Q2.3 Change p_category = 'MFGR#12' to p_brand1 = 'MFGR#2339' and s_region = 'EUROPE'. So FF = $(1/1000)(1/5) = 1/5000$.

Q3. In this flight we place restrictions on three dimensions, including the remaining dimension, customer, based on query TPCQ5. It calculates revenue volume by customer nation, supplier nation and year within a given region, in a certain time period.

select c_nation, s_nation, d_year, sum(lo_revenue) as revenue
        from customer, LINEORDER, supplier, date
    where lo_custkey = c_custkey and lo_suppkey = s_suppkey and lo_orderdate =
    d_datekey and c_region = 'ASIA' and s_region = 'ASIA' and d_year >= 1992 and
    d_year <= 1997
        group by c_nation, s_nation, d_year order by d_year asc, revenue desc;

Q3.1 Q3 as written: c_region = 'ASIA' so FF = 1/5, FF = 1/5 for supplier, and 6-year period FF = 6/7 for d_year; Thus FF = $(1/5)(1/5)(6/7) = 6/175$.

Q3.2 Change restriction to a certain nation, and within that nation, revenue by customer city and supplier city, and year: FF is $(1/25)(1/25)(6/7) = 6/4375$.

Q3.3 Change restriction to *two* cities in 'UNITED KINGDOM' for c_city and s_city and group by c_city, s_city and d_year. FF: $(1/125)(1/125)(6/7) = 6/109375$.

Q3.4 Change date restriction to a specific d_yearmonth. FF = $(1/125)(1/125)(1/84) = 1/1312500$.

---

[1] A Filter Factor (FF) was defined in [14] as the fraction of the table that is retrieved based on the combination of WHERE clause predicates, usually assumed to be indexed.

Q4. This query flight represents a "drill-down" sequence, starting (Q4.1) with a group by on two dimensions and rather weak constraints on three dimensions, measuring aggregate profit defined as (lo_revenue - lo_supplycost).

select d_year, c_nation, sum(lo_revenue - lo_supplycost) as profit from date,
        customer, supplier, part, LINEORDER
    where lo_custkey = c_custkey and lo_suppkey = s_suppkey and lo_partkey =
    p_partkey and lo_orderdate = d_datekey and c_region = 'AMERICA'
    and s_region = 'AMERICA' and (p_mfgr = 'MFGR#1' or p_mfgr = 'MFGR#2')
        group by d_year, c_nation order by d_year, c_nation

Q4.1 Query Q4 as written, FF = $(1/5)(1/5)(2/5) = 2/125$.

Q4.2 Drill down to restrict to years 1997 or 1998 and group by (and order by) p_category and s_nation instead of c_nation. FF = $2/7(2/125) = 4/875$.

Q4.3 Drill down: restrict c_nation & s_nation = 'United States' and p_category = 'MFGR#14', group by d_year, s_city, p_brand1. FF: $(1/5)(1/25)(2/7)(1/25) = 2/21875$.

3 Clustering for Query Performance

Over the past twenty years, performance of indexed retrieval with a moderate sized filter factor [14] has lost its competitive edge compared to sequential scan of a table. We show this with a comparison of Set Query Benchmark (SQB) [9] measurements taken in 1990 on MVS DB2 with those taken in 2009 on DB2 UDB running on Windows Server 2003.

The SQB was originally defined on a BENCH table of one million 200-byte rows, with a clustering column KSEQ having unique sequential values 1, 2, 3 ,…, and a number of randomly generated columns whose names indicate their cardinality, including: K4, K5, K10, K25, K100, K1K, K10K and K100K. Thus for example K5 has 5 values, each appearing randomly on approximately 200,000 rows. Figure 4 shows the form of query Q3B from the Set Query Benchmark.

    select sum(K1K) from BENCH
        where (KSEQ between 40000 and 41000 or KSEQ between 42000 and 43000
        or KSEQ between 44000 and 45000 or KSEQ between 46000 and 47000
        or KSEQ between 48000 and 50000) and KN = 3; -- KN from K5 to K100K

Fig. 4. Query Q3B from SQB (Set Query Benchmark)

In our 2009 measurement on a Windows system, we performed Query Q3B on DB2 UDB with a BENCH table of 10,000,000 rows (instead of the original 1,000,000 rows). DB2 MVS and DB2 UDB results for query Q3B are given in Table 1.

As indicated in Table 1, the query plans for DB2 MVS and DB2 UDB turn out to be identical for the KN cases K100K, K10K (where indexed access finds the single row for K100K = 3 and 10 rows for K10K = 3 in the million rows of DB2 MVS, and about ten times as many in the ten million rows of DB2 UDB), and in the KN case of K5 = 3, where both the old and new approaches perform sequential search on the five KSEQ ranges and simply test that K5 = 3 for each row.

Table 1. Q3B measures: 1990 & 2009

KN Used In Q3B	Rows Read (of 1M)	DB2 MVS Index usage	DB2 UDB Index usage	DB2 MVS Time secs	DB2 UDB Time secs
K100K	1	K100K	K100K	1.4	0.7
K10K	6	K10K	K10K	2.4	3.1
K100	597	K100, KSEQ	KSEQ	14.9	2.1
K25	2423	K25, KSEQ	KSEQ	20.8	2.4
K10	5959	K10, KSEQ	KSEQ	31.4	2.3
K5	12011	KSEQ	KSEQ	49.1	2.1

But there is a great change in query plans for the KN range K100, K25 and K10. In those ranges, 1990 DB2 MVS took a RID-list UNION of the five KSEQ ranges, ANDed that with the appropriate KN = 3 RID-list found by index search, then used list prefetch to access the resulting rows and sum the K1K values. The 2009 DB2 UDB on the other hand, although capable of performing the same indexed access as DB2 MVS, chose instead to perform five sequential accesses on the clustered KSEQ ranges, and summing K1K for qualifying rows with KN = 3. This is the same plan used by DB2 UDB (and DB2 MVS) for K5, and DB2 UDB times for these cases are nearly independent in the range K100 down to K5 compared to growing time for DB2 MVS. In fact, DB2 UDB could have chosen this plan for K10K as well, improving the elapsed time from 3.14 seconds down to about 2.1 seconds. Only at K100K does the use of the KN index actually improve the elapsed time today.

We therefore claim that the K10K case (with filter factor 1/10,000) is near the "indifference point" at which DB2 UDB should start to switch over to a series of sequential scans, rather than using index access to AND these RID lists. With roughly 20 rows per page, a filter factor of 1/10,000 will pick up about one disk page out of 500. The MVS DB2 of 19 years ago had an indifference point between sequential access and indexed access at filter factors that picked up about one disk page out of 13; thus the usefulness of filter factor for indexed access has dropped by about a factor of 500/13 = 38.5 in this period, corresponding with the difference in speed of sequential access in the two Set Query cases, about 1.43 Mbytes/sec for DB2 MVS, and 60 Mbytes/sec for DB2 UDB, a ratio of 60/1.43 = 42. Indexed access performance has changed much less, causing the indifference point shift.

We conclude that clustering, always an important factor for enhancing performance, has become much more important in the last 19 years. Currently, if we are retrieving 1 row out of a thousand from a table that covers an entire disk, sequential access will likely access the entire disk and secondary index access cannot improve on that, but if we have a way to cluster so that the rows we want to retrieve cover only 1/100 of the disk, then sequential fetch will take 1/100 as long. Secondary index access is still useful only in "needle-in-haystack" queries, with very small filter factors, i.e., those below approximately 1/5,000.

3.1 Single Dimensional and Multi-dimensional Clustering

The concept of sorting table data to provide clustering on a column to accelerate queries with range restrictions on that column has been used for many years. In the 1980s there were companies collecting marketing data for up to 80 million U.S. households (see [9], Section 6.1.2) and performing multiple queries to craft sales promotion mailings of the right size, typically for specific regions of the U.S. near Stores owned by a company. Data was sorted by zip code, and a typical direct mail query would be of the Q3B form shown in Figure 4, where KSEQ corresponds to zip code. Of course each zip code would lie on multiple rows in that case, but as in Q3B, each geographic region would typically correspond to a union of disjoint zip code ranges. Additional restrictions, on income class or hobby interests, for example, would correspond to the $KN = 3$ restriction.

Many other companies used queries that accessed recent sales information or compared sales from the most recent month to the period a year earlier, so clustering sales information on order date was a clear winning strategy. Clustering by orderdate is still used in TPC-H benchmark design, though the time-ranges in TPC-H are surprisingly broad (frequently 5 out of 7 years).

Single dimensional clustering does very well when there is one standout among columns to sort the data that will speed up most queries of interest. But what if there is not? The Star Schema pictured in Figure 3 has four dimensions: Date, Product, Store, and Promotion. Thus for SSB we need to consider if it is possible to cluster by multiple commonly restricted columns of these dimensions at the same time to reduce the disk space needed to access in the Fact table. Clustering by some single column of a dimension will not work since restrictions on individual dimensions are often dropped.

DB2 was the first database product to specifically provide an ability to cluster by more than one column at a time, using Multi-Dimensional Clustering (MDC), introduced in 2003 [1, 3, 4, 5, 6, 8, 13]. MDC partitions table data into cells (physically organized as *Blocks* in DB2), by treating some columns *within the table* as orthogonal axes of a cube, each cell corresponding to a different combination of individual values of these cube axis columns. The axes are declared as part of the Create Table statement with the clause ORGANIZE BY DIMENSIONS (col1, col2, ...). A *Block* in MDC is a contiguous sequence of pages on disk identified with a table extent, and a block index is created for each dimension axis. Every value in one such block index is followed by a list of Block Identifiers (BIDs), forming what is called a *Slice* of the multi-dimensional cube corresponding to a value of one dimension. The set of BIDs in the intersections of slices for values on each axis is a *Cell*.

We repeat that the "dimensions" used to cluster a table in MDC are columns *within the table*, not columns in the dimension tables of a star schema! We need to find a way to use MDC to improve performance of Star Schema queries, and indeed we have found an approach to doing this, which we introduce in Section 3.2.

DB2 takes great care to make modifications to the table easy once it is in MDC form. A "Block Map" identifies blocks that are Free, and inserts of new rows into a given cell will either use a block for that cell with space remaining or (in the overflow case) assign a new Free block to the cell. If a row is to be inserted into a new cell (e.g., because of a new month dimension value), the same approach is used to assign Free blocks. MDC can recognize when a block becomes empty after a delete, and Free it. Indeed, it is also a feature that the oldest month slice of cells (say) can be dropped all at once with no cost, a capability known as Rollout [3, 6].

3.2 Adjoined Dimension Columns in LINEORDER Table

Stonebraker and developers at Vertica [15] found a way to create a form of multi-dimensional clustering on a number of other commercial database products, including Vertica and two others that are anonymous. For this paper we took independent measurements and did not measure Vertica; as in [15] we maintain anonymity for results of the three database products measured here. The approach to achieving MDC-like behavior adjoins copies of dimension columns to the LINEORDER table, often by creating a Materialized View (MV or in DB2 an MQT), as shown below, named MVLINEORD containing those columns and all data from LINEORDER. We choose columns at a rather high level in some hierarchy commonly restricted in queries, e.g., c_region or p_category. Since high-level hierarchy columns have low cardinality, this will generate an appropriately small number of conjoint values of the columns making up cells in MVLINEORD so as to ensure that the cells contain enough data that fast sequential disk access within a cell (mainly contiguous on disk) will swamp or at least equal inter-cell access time. The right number of cells depends on the size of the fact table and disk performance but the aim should be to create cells at least one megabyte in length.

Applying ADC to DB2 MDC
We can demonstrate that ADC Indexing works well with the native Block indexing of MDC, given defined block size limits of at least one megabyte. In the MDC user documentation it is noted that a monotonic hierarchy such as day-week-month-quarter-year in the DATE dimension can have rollups functionally defined in LINEORDER based on lo_datekey, but we find no useful suggestions for how other dimensional hierarchies can be defined in LINEORDER. ADC addresses this difficulty, allowing multi-dimensional clustering by adjoined dimension columns in MVLINEORD. Recall that dimensional foreign keys of newly inserted rows in LINEORDER determine the values of adjoined columns, and once these values are known, MDC will always place new rows into an appropriate cell, both in the base table and the MQT named MVLINEORD.

Applying ADC to Other DBMS Products
The Oracle database product has a Partitioning feature [12] that supports dimensional cubing into cells. Various other products can support cubing if they have sufficiently precise indexing. It is simply necessary to create a load file for the LINEORDER data and adjoined columns, ordered by a concatenation of the desired adjoined columns; this can be done by executing a query to retrieve all columns in that order based on a join with dimensions and write it to a file. See Figure 5 for such a query. Then a load of a new LINEORDER table from that file will result in different combinations of

individual values of the columns that make up cells of the cube falling in contiguous bands placed in increasing dictionary order. Given rows sorted by four such columns, c1, c2, c3 and c4, we see the following situation. The leading column c1 in the concatenated order will generate long blocks in the sorted table, one for each increasing value of c1, while the second column c2 of the concatenated order will generate blocks for increasing values of c2 in the range of each individual value of c1, and so on up to column c4. The most finely divided bands will correspond to all combinations of individual columns; in other words they will define the cells of the cube. One can then define a materialized view MVLINEORD with adjoined dimension columns, and the cells will fall in the same order as the base table LINEORDER.

Given an index on each of these adjoined columns, any query with Where Clause range restrictions on the hierarchy for the adjoined columns will select a number of cells comparable to the volume of the conjoined ranges compared to the total volume of the cube. While it might seem that a range of several values on column c1, for example, will select a wide band of fact table rows, efficient indexing will respond to ranges on c2, c3 and c4 by creating a very finely divided foundset to select only the rows that sit in or on the border of the intersection of ranges. This has been experimentally verified. Indeed, these individual column indexes correspond loosely with the Block indexes in MDC, and can be just as efficient if the index performs efficient intersections. Vertica and Sybase IQ are two examples of database products with such indexes.

ADC Problems

There are a number of problems that can arise in adjoining copies of dimension columns to the fact table or view when native support of various features are lacking from the DBMS. However these problems are not so serious that they cannot be dealt with in practice. We start with a listing of missing features and associated problems.

1. When a new row is to be inserted in the LINEORDER table, DB2 and Oracle will materialize a corresponding row in MVLINEORD and place it in the appropriate cell or partition based on the adjoined columns of the view. But some other products will not be able to place the new row in the appropriate cell of MVLINEORD; indeed these rows are likely to end up in the rightmost extent of the materialized view where new inserts are accepted. The combined column indexes will account for the new newly inserted row so future queries will retrieve the proper rows, but the careful clustering we have built up will begin to fail and efficiency will be lost. But note that in an earlier DB2 design of Clustered Indexes [10] the same thing happened with new inserts, and a CLUSTERRATIO statistic was kept to measure this effect, with an advisory to reorganize the table when the statistic fell below 90% (below 80%, the table no longer assumed clustering in query plans). The Vertica product also provides continuously refreshed clustering, because newly inserted rows are kept in efficient memory structures, and are merged out to clustered disk form before the memory space runs out.

2. At present, no database system seems able to keep track of column hierarchies (such as c_region, c_nation, c_city) and use them effectively in predicate AND processing, although this is a common capability in OLAP products (such as Express). If we restrict a query with the dimension value c_city = 'Rome', we must

add a restriction c_nation = 'Italy' (if c_nation is an adjoined column we use, or c_region = 'Europe' if that is the adjoined column). This is true in MDC tables, for example, even though there is no ambiguity in the name 'Rome' as a c_city value. Requiring users to specify a seemingly unnecessary column value in their query is unfortunate, but not such a serious problem that it cannot be dealt with in practice.

3. For database products that don't provide sufficiently robust materialized views (as with one of the products we measured) we need to adjoin dimension columns to the actual base table. This leads to another problem. When a query to a given c_region value for example, we would instead need to restrict the adjoined LINEORDER column lo_cregion (the adjoined version) instead. This type of query modification compares with a need in point (2) for query modification in all database products that do not have native understanding of hierarchies. Furthermore, creating MVLINEORD while the base table LINEORDER still exists can lead to an enormous use of space, whereas adjoining dimension columns to the LINEORDER table will save this space. Indeed we load base tables in ADC form in the Experimental results below. We must also take care when inserting rows into this adjoined LINEORDER table that the adjoined values are added, but this can be done with a simple lo_insert( ) function.

4   Experimental Results

We measured three commercial database products, anonymized with names A, B and C, using star schema benchmark tables at Scale Factor 10 (SF = 10). These tests were run on a Dell 2900 running Windows Server 2003, with 8 GBytes of RAM, 4 dual-core processors (3.20 GHz) and data on RAID0 with 4 Seagate 15000 RPM SAS disks, stripe size 64K. All Query runs were from cold starts. Parallelism to support disk read ahead was employed on all products to the extent possible.

We measured two different forms of load for the LINEORDER table, one with no adjoined columns from the dimension tables (a regular load, known as the Base case), and one with four dimension column values adjoined to the LINEORDER table, d_year, s_region, c_region and p_category, with cardinalities 7, 5, 5, and 25, and LINEORDER data sorted in order by the concatenation of these columns (known as the ADC case). We started with a regular load of the LINEORDER table and ran the query in Figure 5, writing output to an OS file to achieve sorted order.

```
select lineorder.*, d_year, s_region, c_region, p_category
    from lineorder, customer, supplier, part, date
        where lo_custkey = c_custkey and lo_suppkey = s_suppkey
        and lo_partkey = p_partkey and lo_datekey = d_datekey
    order by d_year, s_region, c_region, p_category;
```

Fig. 5. Query to generate sorted data for load of fact table in ADC form

The output data was then loaded into LINEORDER in ADC form, with new columns given names lo_year, lo_sregion, lo_cregion, lo_category; the data remained ordered as it was in the output. Note that in product A the sort was not needed to achieve performance improvements since the load into the clustering units provided a relatively efficient bucket sort. Large enough extent size (1 MB or more) was important in A to keep the clustering units contiguous on disk.

As explained above, the ADC form provides clustering support for improved performance of many queries of SSB. In the Base form, we clustered data by lo_datekey using native database clustering capabilities, but while this improved performance on Q1, it degraded performance on other query flights, so it was dropped.

In the ADC form, the number of the most finely divided cells defined is 4375 (875 in the product where p_mfgr replaced p_category). Since the SF10 LINEORDER table sits on 6 GBytes, this results in cell sizes of about 1.37 MBytes. Disk arm time between blocks was 3 ms on the disks used, and sequential access (on the RAID0 disks) ran at 100-400 MBytes/second (on different products), so the 1.37 MByte cell will be scanned in at most 13.7 ms. Summing the seek and pickup time, each 1.37 MByte block can be read in $3 + 13.7 = 16.7$ ms, an average rate of 1.37 MByte/0.0167 sec = 82 MByte/sec. For larger Scale Factors we could use more cells without increasing inter-cell access.

There are two important points. First, the load of the ADC fact table, since it involves a join and in many cases a sort, will take a good deal longer than an unordered load of Base table. Second, since we adjoin clustering columns to the fact table in ADC, we will expect somewhat more space to be utilized.

4.1 Query Performance

Table 2 contains the Elapsed and CPU time for SSB Queries, with a Table Scan (Q_TS) at the top, originally reported in [2]. For product C, with is vertically partitioned, Q_TS scans a single column. We note in Table 2 that the ADC sorted fact table results, some with native clustering, support much faster execution of all queries on all products than the Base case. There was no native clustering capability available in Product C. All Elapsed and CPU time comparisons that follow reference the Geometric Means. For Product A the ratio of Base Elapsed time to ADC Elapsed time is 6.2 to 1; the CPU ratio is 5.8 to 1. For Product B, the Elapsed time ratio is 8.7 to 1 and for CPU it is 5.8 to 1. For Product C, the Elapsed time ratio is 7.6 to 1 and for CPU it is 3.8 to 1. We note that the best Elapsed times occurred for product C, both in the Base Case and the ADC Case. Note that only a few columns were retrieved in most queries, and vertically partitioned products are known to have an advantage in such queries. In any event, the speedup of Product C going from the Base case to the ADC case is due entirely to the good indexing story; there was no native clustering capability in Product C.

There were a number of cases where the Query Optimizers became confused in the ADC case, since the WHERE clause restrictions on columns in the dimensions could not be identified with the columns brought into the LINEORDER table. Accordingly, we modified queries to refer either to columns in the dimensions or in the LINEORDER table and chose the best performer. This would not normally be appropriate for ad hoc queries, only for canned queries, but we reasoned that a query optimizer upgrade to identify these columns was a relatively simple one, so our modification assumed that could be taken into account.

Table 2. Measured Performance of Queries on Products A, B and C in Seconds

Query	A Base Case		B Base Case		C Base Case		A ADC Case		B ADC Case		C ADC Case	
	Elapsed	CPU	Elapsed	CPU	Elapsed	CPU	Elapsed	CPU	Elapsed	CPU	Elapsed	CPU
Q_TS	17.6	2.2	45	2.7	2.6	0.7	45.2	6.4	53.0	2.75	3.2	0.8
Q1_1	19.7	2.1	43	2.6	10.1	1.9	5.8	0.5	7.9	0.49	2.4	0.7
Q1_2	19.6	1.9	41	2.3	9.1	1.2	6.0	0.4	8.4	0.45	2.7	0.7
Q1_3	19.4	1.9	37	0.5	7.0	1.1	6.0	0.4	8.1	0.4	2.7	0.7
Q2_1	33.9	4.2	49	3.2	17.7	3.1	2.7	0.4	6.4	0.42	1.9	0.6
Q2_2	24.3	2.8	45	2.8	17.4	2.7	2.6	0.3	5.9	0.35	1.2	0.5
Q2_3	22.6	2.6	41	1.4	17.6	1.5	1.9	0.2	5.8	0.33	4.7	0.6
Q3_1	38.5	5.1	58	3.5	16.6	4.9	9.1	1.2	7.8	0.72	4.7	1.3
Q3_2	31.1	3.5	46	1.1	15.4	3.2	3.5	0.5	4.0	0.24	1.5	0.7
Q3_3	11.8	0.2	15	0.4	16.9	1.8	3.0	0.4	3.5	0.18	3.3	0.7
Q3_4	7.9	0.2	6	0.2	8.8	1.3	3.4	0.1	1.8	0.05	0.8	0.4
Q4_1	40.9	5.6	58	3.5	22.8	5.2	7.0	1.0	3.3	0.29	1.7	0.6
Q4_2	36.1	4.6	56	3.1	25.5	3.6	3.6	0.4	1.8	0.15	1.3	0.7
Q4_3	31.7	3.6	49	1.6	27	4.0	1.5	0.1	1.0	0.07	0.8	0.4
Geom. Mean	23.7	2.1	36.8	1.5	15.1	2.4	3.8	0.36	4.23	0.26	2.0	0.64

In addition there were a few cases where clauses that restricted some dimension hierarchy column were not recognized as clustering within one of the columns on which the lineorder table was sorted (as when d_yearmonth = 199401 might not be recognized as falling in d_year = 1994). Clearly, such dimensional hierarchies should be a priority for query optimizers supporting data warehousing, and we added clauses in these few cases. It is particularly interesting that no such problem arose with Product C, which had such precise indexing that it invariably recognized what cells of the ADC various WHERE clause predicates were restricted to.

Note that we got similar results in the SF100 case for two of the products A and C so far measured. We provide graphs of these cases in the slide show presented at the TPC Technical Conference at http://www.cs.umb.edu/~poneil/TPC_Talk082409.pdf.

4.2 Results by Filter Factor

In Figure 6, we plot elapsed time for the queries against the Filter Factor for the query (FF), plotted on a log-scale X-axis. At the low end of the FF Axis, with FF below 1/10000, we see that secondary indexes are quite effective at accessing the few rows that qualify, so ADC holds little advantage over the Base case. For FF = 1, the tablescan case we measured under Q_TS: the whole table is read regardless of ADC, and the times again group together. For FF between 1/10000 and 1 where the vast majority of queries lie, ADC is usually quite effective at reducing query times compared to the Base case, from approximately tablescan-time down to a few seconds (bounded above by ten seconds).

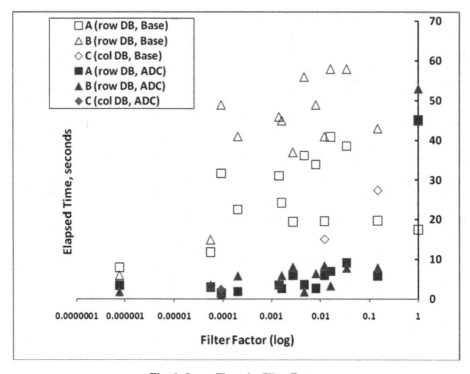

Fig. 6. Query Times by Filter Factor

4.3   Experiments with DB2 Design Advisor

We spoke with a number of with a number of IBM DB2 experts to explain how ADC accelerated MDC performance, and the general reaction was mild interest along with a suggestion from a few people that the DB2 Design Advisor might recommend such a configuration. We explored this, and indeed when the Advisor was provided with the design of the Star Schema Benchmark it generated a number of MQTs that accelerated our queries. However these MQTs did not have any column values at all from the original LINEORDER table. Instead, the generated MQTs simply held aggregated values. Thus if we were to attempt any query with this set of MQTs that differed in a significant way from the SSB queries, a drill down or a restriction on a column not named in the original queries, the Design Advisor solution would have no way to respond. Indeed the MQTs that had been recommended merely materialized the original answers to the SSB, although they did generalize the values on the column restrictions, so if one of our queries restricted c_city to Rome, these MQTs would have answered queries that restricted c_city to any other city.

We tried to specify a set of drill-down queries to add to SSB that would sway the Advisor from simple materialization of aggregate queries, but the Advisor gave no suggestions when we attempted this. We also found that if we requested any aggregates other than sums in a query, such as max or min, the Advisor gave no suggestion.

5 Conclusions and Future Work

Our theory and measurements jibe to demonstrate the value of ADC in accelerating accesses of Star Schema queries, when the ADC columns used are carefully chosen to subdivide dimensional hierarchies commonly queried. Additional dimension columns can be brought into the fact table, but it is important to remember that the entire point of a star schema design is to support a reasonably thin fact table, which means keeping most columns in the dimension tables. Only the dimension-table columns used in clustering earn their place in the fact table.

We should bear in mind that this Star Schema Benchmark is a simple one, with only four Query flights and four dimensions, with a rather simple roll-up hierarchy. With more complex schemas, a larger fraction of queries might fail to be accelerated on the basis of all their restrictions. Of course this has always been the case with clustering solutions: they don't improve performance of all queries. Still, there are many commercial applications where clustering is an invaluable aid.

Our experience with DBAdvisor made us aware of one side effect of the simplicity of SSB: it can be "solved" by statically defined aggregation. However, such an aggregation removes the possibility of drilling down to lower level hierarchies and individual rows, as is expected in a data warehouse. We need to add requirements to SSB to ensure that users can drill down to lower level results of this kind.

One reviewer of this paper suggested that a topic of our future research should be how the TPC could learn from the derivation of this benchmark from TPC-H and how to develop benchmark test patterns relevant to product capabilities and market demands. We appreciate the compliment this suggestion implied, but feel the problems encountered in developing TPC benchmarks are much greater than those we faced. The need to provide a bullet-proof benchmark that will stand up to attempts to gain unforeseen advantage is one such problem, and the requirement that the database companies that make up the TPC vote in favor of releasing each benchmark is another. It is easy for us to point out what we believe might be minor design flaws in a benchmark that has been used for many years, but clearly such benchmarks offer a useful workout of commercial products to compare their effectiveness.

That said, if any of us can be any use to the TPC, we're happy to make the effort.

Acknowledgement. We thank Mike Stonebraker for supporting this benchmark for Vertica and also thanks the reviewers for their comments on this paper.

References

1. Bhattacharjee, B., et al.: Efficient Query Processing for Multi-Dimensional Clustered Tables in DB2
2. Chen, X., O'Neil, P., O'Neil, E.: Adjoined Dimension Column Clustering to Improve Data Warehouse Query Performance. Poster presentation at ICDE 2008 (2008), http://www.cs.umb.edu/~poneil/icde08_adc.pdf
3. Cranston, L.: MDC Performance: Customer Examples and Experiences, http://www.research.ibm.com/mdc/db2.pdf

4. IBM: Designing Multidimensional Clustering (MDC) Tables,
    http://publib.boulder.ibm.com/infocenter/db2luw/v9/
    index.jsp?topic=/com.ibm.db2.udb.admin.doc/doc/c0007238.htm
5. IBM Research: DB2's Multi-Dimensional Clustering,
    http://www.research.ibm.com/mdc/
6. Kennedy, J.: Introduction to Multidimensional Clustering with DB2 UDB LUW. In: IBM
    DB2 Information Management Technical Conference, Orlando, FL (September 2005)
7. Kimball, R., Ross, M.: The Data Warehouse Toolkit, 2nd edn. Wiley, Chichester (2002)
8. Lightstone, S., Teorey, T., Nadeau, T.: Physical Database Design. Morgan Kaufman, San
    Francisco (2007)
9. O'Neil, P.: The Set Query Benchmark. In: Gray, J. (ed.) The Benchmark Handbook for
    Database and Transaction Processing Systems, pp. 209–245. Morgan Kauffmann, San
    Francisco (1993), http://www.cs.umb.edu/~poneil/SetQBM.pdf
10. O'Neil, P., O'Neil, E.: Database Principles, Programming, and Performance, 2nd edn.
    Morgan Kaufmann, San Francisco (2001)
11. O'Neil, P., O'Neil, E., Chen, X.: The Star Schema Benchmark,
    http://www.cs.umb.edu/~poneil/StarSchemaB.pdf
12. Oracle: Partitioning in Oracle Database 10g Release 2 (May 2005),
    http://www.oracle.com/solutions/business_intelligence/
    partitioning.html
13. Padmanabhan, S., et al.: Multi-Dimensional Clustering: A New Data Layout Scheme in
    DB2. In: Proceedings of the ACM SIGMOD Conference (2003)
14. Selinger, P., et al.: Access Path Selection in a Relational Database Management System.
    In: Proceedings of the ACM SIGMOD Conference, pp. 23–34 (1979)
15. Stonebraker, M., et al.: One Size Fits All? Part 2: Benchmarking Results, Keynote address.
    In: Proceedings of CIDR (2007),
    http://www-db.cs.wisc.edu/cidr/cidr2007/papers/cidr07p20.pdf
16. TPC: TPC-DS, TPC Decision Support, under development,
    http://www.tpc.org/tpcds/default.asp
17. Nambiar, R., Poess, M.: The Making of TPC-DS. In: VLDB Proceedings (2006)
18. TPC: TPC-H Version 2.4.0, http://www.tpc.org/tpch/default.asp

An Approach of Performance Evaluation in Authentic Database Applications

Xiaojun Ye, Jingmin Xie, Jianmin Wang, Hao Tang, and Naiqiao Du

Key Laboratory for Information System Security, Ministry of Education
Tsinghua National Laboratory for Information Science and Technology
School of Software, Tsinghua University, Beijing 100084, China
{yexj, jimwang}@tsinghua.edu.cn

Abstract. This paper proposes a benchmark test management framework (BTMF) to simulate realistic database application environments based on TPC benchmarks. BTMF provides configuration parameters for both test system (TS) and system under test (SUT), so a more authentic SUT performance can be obtained by tuning these parameters. We use Petri net and transfer matrix to describe the intricate testing workload characteristics, so configuration parameters for different database applications can easily be determined. We conduct three workload characteristics experiments basing on the TPC-App benchmark to validate the BTMF and the workload modeling approach.

Keywords: Performance testing, benchmarking, test framework.

1 Introduction

In the field of IT systems performance evaluation, testers and hardware/software manufacturers usually focus on different purposes to publish the performance of their IT products with various environments [5]. For example, testers incline to grasp detailed and authentic system status such as its performance, resource utilization or dependability. However, manufacturer's testing purposes are more likely to obtain the performance result of their own product that is comparable with other similar ones. In order to make the evaluation result creditable, tester need to define extremely detailed testing requirements, for example, more authentic business workload, different network delay and every possible think time for each user. It would cost a lot to realize all the detailed requirements modeling in real database systems. On the contrary, some non-profit organizations release performance benchmarks with a high degree of standardization to simplify the testing process and make the performance testing results comparable [12]. These benchmarks not only limit the test database and the database transaction workload, but also the associated performance metrics.

To achieve multiple goals at the same time, emulating test systems, which are close to real database application scenarios and capable to seize comparable performance testing measures, become important for IT system performance evaluation. Two types of approaches are proposed for performance evaluation of emulating systems. One is using general stress testing tools to simulate user requests and responses by invoking

R. Nambiar and M. Poess (Eds.): TPCTC 2009, LNCS 5895, pp. 253–266, 2009.

scripts recorded by testers, and then analyze system performance through the number of concurrent users and maximum throughput [6]. The other type is benchmark testing [12]. Compared with the former, the latter is widely accepted in industry. However, performance benchmarks give too many constraints on the definition of their test database, workload characteristics, performance metrics and SUT (system under test), and benchmark results are rough estimates and only serve the purpose of relative comparison for real systems [10]. To make these components visualized and dynamically configured to satisfy various testing purposes and evaluation targets of different real system characteristic requirements, a domain-independent and model-driven benchmark test management framework (BTMF) emerges from this practice.

Authenticity of simulating different realistic application environments and comparability of various testing results both become important, and this paper aims to find a bridge between them. To better simulate realistic systems based on TPC benchmarks, our BTMF provides configuration parameters in multiple dimensions, so that by tuning these parameters, we can get a more authentic performance result [13]. At the same time, we use Petri net and transfer matrix to describe the intricate and concurrent performance testing workload from business views, various granularity measures and their relationships in real systems under test [3]. With the expandable definition of performance measures [8], customized metrics described by modeling languages, the workload characterization semantics in different test system implementations are explicitly modeled, which is helpful to predict, compare and analyze their corresponding system testing results.

In the next section, we discuss related work of model-driven performance testing and configurable system optimization. In Section 3, the architecture of BTMF is proposed and main components to meet different testing purposes and real system testing environment simulation objectives are detailed. We describe general workload characterization with formal modeling language for simulating different realistic environments in Section 4, and give experimental examples to verify our approach in Section 5. Finally, Section 6 outlines our future considerations.

2 Related Work

Database system performance benchmarking is a well-established area led by Transaction Processing Council (TPC) [12]. With the advance of web technologies and new database application requirements, many benchmarks are updated or replaced in time. For example, TPC-E may supersede the well-known TPC-C lately, and TPC-App derived from TPC-W started to be well accepted by companies [7].

Along with the improvement of performance benchmarks, a variety of performance evaluation methods and techniques ranging from analytical modeling to simulation approaches are designed, including those fault-relevant evaluation methods that focused on specific domains [1, 2], database replay utilities for specific DBMS applications [4]. Therefore, manufacturers need to develop their own performance testing tools for domain-dependent benchmarking, which will add more difficulty for the comparability of the result of test system with other similar products [3, 10].

Literature [10] proposed an application-independent synthetic workload model from the perspective of user's requirements. A high-level specification language, a translator of the language, and a set of generators were created to compose diverse test databases and test transactions of different synthetic database benchmarks. We learn this model-driven method from the perspective of the user's requirements for test database, workload characterization, workload deployment, and collected measures configuration in the benchmark test management framework.

In performance tuning domain of database application systems, literature [9] proposed an algorithm called Quick Optimization via Guessing (QOG). They formally specified how to guess at the performance and when to terminate measurement, and proved that QOG can find a nearly-best configuration with a high probability under common conditions that are frequently assumed in the literature. The idea of measuring the performance of web systems to optimize configuration parameters can be used in performance optimization area [11, 14]. Hence, our BTMF with flexible configurations are significant during test run since the optimal configuration has been a time-consuming task due to the long measurement time needed to evaluate the performance of a given configuration [13], we propose to use formal language to describe high-level workload characterization in order to predict testing system performance.

Inspired by the model-driven thought and the idea of guessing at the performance in parameter tuning, this paper proposes a configurable BTMF: (1) by means of flexible configurations of the data model, workload characterization and deployment, different granularity measures, this framework can be applied for both benchmark and customized applications performance testing; (2) besides, the approaches of using Petri net or transfer matrix to describe workload configurations (which model real system's business processes), database transactions and performance measures, visualize those intricate relationships and make testing result understandable and comparable in performance metric analysis; (3) since the performance can be guessed based on the similar workload configurations, we can predict the performance of a specific test system configuration according to the formal workload descriptions.

3 Benchmark Test Management Framework

3.1 BTMF Design Philosophy

BTMF architecture consists of a test system (TS) and a system under test (SUT). The TS emulates the user-endpoints which issue requests to the SUT. The SUT in turn responds to these transaction requests. Therefore, we can abstract these components, which are either defined by TPC benchmark standard, or customized by external standards or user-requirements, in BTMF with diverse configuration parameters basing on the model-driven concept. So BTMF components can be customized in these dimensions with predefined parameters for the real application simulation.

In the high-level view of the BTMF, TS includes database manager, workload dispatcher, client emulators and performance measure collector, separately manage test database and generate test data, control user requests dispatching, collect and analyze the performance measures produced by the SUT in terms of the system parameters predefined in BTMF configuration files; SUT includes database, transaction and DB engines in terms of the system parameters predefined in BTMF

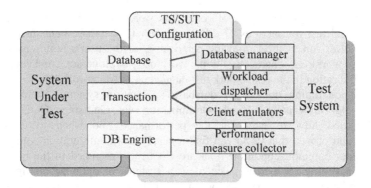

Fig. 1. BTMF design philosophy

configuration files. Therefore, using the model-driven method, we can describe our BTMF design philosophy of SUT and TS as shown in Figure 1.

This architecture is a logical architecture; it does not map functional elements to hardware or software components. Proceeding from these components description to a real IT systems test requires the presence of a complete description of all aspects of the subsystem relevant to the benchmark's performance. This description is called the test system configuration, or the system under test (SUT) configuration.

3.2 BTMF Implementation

The overall components for BTMF implementation include six main modules as shown in Figure 2. *Controller*, *Workload Manager*, *Statistic Collector* and *Data Generator* belong to TS, and *Database* component belong to SUT. *Transactions* component with different granularity measures definition may be in TS or SUT, depending on real system architectures or testing purposes, as we see in different TPC benchmarks. Therefore, BTMF configuration files described by using a high-level language (XML) include configuration parameters for describing workload characteristics, test database, and various measures derived from transactions. These parameters would be analyzed and implemented by the corresponding modules and then be parsed and interpreted by the *Controller* during the testing process.

Data Generator
Data generator mainly has two tasks. One is to model real system data structure by creating divers relations and their semantic restrictions in configuration files, and translate them into real DBMS objects in the form of tables and constraints.

The other task is to generate test database conforming to the data model and data feature definition. We suppose that each independent attribute has a data generation method according to data characteristics predefined in test system (generation rules or user-defined plug-in functions). Like other data generators, BTMF decouples data generation details from user-defined plug-in functions or data generation rules with corresponding configurations in BFM configuration files.

Before populating database, data generator will first analysis table dependence based on foreign key constraints and attribute dependence among attributes of tables

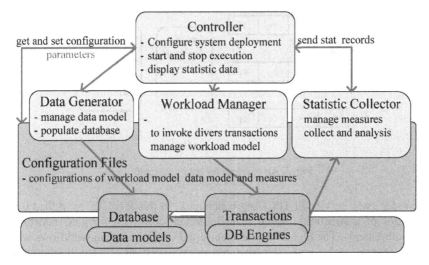

Fig. 2. The benchmark test management framework implementation architecture

based on column level constraints. The connections between output attributes and corresponding input attributes are called as *data dependences*. Before generating test database, the topological structure of these dependences should first be established automatically in order to keep the data semantic. Besides, the acyclic graph of topological structure is divided into several sub-graphs disjointed with each other. Each sub-graph will represent one data generation thread in *Data generator* that BTMF could use to populate table attribute data in order.

The process of database populating has two levels – *table level* and *attribute level*. Taking Figure 3 as an example, A, B, and C are tables; a_i, b_i, and c_i are attributes of tables; the solid and dashed arrows represent dependences between attributes or tables, for example a_1->b_1 means the value of attribute b_1 depends on the value of attribute a_1.

1) Table level: *Data generator* creates the acyclic graph and topological structure of tables, which are listed in Figure 3 (b). Learning from its sub-graphs, BTMF will create two threads to populate data in table A, B and C separately. Considering the broken line in Figure 3 (b), if a_2 depends on b_3, there will be a cycle between table A and table B. In such case, *Data generator* should remove the dependence between a_2 and b_3 first, and then after table A and B is populated, it will recalculate all the values of attribute a_2.

2) Attribute level: When populating data in database tables, the topological structure of all attributes, which represents the order of attributes that the data load module should deal with in each table, should be first established (such as A is listed in Figure 3 (c)). Since there will not be a cycle among these attributes in this example, it is easy for Data generator to populate data in order.

Workload Manager

The workload in database systems can be viewed in two levels. The lower level is manifested by transactions which represent simple business logic unit such as the

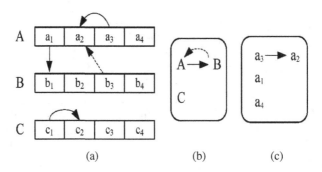

Fig. 3. An example for data generator

"create order" web service in TPC-App benchmark. In this level, the workload is the mixed ratios of transactions, which is an important constraint for TPC benchmark testing requirements. The higher level is manifested by transactional workflows which comprise several tasks with stepwise processes (such as choice, iteration and concurrent execution). The mapping between workflow workloads used in real systems and synthetic transaction workloads used in current benchmarks should be taken into consideration together [3]. By considering more workload characteristics, including the transaction distribution with probabilities, the transaction dependency condition, the input data requirements, etc., the scenarios such as DBMS cache tuning and SQL query optimization during testing process can be more meaningful for real systems performance turning.

As shown in Figure 2, *Workload manager* mainly includes two functions. First, create multi threads to simulate concurrent remote clients to invoke business processes which may be comprised of workflows or transactions. These workflows or transactions are encapsulated in DLL, web service or script according to the realistic environments of simulating systems and the purpose of the comparability of testing results. Second, the mixing ratio of educed database transactions derived from the workflow workload is performed by the *Controller*. These workload characterizations are predefined in configuration files before testing and dynamically invoked by *Controller* during performance evaluation process.

Statistic Collector

During the execution of workflows or transactions, *Statistic collector* will gather performance measures as many as possible, such as begin and end time of a request, submitting number, and throughput. Collected data with the same measure name are connected by a linked list and ordered by submitting time as shown in Figure 4. The linked lists are sorted by hash table. In this way, *Workload dispatcher* can append a line of measure data to the *Statistic collector* and *Controller* can easily get the sorted data from it. With the definition of metrics in configuration files, *Statistic collector* can be also expandable for other specific evaluating purposes.

Statistic collector includes three basic functions: (1) before starting a real test, *Statistic collector* is initialized and ready to receive diverse performance measures from *Client emulators* driven by *Controller*; (2) within an execution, *Workload dispatcher* will add statistic records into *Statistic collector* measure buffer; (3)

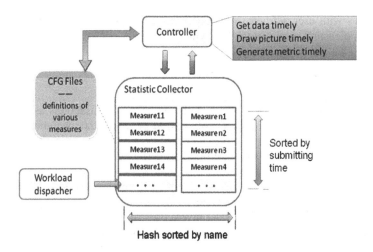

Fig. 4. The store structure and functions of statistic collector

Controller timely gets statistic records from this collector, and then draws performance charts and writes metric data into corresponding BTMF statistic files.

Controller
Controller is used to activate different *Client emulator*'s workloads complying with a fixing ratio from the real system analysis. As listed in Figure 2, *Controller* has three basic functions: (1) getting, parsing and setting configuration parameters predefined by testers in configuration files; (2) starting and stopping data generating and testing execution process, and populating performance measures data in *Statistic collector*; (3) Receiving statistic records, drawing and displaying charts, and writing records into corresponding BTMF statistic files.

The whole testing process of the BTMF includes three steps. First, describe the test database and then populate test data. Second, deploy workload in TS or SUT, design test plan with measures, and initialize *Statistic collector* measure buffer. According to BTMF configuring parameters in configuration files, the *Controller* starts the testing execution and *Statistic collector* records statistic measure data timely.

Transactions, Measures, Database and Configuration Files
Before executing test systems, the transactions and data generating functions should be encapsulated in DLL/web service/scripts programs and their deployed strategies should be described in configuration files in advance. The performance measures are also pre-developed in every workflow/transaction program and predefined in the BTMF functions configuration files.

Apart from workload characterization, data model and feature, performance measures, the configuration items include environment-related parameters (such as database connection string, web service address of *Statistic collector*, store location of statistic files and so on) and testing-related parameters (such as the preheating time of execution, smooth running time etc.). The main objective of configuration files is to build a semantic connection between SUT and TS, and lead our TS to invoke and test various SUTs with user-defined workload characterization, database models, various performance measures, and system deployment strategies, etc.

4 Workload Modeling

The workload of a database benchmark is the amount of transactions assigned to or performed by a database system in a given period of time. Understanding the nature of the workload and its intrinsic features can help to interpret benchmark performance measures. Transaction dependences are usually overlooked in current OLTP workload modeling. To simulate more realistic of real systems and get a comparable performance result from business views, an authentic and visualized workload would be more helpful. So a formal language is required for keeping the consistence between high-level semantic (workflow) invoked by the simulation client threads and low level transaction mixing ratio in OLTP performance benchmarks. In this section, we illustrate how to use workflow model to describe workload characterization in realistic systems and calculate the mixed ratios of their transactions executed in OLTP performance benchmarks from the high level formal model.

4.1 Simple Workloads in Benchmarks

Though TPC-App replaced TPC-W as the new B2B web service performance benchmark, business transactions, such as "create order", "change payment", and "new customer" transactions, are almost abstracted as database transactions workloads. Recursive calling transactions with mixed ratios (transaction distribution with probabilities) in benchmarks can be abstracted and demonstrated as shown in Figure 5 (a) with Petri net models.

This modeling language provides us a practical view of how to construct and analyze the semantic and similarity of business workloads. For instance, the "create order" web service in TPC-App benchmark will asynchronously send a durable message to shipping process after creating an order in DBMS. Figure 5 (b) gives an abstract of the detailed processes of transaction t_1 with an asynchronous process unit like "create order" transaction, which is often required in current benchmarks.

4.2 Complex Workloads in Realistic Systems

Workflow control patterns are used to better represent business process workloads, while transaction control patterns, where mixing ratio is used to keep the semantic workloads mapping with high-level workflow, are workloads for the current TPC benchmarks. In TPC-W benchmark, transfer matrix is adopted to describe the dependence of transactions. Two other kinds of approaches, by using Markov process and Petri-net, have been brought up to model the relationship among workflows and transactions [3]. With these formal models or languages, the connection of independent transactions in OLTP benchmark with the workflow characterizations to meet the user's real workload modeling requirements can be established. These unambiguous and traceable mathematical descriptions of high-level workload characterization would help testers to calculate the mixed ratios of transactions for emulating database systems and then predict the result semantics of performance of

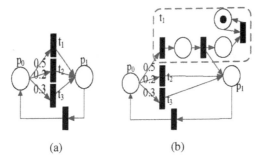

(a)   (b)

Fig. 5. Examples of simple workloads in performance benchmarks

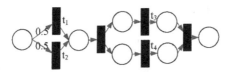

Fig. 6. An example of complex workloads (workflow) in realistic systems

different workflow workloads with the transaction workload for different real systems.

Figure 6 illustrates an example of transactional workflows with a choice of database transaction execution and a concurrent database transaction execution. From the Petri net model, we can calculate that the mixed ratio of transaction t_1, t_2, t_3 and t_4 is 1:1:2:2. In the next section, implementations with different workflows described by Petri net and transfer matrix are tested and analyzed.

4.3 Workload Modeling with Granularity Measures

There are various definitions of the term *performance* in the ISO9126 standard [8]. The most commonly used performance metrics are response time, throughput and utilization. *Response Time* is defined as the time interval between a user request of a service and the response of the system. Some metrics related to response time are *turnaround time, reaction time* and *stretch factor* [8]. *Throughput* is defined as the rate at which tasks can be handled by a system, and is measured in tasks per time. For most IT systems, utilization is defined as the ratio of busy time of a resource and the total elapsed time of the measurement period.

In most existing benchmarks, performance metrics are predefined with detailed mathematical formulas, which should not be changed when test systems are developed. In our BTMF implementation, we decide to parameterize these collected measures and use mark transitions from Petri Net to formally denote different granularity measures for business blocks in the workflow model.

Along with the workflows in Figure 6, measures for high level workloads could be added as showing in Figure 7, where three mark transitions for business blocks represented by shadow rectangles are drawn in Petri net graph. We can obtain one performance metric between mark 1 and mark 2, the other one between mark 2 and

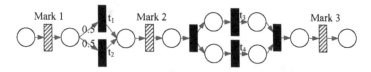

Fig. 7. An example of complex workloads (workflow) with two granularity measures

mark 3. At the appropriate time, these workflow measures data will be sent to *Statistic collector* asynchronously, and high level metrics can be derived timely.

5 Performance Test Result Analysis

In order to validate our BTMF for real database applications, we developed a benchmark test management framework prototype with data models and features, and transaction characteristics derived from TPC-App benchmark [12].

First, we deploy the same database model, transaction characteristics and performance measures as TPC-App benchmark and compare the results with different *active EBs, configured EBs* and *mixed ratio of transactions*. Then, based on the transactions of TPC-App, we add another two transaction processes based on Petri net and transfer matrix separately. Through the formal modeling language, we predict the performance results of them and prove them by using real testing results derived from our BTMF implemented prototype tool. Detailed information for database systems testing environment is listed in Table 1.

The test procedure is carried out as follows:

1) Testers perform TS and SUT component configuration, which is the sequence of actions required to perform a benchmark, including TS and SUT software deployment, OS parameter adjustment, etc.

Table 1. The configuration of testing environment

environments		configurations
Test system (TS)	**Controller Machine (Controller and Web Server 1)**	Intel® Core™2 Quad CPU Q6600 2.40GHz
		8G memory, 1T hard disk
		Microsoft Windows Server 2003 R2
		Internet Information Server (IIS) 6.0
	Web Server 1 (for Statistics)	Intel® Core™2 Quad CPU Q6600 2.40GHz
System Under Test (SUT)	**Web Server 2 Machine**	8G memory, 1T hard disk
		Microsoft Windows Server 2003 R2
		Internet Information Server (IIS) 6.0
	Web Server 2 (for Transactions)	Intel® Xeon® CPU E5420 2.50GHz
	Database Server Machine	8G memory, 1T hard disk
		Microsoft Windows Server 2003 R2
		Oracle Database 10g home1 v10.2.0
	Database Server	Microsoft Visual Studio 2005, C#
Platform	**Development Platform**	Microsoft .NET Framework SDK v2.0

2) Test database initialization, in which we use database generator to create test database structure and populate test database according the data characteristics predefined in BTMF configure files.

3) Workload configuration, which is the set of transactions that simulated users database request during test run, together with the relative frequency and relationship with which transactions occur during the test run.

4) Performance test process: obtain a reliable result within an acceptable period.

5.1 BTMF Usability Analysis

The configuration parameters, such as client number, transaction workload, test database model and scale, supporting our BTMF to test diverse scenarios of web database applications, are based on TPC-App benchmark scenarios. Figure 8 shows the result comparison with different active EBs, configured EBs and mixed ratios.

From the left chart of Figure 8 we can find that along with the larger number of active EBs, the value of SIPS/EB metrics (line 'SIPS/EB' and line 'SIPS/EB with different mixed ratios') is smaller and the values of RT metrics (line '90%RT' and line '50%RT') are larger, which means the performance of SUT is lower. At the same time, in the right chart, the performance does not change much along with the larger of configured EBs.

With different mixed ratios of transactions, the performance of SUT may change a lot. The mixed ratios of [new products], [product detail], [new customer], [create order], [order status], [change payment] and [change item] web service transactions are respectively 7:30:1:50:5:5:2 as TPC-App defined and 3:5:10:60:10:10:2 as the author customized, and the performance of them is shown as line 'SIPS/EB' and line 'SIPS/EB with different mixed ratios'. Since the [new customer], [create order], [order status] and [change payment] web services cost more time to be executed than the others, the performance of the latter SUT with user-defined mixed ratios is much lower than the standard mix ratios in TPC-App benchmark.

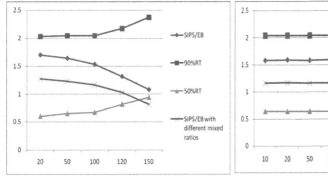
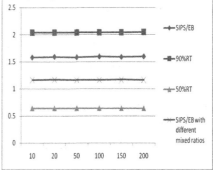

Fig. 8. In the left chart, the x axis represents the number of active EBs, while in the right one the x axis represents the number of configured EBs. The unit of response time (RT) is second.

5.2 Workload Characterization Analysis

In the following, we define three workload scenarios, one is from TPC-App workload model, as shown in Figure 9 (a), one is a transactional workflow with choice and concurrent processes defined by authors described with Petri net as Figure 9 (b), and the third one is a transactional workflow using transfer matrix like Figure 9 (c).

Detailed transfer matrix is shown in Table 2, where the symbol t_1-t_7 represent [new products], [product detail], [new customer], [create order], [order status], [change payment] and [change item] web service in TPC-App. Different workload characterizations, which are represented by Petri net model in Figure 9 (b), transfer matrix model in Figure 9 (c) and Table 2, assures that every web service in each scenarios is still having the same mixed ratios as defined Figure 9 (a). Each value in Table 2 means that when the web service in its row is finished, there will be corresponding possibility to execute the web service in its column, where the blank means that the web service will not be executed after the web service in its row.

We describe these high-level workloads with predefined workflow process definition languages and executed by our BTMF as defined. At the same time, in transaction level, from the mathematic analysis of three types of workloads discussed above (see Figure 9.), we can see that they all have the same mixed ratios of seven types of web services. Table 3 gives the comparable implementation testing results of them. Since they all have the same mixed ratios of the same types of web services, we

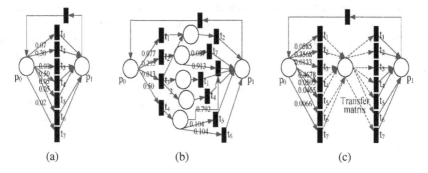

(a)   (b)   (c)

Fig. 9. Three types of workflow workloads with the same mixed ratios of transactions

Table 2. Transfer matrix based on the seven web services in TPC-App benchmark

	t1	t2	t3	t4	t5	t6	t7
t1	0.02	0.02		0.1			
t2				0.3			0.05
t3	0.2	0.3		0.1			
t4	0	0		0.1	0.02	0.03	
t5							
t6	0.2	0.13			0.04		
t7		0.4					
Mixed ratio	0.07	0.30	0.01	0.50	0.05	0.05	0.02

Table 3. Results with different transaction workflows

Workload models	Scenarios in TPC-App benchmark	Scenarios described by Petri net	Scenarios with transfer matrix
Configured EBs	10	10	10
Active EBs	100	100	100
SIPS	157.97	159.19	161.11
SIPS/EB	1.5797	1.5919	1.6111
90%RT (s)	2.04	2.05	2.05
50%RT (s)	0.64	0.64	0.65

can predict that the performance result should be the same or at least very similar. From Table 3 we can see that our prediction comes true, 'SIPS/EB', '90%RT' and '50%RT' metrics are almost the same despite the fact that the implementations have different transactional workflows in high level.

6 Conclusion

We proposed a model-driven benchmark test management framework (BTMF), in which Petri net and transfer matrix are used to describe workload characteristics. The configurable parameters for workload manager, statistic collector, and test database make our BTMF framework applicable for standard benchmarks and authentic applications performance evaluation. The testing results can be predicted according to the mapping of high-level and low-level formal workload descriptions, so the configuration parameters for different database applications can easily be determined.

Both of multiple configuration parameters optimization approaches and workload mathematical modeling with Petri net and other statistical methods will be considered and emphasized in the future. Today's benchmarks do not pay more attentions to the availability issues, such as fault tolerance and recovery cost, thereby, models for performability [8] and analytical method will also be considered together in the BTMS framework.

Acknowledgment

This work was supported by NSFC 60673140 and NHTP (2007AA01Z156, 2008ZX01045-001,2009CB320706).

References

1. Buchacker, K., Tschaeche, O.: TPC Benchmark-c version 5.2 Dependability Benchmark Extensions (2004),
   http://www3.informatik.uni-erlangen.de/Research/FAUmachine/
   papers/tpcc-depend.pdf (accessed in July 2009)

2. Costa, D., Rilho, T., Madeira, H.: Joint Evaluation of Performance and Robustness of a COTS DBMS through Fault-Injection. In: The Proc. of DSN 2000, NY, USA (2000)
3. Du, N.Q., Ye, X.J., Wang, J.M.: Toward Workflow-Driven Database System Workload Modeling. In: The Proc. of DBTest 2009, Providence, USA (2009)
4. Galanis, L., et al.: Oracle Database Replay. In: The Proc. of ACM SIGMOD 2008, Vancouver, BC, Canada (2008)
5. Gray, J. (ed.): The Benchmark Handbook for Database and Transaction Processing Systems. Morgan Kaufmann Publishers, San Francisco (1993)
6. IBM. TPC BenchmarkTM App Full Disclosure Report for IBM® eServerTM xSeries® 366 using Microsoft® .NET 1.1 TPC-App Version 1.1 Submitted for Review (June 21, 2005)
7. HP LoadRunner, http://www.hp.com (accessed in July 2009)
8. Koziolek, H.: Introduction to Performance Metrics. In: Eusgeld, I., Freiling, F.C., Reussner, R. (eds.) Dependability Metrics. LNCS, vol. 4909, pp. 199–203. Springer, Heidelberg (2008)
9. Osogami, T., Kato, S.: Optimizing System Configurations Quickly by Guessing at the Performance. In: The Proc. of SIGMETRICS 2007, San Diego, USA (2007)
10. Seng, J.L., Yao, S.B., Hevner, A.R.: Requirements-Driven Database Systems Benchmark Method. Decision Support Systems 38, 629–648 (2005)
11. Swisher, J.R., Jacobson, S.H., Yucesan, E.: Discrete-Event Simulation Optimization Using Ranking, Selection, and Multiple Comparison Procedures: A Survey. ACM Transactions on Modeling and Computer Simulation 13(2), 134–154 (2003)
12. Transaction Processing Performance Council, TPC-C/App/E BENCHMARKTM Standard Specification, http://www.tpc.org (accessed in July 2009)
13. Xie, J.M., Ye, X.J.: A Configurable Web Service Performance Testing Framework. In: Proc. of IEEE HPCC 2008, Dalian, China (2008)
14. Zhang, Y., Qu, W., Liu, A.: Automatic Performance Tuning for J2EE Application Server Systems. In: Ngu, A.H.H., et al. (eds.) WISE 2005. LNCS, vol. 3806, pp. 520–527. Springer, Heidelberg (2005)

Author Index

Printed in the United States
By Bookmasters